Journalism and Jim Crow

THE HISTORY OF COMMUNICATION

Robert W. McChesney and
John C. Nerone, editors

*A list of books in the series appears
at the end of this book.*

JOURNALISM and JIM CROW

White Supremacy and the Black Struggle for a New America

EDITED BY
**KATHY ROBERTS FORDE
AND SID BEDINGFIELD**

FOREWORD BY ALEX LICHTENSTEIN

UNIVERSITY OF ILLINOIS PRESS
Urbana, Chicago, and Springfield

All Raleigh *News and Observer* political cartoons (ch. 7)
are from the North Carolina Collection, UNC Chapel
Hill Libraries.

Library of Congress Cataloging-in-Publication Data
Names: Forde, Kathy Roberts, editor. | Bedingfield, Sid,
    editor. | Lichtenstein, Alexander C., author of foreword.
Title: Journalism and Jim Crow : white supremacy and
    the black struggle for a new America / edited by Kathy
    Roberts Forde and Sid Bedingfield ; foreword by Alex
    Lichtenstein
Description: Urbana : University of Illinois Press, [2021]
    | Series: The history of communication | Includes
    bibliographical references and index.
Identifiers: LCCN 2021016884 (print) | LCCN 2021016885
    (ebook) | ISBN 9780252044106 (cloth) | ISBN
    9780252086151 (paperback) | ISBN 9780252053047
    (ebook)
Subjects: LCSH: Journalism—Southern States—History—
    19th century. | Journalism—Southern States—
    History—20th century. | American newspapers—
    Southern States—History—19th century. | American
    newspapers—Southern States—History—20th century.
    | African American newspapers—History—19th
    century. | African American newspapers—History—
    20th century. | Journalism—Political aspects—Southern
    States. | Racism in the press—Southern States.
Classification: LCC PN4893 .J68 2021 (print) | LCC PN4893
    (ebook) | DDC 071.5—dc23
    LC record available at https://lccn.loc.gov/2021016884
    LC ebook record available at https://lccn.loc.gov/2021016885

*To the men and women of the Black press who did so much
to raise the alarm during the rise of Jim Crow—and who
have received so little credit for their heroic efforts.*

Contents

Illustrations follow page 186

Foreword

ALEX LICHTENSTEIN

When historians consider newspaper journalism, they tend to treat it as just another primary source. Want to know the unfolding of events during the white supremacist coup d'état in Wilmington, North Carolina, in 1898? Consult the Raleigh *News and Observer*, or perhaps even a local rag, like the *Wilmington Messenger*. Interested in tracing the campaign against convict leasing in Georgia? Turn to the lowcountry African American publication the *Savannah Tribune*. Alternatively, Henry Grady's venerable *Atlanta Constitution*, the (white) New South's leading newspaper, offers plenty of evidence of rationalizations for that brutal system; after all, Grady intoned in its pages, "a convict is a convict." Want to know how whites in Mississippi orchestrated disenfranchisement after the overthrow of Reconstruction? Scroll through the microfilmed pages of the Jackson *Clarion*.

Of course, these sources have long been extraordinarily helpful to historians in uncovering the history of racist violence and the ceaseless Black struggle against it, not least because whites in the Jim Crow South seemed quite unashamed of their behavior and thus happy to broadcast it in the pages of the press. Lurid stories confirming racist stereotypes sold papers. The rapid and widespread digitization of these sources in recent years, making them searchable by keyword, has increased their accessibility, so even undergraduate history students now can get a much fuller and direct glimpse of the hold white supremacy had on the white South's imagination in the late nineteenth and early twentieth centuries and can explore its inner workings. Whether the topic is lynching, segregated public services, crime and punishment, suppression of Black votes by violence or chicanery, peonage and other forms of forced labor, racial pogroms or racial exclusion from the workplace, the region's leading journalists were happy to report positively on what most whites regarded as the legitimate defense of their racial privileges. In many cases, one no longer must endure hours of scrolling through hard-to-read microfilm reels to unearth this material.

Yet, ironically, the ready availability of newspaper sources has sometimes obscured the fact that white Southern journalists and publishers themselves were some of the key architects of Jim Crow, deeply embedded as they were in the very social order on which they reported. This came not only in the form of unmitigated racist propaganda—though there was plenty of that in their pages and columns—but also by way of direct entanglement with the business and political interests that benefited from white supremacy. Corporate control of the media to ensure favorable press treatment long predated our own age, it seems. Arthur S. Colyar, for example, used his control of Nashville newspapers to defend his coal firm's long reliance on convict labor. Railroad magnate Henry M. Flagler invested heavily in Florida newspapers, gaining enough influence to use the press to fend off federal peonage charges in the extension of his Florida East Coast Railway line into the Florida Keys. Flagler's papers engaged in what today would be called "gaslighting," publishing flat-out (and false) denials of the reports of the enslavement of contract workers appearing in the Northern muckraking press.

In short, of the many institutions that made the New South what it was—the sheriff's office and the magistrate's court, the all-white jury, the plantation, the mill, the segregated streetcar, the convict coal mine, the railroad, the peonage camp, the ballot box, the rope on the tree, the White Caps and Red Shirts, the Democratic Party, the merchant's store, the county chain gang, the county courthouse, the Confederate monument standing in front of that courthouse and the Daughters of the Confederacy chapter that put it there—the press must be considered an integral part of the daily fabric of white supremacy as much as any of these. If the monuments are belatedly being toppled, the contributors to this volume give a much-needed shove to the icons of Southern journalism like Henry Grady and Josephus Daniels, who also richly deserve to be displaced from their pedestals still standing in the hall of "great journalists."

This critique of the fourth estate's complicity in white supremacy surely speaks to our own time. Future historians of the current moment will recognize that Fox News, for example, did not just "report" on the news of growing xenophobia, police violence against Black Americans, or the visibility of white supremacists in America's streets. As *Hoax*, Brian Stelter's recent book on the symbiotic relationship between the Trump administration and many journalists working at Fox News reveals, this ultra-partisan television network helped *make* that news by whispering in the president's ear and catering to his prejudices, supplying him with ready-made talking points.[1] In doing so, journalists became active participants in the reconstruction and spread of the white supremacist worldview that emanated from the Trump White House on an almost daily basis.

Much the same phenomenon, the essays in *Journalism and Jim Crow* insist, shaped the world of the segregated South in the years between the end of the First Reconstruction and the first Great Migration. Far from serving as "neutral" transmission belts of "the news," Jim Crow newspapers conjured lynch mobs into action, convened meetings of those determined to expunge Blacks from the political sphere, defended peonage and convict leasing, and deliberately whipped up white anxieties about so-called Black criminality in order to justify such measures. Too often, particularly in cases of organized racial pogroms against Blacks, reportage quickly became a self-fulfilling prophecy. Most of all, if (unlike today) limited to print journalism, popular media in the Southern states played a profound role in crafting white supremacy and its many justifications among whites as everyday "common sense."

This was not simply a matter of publishing racist editorials, opinion pieces, or cartoons; journalistic practice both reflected and shaped deep-rooted assumptions about whites, Blacks, and the nature of their relationships. This might consist of something as seemingly mundane as the use of honorifics—whites received the courtesy of "Mr." and "Miss" in a newspaper's pages while Blacks did not—or as nakedly prejudicial as choices of adverbs and adjectives when describing Black behavior and appearance, let alone the labeling of lynch victims as "black brutes" and lynch mobs as the "best citizens" in a community. We are all too familiar with such tropes today, whether they are the overdue decision on the part of the *New York Times* to capitalize "Black" or the nasty habit of "retweeting" unsourced images of Black men attacking white women—a particularly unfortunate tendency of President Trump's that echoes the most scurrilous press accounts of rumored Black "crime" that often heralded the formation of a lynch mob in the 1890s. In many news outlets today, and especially on the internet, Black Lives Matter protesters, no matter how peaceful and self-disciplined, are transmuted into violent looters; their vigilante antagonists, often well armed, appear in the melodrama favored by the former president and his enablers as honorable defenders of "law and order."

As *Journalism and Jim Crow* illustrates, however, the New South's vibrant Black press did much to defend African Americans against political disenfranchisement, sanctioned violence, and the slandering of the race as an inherently criminal class, often inverting the very tropes relied upon by white reporters and editorialists. Though this may have been "the nadir" of post–Civil War Black life, in fact it was also a golden moment for Black publishers, newspapers, and journalists, despite many obstacles. As Sid Bedingfield and Kathy Roberts Forde note in their introduction to this collection of essays, African American journalists had far more room to challenge racism head-on if they operated above the Mason-Dixon Line; nevertheless, the South had no shortage of courageous, if sometimes more cautious, Black news outlets. More than a few Black Southern journalists, like Ida B. Wells, J. Max Barber, and Alexander Manly, eventually faced forced exile from their home region for their bold challenges to white supremacy, as the pages that follow detail.

Like their white counterparts, Black news journals represent an invaluable source both for charting the course of ordinary events and for understanding the contours of Black politics and resistance to white supremacy, resistance in which they were active participants. Manly, the publisher of Wilmington's *Daily Record*, was very much a protagonist in the attempts of North Carolina's Black citizens to assert their rights—political, civic, and social—for example. If perhaps more willing than most to speak openly against some of the white South's shibboleths about interracial sex, he was hardly the sole Black journalist in the region who saw his role as defending the honor and livelihood of his race under unpromising circumstances. These papers, alas, can be somewhat more difficult to locate than their more long-lived cousins in the North like the *Chicago Defender* or *Pittsburgh Courier*, although the border-state publication the Baltimore *Afro-American* has been made widely available back to its first issue in 1893. Nevertheless, things are different when we move farther south. Manly's *Daily Record* may be digitized, but its up-country counterpart in Charlotte, the *Enterprise*, edited by Republican activist Ed Hagler, seems impossible to find, at least online. Jesse Chisholm Duke's *Montgomery Herald* (1886–1887), referred to in Sid Bedingfield's essay on Alabama Populism, is similarly difficult to lay a hand on. Indeed, uncovering extant copies of the South's Black newspapers of the Jim Crow era, and making them more widely available, remains an important task for scholars, librarians, and archivists. Until then, accounts of Jim Crow journalism will remain skewed to white voices, at least in the Southern states.

Be that as it may, the record of what Thomas Aiello has called "the grapevine of the Black South" remains a stirring one. Aiello focuses on the more than two hundred publications attached to the Black-owned Scott News Syndicate during the 1930s and 1940s, but the preceding period had plenty of examples of Black Southern journalism, even if more fragmentary and fleeting. As Aiello notes, Southern Blacks during the Great Migration did not just read the *Chicago Defender*. Northern papers, he writes, "were supplements to the southern newspapers that provided the news from home, offering a distinct interpretation of events that was decidedly southern and decidedly different from that of papers like the *Defender*. This is evident in the hundreds of newspapers that black southerners created."[2] One might think of the *Richmond Planet* (1883–1938), founded by formerly enslaved people; the *Savannah Tribune*, shuttered from 1878 to 1886 because white printers refused to produce it; Atlanta's bold if short-lived monthly the *Voice of the Negro* (1904–1906); South Carolina's weekly *People's Recorder* (1893–1925), closely bound up with Black fraternal organizations in that state; the *Nashville Globe* (1906–1930s), established to combat that city's segregation of its streetcars; Greenville, Mississippi's *Delta Lighthouse* (1896–1930); Alabama's *Huntsville Gazette* (1879–1894); or the *New Orleans Crusader*, which led the legal fight against segregated railcars that resulted in *Plessy v. Ferguson*, to name but several. Some of the papers have only a few issues extant; others, like the *Planet*, the *Globe*, and the *Gazette*, have hundreds, readily accessible online through the Library of Congress.[3] As D'Weston Haywood observes in his contribution to this volume, in the New South "Black journalism became the incubator of a new tide of Black activism."

That activism could come at a high price, however. J. Max Barber, who defended Black boycotts of segregated public transportation in the pages of the *Voice of the Negro*, found himself a target when Atlanta whites went on an anti-Black rampage in 1906, a pogrom not incidentally inflamed by the city's white newspapers. As Blair LM Kelley shows in the closing chapter, when Barber publicly called these newspapers to account, he was threatened with a stint on the Georgia chain gang and chose, wisely, to flee to Chicago, much as Ida B. Wells had done more than a decade before. "How," Kelley concludes forcefully, "can we begin to calculate the loss of free Black voices?" A fitting question to ask at a moment when those voices courageously are crying out to be heard again. This time, the nation would be wise to listen more closely to what they have to say.

Notes

1. Brian Stelter, *Hoax: Donald Trump, Fox News, and the Dangerous Distortion of Truth* (New York: Simon and Schuster, 2020).

2. Thomas Aiello, *The Grapevine of the Black South: The Scott Newspaper Syndicate in the Generation before the Civil Rights Movement* (Athens: University of Georgia Press, 2018), 10.

3. The Library of Congress website "Chronicling America: Historic American Newspapers" can be searched for African American publications. See https://chronicling america.loc.gov/. The *Huntsville Gazette*, for example, can be found at https://chroniclingamerica.loc.gov/lccn/sn84020151/.

Acknowledgments

Ten of us produced this collection, but it would not have reached a single reader without the generosity and goodwill of dozens of others. The editors are especially grateful for the support we received from our home institutions. The University of Minnesota's Hubbard School of Journalism and Mass Communication and its indefatigable director, Elisia Cohen, provided generous financial support for the project and hosted a symposium that brought us together early in the process and played an invaluable role in shaping this book. The College of Social and Behavioral Sciences at the University of Massachusetts Amherst helped fund this gathering as well. Financial support for the book itself was provided by the Office of the Vice Chancellor for Research and Engagement, University of Massachusetts Amherst. This book also received valuable feedback and support during sessions at the Media and Civil Rights History Symposium, a biennial event sponsored and hosted by the School of Journalism and Mass Communications at the University of South Carolina. Finally, a UMass Amherst Faculty Research Grant funded archival research with undergraduate students in Georgia.

We also want to thank the University of Illinois Press, particularly acquiring editor Danny Nasset, an early champion of the project, and the reviewers whose comments shaped revisions of the manuscript. We are honored to have it published in the History of Communication series and to be associated with two of the most respected and intellectually ambitious scholars in journalism and media history—John Nerone and Robert W. McChesney. We also want to thank the University of Georgia Press, which expressed support for this project and provided useful and time-consuming feedback—despite knowing we were leaning toward another publisher.

The editors must thank the contributors to this collection—the historians and scholars who did the research, wrote the chapters, and put up with our questions and edits. They constitute the backbone of this project. And their work could not have been accomplished without the librarians and archivists who worked tirelessly to help ensure our research was thorough and comprehensive. We also thank Kathy's exceptional undergraduate students at UMass (all now graduates)—Bryan Bowman, Ethan Bakuli, and Natalie DiDomenico—who worked with her in archives, library microfilm rooms, newspaper databases, and classrooms in the Journalism Department. Their curiosity and intelligence made this project stronger. Bryan's contribution was so substantial that he coauthored this volume's chapter on Florida. He received the Alan L. and Carol S. Lebovidge undergraduate research scholarship from the College of Social and Behavioral Sciences and the UMass Rising Researcher Award for this work.

We believe the best research emerges through rich and meaningful conversation with work that came before, and we encourage readers to note the cited sources throughout the book; they undergird our arguments and, occasionally, challenge and debate us in ways that deepen and enrich the discussion. We also want to note sources who were especially important to the project. On the issue of criminal justice in the New South, which is central to our understanding of the Jim Crow political economies, we greatly appreciate the contributions made by Alex Lichtenstein and Douglas A. Blackmon. Through their published works, and their willingness to engage with us at the symposium and throughout the process, Lichtenstein and Blackmon helped us think in new ways about the New South, criminal justice, journalism, and power.

We also thank our families for their support and forbearance during the past several years—Jack and Zada Forde; and Dana, Walter, and Kate Bedingfield (who has been hard at work on her own democracy project over the past two years).

We want to end by paying special tribute to the Black journalists and activists whose valiant struggle against Jim Crow serves as the heart and soul of this book. Since the Civil War, liberal and illiberal forces have been fighting to define the American story. During the rise of the New South, the forces of illiberalism won, with tragic consequences for the nation. But their victory was not uncontested. Black journalists and activists left a legacy of dissent that should serve as a road map for all of us in the ongoing struggle for the soul of the nation. Some of those African American journalists later gained national and historical recognition—W.E.B. Du Bois, Ida B. Wells-Barnett, T. Thomas Fortune, and others. But we want to end with a special tribute to those who are less well known and have never received the popular acclaim they deserve. These include such editors and writers as Alex Manly, J. Max Barber, Charles Hendley Jr., Jesse Chisholm Duke, John Deveaux, and many, many more. We humbly dedicate this book to them.

Journalism and the World It Built

SID BEDINGFIELD AND
KATHY ROBERTS FORDE

Journalism and Jim Crow offers a fresh take on the creation of Jim Crow and the New South by taking seriously the role of journalism in American history. Journalism is neither a neutral institution nor a neutral cultural product. And journalists are not neutral actors, even when they pursue the technocratic goals of objectivity and impartiality. Journalists engage deeply in the politics and culture of their communities, not merely as observers but as participants too. They have often used their status and influence to shape outcomes, particularly during transformative moments of heightened political and cultural tension. These are fundamental realities that, when considered, open up new ways of understanding political change in the past—and political conflict in the present.

Our central argument is surprisingly new. After Reconstruction, white publishers and editors used their newspapers to build, nurture, and protect white supremacist political economies and social orders across the South that lasted for generations. Black journalists fought these regimes as they were being built. The stakes could not have been higher: the future of liberal democracy in the newly restored United States was on the line. *Journalism and Jim Crow* is the first extended work to examine the foundational role of the press at this critical turning point in U.S. history. It documents the struggle between two different journalisms—a white journalism dedicated to building an anti-Black, antidemocratic America and a Black journalism dedicated to building a multiracial, fully democratic "New America."[1] The Southern white press and its political and business allies carried the day, effectively killing democracy in the South for nearly a century and shaping a tragically durable system of racial caste in America.

In the summer of 2020, when we first drafted this introduction, the country was exploding with pent-up rage over the wanton police killing of a Black citizen, George Floyd, in Minneapolis, where one of us works and the other used to work. We watched and read the ongoing news coverage as we wrote about the historical roots of the anti-Black racism built into the U.S. criminal justice system and the American way of life. We watched a U.S. president and his right-wing journalistic allies spread disinformation and racist rhetoric, attacking other journalists as "fake news" and "enemies of the people," with the goal of destroying public faith in both a consensus notion of truth and an independent press committed to the democratic values of transparency, exposure, and honest public debate.

A few months later, in November, when President Donald J. Trump lost the election to Joseph R. Biden Jr., he and the right-wing news media spread the big lie that the election was stolen through widespread voter fraud, a racist lie meant as an attack on Black and Brown voters. With the lie on repeat and couched in incendiary rhetoric, Trump and his right-wing media allies whipped up white supremacist and extremist fury and promoted rallies to coincide with the pro forma certification of the electoral results in the U.S. Congress. On January 6, 2021, the president sent a mob of extremist supporters to the Capitol to disrupt the certification process and "Stop the Steal." The result was a violent, antidemocratic, white supremacist insurrection against the legislative branch of the U.S. government in an attempt to overturn a free and fair presidential election.

We hope this study of journalism, democracy, and race during a tragic, consequential moment in our nation's past will help readers think in new ways about two important concerns: the complicated relationship between journalism and power in American democracy and the systems and structures of white supremacy in American life. While these subjects may appear to have little to do with one another, *Journalism and Jim Crow* demonstrates that they are historically, and ineluctably, intertwined. The unpleasant truth is that journalism in America has often not been devoted to democratic values. For decades after Reconstruction in the South, white newspaper publishers and editors worked closely with political and business allies in the Democratic Party to build a white supremacist society and, in the process, destroy interracial democracy for generations to come.

In Georgia, for example, Henry W. Grady is lionized as the progressive editor who championed reconciliation with the North in the 1880s and turned the *Atlanta Constitution* into the most prominent booster of New South ideology. But Grady also led a political machine, with the *Constitution* as its mouthpiece, that controlled state government, influenced federal policies, championed white supremacy, and spread the use of convict leasing to lure industry to Georgia. After Grady's death in 1889, his successors at the *Constitution* incorporated lynching into the paper's business model. To increase circulation and grow advertising revenue, the *Constitution* and its competitor, the *Atlanta Journal*, fabricated Black criminal acts, transformed mob violence into sensational melodrama, and legitimized acts of terror. In neighboring Alabama, editor and politician William Wallace Screws received a secret subsidy from the Louisville and Nashville Railroad to prop up his financially ailing *Montgomery Daily Advertiser*, the state's largest newspaper. In return, Screws launched a vicious campaign against a populist insurgency that had united white and Black farmers and industrial workers against the railroads, mining interests, and big planters who controlled the state. In Florida, Standard Oil tycoon Henry M. Flagler purchased a controlling stake in Jacksonville's *Florida Times-Union*, the state's largest newspaper, and other newspapers and used these journals to rally support for his railroad projects and to undermine federal investigations into debt peonage and other brutal labor practices. In North Carolina, Josephus Daniels used his newspaper, the Raleigh *News and Observer*, as the propaganda organ for the Democratic Party's violent, racist campaign to destroy the fragile Fusionist alliance of Black Republicans and white Populists, a biracial coalition that had gained control of the governor's office, the state legislature, and the municipal government of Wilmington. The Democrats took back power by fraud and violence at the ballot box; a murderous coup d'état, exile of Black citizens, and destruction of the Black press in Wilmington; and a constitutional amendment instituting Black disenfranchisement.[2]

Ida B. Wells, T. Thomas Fortune, Mary Church Terrell, W.E.B. Du Bois, Alexander Manly, J. Max Barber, John Mitchell Jr., W. Calvin Chase, and other Black journalists fought ferociously against these anti-Black actors, events, and ideologies. Their efforts did little then to stem the growth of white supremacy, but they built a formidable Black public sphere that forever after organized and rallied dissent against African American exclusion from the project of democracy in the United States. Some survived lynching threats and forced exile. Many were traumatized by the racial terror that turned the New South, as W.E.B. Du Bois trenchantly observed in *The Souls of Black Folk*, into "an armed camp for intimidating Black folk."[3] But their work has endured, providing a clear documentary record and a searing indictment of what happened as it happened. Their stories show us what it looked like then to stand up to the exercise of antidemocratic, racist, and often illegal political and economic power.

For example, T. Thomas Fortune, the most influential Black newspaper editor of the late nineteenth century and founder of the short-lived but trailblazing Afro-American League, repeatedly critiqued New South doctrine in general and Henry W. Grady in particular. In writing about Grady's famous 1886 New South speech in New York, in which Grady claimed that white Southerners honored the political rights of Black Southerners, Fortune wrote, "The white men of the South—in legislatures, in courts of justice, in convict camps, in churches, in hotels and theatres, in railroad and steamboat accommodations— do not do justice to their colored fellow-citizens; and when a man like Grady stands up and lies about these matters, we are here to strike the lie on the head." Fortune, who was well acquainted with violent Southern white supremacy from growing up in a political family in Florida, made good on his promise, challenging Grady's anti-Black New South claims in his New York newspapers (the *Globe*, then the *Freeman*, then the *New York Age*) and other press venues even after Grady's unexpected and premature death. What's more, Fortune championed a "race-first" Black politics divorced from party that fought for the enforcement of the Reconstruction era amendments rather than kowtowing to the increasingly racially conservative Republican Party. Ida B. Wells, the militant Black journalist who was radicalized after her friends, successful Black businessmen, were lynched in Memphis, drew a straight line from Grady and his New South doctrine to the practice of lynching, which she explained and documented in *Southern Horrors*.[4]

This book joins the growing effort to reconsider the influence of news media during times of political change. Newspapers and other news outlets have played "an enormous role in American politics," historians Bruce J. Schulman and Julian E. Zelizer argued recently, but their political influence has not received the detailed attention it deserves.[5] Journalism historian Andie Tucher attributes the blind spot in part to the quotidian nature of news content. Journalism "seems too common—in every sense of the term—to merit serious attention," she writes.[6] Professional journalists have also discouraged closer scrutiny of journalism's political influence. The norms of neutrality and objectivity that emerged in the twentieth century were supposed to enhance democratic discourse by elevating journalists above partisan politics. But the objectivity movement had less-idealistic goals as well. The vow of strict impartiality made it easier for commercial newspapers to pursue readers of all ideological persuasions. And while objective journalists defended their right to referee the public sphere aggressively, they downplayed any role in shaping political outcomes in their communities. Yet the decisions journalists made about what news to cover and how to contextualize it were inherently political.[7] When political historians have taken journalism seriously as an agent of change, they have emphasized the soft power that news media exerts through its contributions to public discourse and have often ignored the hard power wielded by journalists who formed alliances with political, industrial, and financial leaders, or who operated as such leaders themselves. Since the rise of talk radio, cable news, hyperpartisan online media, and—most prominently—the 2016 election of Donald Trump, scholars have begun to rethink the connection between news media and political power. As Schulman and Zelizer write, "Nearly every serious analyst of recent American politics concedes that the relationship between political actors and the mass media is central to understanding the political history of the last century."[8]

We believe the relationship between white newspaper leaders and their Democratic Party and business allies in the New South project is central to understanding how Jim Crow political economies and social orders emerged in the South, how anti-Black ideologies corrupted our criminal justice system and transformed it into a tool of racial control, and how white supremacy metastasized across twentieth-century America and remains a powerful force in American life to this day. More than mere peddlers of racist tropes and stories, many white editors and publishers in the Jim Crow South were straight-out political actors, deeply entrenched in Democratic Party campaigns, machines, and policy making. They used their positions and their newspapers to unite white publics in support of Black disenfranchisement and economic exploitation; to build and sustain punitive penal systems that criminalized Blackness and stole the labor and lives of Black men, women, and children; to defend and foment lynching and other forms of racial terror used to enforce white supremacy; to spread racist political propaganda that disrupted interracial political alliances and built the one-party so-called Solid South; and to propagate misinformation campaigns against enemies, the Justice Department, and other investigative entities to protect white Southern political and business interests. Many of these publishers and editors served as political leaders themselves—as officials in municipal, state, and federal government and as delegates to the constitutional conventions that codified the Jim Crow political system. In certain instances, they ran industrial enterprises that profited enormously from convict labor and debt peonage. Finally, many white Southern newspaper leaders worked directly and indirectly with both state and federal election campaigns and thus helped constitute the white supremacist Democratic Party network and its communication power within Southern states, between Southern states, and between the Solid South and its elected officials in the federal government.

Historians have produced voluminous literature on the rise of the New South since C. Vann Woodward published his masterwork, *Origins of the New South, 1877–1913,* in 1951.[9] While they have challenged some of his ideas, his central thesis still stands: the ex-Confederates who "redeemed" the South after Reconstruction built a region quite different from the one that preceded the Civil War through the promotion of industrial capitalism, corruption of democracy, and crafting of a new political economic and social order based on the brutal subjugation of Black Southerners.[10] This understanding of the New South informs the overarching framework of *Journalism and Jim Crow.*

Forty years after Woodward forever changed the terrain of New South historiography, Edward L. Ayers published his synthesis *The Promise of the New South,* focusing on the familiar New South historical tropes of the region's "stunted economic growth, narrow political alternatives, poisoned race relations, confined roles for women, and shallow intellectual life."[11] But he also developed an especially vivid portrait of populism in general and the Farmers' Alliance in particular—those remarkable if short-lived movements that critiqued key tenets of New South boosterism and offered new ways of thinking about the possible structure of social, political, and economic relations, including biracial cooperation. Other work on populism in the South provides nuanced understandings of these movements, including the existence of an independent Black populist movement.[12] *Journalism and Jim Crow* documents and dramatizes the role newspaper owners and editors played in spreading the concepts of New South ideology and populist critique.

Much of *Journalism and Jim Crow* could not have been written without another body of recent New South literature. For several decades now, historians have produced painstakingly sourced work documenting the role of convict leasing and debt peonage and lynching in the creation of the New South.[13] While the resulting works have not addressed the role of the press in constituting or resisting these systems and practices, they have drawn rich, detailed explanations and portraits of forced labor regimes and racial terror, leaving important clues in the footnotes that point toward press involvement. Alex Lichtenstein's argument that so-called progressive New South leaders built a distinctive Southern political economy based on convict leasing—a cruel penal slavery that targeted Black Southerners—is of particular importance to our book's arguments.[14]

Historians have also produced an outpouring of work exploring the nexus of journalism and the African American freedom struggle, including work on the Black press.[15] Biographies of Black journalists in the late nineteenth and early twentieth centuries are essential to the stories we tell in *Journalism and Jim Crow*.[16] Other work—on the mainstream press during the civil rights movement and Black Power era,[17] and on the relationship of the white Southern press to these struggles[18]—has inspired if not directly informed our work.

The new subfield known variously as "Jim Crow North" and "Freedom North Studies" has challenged historical narratives of "Jim Crow" as a Southern invention of the late nineteenth century. This work has established important new understandings about the history of structural anti-Black racism in the United States: the term "Jim Crow" originated decades earlier in the North as free Black citizens battled segregated schools and housing as well as gerrymandering meant to weaken Black voting power; liberals in the North and the federal government claimed the mantle of color-blindness while embedding unconstitutional race-based discrimination in housing and education policies and practices; and Black activists worked tirelessly against segregation and racial inequality in Northern cities across much of the twentieth century. But understanding the creation of Jim Crow in the New South remains massively important. The New South was a regional political economic project that produced a highly distinctive Jim Crow regime—an exceptionally violent, rapacious, and near-totalizing regime with a racial ideology that crept far beyond Southern borders. Put plainly, the North had racist systems, but the South became a murderously racist totalitarian state. As we demonstrate repeatedly, the political actors involved in creating both the New South and its Jim Crow system exercised considerable power in American life, including Congress, leading the rest of the country to become, as others have argued, "a southern nation."[19]

Journalism and Jim Crow also complicates the popular narrative of the American press in the late nineteenth century, which tends to focus myopically on white urban dailies in the North. It's a familiar story. As the country industrialized, many newspapers in Northern cities became mass commercial enterprises, propelling and propelled by the rapid growth of consumer culture and increased demand for advertising. To appeal to more readers, they gradually began to jettison partisanship and embrace political independence. It was an age of mass politics, and while some Northern papers maintained a partisan identity, the trend toward nonpartisan, commercialized journalism that dominated the twentieth century had begun to take hold.

The landscape of American journalism in the late nineteenth century was actually vast and variegated, containing the most diverse array of print publication types, ideological and political positions, languages, topical interests, and intended audiences of any period before or after. While many kinds of news publications and journalism appear in the stories we tell—country weeklies, religious newspapers, muckraking magazines, populist papers—*Journalism and Jim Crow* concentrates on the white urban dailies in the South that actively built the world of Jim Crow and the Black press in both the South and the North that fought against this construction. Historians have done surprisingly little work on the urban Southern press during this period. They have focused primarily on Henry W. Grady in Atlanta, Francis Warrington Dawson in Charleston, Henry Watterson in Louisville, and a handful of other editors who were eager to join the new age of newspaper prosperity by adapting some aspects of the so-called new journalism of the urban North and enticing industry below the Mason-Dixon Line with their New South boosterism.[20] Yet Southern newspapers during this period developed in economic conditions that lagged far behind those of their Northern counterparts. Operating in a mostly agrarian and rural economy that suffered a steep decline after the Civil War, Southern newspapers bore only a passing resemblance to the commercial powerhouses that were emerging in the North. Partisan commitment was the rule rather than the exception. In many ways, the Southern press operated much as the partisan press had before the Civil War. Publishers and editors, even of white urban dailies, eagerly accepted subsidies from political parties, railroad companies, and powerful industrialists; in return, they engaged in political struggle on behalf of their benefactors. In notable instances, Southern publishers and editors themselves held political office and owned industrial enterprises.[21]

In the South, Black newspapers began appearing immediately after the Civil War and proliferated across the late nineteenth century, but after Reconstruction, when the political activism that animated their pages and mission became increasingly dangerous, editors were often forced to pull their punches. Meanwhile, many important Black newspapers emerged in the North after Reconstruction, where white supremacy posed a less existential threat. Anti-Black racism existed beyond the South, of course, but there was nonetheless open space for frank discussion of the "race problem" and militant agitation for Black civil and political rights. The accommodation with white supremacists that Booker T. Washington promoted was a much safer approach for Black publishers and editors in the South. As *Journalism and Jim Crow* shows, Washington offered public support and often exerted behind-the-scenes control of Black newspapers that embraced the New South's focus on industrial capitalism and accepted its doctrine of separate but equal. Black Southern journalists who were brave enough to condemn lynching or to otherwise challenge white supremacy were frequently forced to flee for their lives to the North by angry mobs that were often incited by white press leaders. These exiled Black journalists included Alexander Manly in North Carolina, Ida B. Wells in Tennessee, Jesse C. Duke in Alabama, and J. Max Barber in Georgia, to name just a few. That so many Black journalists in the South had the courage to stand up against white supremacy is remarkable. That so many white journalists in the South actively built white supremacy—and actively threatened, excluded, and silenced Black journalists—is a historical truth that demands recognition and acknowledgment. Black leaders and journalists in the North, like Fortune in New York City, Wells in Chicago, and William Monroe Trotter in Boston, were much better positioned to launch attacks on white supremacy as it spread across the South and the country. Many met the New South and its creeping systems and ideology of racial caste with fierce, militant resistance and used their newspapers to nurture new forms of Black activism and to constitute a national Black public sphere.[22]

* * *

The story we tell begins at the end of Reconstruction, the country's extraordinary experiment in biracial democracy, which lasted barely twelve years after the Civil War. During that brief period, Black Southerners made notable gains across many areas of life, participating politically in public affairs, expanding productive skill sets, building economic capacity, gaining literacy and education, and creating connected communities. They also launched newspapers to serve their communities. The three Reconstruction amendments meant to endow newly freed people with citizenship rights, along with the federal legislation meant to enforce the amendments, were such a profound revision of the U.S. charter—such a revolutionary remaking of U.S. society—that Eric Foner has deemed the era of their creation "the second founding."[23] The Thirteenth Amendment forbade slavery and involuntary servitude, thus introducing the word "slavery" to the Constitution and dismantling an institution that had been central to the American way of life long before and long after the country's founding. The Fourteenth Amendment granted citizenship to all "persons born or naturalized in the United States" and promised equal protection under the law, laying waste the U.S. Supreme Court's infamous *Dred Scott* ruling that Black people in the United States could not be citizens. And the Fifteenth Amendment guaranteed the right to vote to all citizens, regardless of "race, color, or previous condition of servitude."[24] The nation's charter had been remade to include Black Americans in the collective project of democracy.

Once congressional Republicans took charge of Reconstruction in 1867, Democratic Party newspapers were the only institutions to remain under native white control in the South, and they wielded surprising influence in the North. The epithet of "carpetbagger"—indicating a Northern white man who came to the South to manipulate politically naïve Blacks and steal from white taxpayers—first appeared in Alabama's *Montgomery Daily Mail* in late 1867. The slur spread across the South and into the Northern press, including such influential Republican outlets as Horace Greeley's *New-York Tribune* and E. L. Godkin's magazine, *The Nation*. In 1873 the *Tribune* published excerpts from *The Prostrate South*, a devastating depiction of supposed Black corruption and incompetence in South Carolina's biracial government. The *New York Herald* followed with a similar diatribe against Reconstruction, and the momentum of pack journalism soon took hold. Articles from nationally prominent journalists denouncing corruption in the South appeared in *Harper's*, *Scribner's*, the *Atlantic Monthly*, and other popular publications. The nation's experiment in biracial democracy in the South, where 90 percent of Black Americans lived, was losing the battle over public opinion in the North.[25]

The "best men" of the South, including white newspaper publishers and editors, rejected and resisted the "second founding" of Reconstruction. Its demise was hurried along by the infamous bargain of 1877 that settled the contested 1876 U.S. presidential election, when national leaders of both parties, under pressure from white Southern leaders, agreed to support Republican Rutherford B. Hayes over Democrat Samuel Tilden. The bargain was straightforward if craven. Hayes would recognize Democratic control of the South and end federal "interference" in Southern affairs. In return, Democrats agreed to safeguard the citizenship rights of Black people, a promise they never intended to keep. Instead, they began the process of building the world of Jim Crow.

The political world of the South from the end of Reconstruction to the turn of the century was neither monolithic nor uniform, but it was dominated by the Democratic Party, which jealously guarded and leveraged its power to create the perception and near reality of a white, one-party Solid South. Many of the white Democratic Party leaders who had "redeemed" their states from "radical" Republicanism and "Negro rule" in the 1870s were former Confederate officers. Outraged by federal intervention in the South—and by Republican efforts to spend tax dollars on education and infrastructure and to build biracial governments—the new Democratic leaders proudly declared themselves to be low-tax, small-government conservatives. They were also, of course, white supremacists. Their close allies in the press had been fighting at their side throughout the battle against Reconstruction, and they were now some of the best-known names in Southern journalism—Francis Dawson at the *Charleston News and Courier*, for example, and William Wallace Screws at the *Montgomery Daily Advertiser*. The Democrats who regained power in the late 1870s preferred the "conservative" label, but they were also called "Bourbon Democrats," a moniker that gained traction in the Northern press. Evoking both the Southern whiskey and the restoration of the Bourbon monarchy after the French Revolution, the "Bourbon" political label suggested a reactionary mind-set—an absolute rejection of Reconstruction and a desire to return to the glorious past before the Civil War.[26]

The Reconstruction amendments, which empowered formerly enslaved persons as citizens with political and civil rights and transferred state authority over these rights to the federal government, were formidable obstacles to the world of white supremacy that the Democrats were bent on building. White newspaper publishers and editors in the New South actively worked to strip the new amendments of their power and meanings. In 1883 Grady and his *Atlanta Constitution* celebrated the U.S. Supreme Court decision in the *Civil Rights Cases* that laid waste to the Civil Rights Act of 1875, which required equal treatment across the color line in public venues, accommodations, transportation, and juries. In deciding that the Fourteenth Amendment prohibited unequal treatment by the state, not individuals and businesses, the court had drawn the line, Grady argued in an editorial, "just where it should be." In 1885 he elaborated on his earlier editorial, popularizing the idea of "equal but separate" social spaces for white and Black Southerners in a widely read essay in a national magazine. It was an idea later enshrined by the U.S. Supreme Court's decision in *Plessy v. Ferguson* in 1896, holding that state laws mandating segregation were permissible under the Fourteenth Amendment if accommodations were "separate but equal," a constitutional doctrine that galvanized the social order of Jim Crow. In 1889, in an invited speech before an elite group of political and businessmen in Boston that included former president Grover Cleveland, Grady attacked the federal Lodge Bill, which was meant to enforce voting rights for Black men in the South. Grady's unexpected death just days later at the height of his popularity as New South spokesperson transformed the speech, already widely praised in newspapers across the country, into a virtually unassailable philosophy of the way forward for a New South and a unified nation: the Southern Black man could not be entrusted with the vote, and the "race problem" must be left to the white South to solve. The near deification of Grady and his New South doctrine laid the ideological groundwork for the bill's defeat in the Senate by Southern filibuster and the institution and spread of the 1890 Mississippi Plan, designed to disenfranchise Black citizens. Lynching coverage in Grady's *Constitution* and other white Southern newspapers—which sometimes began well in advance of a lynching—tended to glorify and even foment lynching, normalizing white social acceptance of racial terror as a legitimate if extralegal tool for controlling Black people.[27]

White Southern journalists thus used the soft power of narrative and propaganda in their newspaper coverage to shape culture and society. This soft power, wielded through newspaper content, produced shared understandings—the social attitudes and norms—necessary to sustain the white supremacist world they built with their allies. But these journalists, and the newspaper institutions they ran, exercised hard power too. They assumed active roles in constructing state and municipal political, economic, and social policies meant to supplant the Reconstruction era amendments and their supporting legislation. They helped devise laws and systems that disenfranchised Black men; unjustly imprisoned Black men, women, and children and exploited their labor; stripped Black men of the ability to serve on juries and hold positions of authority in the criminal justice system; built a segregated social landscape providing little economic opportunity for their Black neighbors; and actively fomented and justified racial terror lynchings to control the New South's system of racial caste.

In Georgia, for example, Grady's political ring, with the *Atlanta Constitution* as its organ, protected, extended, and sustained the state's convict leasing system. In Tennessee, Arthur S. Colyar, a leading industrialist, politician, and editor, followed Grady's lead, lining his own pockets with the wealth he accrued through the convict labor he employed in his coal mines and supported in campaigns orchestrated through his own and other newspapers. In Alabama, the South's most industrialized state, white newspaper editors worked with executives at the Louisville and Nashville Railroad and the Tennessee Coal, Iron and Railroad Company to marshal legislative votes to protect convict leasing, despite rising public opposition driven in part by a new populist reform press. In Florida, Flagler built a tourist empire of hotels, resorts, and railroads using convict and peon labor, controlling public knowledge of his practices and shaping public opinion through his control of the Florida press. Grady, Colyar, Flagler, and their peers exploited a clause in the Thirteenth Amendment: slavery was unconstitutional "except as a punishment for crime." Black journalists challenged the lease system and tried to rally white opposition in the North. T. Thomas Fortune warned that a system in which "honest wage earners" are forced to compete with convict labor will eventually cause "wage earners of the entire country [to be] damaged and degraded." While convict lease laws emerged during Reconstruction, the laws were sustained and the system expanded in scale and brutality under Democratic rule across Southern states in the decades following the end of Reconstruction. It was a system that essentially criminalized Blackness and set in place anti-Black policing and criminal justice structures, practices, and attitudes that endure today.[28]

White Southern newspapermen also exercised hard power in the historically consequential arena of Black suffrage, helping to build the white supremacist, one-party "Solid South" that endured until the Voting Rights Act of 1965. In 1875 the white editor of the Jackson *Clarion*, Mississippi's leading Democratic newspaper, helped devise and execute a campaign of public rhetoric and terrorist violence intended to suppress the Black vote in state elections, replace Republican with Democratic rule, and overwhelm Reconstruction in the South. Editor Ethelbert Barksdale joined forces with Democratic Party leader James Z. George to launch the "Mississippi Plan," a combination of newspaper commentary, voter fraud, and vicious guerilla warfare designed to overthrow "Negro rule" in the state. While "white line" militias attacked Black communities, burned homes, and murdered civilians, Barksdale and George used the *Clarion* and other newspapers to blame the violence and chaos on the "carpetbagger" governor, Adelbert Ames, and his "venal and incompetent" administration. As the 1875 elections approached in Mississippi, Ames pleaded with President Ulysses S. Grant to send federal troops to stop the slaughter. Grant refused, deciding the Republican Party would have to concede Mississippi to the white Democrats if they wanted any chance of retaining control in Northern states such as Ohio, where white voters had turned against Reconstruction and opposed sending federal troops to maintain biracial democracy in the South.[29]

The Mississippi Plan spread to other Southern states. With significant help from their newspapers, white Democrats in South Carolina executed a textbook example of the scheme in 1876. A young Benjamin Ryan Tillman and other militia leaders carried out violent attacks on Black communities and sowed fear among potential Black voters, while former Confederate general

Wade Hampton and Democratic newspaper editors blamed the chaos and conflict on the Republican governor and Black state militia units. In a message aimed directly at Northern politicians and newspaper editors, South Carolina's white Democratic press trumpeted Hampton's pledge to protect African American rights and pursue peaceful reconciliation with the North. The former Confederate won the race for governor in an election marked by widespread voter intimidation and outright fraud. The following year, President Rutherford Hayes recalled the remaining federal troops in the South, formally ending Reconstruction.[30]

Barksdale, the white newspaper editor at the helm of the 1875 Mississippi Plan, served two terms in the U.S. House in the 1880s and was part of the Solid South political bloc. When the federal Lodge Bill meant to protect Black voting rights in the South became a matter of national discussion in 1889, and after Henry Grady dedicated the final speech of his life to its opposition, Barksdale put his rhetorical and political skills to work in an essay for a propaganda hit piece opposing the Lodge Bill and Black voting rights titled *Why the Solid South?* He paved the way for the 1890 Mississippi Plan, a state constitutional amendment, written in contravention of the Fifteenth Amendment, that effectively disenfranchised Black men through literacy and so-called understanding provisions.[31]

This strategy of revising suffrage laws, thus giving local white officials the power to decide who could vote and effectively disenfranchising Black citizens, spread across the South. White Democrats stated their primary goal explicitly: "To ensure white supremacy," as one South Carolina editor declared. U.S. Representative James K. Vardaman stated it more crudely: the Mississippi constitution was designed "for no other purpose than to eliminate the nigger from politics." When Henry Williams, a Black man from Mississippi, challenged the state's new constitution on grounds that it disenfranchised African Americans and excluded them from jury service, the U.S. Supreme Court sided with Vardaman and Mississippi's white Democrats. The justices voted unanimously, 9–0, to uphold the new suffrage restrictions, claiming Williams had been unable to prove the new rules were discriminatory. It's no coincidence that North Carolina Democrats carried out a murderous coup d'état against Black political leaders in Wilmington and wrested control of the state from the biracial Fusionists the same year the Supreme Court's *Williams* decision validated the Mississippi Plan in the South. As with *Plessy v. Ferguson's* "separate but equal" ruling on segregation in 1896, the *Williams v. Mississippi* decision undermining Black voting rights showed how far the nation would go in ceding local control to white Southern Democrats. Thus was born a powerful Southern voting bloc in the federal government that exercised control for decades.[32]

Despite the Democratic Party's efforts to project total control in the New South, political factions periodically arose to challenge its power, including various short-lived independent movements in the late 1870s and early 1880s and the more robust populist revolts of the 1880s and early 1890s. The news publications associated with these movements, and their leaders, are also important political actors in the making of the New South. Yeoman farmers in the New South found themselves on the losing end of the modernizing agricultural economy. The opening of the Suez Canal in 1869 had flooded British markets with cotton from Egypt and India, causing global cotton prices to plummet. Under the onerous crop-lien system, small Southern farmers grew dependent on credit from merchants and banks, but declining cotton prices made it nearly impossible to pay the steep interest rates. Many lost their land and were forced into sharecropping or wage labor.[33] As the agrarian economy fell apart, populist reform movements emerged—both white and Black—fueled by struggling small farmers demanding change in the New South. These political movements peaked and then fell quickly in the 1890s, but for a brief historical moment, populism raised tantalizing prospects for biracial democracy to reemerge in the region.[34] In Alabama, for example, a biracial coalition of farmers and workers delivered a clear majority of votes against the Democrats in the 1892 governor's race, only to have the election stolen by blatant voter fraud. The state's colorful and combative populist press, bearing names such as the *Living Truth*, the *Weekly Toiler*, and the *New Leader*, fought back valiantly and ensured the ballot-box stuffing received national attention. But the populist movement lacked the cohesiveness to challenge the Democrats over time. In the end, white Democratic leaders played on racial loyalty to split the biracial Populist coalition and build support for new suffrage laws that restricted Black voting. Always struggling financially, the beleaguered populist press faded quietly in the mid-1890s, many of these white and Black publications lost to history forever.[35]

Railroads were vital to the political economy of the New South, and, perhaps surprisingly, to the livelihoods of many white newspaper editors and publishers featured in *Journalism and Jim Crow*. Consequently, railroads appear throughout the stories we tell. Transportation and communication systems in the late nineteenth century were mutually dependent, and virtually every arena of public and private life depended on both. Industrialists took a great interest in rebuilding the South's decimated railway network after the Civil War and mostly used convict labor, vastly reducing their expenses and financial exposure. Political leaders, many of whom held convict leases, encouraged rail development to develop the region and pursue personal profit. Railroads were essential to newspapers, too, and vice versa. The press needed railroads to deliver paper and printing supplies and to distribute newspapers across the region and country; railroads needed the press to advertise ticket costs and travel schedules and to advocate for railroad interests to state legislatures. Railway leaders spent a great deal of time and money currying favor, providing business loans and insider stock tips to newspapermen and political leaders, as well as free passes, which were also shared with judges, lawyers, and police officials.[36]

The Louisville and Nashville Railroad, commonly called the L&N and nicknamed the "Old Reliable," was especially active in the New South and forged close relationships with prominent newspapermen. From the end of the Civil War to 1920, it grew from roughly three hundred to five thousand miles of track, with lines running across fourteen states, connecting coalfields and cities, including Atlanta. In 1880 Henry Grady accompanied Victor Newcomb, then vice president of the L&N, on a cross-country railroad trip from the South to New York City, publishing an admiring series on "Newcomb's Octopus" in the *Atlanta Constitution* along the way. His goal was to soften the political ground in Georgia to make way for the L&N's incursion and thus make Atlanta the gateway to the South. He succeeded, and he also scored a major personal victory. In New York, Newcomb introduced Grady to financier Cyrus W. Field, who floated Grady a loan to buy a quarter interest in the *Atlanta Constitution*. Grady immediately was named managing editor, and Newcomb advised him through stock trades so that he could reimburse Field. Grady promoted both the L&N and Field's brother, who was pursuing a bid for the U.S. presidency, in the pages of his newspaper. As chapter 1 recounts, the L&N set up Grady to become a chief architect of white supremacy in the New South.[37] In Tennessee the L&N loaned substantial sums to convict-labor industrialist Arthur S. Colyar to fund Nashville newspapers he edited in the 1880s. In Alabama the railroad subsidized the cash-strapped *Montgomery Advertiser*, the propaganda arm of the state's Democratic establishment, allowing it to crush a biracial populist uprising, protect the convict lease system, and defend white supremacy.

* * *

From its inception, *Journalism and Jim Crow* was designed to be an especially coherent collection, more like a traditional monograph than the typical edited book. When we began talking about documenting and writing this history, we realized we couldn't do it alone if we wanted to make timely progress. Many topics required time-consuming work in far-flung archives and vast wells of primary sources, as well as intense reading and detective work across multiple subfields of historiography. So we reached out to scholars with relevant expertise to join us in this significant reinterpretation of the making of white supremacy after Reconstruction, with the white and Black press centered in the story as critical political actors engaged in a fierce, and momentous, democratic struggle.

As we worked on this book, we sometimes worried whether we were inadvertently assessing the past using the standards of the present. Presentism is a cardinal sin of the historical profession, of course, and we don't believe we are guilty of it. While many historians have called Henry W. Grady a "moderate" on race for his era, many Black leaders of his own era viewed him as a serious threat to Black American life. And some prominent white people, like George Washington Cable, agreed. When we say that Grady was a chief architect of white supremacy in the New South, we aren't saying anything new. T. Thomas Fortune said as much in the late 1880s. Does his race disqualify his point of view? Obviously, no. And, like Fortune, we provide robust evidence to support our case. And, yes, the use of the term "white supremacy" and its variants has increased dramatically in public discourse this past decade as Americans have discussed race and efforts to dismantle structural racism. But when we use "white supremacy" to describe the efforts of white Democrats, including white press leaders, to build a society built on racial caste after the Civil War, we are using the term in a historical context. It appears as early as 1867 and 1868 in *New York Times* articles about Democrats in the South, and its use increases notably across the late nineteenth century. By 1898 the Democratic Party in North Carolina used the term repeatedly in its election campaign handbook.[38]

Journalism and Jim Crow examines the role of the press in making and resisting white supremacy in the New South by focusing on prominent macro-level issues and initiatives that spanned the region and state-level case studies that demonstrate how political economies and social orders were built at the state level. We had neither space nor time to include studies of every Southern state or to tell every story worth telling about every Southern state. There is still much work to be done, and we hope other historians, especially graduate students, will pick up the torch (see the epilogue for ideas). But we have tried to tell the stories of people, events, and issues that illuminate how the Southern white press worked to build anti-Black and antidemocratic political economies and social orders in the South—and how the Black press fought to disrupt these efforts.

The first two chapters provide a comprehensive narrative and analytical framework for the book. Kathy Roberts Forde examines how the prominent managing editor of the *Atlanta Constitution* and national spokesperson of the New South, Henry W. Grady, led his "Atlanta Ring" of powerful Georgia Democrats in building white supremacy in the state and the region. "More than any other New South leader," Forde argues, "Grady provided the intellectual predicate and political blueprint for the erection of white supremacist political economies and social orders across the South." She examines his support and protection of convict leasing; normalization of inflammatory reporting practices in lynching coverage; promotion of the idea of "equal but separate," which became *Plessy v. Ferguson*'s "separate but equal" doctrine; use of the *Atlanta Constitution* as the propaganda machine of New South Democrats; and his national advocacy for the disenfranchisement of Black Southerners.

D'Weston Haywood explores the work of militant Black journalists like T. Thomas Fortune, Ida B. Wells, and W.E.B. Du Bois, who mobilized to combat the political economies and social orders of the New South—and directly attacked Grady. "Black journalism," he writes, "became the incubator of a new tide of Black activism." The men and women of the Black press built a critical Black discursive space for Black Americans to debate, organize, and mobilize and exposed "the New South for what it really was." They rejected the New South narrative and the anti-Black systems and structures it spawned and fought instead to build a "New America" that respected Black civil, political, and human rights, a truly multiracial and democratic America.

Chapters 3 and 4 explore racial terror and disenfranchisement as tools of white supremacist newspaper power. Fitzhugh Brundage documents the complex relationship between lynching and newspapers, which previously has received inadequate attention. As he writes, "Any understanding of the phenomenon of lynching in the United States must begin with news accounts of lynchings." Between 1890 and 1920, newspapers in America carried news and discussions about lynching on an almost daily basis. White papers legitimized and at times even incited lynching through the use of sensationalism, melodrama, and racist stereotypes of white female victimhood and "black brutes." The Black press fought back, documenting lynchings, exposing the racist lies used to justify them, and organizing public protest and support for federal anti-lynching bills.

Robert Greene II documents the role of newspapers and print culture in what became white Mississippi's long-range disenfranchisement scheme. The first phase of the "Mississippi Plan" emerged in 1875 when Ethelbert Barksdale, editor of that state's leading Democratic paper, devised a campaign of violence, fraud, and propaganda to undermine the Republican government and end Reconstruction. The second phase began in 1890, when Mississippi became the first state to rewrite its constitution to include discriminatory provisions like literacy tests to keep Black men from voting and exercising political power. In the years between, Greene says, African Americans, like George Washington Williams, T. Thomas Fortune, and W. Calvin Chase, fought back the best way they could: by raising their voices in opposition and challenging their erstwhile allies in the federal government to reject these unconstitutional and antidemocratic acts. "Newspaper editors, historians, and writers become the center of this story," Greene writes, "as they revitalized African American print culture in service of civil, political, and social rights."

Chapters 5 through 9, each a state-level case study, examine the role of journalism in building the Solid South. Sid Bedingfield shows how the "Big Mules"—the new industrialists who were reshaping northern Alabama—used the press to help turn back a populist insurgency that threatened to empower Black voters and bring convict leasing to an end in that state. Desperate to save his failing newspaper, *Montgomery Daily Advertiser* publisher and editor William Wallace Screws sought help from the L&N railroad and its brash leader, Milton H. Smith. In return for his paper's financial subsidy, the *Advertiser* spread disinformation, dismissed voter fraud, and published opposition research provided by the railroad against Populist candidate Reuben F. Kolb during three contentious gubernatorial elections between 1890 and 1894. Kolb's allies in the "reform press" fought back valiantly, denouncing the *Advertiser* and other Democratic establishment newspapers as "hirelings of the plutocrats" and "tools of Wall Street."

Sid Bedingfield also documents the role of the South Carolina white press, including the *Charleston News and Courier*, in facilitating the rise of Benjamin Ryan Tillman and the spread of his ideology of an all-encompassing white supremacy. Unlike agrarian rebellions in other Southern states, South Carolina's angry farmers dismissed the populist call for biracial democracy and embraced Tillman's draconian views of race and society. Bedingfield attributes much of Tillman's success to his mastery of the press. "Like any successful demagogue," he writes, "Tillman developed a symbiotic relationship with the press; he injected drama and excitement into the state's political culture, and the newspapers ensured Tillman remained front and center in the public's imagination."

Kristin Gustafson shows how Josephus Daniels used the Raleigh *News and Observer* to spread white supremacist Democratic Party propaganda in the

North Carolina election of 1898 and foment the Wilmington Massacre. The propaganda demonized Black men as unfit for suffrage and elective office and as sexual predators of white women, a strategy meant to disrupt the state's fragile, biracial Fusionist government. Alexander L. Manly, editor of the Black Wilmington *Daily Record*, fought back with a blistering editorial exposing white hypocrisy, which the Democrats weaponized against him and the Fusionists. The immediate results were the killing and exile of untold numbers of African Americans from Wilmington, the destruction of a fighting Black press, the overthrow of democratic institutions and norms, and the erection of white supremacy. Black disenfranchisement soon followed.

Razvan Sibii demonstrates how the ideology and mechanisms of convict labor and New South industrialism were built across state lines, with newspapers as a critical tool. Arthur S. Colyar was to Tennessee who Henry Grady was to Georgia: a leading proponent of New South ideology, political power broker, and newspaper editor. But, unlike Grady, Colyar was an industrialist, with vast holdings in coal mines—he was a founder of the Tennessee Coal, Iron and Railroad Company—and a proponent and holder of the state convict lease. He used newspaper campaigns to protect the convict lease and his business interests and to fight against free labor. In Tennessee free labor repeatedly fought against the convict lease system, producing dramatic episodes of labor insurrection.

Kathy Roberts Forde and Bryan Bowman examine how captains of industry built the modern state of Florida and controlled newspapers to protect their business interests and shape public opinion. Standard Oil tycoon Henry M. Flagler and railroad magnate Henry B. Plant held controlling interests in the most powerful white newspapers in the state, including the Jacksonville *Times-Union*, to dictate information flow and public opinion about their use of convict and immigrant labor to build their respective railroad and hotel empires. Using his control of the press and related business and political interests, Flagler was able to successfully quash a robust Justice Department investigation of his slave labor camps in the Florida Keys.

In the final chapter, Blair LM Kelley takes readers inside the world of Southern Black journalism after the rise of Jim Crow, when hundreds of editors and writers persisted across the region despite the constant threat of white supremacist violence. For those who spoke boldly, "journalism in the age of lynching was dangerous work," Kelley writes. She circles back to Georgia, where this book begins with the story of Henry W. Grady, and tells the story of one such Black journalist, J. Max Barber, editor of the *Voice of the Negro*, an ambitious national journal based in Atlanta that challenged the accommodationist views of Booker T. Washington. Barber's account of race riots in the city in 1906—particularly his debunking of white newspaper reports accusing Black men of rape—incurred the wrath of white politicians and the white press. Kelley documents the successful campaign to silence the *Voice of the Negro* and force its editor to flee the city.

Finally, the epilogue looks to the recent past, the present, and the future, tracing the outcomes of the events documented across the book and considering, also, the reality of Jim Crow in the North. How does the history of *Journalism and Jim Crow* shape our present and with what consequences—and possibilities—for journalism, democracy, and racial justice? Where can we go from here?

For generations after the Civil War, the white Southern press was committed to constructing an antidemocratic world of white supremacy, with little regard for Black civil, social, political, or even human rights. The Black press fought for a multiracial democracy of equality, justice, and opportunity for all. The white Southern press, allied with white political and business interests, achieved far-reaching and long-lasting results, with tragic consequences for the American experiment. This is the story we tell in *Journalism and Jim Crow*.

Notes

1. See D'Weston Haywood, "Fight for a New America," in *Journalism and Jim Crow*.

2. Kathy Roberts Forde, "Architect of the New South"; W. Fitzhugh Brundage, "The Press and Lynching"; Sid Bedingfield, "Populist Insurgency, Alabama"; Kathy Roberts Forde and Bryan Bowman, "Tourist Empires, Florida"; and Kristin Gustafson, "Death of Democracy, North Carolina," all in *Journalism and Jim Crow*.

3. W.E.B. Du Bois, *The Souls of Black Folk* (Chicago: McClurg, 1903), 105.

4. T. Thomas Fortune, *New York Freeman*, January 22, 1887, in C. Calloway-Thomas, "T. Thomas Fortune on the 'Land of Chivalry and Deviltry,'" *Negro History Bulletin* 42, no. 2 (1979): 40–45, 41; Kerri K. Greenidge, *Black Radical: The Life and Times of William Monroe Trotter* (New York: Liveright Publishing, 2020), 25–26; Ida B. Wells, *Southern Horrors: Lynch Law in All Its Phases* (New York Age Print, 1892), http://www.gutenberg.org/files/14975/14975-h/14975-h.htm.

5. Bruce J. Schulman and Julian E. Zelizer, eds., *Media Nation: The Political History of News in Modern America* (Philadelphia: University of Pennsylvania Press, 2017), 2.

6. Andie Tucher, "Why Journalism History Matters: The Gaffe, the 'Stuff,' and the Historical Imagination," *American Journalism* 31, no. 4 (2014): 434.

7. On objectivity norm, see Michael Schudson, *Discovering the News: A Social History of American Newspapers* (New York: Basic Books, 1978); Richard L. Kaplan, *Politicians and the American Press: The Rise of Objectivity, 1865–1920* (Cambridge, UK: Cambridge University Press, 2002); Michael Schudson, "Persistence of Vision: Partisan Journalism in the Mainstream Press," 140–50, in *A History of the Book in America*, vol. 4, *Print in Motion: The Expansion of Publishing and Reading in the United States, 1880–1940*, ed. Carl F. Kaestle and Janice A. Radway (Chapel Hill: University of North Carolina Press, 2009; John Nerone, *The Media and Public Life: A History* (Cambridge, UK: Polity Press, 2014), 167–83; Richard L. Kaplan, "From Partisanship to Professionalism: The Transformation of the Daily Press," 116–39, in Kaestle and Radway, *History of the Book in America*.

8. Schulman and Zelizer, *Media Nation*, 2.

9. C. Vann Woodward, *Origins of the New South, 1877–1913* (1951; repr., Baton Rouge: Louisiana State University Press, 1971). For examples of some of this early literature, see George B. Tindall, *The Emergence of the New South, 1913–1945* (Chapel Hill: University of North Carolina Press, 1967), and Paul Gaston, *The New South Creed: A Study in Southern Mythmaking* (Montgomery, AL: NewSouth Books, 1970).

10. See John B. Boles and Bethany L. Johnson, eds., Origins of the New South *Fifty Years Later: The Continuing Influence of a Historical Classic* (Baton Rouge: Louisiana State University Press, 2003).

11. Edward L. Ayers, *The Promise of the New South: Life after Reconstruction*, 15th anniversary ed. (1992; New York: Oxford University Press, 2007), viii.

12. See, for example, Omar H. Ali, *In the Lion's Mouth: Black Populism in the New South, 1886–1900* (Oxford: University Press of Mississippi, 2010); James M. Beeby, ed., *Populism in the South Revisited: New Interpretations and New Departures* (Oxford: University Press of Mississippi, 2012); Gerald H. Gaither, *Blacks and the Populist Movement: Ballots and Bigotry in the New South* (Tuscaloosa: University of Alabama Press, 2005); Matthew Hild, *Greenbackers, Knights of Labor, and Populists: Farmer-Labor Insurgency in the Late-Nineteenth-Century South* (Athens: University of Georgia Press, 2007); Robert C. McMath Jr., *American Populism: A Social History* (New York: Hill and Wang, 1992); Steven Hahn, *A Nation Under Our Feet: Black Political Struggles in the Rural South from Slavery to the Great Migration* (Cambridge: The Belknap Press of Harvard University Press, 2003), 364-464; Steven Hahn, *The Roots of Southern Populism: Yeoman Farmers and the Transformation of the Georgia Upcountry, 1850–1890*, updated ed. (New York: Oxford University Press, 2006); Barton C. Shaw, *The Wool-Hat Boys: Georgia's Populist Party* (Baton Rouge: Louisiana State University Press, 1984); Lawrence Goodwyn, *The Populist Moment: A Short History of the Agrarian Revolt in America* (New York: Oxford University Press, 1978); Robert C. McMath Jr., *Populist Vanguard: A History of the Southern Farmers' Alliance* (Chapel Hill: University of North Carolina, 1975);

William Warren Rogers Sr., *The One-Gallused Rebellion: Agrarianism in Alabama, 1865–1896* (1970; repr., Tuscaloosa: University of Alabama Press, 2001); Sheldon Hackney, *Populism to Progressivism in Alabama* (1969; repr., Tuscaloosa: University of Alabama Press, 2009); C. Vann Woodward, *Tom Watson, Agrarian Rebel* (1938, 1955; repr., Eastford, CT: Martino, 2014).

13. On debt peonage, see, for example, Douglas A. Blackmon, *Slavery by Another Name: The Re-Enslavement of Black Americans from the Civil War to World War II* (New York: Anchor Books, 2009); Mary Ellen Curtin, *Black Prisoners and Their World: Alabama, 1865–1900* (Charlottesville: University Press of Virginia, 2000); Pete Daniel, *The Shadow of Slavery: Peonage in the South, 1901–1969* (1972; repr., Urbana: University of Illinois Press, 1990); Talitha LeFlouria, *Chained in Silence: Black Women and Convict Labor in the New South* (Chapel Hill: University of North Carolina Press, 2015); Sarah Haley, *No Mercy Here: Gender, Punishment, and the Making of Jim Crow Modernity* (Chapel Hill: University of North Carolina Press, 2016); Alex Lichtenstein, *Twice the Work of Free Labor: The Political Economy of Convict Labor in the New South* (London: Verso, 1996); Matthew J. Mancini, *One Dies, Get Another: Convict Leasing in the American South, 1866–1928* (Columbia: University of South Carolina Press, 1996); Vivien M. L. Miller, *Hard Labor and Hard Time: Florida's "Sunshine Prison" and Chain Gangs* (Gainesville: University Press of Florida, 2012); Paul Ortiz, *Emancipation Betrayed: The Hidden History of Black Organizing and White Violence in Florida from Reconstruction to the Bloody Election of 1920* (Berkeley: University of California Press, 2005); David M. Oshinsky, *Worse Than Slavery: Parchman Farm and the Ordeal of Jim Crow Justice* (New York: Free Press, 1997); Karin A. Shapiro, *A New South Rebellion: The Battle against Convict Labor in the Tennessee Coalfields, 1871–1896* (Chapel Hill: University of North Carolina Press, 1998). On lynching, see, for example, W. Fitzhugh Brundage, *Lynching in the New South: Georgia and Virginia, 1880–1930* (Urbana: University of Illinois Press, 1993); W. Fitzhugh Brundage, ed., *Under Sentence of Death: Lynching in the South* (Chapel Hill: University of North Carolina Press, 1997); Philip Dray, *At the Hands of Persons Unknown: The Lynching of Black America* (New York: Modern Library, 2002); Crystal N. Feimster, *Southern Horrors: Women and the Politics of Rape and Lynching* (Cambridge: Harvard University Press, 2009); Daniel Kato, *Liberalizing Lynching: Building a New Racialized State* (New York: Oxford University Press, 2016); Michael J. Pfeifer, *Rough Justice: Lynching and American Society, 1878–1946* (Urbana: University of Illinois Press, 2004); Stewart E. Tolnay and E. M. Beck, *A Festival of Violence: An Analysis of Southern Lynchings, 1882–1930* (Urbana: University of Illinois Press, 1995); Margaret Vandiver, *Lethal Punishment: Lynchings and Legal Executions in the South* (New Brunswick, NJ: Rutgers University Press, 2005); Christopher Waldrep, *The Many Faces of Judge Lynch: Extralegal Violence and Punishment in America* (New York: Palgrave Macmillan, 2002); Christopher Waldrep, *African Americans Confront Lynching: Strategies of Resistance from the*

Civil War to the Civil Rights Era (Lanham, MD: Rowman and Littlefield, 2008); Kidada E. Williams, *They Left Great Marks on Me: African American Testimonies of Racial Violence from Emancipation to World War I* (New York: New York University Press, 2012).

14. Lichtenstein, *Twice the Work of Free Labor.*

15. See, for example, Jacqueline Bacon, *Freedom's Journal: The First African American Newspaper* (Lanham, MD: Lexington Books, 2007); Jinx Coleman Broussard, *African American Foreign Correspondents: A History* (Baton Rouge: Louisiana State University Press, 2013); Fred Carroll, *Race News: Black Journalists and the Fight for Racial Justice in the Twentieth Century* (Urbana: University of Illinois Press, 2017); Juan Gonzalez and Joseph Torres, *News for All the People: The Epic Story of Race and the American Media* (New York: Verso, 2011); William G. Jordan, *Black Newspapers and America's War for Democracy, 1914–1920* (Chapel Hill: University of North Carolina Press, 2001); Armistead Scott Pride and Clint C. Wilson, *A History of the Black Press* (Washington, DC: Howard University Press, 1997); Henry Lewis Suggs, ed., *The Black Press in the South* (Westport, CT: Greenwood Press, 1983).

16. See, for example, Ann Field Alexander, *Race Man: The Rise and Fall of the "Fighting Editor," John Mitchell Jr.* (Charlottesville: University of Virginia Press, 2002); Paula J. Giddings, *Ida: A Sword among Lions: Ida B. Wells and the Campaign against Lynching* (New York: Amistad, 2009); Greenidge, *Black Radical*; Emma Lou Thornbrough, *T. Thomas Fortune: Militant Journalist* (Chicago: University of Chicago Press, 1972).

17. See, for example, Aniko Bodroghkozy, *Equal Time: Television and the Civil Rights Movement* (Urbana: University of Illinois Press, 2012); Gene Roberts and Hank Klibanoff, *The Race Beat: The Press, the Civil Rights Struggle, and the Awakening of a Nation* (New York: Vintage Books, 2006); Jane Rhodes, *Framing the Black Panthers: The Spectacular Rise of a Black Power Icon* (New York: New Press, 2007).

18. See, for example, Sid Bedingfield, *Newspaper Wars: Civil Rights and White Resistance in South Carolina, 1935–1965* (Urbana: University of Illinois Press, 2017); Doug Cumming, *The Southern Press: Literary Legacies and the Challenge of Modernity* (Evanston, IL: Northwestern University Press, 2009); John T. Kneebone, *Southern Liberal Journalists and the Issue of Race, 1920–1944* (Chapel Hill: University of North Carolina Press, 1985); Carl R. Osthaus, *Partisans of the Southern Press: Editorial Spokesmen of the Nineteenth Century* (Lexington: University Press of Kentucky, 1994).

19. Thomas J. Sugrue, *Sweet Land of Liberty: The Forgotten Struggle for Civil Rights in the North* (New York: Random House, 2008); Jeanne F. Theoharis and Komozi Woodard, eds., *Freedom North: Black Freedom Struggles outside the South, 1940–1980* (New York: Palgrave Macmillan, 2003); Jeanne Theoharis, *A More Beautiful and Terrible History: The Uses and Misuses of Civil Rights History* (Boston: Beacon Press,

2018); Brian Purnell and Jeanne Theoharis, "Introduction: Histories of Racism and Resistance, Seen and Unseen: How and Why to Think about the Jim Crow North," in *The Strange Careers of the Jim Crow North: Segregation and Struggle Outside the South*, ed. Brian Purnell and Jeanne Theoharis with Komozi Woodard, 1–42 (New York: New York University Press, 2019); Sundiata Keita Cha-Jua and Clarence Lang, "The 'Long Movement' as Vampire: Temporal and Spatial Fallacies in Recent Black Freedom Studies," *Journal of African-American History* 92, no. 2 (2007): 265–88, 283; David A. Bateman, Ira Katznelson, and John S. Lapinski, *Southern Nation: Congress and White Supremacy after Reconstruction* (Princeton, NJ: Princeton University Press, 2018).

20. Kathy Roberts Forde and Katherine A. Foss, "'The Facts—the Color!—the Facts'": The Idea of a Report in American Print Culture, 1885–1910," *Book History* 15 (2012): 123–51; Osthaus, *Partisans of the Southern Press*; E. Culpepper Clark, *Francis Warrington Dawson and the Politics of Restoration: South Carolina, 1874–1889* (Tuscaloosa: University of Alabama Press, 2002); Lewis P. Jones, *Stormy Petrel: N. G. Gonzales and His State* (Columbia: University of South Carolina Press, 1973); Daniel S. Margolies, *Henry Watterson and the New South: The Politics of Empire, Free Trade, and Globalization* (Lexington: University Press of Kentucky, 2006).

21. See, for example, Bedingfield, "Populist Insurgency, Alabama," in *Journalism and Jim Crow*.

22. Jordan, *Black Newspapers and America's War for Democracy*, 16–22; Blair LM Kelley, "Silencing a Generation," in *Journalism and Jim Crow*; Haywood, "Fight for a New America," in *Journalism and Jim Crow*.

23. Eric Foner, *The Second Founding: How the Civil War and Reconstruction Remade the Constitution* (New York: W. W. Norton, 2019); Eric Foner, *Forever Free: The Story of Emancipation and Reconstruction* (New York: Vintage Books, 2006), 197–99.

24. Foner, *Second Founding*, xvi-xxvi, 14.

25. Ted Tunnell, "'Creating 'the Propaganda of History': Southern Editors and the Origins of Carpetbagger and Scalawag," *Journal of Southern History* 72, no. 4 (2006): 790; Eric Foner, *Reconstruction: America's Unfinished Revolution* (1988; repr., New York: Harper and Row, 2008), 524–26.

26. Woodward, *Origins of the New South*, 1–22; Ayers, *Promise of the New South*, 7–8; William J. Cooper Jr., *The Conservative Regime: South Carolina* (1968; repr., Baltimore: Johns Hopkins Press, 1991), 13–40; Clark, *Francis Warrington Dawson*, 1–13.

27. James C. Cobb, "Segregating the New South: The Origins and Legacy of *Plessy v. Ferguson*," *Georgia State University Law Review* 12, no. 4 (1996): 1024–26; Ibram X. Kendi, *Stamped from the Beginning: The Definitive History of Racist Ideas in America* (New York: Nation Books, 2016), 265–66; Raymond B. Nixon, *Henry W. Grady: Spokesman of the New South* (New York: Russell and Russell, 1943),

213–14; Sharon D. Kennedy-Noelle, *Writing Reconstruction: Race, Gender, and Citizenship in the Postwar South* (Chapel Hill: University of North Carolina Press, 2015), 281; Michael Perman, *Struggle for Mastery: Disfranchisement in the South, 1888–1908* (Chapel Hill: University of North Carolina, 2001), 50–51; Ayers, *Promise of the New South*, 146–47; David A. Bateman, Ira Katznelson, and John S. Lapinski, *Southern Nation: Congress and White Supremacy after Reconstruction* (Princeton, NJ: Princeton University Press, 2018), 393; Alexander Keyssar, *The Right to Vote: The Contested History of Democracy in the United States*, rev. ed. (2000; New York: Basic Books, 2009), 92.

28. Forde, "Architect of the New South," Sibii, "Convict Wars, Tennessee," Bedingfield, "Populist Insurgency, Alabama"; Forde and Bowman, "Tourist Empires, Florida," all in *Journalism and Jim Crow*; T. Thomas Fortune, "Whose Problem Is This?" *AME Church Review*, 1894, in *T. Thomas Fortune: The Afro-American Agitator: A Collection of Writings, 1880–1928*, ed. Shawn Leigh Alexander, 221–29 (Gainesville: University Press of Florida, 2008).

29. Nicholas Lemann, *Redemption: The Last Battle of the Civil War* (New York: Farrar, Straus and Giroux, 2006), 170–95; Keyssar, *Right to Vote*, 89–90; Timothy B. Smith, *James Z. George: Mississippi's Great Commoner* (Oxford: University Press of Mississippi, 2012), 101, 111–13; Foner, *Reconstruction*, 560–63.

30. Sid Bedingfield, "Tillman's Rebellion, South Carolina," in *Journalism and Jim Crow*; Stephen Kantrowitz, *Ben Tillman and the Restoration of White Supremacy* (Chapel Hill: University of North Carolina Press, 2000), 64–78; Eric Foner, *Reconstruction*, 573–75.

31. Bruce E. Baker, *What Reconstruction Meant: Historical Memory in the American South* (Charlottesville: University of Virginia Press, 2007), 23–25; K. Stephen Prince, "Jim Crow Memory: Southern White Supremacists and the Regional Politics of Remembrance," in *Remembering Reconstruction: Struggles over the Meaning of America's Most Turbulent Era*, ed. Carole Emberton and Bruce E. Baker, 20–21 (Baton Rouge: Louisiana State University Press, 2017).

32. "Constitutional Convention," *Columbia Daily Register*, March 23, 1895; Perman, *Struggle for Mastery*, 76; Richard Wormser, *The Rise and Fall of Jim Crow* (New York: St. Martin's Press, 2004), 70; Keyssar, *Right to Vote*, 92; Litwack, *Trouble in Mind*, 224.

33. Hahn, *Roots of Southern Populism*, 186–203; McMath, *Populist Vanguard*, 1–11.

34. Hahn, *Roots of Southern Populism*, 204–230; Ayers, *Promise of the New South*, 249–83; Rogers, *One-Gallused Rebellion*, 249–51; Shaw, *Wool-Hat Boys*, 45–102; Ali, *In the Lion's Mouth*, 3–11; Woodward, *Origins of the New South*, 235–63.

35. Bedingfield, "Populist Insurgency, Alabama"; Anthony J. Adams and Gerald H, Gaither, *Black Populism in the United States: An Annotated Bibliography* (Westport, CT: Praeger, 2004).

36. Scott Reynolds Nelson, *Iron Confederacies: Southern Railways, Klan Violence, and Reconstruction* (Chapel Hill: University of North Carolina Press, 1999), 153–56; Maury Klein, *History of the Louisville & Nashville Railroad* (1972; repr., Lexington: University Press of Kentucky, 2013), 375–76.

37. Klein, *History of the Louisville & Nashville*, 375–76; Forde, "Architect of the New South."

38. Michael Powell, "'White Supremacy' Once Meant David Duke and the Klan. Now It Refers to Much More," *New York Times*, October 17, 2020; "Southern Conservatism," *New York Times*, December 10, 1867; "Future Course of the South," *New York Times*, June 9, 1868; "Southern Idea of Democratic Duty," *New York Times*, June 17, 1868; *The Democratic Handbook, 1898*, State Democratic Executive Committee of North Carolina, https://docsouth.unc.edu/nc/dem1898/dem1898.html.

PART ONE

The Contested New South

CHAPTER 1

Architect of the New South

KATHY ROBERTS FORDE

In the 1880s, Henry W. Grady was the most prominent New South spokesperson in the nation and the most influential newspaper editor in the South. He was also the master of the "Atlanta Ring" of Democrats who traded seats for almost two decades in the Georgia governor's office and the U.S. Senate. With Grady at the helm of the ring and the *Atlanta Constitution* as its organ, these men became the chief architects of a white supremacist political economy and social order in Georgia that lasted for generations. Their work in Georgia became a template for leading white men in states across the South.

Grady did not invent the idea of a New South. Other white Southerners did that work in the 1870s in prominent magazine essays exploring how best to rebuild the South after the Civil War. They advocated industrial and railroad development, immigration, Northern investment, technical training, college education, and sectional reconciliation. When Grady became managing editor and part owner of the *Atlanta Constitution* in 1880 at the young age of thirty, he acquired the vehicle and social position to spread a "contagious narrative" about the New South—a story convincing enough and dispersed widely enough to influence collective behavior.[1] To attract Northern investment for Southern industry, and Northern immigrants to build out the labor force and enliven the economy, Grady needed to convince white Americans that race relations in the South were happy and peaceful and that the "race problem" must be left to Southerners to solve. He meant, of course, white Southerners. Grady catapulted to national prominence in 1886 when he gave what became his famous New South speech at Delmonico's restaurant in New York City to an audience of wealthy Northern industrialists and financiers at the invitation of the New England Society of New York. The New South creed was born.[2]

Henry W. Grady's outsize role in crafting white supremacy in Georgia and the South is poorly understood in both professional historiography and popular historical narratives. With a few notable exceptions, historians have largely neglected the antidemocratic purposes to which Grady put his newspaper, voice, and political machine.[3] They have instead discussed him as a "mild" racist for his era, the leading proponent of the New South movement, a booster and builder of Atlanta, a political kingmaker, a conciliator of Northern and Southern sectional tensions, and, finally, a brilliant Southern newspaper editor and orator.[4] Even C. Vann Woodward, who, in his landmark *Origins of the New South*, famously toppled the cheery historical interpretation of the New South movement as one of humanitarian reform and industrial transformation, declined to draw a full portrait of the man.[5] Grady was, Woodward wryly observed in his early work, "an irrepressible good caliph-at-large in Georgia, dispensing a gospel of optimism, charity, and fun. . . . To question the motives of such a man would be churlish."[6]

It is time to be "churlish" and tell a more complete story about Henry W. Grady and his life's work. More than any other New South leader, Grady provided the intellectual predicate and political blueprint for the erection of white supremacist political economies and social orders across the South. In his most famous New South speech, he popularized the idea of "equal but separate" that shaped the accommodationist approach of Booker T. Washington, was enshrined in *Plessy v. Ferguson* in 1896 as "separate but equal," and became the constitutional framework for segregation in public schools and public spaces that lasted in the South until the Civil Rights Act of 1964.[7] In the years that followed his 1886 address in New York City, Grady advocated for the disenfranchisement of Black Southerners as the only way to guard against the supposed behemoth of "Negro domination." In speech after speech, he delivered sotto voce threats against Black Southerners and their efforts to exercise their civil rights. During his decade at the helm of the *Atlanta Constitution*, he used the newspaper as a propaganda machine for the political and business interests of elite white New South Democrats in Georgia and the South. He championed industrial growth and romanticized the dire financial straits of agrarian life as he spread and normalized the ideology of white supremacy. Relatedly, he used his newspaper as a blunt weapon against the political, economic, and social interests of Black Georgians and Southerners. His lynching coverage shifted between tones of callous humor and menace and contributed to white Southern reporting practices that normalized lynching and increasingly fomented mob frenzy and violence against Black bodies. While his friend Robert Alston lost his life attempting to end Georgia's brutal convict leasing system that targeted Black men, women, and children, Grady defended it in the *Constitution* and made sure the powerful men of his Atlanta Ring were able to use it to build their fortunes. He peddled disinformation to serve special interests and masterminded a secretive and corrupt political deal to keep power in the hands of his ring members. He helped build the single-party Democratic framework for white political domination known as the "Solid South." In the final speech of his short life, he advocated against the federal Lodge Bill meant to protect Black voting rights in the South, thus contributing to the bill's demise in the Senate and the later success of the 1890 Mississippi Plan's disenfranchisement scheme that was replicated in other Southern states and lasted until the Voting Rights Act of 1965.[8]

Grady yoked the soft power of his contagious New South narrative, spread through the powerful newspaper he controlled and his nationally publicized speeches, to the hard power of Democratic Party politics and industrial business interests in Georgia, the South, and the nation. This early New South collaboration between a powerful white newspaper editor and powerful white public officials, politicians, businessmen, and industrialists served as a template for similar combinations that would form in other Southern states as Jim Crow regimes were erected and solidified. These combinations, relying on the tools of racial terror such as lynching, convict leasing, and mob violence, allowed little space for African American aspiration and collective effort. They also provided little space for Black or white dissent.

These claims about Henry W. Grady may strike some readers as overblown and unfair, an error of presentist thinking that evaluates the man by contemporary values and standards. But during Grady's era, Black leaders in the South and across the country recognized clearly the New South's threat to Black lives. While many white leaders across the country celebrated Grady's New South creed, most Black leaders denounced it. Black critique during Grady's lifetime and after—clear-eyed, analytical, and often brave—provides the inspiration for the story told here. Black men and women with national reputations and platforms, such as T. Thomas Fortune and Ida B. Wells, called out Grady's lies and antidemocratic ideology. Black journalists in Georgia were less direct, focusing their critique more on the issues raised by white supremacy than on the specific people who built it. As D'Weston Haywood argues in the following chapter, these Black leaders, journalists all, built a distinctive public sphere and critical discursive space, along with civil rights organizations, that rejected Grady's white supremacist New South and pointed the way toward a "New America" of Black inclusion. The white supremacist systems Grady and his peers built have been so durable that, despite many civil rights achievements, later generations of Black leaders and journalists have necessarily continued the "New America" project to the present day.[9]

Murder in the Georgia Capitol

Henry W. Grady ascended simultaneously to the rank of managing editor and part owner of the *Atlanta Constitution* and leadership of the Atlanta Ring in May 1880. But just one year earlier, he had rushed to the Georgia statehouse to attend to his dying friend and former partner at the *Atlanta Herald*. Robert A. Alston had been shot in the head in the state treasurer's office in a dark dispute over the state's lucrative convict leasing system, in which all three Democratic officeholders of the Atlanta Ring held a financial stake.[10]

From 1872 to 1876, Grady and Alston had become close friends as they launched a fierce challenge to the *Atlanta Constitution* with the *Herald*'s sensational, hard-hitting coverage of state politics. But their partnership ended abruptly when Joseph E. Brown—former governor, future U.S. senator, and future member of the Atlanta Ring—foreclosed his bank's mortgage on the newspaper. Brown's move was brass-knuckle retaliation against the *Herald*'s relentless attacks on his shady business practices, collusion with state officials, and bribery of editors across Georgia to gain favorable coverage. When the *Herald* folded, Grady began stringing for the *Atlanta Constitution* and at least five other newspapers, including the *New York Herald*. Alston shifted his talents to politics. In short order, as chairman of the penitentiary committee of the Georgia General Assembly, Alston authored a shocking report on the inhumane treatment of convicts caught in the state's convict leasing system.[11]

Alston's report, released in November 1878, provoked widespread press coverage in Georgia. Men and women were shackled together, he reported, in often filthy conditions in convict camp bunkhouses, where twenty-five children had been born and now lived. Women were subject to sexual assault. The convict death rate was 10 percent on average but as high as 16 in one camp; escape rates were even higher. Many convicts suffered cruel punishments and inhumane treatment. And the state did not comply with its own laws requiring physicians and chaplains to care for the convicts and the "principal keeper of the penitentiary" to make monthly camp inspections. While Alston's report was careful to clear former governor Brown's camps of these abuses (future historians set the record straight), Alston noted in an interview with the *Atlanta Constitution* that "the same lease-law that gives him [Brown] his convicts gives hundreds to other men who inhumanly treat them." Alston was continuing to collect "facts and figures" and already had "enough for a two hours' speech that will absolutely shock the public sentiment into protest and repeal." An outraged state senator introduced a resolution to abolish the lease system, scheduled for debate in the next legislative session in spring 1879.[12]

Georgia began convict leasing in 1866, soon after the Civil War ended. In 1876, with the state fully "redeemed" from "radical Republican" rule, the state leased convicts for twenty years to three penitentiary companies for a total of five hundred thousand dollars, with each company paying twenty-five thousand dollars per year, regardless of the number of convicts received. It was a system devised to increase arrests of Black citizens on the one hand and the wealth of white industrialists on the other.[13]

The onslaught against Alston and his report began immediately. Democratic newspapers across the state denounced him as a traitor. White Leaguers, a white paramilitary organization that terrorized Black Southerners and their allies, hounded him. In early 1879 Alston confided to Dr. William H. Felton, representative from Georgia's seventh district in the U.S. House and leader of the Independents, and his wife, Rebecca Latimer Felton, that his life was being threatened by those connected with the convict lease. He confided the same to well-known Northern journalist George A. Townsend, whom Alston visited two weeks before his death. In an exposé after Alston was killed, Townsend, one of the few white journalists to disapprove in print the disproportionate number of Black convicts in Georgia, wrote that Alston had asked him to publicize the inhumane convict lease system while being careful "not to antagonize the leading public men of the State against him." Townsend made a bold claim: "I have little doubt myself that the contractors for that labor had him murdered." The *New York Times* seemed to agree: "Of the causes which really led to it no mention is made [in Georgia newspapers], but it is, nevertheless, well known to those who have watched the course of recent political events in Georgia, that the killing of Colonel Alston was directly the result of his laudable effort to reform the penitentiary system of that state."[14]

Senator John B. Gordon, a celebrated Confederate general and soon-to-be member of the Atlanta Ring, held a share of a twenty-year convict lease. He worked some convicts on his Beechwood plantation and subleased others to area farmers, including Edward Cox, who helped manage Beechwood and was mentioned in Alston's investigative report. A longtime supporter of Senator Gordon, Alston entreated Gordon to sell his share in the lease; Gordon agreed, asking Alston to sell his share on his behalf. Cox wanted Gordon's share, and when Alston informed him that it was promised to someone else, Cox grew enraged and demanded that Alston arm himself for a duel. Alston repeatedly attempted to soothe Cox, saying he had no interest in a "difficulty." As Cox hounded and pursued him throughout downtown Atlanta on March 11, 1879, Alston asked Governor Alfred H. Colquitt, the third future member of the Atlanta Ring, to protect him. Several hours later, Alston took refuge in the treasurer's office at the capitol building, where he found the treasurer and principal keeper of the penitentiary, who had disputed Alston's convict lease report. Cox barged into the office and shot Alston in a loose approximation of a duel. It was a strange and suspicious affair.[15]

As Alston lay dying, Henry W. Grady stood vigil. Two days later, Grady penned a tribute to his former *Atlanta Herald* business partner that ran on the front page of the *Atlanta Constitution*: "For ten years he was my friend—knit to my heart by a thousand ties." A year later Grady had a new business partner, Evan Howell, with a different newspaper, the *Atlanta Constitution*.[16] What's more, at the very moment Grady became managing editor of the most influential newspaper in the South, he masterminded a secret political and business plot that established him as the leader of the Atlanta Ring. That ring included Colquitt, Brown, and Gordon, who would go on to trade seats in the Georgia governor's office and the U.S. Senate for years to come. Along the way, they reaped vast fortunes from the convict lease system Alston had tried to end.

Alston's killer, Edward Cox, was found guilty of murder and sentenced to life in prison in May 1879, less than two months after the event. Newspapers across the country covered both the murder and the trial. In a strange turn, Cox was sent to serve his life term at former governor Joseph E. Brown's convict camp at the Dade Coal Company mines. But Cox did not work in the mines with the other convicts, most of whom were Black. Instead, he milked cows and took care of livestock. In a letter to the editor of the *New York Times* in 1881, an observer of Georgia politics claimed that Brown had an interest "in covering up the ugly features of the shameful combination" involved in Alston's murder and predicted that Cox would eventually be pardoned. That's exactly what happened one year later. Henry W. Grady even signed the petition asking Governor Alexander Stephens for the pardon. Cox served only three years of his life sentence and later became superintendent of the same Brown convict camp where he served time.[17]

For three years after Alston's death, Black leaders in Atlanta's Dekalb County, where Alston lived and was buried, organized an annual event at his grave to memorialize his efforts to end the convict lease system. A broadside shared in the Black community in 1881 urged all to attend a decoration of his tombstone "to testify exalted admiration of the life and services of him who was first and foremost to expose, condemn, and denounce the workings of the abominable, blasphemous and vile penitentiary lease system, under which so many of our race are doomed to horror, agony and pollution."[18]

Grady's Ascent

A year after his former newspaper partner was buried, Henry Grady found himself on the railroad beat for the *Atlanta Constitution*, traveling the roads across twelve states with Victor Newcomb, soon-to-be president of one of the South's largest railroad companies, the Louisville and Nashville, which Grady dubbed "Newcomb's Octopus." The men, both of them gregarious and charismatic, became quick friends. Grady viewed railroad development as critical to Atlanta's fortunes, and his journey with Newcomb introduced him to not only the intricacies of railroad combinations and expansions but also the value of having friends in high places. In New York, Newcomb introduced Grady to the financier Cyrus W. Field. When Howell telegrammed Grady that a quarter interest in the *Constitution* was available, Field loaned Grady the twenty thousand dollars needed to purchase it. Newcomb then advised Grady in stock speculation so that Grady could repay the loan. In return for these life-changing favors, Grady wrote glowingly in the *Atlanta Constitution* about Newcomb's railroad and Field's brother, an associate justice on the U.S. Supreme Court, who was vying for the Democratic nomination for the presidency. It was an early lesson in the personal and professional advantages of quid pro quo.[19]

Grady put the lesson to use in short order. In May 1880, the same month he elevated himself from stringer to part owner and managing editor of the *Atlanta Constitution*, he orchestrated a corrupt backdoor political deal that secured his status as the ringmaster of Georgia politics. Senator Gordon, who had served as Grand Dragon of the Ku Klux Klan in Georgia and lied about it to a U.S. congressional investigating committee in 1871, had accomplished little during his seven years in the U.S. Senate. His finances were in disarray. (A few years later, he would be exposed for accepting bribes from the railroad lobby while in the Senate in exchange for promoting favorable legislation, an involvement the *Constitution* helped keep quiet in Georgia.) Meanwhile, Joe Brown wanted the honor of holding public office again—in particular, the prestige and power of a U.S. Senate seat. Brown held a twenty-year leasing contract for the state's convicts, served as president of the powerful Western and Atlantic Railroad leased from the state of Georgia, and owned multiple coal and iron companies. He was wealthy and powerful and well positioned to purchase Gordon's senate seat, and he knew the man to make things happen. Grady had covered Brown's legal efforts in Florida to win the state for the Democrats in the contested Tilden-Hayes presidential election of 1876. Of course, the state and ultimately the presidency went to Republican candidate Rutherford B. Hayes, marking the end of Reconstruction in the South. Brown did not succeed in his mission, but he impressed the young Grady with his intelligence and hard work. The men began a friendship that several years later led to political collusion with Newcomb, Senator Gordon, and Governor Colquitt. Grady was the mastermind, devising a secret plan and a secret code for the group's telegraphed negotiations.[20]

Newcomb, who wanted an alliance with Brown because the Western and Atlantic Railroad was critical to the expansion of the Louisville and Nashville, created a position for Senator Gordon as counsel to the L&N, with a generous annual salary to be paid by both railroads. Grady helped arrange Gordon's resignation and Governor Colquitt's appointment of Brown to his Senate seat. What's more, Grady stage-managed the *Atlanta Constitution*'s coverage of the entire affair, spreading false news accounts to cover up the undemocratic backdoor deal and to quell the public outcry of corruption. Meanwhile, Colquitt, whose administration had been censured for all manner of fraud and corruption, faced a serious reelection challenge. Grady took charge of Colquitt's campaign and pressed Gordon and Brown into active service stumping for the governor across the state. Colquitt retained the governorship. Brown became a U.S. senator. Gordon secured a lucrative job with the ever-cunning Louisville and Nashville. Newcomb cultivated a powerful business ally. And Grady became the leader of the Atlanta Ring until his death in 1889, managing to keep his role in the affair secret until historians discovered archival evidence one hundred years later.[21]

Convict Leasing and Lynching

From the moment he ascended to power in Georgia public life, Grady was knee-deep in convict leasing controversy. The Independents who opposed

Governor Colquitt in the 1880 gubernatorial race circulated an anonymous pamphlet exposing the brutalities of Georgia's convict system. Titled "The Convict Catechism!" it called out Colquitt, Brown, and Gordon for their involvement in the convict lease. It also reported on the convict abuses Robert Alston had discovered as chair of the penitentiary committee and named both Colquitt and Gordon as former leaders of Georgia's KKK. The pamphlet was intended to secure the Black vote for Thomas M. Norwood, an Independent and Colquitt's opponent, and to encourage reform of Georgia's convict leasing system, which competed with free white labor. Grady did all he could to discredit the document in the *Constitution*. The catechism, reprinted in Northern newspapers, was responsible for "slandering the south" and "enflaming the minds of the north" against the South, the *Constitution* complained. Evincing no interest in democratic debate or the role of newspapers in informing the electorate, Grady denounced the catechism for bringing the question of convict leasing "into politics, for it is a matter to be discussed at leisure by the best minds of the state." Calling the catechism "a parcel of lies," even though it reiterated information from his friend Alston's legislative report, Grady also chastised the *New York Times* for printing excerpts and condemning the Georgia system's brutalities. In a campaign speech in Savannah, Governor Colquitt claimed the catechism was entirely untrue, especially the claim that he had any financial connection to the lease. "A fouler lie," he bellowed to applause, "never escaped from the smoke of the infernal regions!" But the catechism told the truth, no matter what Colquitt or Grady told the people of Georgia.[22]

Colquitt was personally involved in convict leasing through his investment in Joe Brown's Dade Coal Company. For decades Brown built a personal fortune by working state convicts in his industrial empire. In the early 1870s, Brown launched multiple mining companies in the hills of northwest Georgia. Expanding his holdings across time, he eventually consolidated them under the parent company of Dade Coal, which competed successfully with Arthur S. Colyar's Sewanee Mines in Tennessee (see chapter 8). From the beginning, his mines made immense profits not only using convict labor but also leveraging cheap transportation rates from the state railroad he controlled. Brown first secured a five-year lease from the state in 1874 for one hundred convicts, even though he submitted his bid a day after the deadline. (He was a man not beholden to rules, honest governance, or human decency.) In 1876, when the state extended the previous leases by twenty years, Brown received three hundred prisoners, and he was no longer constricted by the previous contract's maximum ten-hour working day. Gordon also owned a share in the twenty-year state convict lease, working convicts on his plantation and eventually subleasing them to other men, including the man who killed Robert Alston in the statehouse, to work in agricultural ventures.[23]

The degree of cronyism involved in Georgia's convict leasing scheme was stunning. In addition to Colquitt, John B. Gordon's brother was invested in Joe Brown's Dade Coal Company. The brother of Evan Howell, the *Atlanta Constitution*'s publisher and editor in chief, held part of a convict lease contract, which spread its allotted prisoners among multiple interests, including Dade Coal and the Chattahoochee Brick Company. Howell himself recommended a man to work as a convict boss at Joe Brown's camps. James W. English—mayor of Atlanta from 1881 to 1883 and Atlanta police commissioner for decades, considered by some to be a member of Grady's Atlanta Ring—owned a large share in the convict lease and built a vast industrial enterprise using convict labor. He worked convicts at the Chattahoochee Brick Company, which made bricks used to build homes, buildings, and roads of Atlanta, as well as the Durham Coal and Coke Company, the Iron Belt Railroad and Mining Company, the Georgia Pacific Railroad, and a sawmill company. English grew rich working convicts leased from the state, the city of Atlanta, and various counties; in one year, he made almost two million dollars in profits alone, a staggering figure for the period. As part of Atlanta's police administration, English was perfectly placed to ensure that Black citizens were arrested at a sufficient rate to fulfill his labor needs as his industrial enterprises proliferated and expanded across the late nineteenth century and into the twentieth. Eventually he was wealthy enough to start the First National Bank of Atlanta, with descendant banks ultimately absorbed into today's vast, multinational financial services company Wells Fargo.[24]

At Dade Coal, Joe Brown's overseers worked convicts on the capricious task system: if convicts were not able to produce the day's quota of coal in the mines, they were punished. Punishments were inventive in their cruelty and sadism. It was, in fact, an organized system of torture. Prisoners were secured by the legs and waist to one pole with their hands tied to another pole about six feet away; they were thus bent at the waist with their backs exposed for flogging with a wide leather whip, which was often dragged through wet sand so as to take off the skin. This style of whipping was called "bucking." Other punishments included the "water cure," a form of torture akin to waterboarding; the "sweat box," in which a prisoner was locked in a narrow box and left in the sun to bake; and the "blind mule." Carrie Massie, a Black teenage girl, endured this latter torture for six hours. Her wrists were tied with rope and she was hoisted by being pulled over a ceiling beam, until her toes just grazed the ground. While a convict, she was raped repeatedly and bore a child in the camp.[25]

James English worked convicts at his Chattahoochee Brick Company on the task system too. The brickmaking process was archaic, using old handmade methods under a modern productivity regime. Convicts filled brick molds by hand with clay, worked fire-breathing kilns, and carried pallets of hot bricks on their backs at a run under the lash of guards wielding horse whips. At its worst, the camp flogged fifteen to twenty prisoners a day. Community members heard bloodcurdling screams emanate from the camp whenever they came within a quarter mile of it. In 1885 a Macon newspaper reported a death rate of 20 to 25 percent at the Chattahoochee camp, noting that the deaths were not due to illness, implying they were due instead to accidents and mistreatment. Meanwhile, a legislative penitentiary report the same year stated that convicts across all Georgia camps were in excellent health. The newspaper explained the discrepancy by correctly noting that public information about the convict leasing system was controlled by "influential political rings" that included the lessees themselves. When Governor Gordon presided over an investigation of the convict leasing system in 1887, prodded by reports of cruelty, it was found that prisoners at the Chattahoochee camp had been flogged so viciously that "stripes of flesh had been cut out with the lash" from their backs. Their offense? They had reported inhumane treatment to a legislative committee.[26]

Grady was well aware of his colleagues' involvement in the convict lease and the brutalities of the system. After all, Gordon's sublessee had murdered Grady's friend for his attempts to expose convict leasing as an inhumane system. And Grady had covered the entire affair in the *Atlanta Constitution*. But Grady's knowledge far exceeded Alston's legislative report and the convict catechism. As a reporter, he developed granular knowledge of government in Georgia and Atlanta and the convict leasing system; the *Constitution* reported on state government affairs, including the penitentiary keeper's annual report, as well as the multiple legislative investigations of convict abuse that occurred during his tenure as managing editor. Even before then, Grady wrote a report for the *Philadelphia Times* on Georgia's convict labor system, explaining "how the system operates, its merits and its faults." While Alston's report impugned the system, Grady defended it, even as he explained how lucrative it was for the companies with twenty-year leases and documented brutal treatment of convicts and high death rates. "The disposition in Georgia is to adhere to the present system, as the best for the State and for the negro," he wrote, noting, as if to reassure his white readers, that most of the convicts were Black. "I cannot deny many of the stories of cruelty or of excessive mortality that are told. Most of the reports, however, are colored for sinister effect." Apparently,

Grady found nothing authentically sinister about a cruel and lethal system targeting Black Georgians.[27]

Black leaders in Georgia understood early and clearly the sinister nature of leasing. Black legislators consistently condemned and opposed the system during Reconstruction. In 1879 Republican Thomas M. Butler introduced a bill to conduct more thorough and honest inspections of the convict camps. It failed. The same year he introduced a bill to abolish the system. It too failed. In 1892 W. H. Stiles, a Black member of the Legislative Committee on the Penitentiary, visited Brown's Dade Coal Mines, which employed one thousand convicts. He reported appalling working conditions in mines three hundred feet underground with standing water up to the knees and suffocating gases. Some convicts worked and slept nearly naked for lack of clothes; food was inadequate. The convicts were reluctant to speak to the visitors for fear of retribution after the legislative visitors had left. Nothing was done. Reverend William J. White, editor of the long-lived *Georgia Baptist* and founder of what became Morehouse College, laid bare the ugly truth: "The fortunes of many a prominent white Georgia family [are] red with the blood and sweat of Black men justly and unjustly held to labor in Georgia prison camps." John H. Deveaux's *Savannah Tribune*, a Black newspaper forced to shutter from 1878 to 1886 because white printers refused to print it, consistently criticized and opposed the system.[28] Its most vigorous coverage happened before the turn of the century, the point when white supremacy formed a hardened crust over Southern social life and made forthright Black dissent ever more dangerous. White tools to silence Black protest ran the gamut from refusing printing contracts to Black newspapers to threatening violence against Black publishers and editors. A few white Georgians, particularly Rebecca Latimer Felton, repeatedly condemned convict leasing in newspaper columns and national magazine articles, focusing especially on the plight of women caught in the system, but hers was an effort guided by a white supremacist fear of "miscegenation."[29]

Black leaders outside the South were better positioned to mount a counteroffensive to convict leasing and other tools of white supremacy, such as lynching, during Grady's short lifetime and the years after. T. Thomas Fortune, the brilliant journalist and activist working from New York City, attacked Grady directly, calling Georgia's convict system a "cesspool of degradation and crime . . . under the very nostrils of the prophet Grady." Selena Sloan Butler exposed the plight of women and girls caught up in Georgia's convict system—rape by camp guards, in addition to other brutalities—in a paper presented to the

National Association for Colored Women (NACW) and widely circulated as a pamphlet to the Woman's Christian Temperance Union. Inspired by Butler, Mary Church Terrell, president of the NACW, took up the same issue. She spoke openly about "the rape of black girls" in Georgia convict camps—a stunningly forthright use of language for her era, when the word "outrage" was preferred—and published a deeply researched article, in a widely circulated national magazine, detailing the horrifying conditions and practices in Georgia convict camps. The *Atlanta Constitution* was an essential primary source for her work. "It is well known that some of the wealthiest men in the State have accumulated their fortunes by literally buying coloured men, women, and children, and working them nearly, if not quite, to death," she wrote. Georgia's convict camps also contained large numbers of boys, some as young as eight years old; in 1896 half the almost twenty-five hundred convicts were minors.[30]

Ida B. Wells documented and condemned "the twin infamies" of convict leasing and lynching in *The Reason Why*, a pamphlet she published with Frederick Douglass to protest the attempted exclusion of African Americans from the World's Columbian Exposition in Chicago in 1893. In her anti-lynching pamphlet *Southern Horrors*, published just a few years after Grady's death, Wells connected the dots from Grady's New South doctrine to lynching, that white supremacist tool of terror that grew in prominence across the late nineteenth century and into the twentieth. "Henry W. Grady in his well-remembered speeches in New England and New York pictured the Afro-American as incapable of self-government," Wells wrote. "Through him and other leading men the cry of the South to the country has been 'Hands off! Leave us to solve our problem.' To the Afro-American the South says, 'the white man must and will rule.' There is little difference between the Antebellum South and the New South."[31]

Across the 1880s, Henry W. Grady established reporting practices that actively encouraged lynching, such as identifying lynching victims and egging on mobs through incendiary stories and headlines. A professor at the University of Georgia wrote to Grady, chastising him for irreverent headlines and language in articles about legal hangings and lynchings. For decades after Grady's death, the *Atlanta Constitution* continued these practices, leading to the role white Atlanta newspapers played in fomenting the 1906 Atlanta Race Riot. Ten years after Grady's death, Wells published the pamphlet *Lynch Law in Georgia*, using coverage from the pages of the *Atlanta Constitution* to document and indict the role of the white press in inciting the lynching of twelve Black men in Georgia in March and April 1899, including the extraordinarily brutal lynching of Sam

Hose. In the preface, Wells wrote, "The Southern press champions burning men alive." She then provided damning evidence from the pages of the *Constitution*.[32]

Henry W. Grady never wavered in his defense of Georgia's convict lease system, even as he and his paper reported repeatedly across the years on its enduring abuses. His defense strategy relied on several rhetorical tactics. One was to blame the Reconstruction-era Republican government for creating the system in the first place, even though Redemption Democrats, many of whom were Grady's close associates, radically expanded and prospered personally from it as they built industrial empires. Another was to insist that crime required social retribution and criminals deserved little sympathy. "Criminals must be punished," the *Constitution* insisted in 1885. When a public outcry led to legislative investigations of the convict lease system in 1886, the paper mocked the "sickly sentimentality" of proposed reforms, suggesting they were tantamount to providing that "the convicts shall be clothed in fine linen and purple, lodged in marble palaces, and fed three times daily upon ice cream from a silver dish." Do not forget, the paper warned the legislature, "that a convict is a convict" and "he deserves just punishment for his violation of the law." When the *New York Times* criticized Georgia's convict lease system as barbaric, the *Constitution* denied all charges and mocked the concern: "It is true, they are not allowed to attend picnics, nor are they taught to perform on the piano." Yet another tactic involved blaming the authorities for not enforcing the laws the lessees were meant to follow—while insisting that the lease law itself was fair and just. Punish those very few lessees who abuse the system, the *Constitution* editors argued, and let that punishment "be a reformatory principle among the convicts themselves. It will teach them that in Georgia the law is supreme and must be obeyed from the highest to the lowest, and that its violation means punishment adequate and certain." Meanwhile, Grady's friends Brown and English grew wealthy as they operated some of the most brutal camps in the history of convict leasing, breaking the law requiring humane treatment with impunity.[33]

In 1886 Grady sent a reporter to cover a convict mutiny at Joe Brown's mines in Dade County. Led in part by a former Black schoolteacher convicted for forgery, 125 convicts barricaded themselves in their bunkhouses and refused to work unless their demands were met. They asked for the removal of a brutal camp boss, the abolition of flogging as a punishment, and adequate food. One Dade prisoner, testifying to the convicts' collective desperation, said they were "ready to die, and would as soon be dead as to live in torture." On order of the governor, camp overseers starved the convicts into submission and then administered brutal whippings as punishment. Grady's reporter was amused. He called the scene, which he witnessed, a "special matinee" in his report for the *Constitution*.[34]

Henry Grady and the New South

In December 1886, just six months after the convict uprising at Brown's mines, Grady found himself giving a speech about the New South before the New England Society of New York at the famed Delmonico's restaurant in New York City. His audience included many of the wealthy industrialists of the day, including Henry M. Flagler, John D. Rockefeller's business partner in Standard Oil, who the previous year had begun building his own industrial empire on the east coast of Florida (see chapter 9).[35] John H. Inman, a member of the society with roots in both Atlanta and Tennessee, had invited Grady to give the speech. Inman was well positioned to understand the industrial and financial promise of the New South; after all, he was invested in many railroad and iron enterprises across the South, most of which profited from the use of convict labor. Inman's brother Samuel was Grady's close friend and a stockholder in the *Atlanta Constitution*.[36]

Grady had gained national recognition the previous year when he published a reply to George Washington Cable's much-discussed article in *Century Magazine* titled "The Freedman's Case in Equity." Cable, a white novelist from Louisiana, defended Black civil rights and denounced Southern white supremacy, racial segregation, and the convict lease system, insisting that the fate of Black Americans was a national issue. The blowback in white Southern newspapers and from white Southern letter writers was immediate and harsh. Grady's response essay, "In Plain Black and White: A Reply to Mr. Cable," claimed to speak for the entire South. "The assortment of the races is wise and proper, and stands on the platform of equal accommodations for each race but separate," Grady wrote. Both Black and white people had a "race instinct" that led them to separation. Without it, he said, there would be "disorganization of society" and "internecine war." But even if Black people wanted to mingle across the color line, white people would never allow it. "The whites, at any cost and at any hazard, would maintain the clear integrity and dominance of the Anglo-Saxon blood," he proclaimed. With this essay, Grady began to popularize the idea, if not the actual phrase, of "equal but separate" that he would spread throughout white America with his New South speeches. He demonstrated his willingness to threaten violence against those who would dare to cross the color line. And he insisted that Northerners must leave racial matters to the white South to solve. The South, he wrote, "has reserved to herself the right to settle the still unsettled element of the race problem, and this right she can never yield. As a matter of course, this implies the clear and unmistakable domination of the white race in the South."[37]

When Grady stood before his elite audience at Delmonico's, he was speaking as the most recognizable voice of the New South movement. And he had a message to sell to those with deep pockets and entrepreneurial industrial interests. The South was ripe for industrial development and Northern capital, he said. Its doors were open to immigrants from the North, both industrialists and workers. And the South had buried any resentment toward the North, he said. But Grady's message was also laced with calculated lies. "The relations of the Southern people with the negro are close and cordial," he said. And the "new South presents a perfect democracy . . . a social system compact and closely knitted . . . and a diversified industry that meets the complex need of this complex age." Race relations were not cordial, and the "New South" was hardly a democracy, as any Black Southerner could attest. One of Grady's points about "the Negro" was true enough and meant to attract the avid interest of affluent white industrialists: "No section shows a more prosperous laboring population than the Negroes of the South." Grady did not have to say out loud that convict leasing provided a robust "laboring population" of Negroes in the South. Everyone in Delmonico's read newspapers, so everyone in Grady's audience already knew the Southern system of convict leasing would provide large numbers of incredibly cheap, easily controlled, enslaved Black labor.[38]

Grady's audience at Delmonico's loved his speech. Newspapers across the country reprinted it and pronounced it, and its author, brilliant. Congratulatory telegrams and letters poured into the offices of the *Atlanta Constitution*. The New York *Sun* even suggested Grady would make a strong candidate for vice president of the United States. Grady was suddenly well known not only in the South but across the nation as well. But not everyone was enchanted with his speech. T. Thomas Fortune, the leading Black newspaper editor of the period, directly attacked Grady's speech in the *New York Freeman*: "The white men of the South—in legislatures, in courts of justice, in convict camps, in churches, in hotels and theatres, in railroad and steamship accommodation—do not do justice to their colored fellow-citizens, and when a man like Grady stands up and lies about these matters, we are here to strike the lie on the head." In an article published slightly before Grady's speech at Delmonico's, Fortune attacked Grady's response to Cable, calling Grady the "editor of a leading but hide-bound Georgia newspaper" and pointing out the irony of Grady insisting on social separation of the races when "the entire African race in this country has not only had its blood tainted but *actually corrupted* by unholy contact with his much vaunted 'superior race.'" Fortune rebuked and corrected Grady's arrogant assumption that Black people were somehow not included in the "we" of the South. "Grady appeals to the North to leave the race question to '*us*' and '*we*' will settle it," Fortune wrote. "So *we* will; but the *we* Mr. Grady had 'in his mind's eye' will not be permitted to settle it alone. Not by any means, Mr. Grady. Not only the White *we*, but the Colored *we* as well, will demand a share in that settlement."[39]

Fortune could not abide the anti-Black racism at the heart of the New South message and emerging political economies. He kept his pencil sharpened as he laid bare, again and again, the rapacious capitalism and racial exploitation at the heart of the New South system. By 1887 he was leading the effort to create a national "Afro-American League" to enforce and protect constitutional rights for Black Americans, a short-lived organization that nonetheless lit the way to the formation of the National Association for the Advancement of Colored People two decades later. That same year, Grady gave another New South speech, but this time in the South, where he expressed his white supremacist views clearly and directly to a cheering audience at the Texas State Fair: "The supremacy of the white race of the South must be maintained forever, and the domination of the negro race resisted at all points and at all hazards—because the white race is the superior race. This is the declaration of no new truth. It has abided forever in the marrow of our bones, and shall run forever with the blood that feeds Anglo-Saxon hearts." With his menacing words and antidemocratic actions, Grady was the distillation of the white supremacy that Black Americans, including Fortune, fought against in the late 1880s.[40]

In the last speech of his life, given at Faneuil Hall before the Boston Merchants Association in December 1889, Grady spoke yet again of the New South and its industrial "splendor." As usual, his speech was an invitation to Northern investment and immigration, but the focus of the speech was the "problem" of the "freedmen." It was Grady's most open explanation to a Northern audience of the ideology of white supremacy that animated the New South program. And he couched it in a full-throated defense of the country's long history of violent discrimination against people of color. "Never before in this Republic has the white race divided on the rights of an alien race," Grady said. "The red man was cut down as a weed, because he hindered the way of the American citizen. The yellow man was shut out of this Republic because he is an alien and inferior. The red man was owner of the land—the yellow man highly civilized and assimilable—but they hindered both sections and are gone!" His point was the same he had made in his celebrated speech in New York City several years earlier: white America must allow the white South to handle the "problem" of "the blacks" without interference.[41]

Grady's goal in Boston was to persuade Massachusetts business leaders and public officials, including the governor, that their own representative, Henry Cabot Lodge, was misguided in drafting a bill authorizing the federal government to supervise congressional elections. The primary purpose of the Lodge Bill, or the "Force Bill" as it was called derisively in the white South, was to protect the Black vote in the South, where anti-Black voter suppression tactics—such as poll taxes, literacy tests, and intimidation—were proliferating. For Grady, maintaining the Solid South in one-party white political rule was essential to building the New South. In his speech he attacked Black Southerners as a "vast ignorant and purchasable vote—clannish, credulous, impulsive and passionate—tempting every art of the demagogue, but insensible to the appeal of the statesman." The only protection for the South against this danger, he maintained, was not "the cowardly menace of mask or shotgun" but rather "the peaceful majesty of intelligence and responsibility, massed and unified for the protection of its homes and the preservation of its liberty." By "intelligence and responsibility" he clearly meant voter suppression tactics increasingly enshrined in laws of the Southern states, but his remarks two years earlier in Texas suggested he understood and at times embraced the tactics of "the mask or shotgun." Years earlier, in fact, he had addressed his "friends" and "brothers" in the Ku Klux Klan in a chilling editorial in the *Rome (GA) Commercial*, cautioning them not to waste their power by stopping "innocent men and forcing them to dance" in the streets. "The strength and power of any secret organization rests in the attribute of mystery and hidden force," he wrote. Its members "can be called together by a tiny signal, and when the work is done, can melt away into shadowy nothing."[42]

Grady died unexpectedly of pneumonia less than two weeks after his Boston speech, in which he attacked the "Afro-American agitator" for "stirring the strife in which he alone prospers." The agitators Grady had in mind were, at the local level, *Athens (GA) Blade* editor William Pledger, who called for a reduction in the number of U.S. congressmen, since they did not represent Black Georgians, and, at the national level, T. Thomas Fortune, whose Afro-American League was scheduled to hold its inaugural meeting the following month. Fortune took note, challenging Grady's speech in a *New York Age* editorial published two days before Grady's death. If Black Georgians were so "happy in their cabin homes," Fortune asked, why had they just held a convention in Atlanta, two hundred strong, to protest disenfranchisement, lynching, racial violence, and civil rights violations in the state capital itself. Just six months after Grady's speech and death, Fortune published his own take on "The Race Problem," subtitled "The Negro Will Solve It," a pointed rejoinder to Grady's repeated insistence that the white South must be left alone to solve it. Grady knew, Fortune argued, that the point of the Afro-American League was to organize Black America to find and enact the solution. "Mr. Grady, with the vision of a prophet," Fortune wrote, "singled out the agent who, in the mysterious providence of God, must and will lead the Afro-American out of the darkness in which he now gropes into the sunshine of manhood and citizenship."[43]

In 1890, the year after Grady's death, Mississippi held a constitutional convention meant to disenfranchise its Black citizens, who outnumbered white Mississippians by half a million (see chapter 4). Among other provisions meant to suppress the Black vote, white Democrats crafted the infamous "understanding clause," which required Black citizens to interpret the state constitution to the satisfaction of the registrar when registering to vote. And thus the second Mississippi Plan was born at the same time Southern senators filibustered the Lodge Bill (including Colquitt, who by then was a U.S. senator from Georgia), defeating it for good in 1891. The federal bill's animating principle—the protection of the franchise for African Americans across the South and the nation—was repudiated in the Mississippi Plan of 1890. The goal of the Lodge Bill, which Grady spoke against in Boston, was not realized until the Voting Right Act of 1965. Grady's idea of "equal but separate" shaped Southern social and political economic relations, not to mention constitutional law, from *Plessy* in 1896 to *Brown v. Board of Education* in 1954 and the Civil Rights Act of 1964. But in the long arc of history, Fortune had the final say over Grady. It was indeed the "Afro-American agitator" who solved, at least in part, the so-called race problem and achieved a degree of racial justice through grassroots organization, protest, and activism stretching from the late nineteenth century, to the civil rights movement, to the present.[44]

Conclusion

As kingmaker of the Democratic Party in Georgia in the critical decade of the 1880s, when key mechanisms of Jim Crow were being devised, and as managing editor of the most powerful newspaper in the South and the most powerful

Southern newspaper in the nation, Grady helped plan, build, promote, and sustain the white supremacist political economies and social orders of Georgia and the South. His work fused the shared interests of white news leaders, politicians, business elites, and industrialists, providing a blueprint that the "best men" across the South adapted to their own purposes as they built Jim Crow regimes across the last two decades of the nineteenth century.

Under Grady's guidance, the *Atlanta Constitution* grew to have the largest circulation and influence of any Southern or regional newspaper in the United States. Through the newspaper and his speeches, he spread his New South narrative across the country; served up heaping doses of propaganda that served the political and personal financial interests of his Atlanta Ring of Democratic leaders; hid his and the ring's backdoor, antidemocratic dealmaking; defended and protected convict leasing to enrich his political allies and friends; established lynching reportorial practices that helped to normalize lynching for decades; and advocated for Black disenfranchisement and "equal but separate" laws and practices.

Nationally prominent Black journalists and scholars understood Henry W. Grady, his newspaper the *Atlanta Constitution*, and his New South doctrine for what they were: anti-Black, antidemocratic, and anti-civil. When he learned of Grady's death in late December 1889, *Washington Bee* editor W. Calvin Chase wrote that "the Negroes of this country . . . have no tears to shed" for this "dead tyrant . . . who made a mockery of American freedom and civil liberty." In *Black Reconstruction in America*, published in 1935, W.E.B. Du Bois called Grady's New South "a phantasmagoria" of "five thousand lynchings, jails bursting with black prisoners incarcerated on trivial and trumped-up charges, and caste staring from every train and street car." When Emory University professor Raymond B. Nixon's hagiographic biography of Grady appeared in 1943, Rayford Logan observed that the author "stands for the same kind of 'New South' as that which Grady advocated." Logan wryly titled his review "Plus ça change, plus c'est la même chose": The more things change, the more they remain the same.[45]

Notes

Ethan Bakuli and Natalie DiDomenico, now graduates of the University of Massachusetts Amherst, contributed research used in this chapter.

1. Robert J. Shiller coined the terms "contagious narrative" and "contagious story" in his work on narrative economics. See Robert J. Shiller, *Narrative Economics: How Stories Go Viral and Drive Major Economic Events* (Princeton, NJ: Princeton University Press, 2019).

2. Harold E. Davis, *Henry Grady's New South: Atlanta, a Brave and Beautiful City* (Tuscaloosa: University of Alabama Press, 1990), 41, 134–37, 175–78; Henry W. Grady, "In Plain Black and White: A Reply to Mr. Cable," *Century Magazine*, April 1885, 909–917; Paul M. Gaston, *The New South Creed* (New York: Alfred A. Knopf, 1970), 32–33.

3. Among the exceptions are William A. Link, *Atlanta, Cradle of the New South: Race and Remembering in the Civil War's Aftermath* (Chapel Hill: University of North Carolina Press, 2013), and James C. Cobb, *Away Down South: A History of Southern Identity* (New York: Oxford University Press, 2005).

4. See, for example, Davis, *Henry Grady's New South*; Raymond B. Nixon, *Henry W. Grady: Spokesman of the New South* (1943; repr., New York: Russell and Russell, 1969); Carl R. Osthaus, *Partisans of the Southern Press: Editorial Spokesmen of the Nineteenth Century* (Lexington: University Press of Kentucky, 1994).

5. C. Vann Woodward, *Origins of the New South, 1877–1913* (1951; repr., Baton Rouge: Louisiana State University Press, 1971).

6. C. Vann Woodward, *Tom Watson, Agrarian Rebel* (1938; repr., New York: University Press, 1963), 89.

7. James C. Cobb, "Segregating the New South: The Origins and Legacy of *Plessy v. Ferguson*," *Georgia State University Law Review* 12, no. 4 (June 1996): 1024–26; Ibram X. Kendi, *Stamped from the Beginning: The Definitive History of Racist Ideas in America* (New York: Nation Books, 2016), 265–66.

8. Henry W. Grady, Speech at the Annual Banquet of the Boston Merchants' Association, December 1889, in Joel Chandler Harris, ed., *Joel Chandler Harris' Life of Henry W. Grady Including His Writings and Speeches*, vol. 1 (New York: Cassell Publishing, 1890), 180–98; Cobb, *Away Down South*, 70–71; Link, *Atlanta, Cradle of the New South*, 155; Paul M. Gaston, *The New South Creed: A Study in Southern Mythmaking* (New York: Alfred A. Knopf, 1970), 149; Michael Perman, *Struggle for Mastery: Disfranchisement in the South, 1888–1908* (Chapel Hill: University of North Carolina, 2001), 50; Sharon D. Kennedy-Noelle, *Writing Reconstruction: Race, Gender, and Citizenship in the Postwar South* (Chapel Hill: University of North Carolina Press, 2015), 281.

9. D'Weston Haywood, "Fight for a New America," in *Journalism and Jim Crow*.

10. Davis, *Henry Grady's New South*, 40–41, 62; Derrell Roberts, "Duel in the Georgia State Capitol," *Georgia Historical Quarterly* 47, no. 4 (1963): 420–24.

11. Davis, *Henry Grady's New South*, 35–37; "Report of the Legislative Committee on Penitentiary," *Atlanta Constitution*, December 17, 1878.

12. "Georgia's Convicts: The Manner of Their Treatment," *Atlanta Constitution*, December 17, 1878; "Report of the Legislative Committee on Penitentiary," *Atlanta Constitution*, December 17, 1878.

13. Alex Lichtenstein, *Twice the Work of Free Labor: The Political Economy of Convict Labor in the New South* (New York: Verso, 1996), 41, 68–69.

14. George Alfred Townsend, "A Bloody Chapter of Southern Life," *Brooklyn Eagle*, March 30, 1879; "The Latest Georgia Murder," *New York Times*, March 13, 1879; Pamela Chase Hain, *Murder in the State Capitol: The Biography of Lieutenant Colonel Robert Augustus Alston (1832–1879)* (Macon, GA: Mercer University Press, 2013), 200.

15. Ralph Lowell Eckert, *John Brown Gordon: Soldier, Southerner, American* (Baton Rouge: Louisiana State University Press, 1989), 263–64; "Bathed in Blood: Horrible Tragedy in the Capitol," *Atlanta Constitution*, March 12, 1879, scrapbook 3, 1877–79, Henry Woodfin Grady Papers, Stuart A. Rose Manuscript, Archives, and Rare Book Library, Emory University (hereafter cited as Grady Papers); "The Convict System of Georgia," Letter to the Editor, signed TRUTH, *New York Times*, November 24, 1881.

16. H.W.G., "Colonel R. A. Alston: Incidents of His Life and Family," *Atlanta Constitution*, March 13, 1879, scrapbook 3, 1877–79, Grady Papers.

17. Trial coverage in the *Atlanta Constitution*, May 1–8, 1879; "The Convict System of Georgia," Letter to the Editor, signed TRUTH, *New York Times*, November 24, 1881; "Ed. Cox Pardoned," *Atlanta Constitution*, December 12, 1882; "The Code in Georgia: Feuds and Duels That Make a Dark Page in History," *Indianapolis Journal*, June 14, 1896; "Evidence Still Pouring In: The Court of Inquiry Held a Most Important Session Yesterday," *Atlanta Constitution*, February 15, 1896.

18. Emma Edmunds, "Robert Alston: An Authentic Georgia Martyr," *Atlanta Constitution*, March 10, 1978.

19. Davis, *Henry Grady's New South*, 40–41; Woodward, *Origins of the New South*, 146–47; Eckert, *John Brown Gordon*, 225.

20. Davis, *Henry Grady's New South*, 66–68; Eckert, *John Brown Gordon*, 145, 216–17; Joseph H. Parks, *Joseph E. Brown of Georgia* (Baton Rouge: Louisiana State University Press, 1977), 487–89, 514–18; Woodward, *Tom Watson*, 59–63, 121. The secret code and telegrams can be found in the Joseph E. Brown Papers, box 3, folder 12, Hargrett Rare Book and Manuscript Library, University of Georgia (hereafter cited as Brown Papers).

21. Numan V. Bartley, *The Creation of Modern Georgia*, 2nd ed. (Athens: University of Georgia Press, 1990), 82–83; Eckert, *John Brown Gordon*, 225–34; Davis, *Henry Grady's New South*, 68–70; Ralph L. Eckert, "The Breath of Scandal: John B. Gordon, Henry W. Grady, and the Resignation-Appointment Controversy of May 1880," *Georgia Historical Quarterly* 69, no. 3 (1985): 315–37.

22. "Convict Catechism!" Independent Democratic Committee of Georgia, 1880, Digital Collections, Beinecke Rare Book and Manuscript Library, Yale University, https://brbl-dl.library.yale.edu/vufind/Record/3576572?image_id=1325368; "The Convict Catechism Once More," *Atlanta Constitution*, September 15, 1880; "Mr. Norwood and the Colored People," *Atlanta Constitution*, September 1, 1880; "The New York Times and the Convict Catechism," *Atlanta Constitution*, October 21,

1880; 1880 Scrapbook, box 1, Gov. Alfred H. Colquitt Collection, Hargrett Rare Book and Manuscript Library, University of Georgia.

23. Rebecca Latimer Felton, *My Memoirs of Georgia Politics* (Atlanta: Index Printing Company, 1911), 259; Donald L. Grant, *The Way It Was in the South: The Black Experience in Georgia* (Athens: University of Georgia Press, 1993), 155; Allison Dorsey, *To Build Our Lives Together: Community Formation in Black Atlanta, 1875–1906* (Athens: University of Georgia Press, 2004), 148; Derrell Roberts, "Joseph E. Brown and His Georgia Mines," *Georgia Historical Quarterly* 52, no. 3 (1968): 285–92; Roberts, "Joseph E. Brown," 286; Matthew J. Mancini, *One Dies, Get Another: Convict Leasing in the American South, 1866–1928* (Columbia: University of South Carolina Press, 1996), 84–88; Lichtenstein, *Twice the Work of Free Labor*, 108–112; Eckert, *John Brown Gordon*, 263–65; Penitentiary Committee Report, December 11, 1878, *Journal of the Senate of the State of Georgia 1878*, 243–44; Razvan Sibii, "Convict Wars, Tennessee," in *Journalism and Jim Crow*.

24. A. Elizabeth Taylor, "The Origin and Development of the Convict Lease System in Georgia," *Georgia Historical Quarterly* 26, no. 2 (1942): 119, 125; Georgia Penitentiary Company convict lease bid, June 15, 1876, Evan P. Howell to Joseph E. Brown, February 13, 1888, Brown Papers, box 3, folder 4; Mancini, *One Dies, Get Another*, 90; Douglas A. Blackmon, *Slavery by Another Name: The Re-enslavement of Black Americans from the Civil War to World War II* (New York: Anchor Books, 2008), 342–43, 391–92.

25. Kathy Roberts Forde, "Afterword: Ida B. Wells-Barnett and the 'Racist Cover-Up,'" in *Political Pioneer of the Press: Ida B. Wells-Barnett and Her Transnational Crusade for Social Justice*, ed. Lori Amber Roessner and Jodi L. Rightler-McDaniels (Lanham, MD: Lexington Books, 2018), 177; Matthew J. Mancini, *One Dies, Get Another*, 90; Lichtenstein, *Twice the Work of Free Labor*, 129; Talitha L. LeFlouria, *Chained in Silence: Black Women and Convict Labor in the New South* (Chapel Hill: University of North Carolina Press, 2015), 74–77.

26. Blackmon, *Slavery by Another Name*, 343–46; "The Convict Camps: Their Management and the Death Rate—Who Is Responsible?" *Macon Telegraph*, December 18, 1885; "Inhumanity to Convicts," *North Carolina Prohibitionist* (Archdale, NC), September 2, 1887.

27. H.W.G., "Convict Labor: An Explanation of the Penal System of the Southern States," *Philadelphia Times*, December 14, 1879, in scrapbook 4, 1877–79, Grady Papers.

28. The *Savannah Tribune* became an important and influential Black newspaper in Georgia when it resumed operations in 1886. When founder and editor John H. Deveaux received a commission as collector of customs in Brunswick in 1889, the year of Grady's death, he gave the editorship to Sol C. Johnson. The *Tribune* never wavered in its opposition to convict leasing, the chain gang, and the anti-Black nature of Georgia's criminal justice system. It carried out a pragmatic editorial

policy, shifting between accommodation and protest. See Jeffrey Alan Turner, "Agitation and Accommodation in a Southern Black Newspaper: The *Savannah Tribune*, 1886–1915" (PhD diss., University of Georgia, 1993).

29. Rebecca Latimer Felton, a vocal supporter of lynching, was decidedly not committed to Black equality. "An American Siberia: Horrible Treatment of Convicts in Georgia Mines," *Farmers' Leader* (Canton, SD), November 25, 1892; Jay Winston Driskell Jr., *Schooling Jim Crow: The Fight for Atlanta's Booker T. Washington High School and the Roots of Black Protest Politics* (Charlottesville: University of Virginia Press, 2014), 49; Jeffrey Alan Turner, "Agitation and Accommodation in a Southern Black Newspaper: *The Savannah Tribune*, 1886–1915" (master's thesis, University of Georgia, 1993), 55–57; Rebecca L. Felton, "The Convict System of Georgia," *Forum* 2 (January 1887), 484–90; Sarah Haley, *No Mercy Here: Gender, Punishment, and the Making of Jim Crow Modernity* (Chapel Hill: University of North Carolina Press, 2016), 141–44.

30. *New York Freeman*, July 30, 1887, in Grant, *The Way It Was*, 187; Haley, *No Mercy Here*, 125–36; Mary Church Terrell, "Peonage in the United States: The Convict Lease System and the Chain Gangs," *Nineteenth Century and After* 57 (August 1907): 313; "The Boy Convicts," *Atlanta Constitution*, October 3, 1884; Mancini, *One Dies, Get Another*, 87.

31. Ida B. Wells, ed. *The Reason Why the Colored American Is Not in the World's Columbian Exposition* (Chicago, 1893), http://digital.library.upenn.edu/women/wells/exposition/exposition.html; Ida B. Wells, *Southern Horrors: Lynch Law in All Its Phases* (New York Age Print, 1892), http://www.gutenberg.org/files/14975/14975-h/14975-h.htm; Ida B. Wells, *Lynch Law in Georgia* (Chicago, 1899), https://babel.hathitrust.org/cgi/pt?id=emu.010000667705&view=1up&seq=1; Davis, *Henry Grady's New South*, 149–51; W. Fitzhugh Brundage, "The Press and Lynching," in *Journalism and Jim Crow*.

32. Davis, *Henry Grady's New South*, 149–51; William Rutherford to Henry W. Grady, May 9, 1877, scrapbook 4, 1877–79, Grady Papers; David Fort Godshalk, *Veiled Visions: The 1906 Atlanta Race Riot and the Reshaping of American Race Relations* (Chapel Hill: University of North Carolina Press, 2005), 46–56; Wells, *Lynch Law in Georgia*.

33. From 1880 to 1889, when Henry W. Grady was managing editor, the *Atlanta Constitution* published more than five hundred news items, editorials, and advertisements referencing convict leasing or convict labor in Georgia and elsewhere (author's analysis). Lichtenstein, *Twice the Work*, 62–64; "The Lease System," *Atlanta Constitution*, January 16, 1885; "The Convict Question," *Atlanta Constitution*, December 18, 1886; "Enter Master Carroll," *Atlanta Constitution*, December 20, 1882; "A Word about the Convicts," *Atlanta Constitution*, August 28, 1887. For detailed accounts of the brutality in English's and Brown's camps, see Blackmon, *Slavery by Another Name*.

34. Grady's biographer Harold E. Davis claimed that the Dade camp "never was accused of being one of the worst in Georgia," but many historians of convict labor in Georgia have proved him wrong. See Davis, *Henry Grady's New South*, 146–47. "Starving Convicts: Mutiny in the Camp at Cole City," *Atlanta Constitution*, July 14, 1886; "All Quiet in Dade: The Full Story of the Insurrection," *Atlanta Constitution*, July 15, 1886; Derrell Roberts, "Joseph E. Brown and the Convict Lease System," *Georgia Historical Society* 44, no. 4 (1960): 403.

35. Kathy Roberts Forde and Bryan Bowman, "Tourist Empires, Florida," in *Journalism and Jim Crow*.

36. "John H. Inman Is Dead" (obituary), *New York Times*, November 6, 1896; Davis, *Henry Grady's New South*, 175. See also Karin A. Shapiro, *A New South Rebellion: The Battle against Convict Labor in the Tennessee Coalfields, 1871–1896* (Chapel Hill: University of North Carolina Press, 1998).

37. George W. Cable, "The Freedman's Case in Equity," *Century* 29 (January 1885), 409–18; Henry W. Grady, "In Plain Black and White: A Reply to Mr. Cable," *Century* 29 (April 1885), 909–17; K. Stephen Prince, *Stories of the South: Race and the Reconstruction of Southern Identity, 1865–1915* (Chapel Hill: University of North Carolina Press, 2014), 129–31.

38. Harris, *Life of Henry W. Grady*, 89, 91.

39. For copious examples of positive newspaper coverage of Grady's New South speech at Delmonico's, see scrapbook 10, 1886–87, Grady Papers. Davis, *Henry Grady's New South*, 178; Prince, *Stories of the South*, 131; Donald E. Drake II, "Militancy in Fortune's *New York Age*," *Journal of Negro History* 55, no. 4 (1970): 314–15; T. Thomas Fortune, "Civil Rights and Social Privileges," *AME Church Review* 2 (1886): 119–31, in *T. Thomas Fortune, the Afro-American Agitator: A Collection of Writings, 1880–1928*, ed. Shawn Leigh Alexander (Gainesville: University Press of Florida, 2008), 126–26.

40. Cobb, *Away Down South*, 92–93; Shawn Leigh Alexander, *An Army of Lions: The Civil Rights Struggle before the NAACP* (Philadelphia: University of Pennsylvania Press, 2012), 19, 25–26; Henry W. Grady, "The South and Her Problems," speech, October 26, 1887, in Harris, *Life of Henry W. Grady*, 94–120, 100.

41. Henry W. Grady, "At the Boston Banquet," speech, Boston Merchants' Association, December 1889, in Harris, *Life of Henry W. Grady*, 183–84.

42. Edward L. Ayers, *The Promise of the New South: Life after Reconstruction*, 15th anniversary ed. (1992; New York: Oxford University Press, 2007), 50–51; Grady, "At the Boston Banquet," 190, 193; Nixon, *Henry W. Grady*, 83, 319.

43. Alexander, *Army of Lions*, 21; Davis, *Henry Grady's New South*, 7, 158–60; T. Thomas Fortune, "The Race Problem," *Belford's Magazine* 5, no. 28 (1890), 489–95, 489.

44. Robert Greene II, "Mississippi Plan," in *Journalism and Jim Crow*; Grant, *The Way It Was in the South*, 197–99; Ayers, *Promise of the New South*, 146–49; Wood-

ward, *Origins of the New South*, 332; Eric Foner, *The Second Founding: How the Civil War and Reconstruction Remade the Constitution* (New York: W. W. Norton, 2019), 158; Perman, *Struggle for Mastery*, 51, 76.

45. W. Calvin Chase, "Aliens Forever?" *Washington Bee*, December 28, 1889; W.E.B. Du Bois, *Black Reconstruction in America, 1860–1880* (1935; repr., New York: Free Press, 1998), 705–706; Rayford Logan, "Plus ça change, plus c'est la même chose," *Journal of Negro Education* 13, no. 4 (1944): 522–24.

CHAPTER 2

Fight for a New America

D'WESTON HAYWOOD

In December 1886, Henry Grady, editor of the popular *Atlanta Constitution*, spoke before the annual banquet of the New England Society of New York City. He announced, "There is a New South." He had used the phrase "New South" before in an article he authored in 1874 to promote industrialization in the region. But standing before many Northern politicians, businessmen, and investors, he continued promoting, though this time he outdid himself. For Grady, the "Old South," which had rested on slavery and undemocratic regimes vesting political and economic power in an elite planter class, was dead. The New South marked a definitive break with the past, "not through protest against the Old, but because of new conditions, new adjustments and, if you please, new ideas and aspirations." Illustrating this departure even more was the new status of the formerly enslaved, Grady argued, reflecting prevailing beliefs among whites in the South, beliefs that his speech would help popularize further. "But what of the Negro? . . . Let the record speak to the point. No section shows a more prosperous laboring population than the Negroes of the South; none in fuller sympathy with the employing and land-owning class." Grady wanted to portray the conditions of Black Southerners as wholly positive, given the promise of the New South. "He shares our school fund, has the fullest protection of our laws and the friendship of our people. Self-interest, as well as honor, demand that he should have this," he affirmed. "Our future, our very existence depend upon our working out this problem in full and exact justice," a problem that he and others like him believed was best handled by Southerners. Grady insisted that tensions between Black and white people were now virtually reconciled, that "in general . . . the free Negro counts more than he did as a slave," that in putting "business above politics," "the relations of the Southern people with the Negro are close and cordial."[1]

Grady touted the New South as a literal and figurative space of boundless opportunities for the entire country as well as its inhabitants. And to make the point, he made an ideological and rhetorical move that was characteristic of many white people at the time: he claimed to know precisely the conditions of Black people at this juncture of immense and precarious transition in America.[2] His speech circulated widely across the country and received a great deal of praise.[3] But many members of the contemporary Black press knew that the speech and the ideas behind it smacked of paternalism and worse. To them, the speech was rooted in problematic ideas that helped generate dangerous untruths about the realities of Black life in the South and elsewhere. For many Black journalists, the New South would not herald a complete break—it would herald a new fight.

This chapter examines the cadre of militant Black journalists who emerged in the late nineteenth and early twentieth centuries to mobilize the Black press to combat the political economies and social orders of the New South. They marshaled Black newspapers to resist amid what historian Rayford Logan called the "nadir" of race relations, an era when white supremacists rolled back the constitutional rights that Black people had gained during Reconstruction, instituted Jim Crow segregation, and deployed violence to control the labor, mobility, autonomy, and aspirations of Black people.[4] It was also an era when print media exerted a tremendous influence on public opinion and the public sphere. This influence proceeded much to the detriment of Black people, as the white press virtually shut them out of any serious public discourse, except in terms of discussing them along a spectrum of problematics: from a menacing criminal race to a perpetual societal problem. Racial discourses in the press often paralleled racial discourses in the law with one helping to reinforce the other. Consequently, there was little safe space for Black people both in public and within the columns of white newspapers.

It was against this backdrop that Black journalism became the incubator of a new tide of Black activism. Thus, Black journalists worked to expose the New South for what it really was and to raise public consciousness to the realities of racial injustice that proponents of the New South attempted to mask. This difficult work required Black newspaper men and women to build a critical discursive space of their own.[5] It also required the "unmasking" of Black people. In 1895 Black poet and writer Paul Laurence Dunbar published "We Wear the Mask," a poem that spoke to a certain public self that Black people were expected to perform and project before white publics in order to avoid insult and violence.[6] Militant Black newspaper workers rejected the proverbial mask that Black people were expected to don and embraced instead vocal, outright resistance through pointed protest in deed and in print.

The antebellum Black press had fought relentlessly against slavery. Building on this foundation, the new generation of Black journalists confronted a new target: Jim Crow and the racial ideologies and political economies that underpinned it. Their literacy and formal education convinced them that they must act on behalf of the Black masses to mount a discursive assault on the false narratives of the New South and the structures of white supremacy those narratives protected.[7] Indeed, if there was going to be anything truly new about the New South, it would be the counterpublic Black journalists would forge by carving out their own critical discursive space predicated on militant Black resistance.[8] Here, Black journalists appeared to be situated outside the mainstream, dangling somewhere beyond even the margins of the pages of the white press, South and North, which made it extremely challenging to gain a substantial hearing. Yet a closer analysis shows that their critical discursive space seemed peripheral only because it was at the center of an America that did not yet exist. Embracing "new" as the watchword of the era, but in terms cut from the particular contexts of urgent Black protest, Black journalists worked from different corners of the country while essentially sharing the same singular objective: to expose the fallacies of the New South, reveal the truth about Black life, and outline the social, political, and racial contours of America as it should be.

Indeed, many Black journalists immediately rejected the "New South" as a signifier with any real meaning, recognizing it for what it actually was: a concept and brand reflecting the construction and promotional work of white journalists like Henry Grady.[9] The term seemed not to register much in the publications and public utterances of most Black newspaper men and women in the North or South, unless as a problematic. Joseph Charles Price and Simon Green Atkins, founders of the North Carolina *Southland* in 1890, dedicated their newspaper to, as its motto announced, "Not the Old South nor the New South, but the Southland as it ought to be."[10] T. Thomas Fortune, the talented editor and writer for numerous Black papers, known best for his fiery editorship of the *New York Age*, became a constant critic of the façade of the New

South. Fortune labeled Grady and his ilk "false prophets" and determined to contest their vision and its adroit masking of Black discontent in the South. "Mr. Grady appeals to the North to leave the race question to '*us*' and '*we*' will settle it. So *we* will; but that *we* Mr. Grady had 'in his mind's eye' will not be permitted to settle it alone. Not by any means, Mr. Grady," Fortune wrote. "Not only the White *we*, but the Colored *we* as well, will demand a share in that settlement. . . . Unlike in times past, *we have a voice, and we propose to make that voice heard,* in all future phases of the discussion of this race question," Fortune thundered.[11]

Even less-sanguine Black journalists also failed to relate to the idea of the New South. They instead seemed more enthusiastic about the prospects of the coming new century and the active role they thought the Black press needed to take in it, as evidenced by Irvine Garland Penn's 1891 volume, *The Afro-American Press and Its Editors*. Penn, himself a Black journalist, profiled an array of Black publishers, working across the country to shepherd a diverse body of religious and secular periodicals. Penn's book testified to the explosion of Black newspapers at this crucial time, due in no small part to the continued erosion of Black people's rights. He even apologized that he could not feature all the "hundreds of men and women laboring in journalism."[12] But collectively the Black press had "proven a power in the promotion of truth, justice and equal rights for an oppressed people," he insisted, and at a great cost for many Black publishers. Publishing Black newspapers was no easy task. The efforts of Black publishers and editors involved a labor of resistance, a certain "magnitude," "heroic labors," and "responsibilities" that demanded "the greatest sacrifice" to address the "social, moral, political and educational ills of the Afro-American" at a time when Black people's rights were "being questioned." But Penn remained hopeful that with the new century approaching, the Black press would continue to expand and the public would rally to its cause of racial equality. And while there existed a group of white publishers "prevailing in the South to an alarming extent" who were "abusive" and "glory in encouraging lynch law," he was confident that they would disappear over time through greater education.[13] Yet not too long after the book's publication, one of the publishers that Penn profiled, Ida B. Wells, came to know firsthand what the new century would actually look like for many Black people. In 1892, after using her *Memphis Free Speech and Headlight* to protest the lynching of three of her friends, a mob destroyed her office and printing press. The assailants left a note: "anyone trying to publish the paper again would be punished with death."[14]

What Wells experienced was no anomaly but very much characteristic of the racial terror that pervaded the South during the "nadir."[15] Undaunted, Wells continued to mobilize Black protest through journalism. Several other Black journalists did too. And there was much to attack: "Redeemers," Southern Democrats and elites determined to solidify white supremacy throughout the South, took over state legislatures to dismantle cross-racial democracy in the region, expel Black officeholders, undercut Black male suffrage, and institute Jim Crow segregation. Additionally, "whitecapping" rose, the violent means by which white people forced Black landowners from their property in order to seize it, all while lynching soared. By 1883 the U.S. Supreme Court overturned the Civil Rights Act of 1875.[16]

Compounding matters was a slew of white writers, academics, and pseudo-scientists who published numerous works that helped instantiate what historian George M. Fredrickson called "Southern Negrophobia." Charles Carroll's *The Negro a Beast* (1900) and Thomas Dixon's *The Leopard's Spots* (1902) and *The Clansman* (1905), which would be adapted as the film *The Birth of a Nation* in 1915, were popular examples of "virulent anti-Negro propaganda" that helped give whites cultural and intellectual authority and legitimacy in attacking Black people's public image, bodies, and rights.[17] And the white press served as a crucial weapon in the arsenal of white supremacy, justifying and reflecting the false logics of these developments and shaping white public opinion accordingly in powerful ways. As Wells discerned, part of the branding of the New South involved branding Black people "a race of rapists." This pernicious representation of Black people performed crucial political and cultural work for the Redemption project, serving as reason enough for many white people to support racially discriminatory laws, on one hand, and wanton racial violence, on the other, projecting what was printed about Black people onto the bodies of actual Black people. Not only did this representation help remove Black people's legitimate claims to citizenship rights from public discourse, but it was also "bound to rob us of all the friends we had," Wells wrote, "and silence any protests that they might make for us."[18] The rapist brand that white media helped fix against Black men emphasized the purity of white women while impugning that of Black women. For the president of the Missouri Press Association, Black women were incapable of "true womanhood." Unlike white women, Black women lacked any "sense of virtue" and were "altogether without character," he argued in an 1895 open letter denouncing Wells's anti-lynching activism. This printed attack, yet another racist calculation from a member of the Southern white press, was enough to motivate Black women activists to respond in full force in July 1895 through collective organization. In 1896 they formed the National Association of Colored Women (NACW), with journalist and essayist Mary Church Terrell as their president.[19] Member and journalist Fannie Barrier Williams explained that because there had been "no fixed public opinion to which they could appeal; no protection against the libelous attacks upon their characters," their organization was in part determined to carve out a critical discursive space "to change public opinion concerning the character and worth of colored women." One of their publications, *Woman's Era*, among the many "leaflets and tracts" they issued, was hailed proudly as the "first newspaper ever published by colored women in this country." Invoking the "newness" of the era, and in gendered terms, they represented the "real new woman in American life" who "has come to the front in an opportune time."[20]

Wells was a member of the NACW, among several other activist organizations, drawing on their concerted organizing to wage her journalistic fight. Having lost her friends and paper to a violent mob, she waged an especially personal crusade. Ultimately, however, she believed the destruction of her press was a boon to her journalism, freeing her from the South and enabling her to "tell the whole truth now."[21] And her investigative journalism quickly showed what that truth was. In order to justify the open murder of lynching, many white leaders and newspapers argued that lynch mobs descended to defend white womanhood against Black men, encouraged by their belief in a Black male propensity for raping white women. But Wells found that her friends had committed no such crime. Their only offense was that they owned a successful grocery store. And "this is what opened my eyes to what lynching really was," she explained, an "excuse to get rid of Negroes who were acquiring wealth and property and thus keep the race terrorized and 'keep the nigger down.'" The promise of the New South, which proponents argued hinged on economic freedom for all and putting "business above politics," as Grady had insisted, clearly did not extend to upwardly mobile and economically successful Black people. "For all these reasons it seemed a stern duty to give the facts I had collected to the world."[22]

Though Black publishers like John Mitchell Jr. of the *Richmond Planet* for many years had used their papers to condemn lynching in unequivocally militant terms, Wells was the first to mount a sustained campaign to challenge lynching and debunk the myths of a rapacious Black male sexuality that sustained the barbaric practice.[23] Wells relocated to New York, and later Chicago, and began writing for T. Thomas Fortune's *New York Age* as she built an anti-lynching campaign that placed her before publics as far as England. Just when members of the Southern white press instigated racial violence and the

Northern white press often remained indifferent, if not complicit, Wells took her work internationally, extending the Black counterpublic. Even Frederick Douglass, the famous abolitionist and a premier leader of the antebellum Black press, acknowledged that Wells's work had been a revelation to him too. He admitted to her that without countervailing evidence, he, too, had begun to believe white supremacists' arguments behind lynching until she exposed the truth.[24] *Exiled*, the account of her expulsion from Memphis, published as an article in June 1892 in the *New York Age*, and the pamphlet, *Southern Horrors: Lynch Law in All Its Phases*, released in October 1892, were the first of Wells's many meticulously researched and powerfully presented anti-lynching tracts.[25]

And in her effort to elevate lynching as a national problem that required a federal solution, Wells not only railed against racial violence but also castigated the white press for encouraging it. To be sure, many Black activists and journalists well understood that white newspapers were one part of a broader oppressive and violent racial regime stretching across the country, but tremendously important parts no less, as they served as fonts for the racist ideologies and discourses that underpinned that regime. Acting as the printed arm of white supremacy, the white press was crucial to helping influence the white public to unite across otherwise deep class cleavages to destroy Black people's freedom. In *Southern Horrors*, Wells called out the "Malicious and Untruthful White Press." Her pamphlet reprinted the comments of the *Daily Commercial* and *Evening Scimitar* specifically, two white papers in Memphis that condoned the lynching of her friends. "Nothing but the most prompt, speedy and extreme punishment can hold in check the horrible and bestial propensities of the Negro race," the *Commercial* asserted. The *Evening Scimitar* echoed the claim: "Aside from the violation of white women by Negroes, which is the outcropping of a bestial perversion of instinct, the chief cause of trouble between the races in the South is the Negro's lack of manners. . . . He has taken up the idea that boorish insolence is independence," to which the *"response will be prompt and effectual"* (original emphasis). But Wells also identified Henry Grady as the leading white voice promoting anti-Black discourses that shaped racial violence and structures of white power throughout the South in particular and the nation more broadly: "Through him and other leading men the cry of the South to the country has been 'Hands off! Leave us to solve our problem.' To the Afro-American the South says, 'the white man must and will rule.'" For Wells, Grady's ideology pointed to a much larger problem, exposing a deeper line of continuity that showed "there is little difference between the Ante-bellum South and the New South."[26] This point, collapsing time and space in order to illuminate Black life and the nation as they really existed, was a sentiment to which many Black Southerners could relate.[27] And many Black activists and journalists agreed, sharing the same consciousness of resistance as they mobilized Black newspapers to map from inside a growing critical Black discursive space the contours of an America that should be.

By the mid-1890s sustained Black resistance became even more urgent. A cascade of segregation laws at the state level during the decade and soaring racial violence made the need for strident Black protest especially clear. The stance of Black educator Booker T. Washington helped make this even clearer. A former slave, who became the leader of the Black vocational Tuskegee Institute in Alabama, Washington was featured in Irvine Garland Penn's 1891 book. In a section titled "Opinions of Eminent Men on the Afro-American Press," Penn quoted Washington's comment that Black newspapers "served as educators to the white race, in matters that pertain to the progress of the Negro. The white press readily sees our dark side," hardly ever "letting the world know of the Negro's advancement."[28]

But in 1895 Washington sounded a somewhat different note. Before a large gathering of white Southern and Northern industrial leaders, public officials, and businessmen attending the Cotton States Exposition in Atlanta, Georgia, a promotion and celebration of economic progress in the South, Washington delivered a speech that appealed to New South exponents, even segregationists. From Henry Grady's home base, and rehearsing many of the themes of his famous oration, including Grady's glowing take on the conditions of Black people in the South, Washington asserted, "Whatever other sins the South may be called to bear, when it comes to business, pure and simple, it is in the South that the Negro is given a man's chance in the commercial world." Again, a promoter of the New South intentionally masked the widespread labor exploitation, whitecapping, debt peonage, convict leasing, and racial violence that had come to typify Black Southern life.[29] In fact, in 1895, six years after Grady's death, the *Atlanta Constitution* chastised the *New York World* for circulating photographs of a lynching in Texas because the image amounted to "pictorial libeling" that gave the impression that the "South was a land of barbarians."[30] Grady's newspaper had fully absorbed his New South teachings, as had Washington. In this "new era of industrial progress," Washington advised Black people against allowing their "grievances to overshadow our opportunities," a point that only served as an entrée to his resounding capitulation to the Jim Crow regime. "In all things that are purely social," he said, "we can be as separate as the fingers, yet one as the hand in all things essential to mutual progress." "The wisest among my race understand that the agitation of questions of social equality is the extremist folly," he continued in a veiled shot at some Black activists and Black publishers.[31] Indeed, that same year, Wells would publish yet another thorough investigation of lynching, *A Red Record: Tabulated Statistics and Alleged Causes of Lynching in the United States*. This one was a hundred-page pamphlet.[32] Washington instead counseled Black people to begin "making friends, in every manly way, of the people of all races by whom we are surrounded." "I pledge," he declared in paternalistic terms that conceded leadership on racial issues to white elites, "that in your effort to work out the great and intricate problem which God has laid at the doors of the South, you shall have at all times the patient, sympathetic help of my race" to support the New South in producing something even greater: "a new heaven and a new earth."[33]

The speech, which became popularly known as the "Atlanta Compromise," launched Washington to national fame and racial leadership, due in no small part to its conciliatory vision, as well as the fact that a notable Black leader had articulated the opposite of what many Black activists and journalists were demanding at the time. It might seem that Washington, an adept public speaker, a talent he wielded in successful fund-raising for Tuskegee, could have been merely posturing in order to win white support for certain Black causes. But the speech represented the accommodationist public position he would hold until his death in 1915.[34] Many white leaders, North and South, seized on it as another signal to retreat from racial issues. It was a move they were already more than willing to make, for national white public interest in debates and efforts around protecting Black people's rights had declined precipitously.[35] To his credit, Washington actually believed in the economic promise of the New South, that business and free market forces would steadily improve the oppressed plight of Black people in and outside of the region.[36] However, a Black leader's promotion of the New South and endorsement of the social, political, and legal subordination of Black people gave a white public increasingly indifferent to racial issues yet another convenient excuse to further absolve themselves of their part in the consolidation of the political economies of the Jim Crow South. Washington was a "sensible and progressive negro educator," who had rendered the "most remarkable address delivered by a colored man in America," the *Atlanta Constitution* opined. "Washington knows he's on the right line."[37] White leaders now cited Washington as *the* authority on racial issues, preferring his approach to Black agitation, of course.

Testifying to his new position of leadership, President Theodore Roosevelt hosted Washington as a guest at the White House in October 1901.[38] Juxtaposed to Washington, many Black journalists appeared even more militant, despite their demands being fully consistent with the promise of American democracy and constitutional rights. They were not wholly convinced, as Washington and his supporters were, that moral and economic uplift alone could protect Black people's public image, bodies, and rights. For them, Washington was advising outmoded strategies of racial uplift that reified the "mask" of the New South and Black people at a time when the exigencies of Black life demanded vocal and consistent critique, protest, organization, and legal recourse.[39] These journalists resisted with a zealous fervor poised to outmatch all the disciples of the New South, Black and white alike. As T. Thomas Fortune put it, "The great need of the times is well directed agitation which will vex the soul of the nation until it shall be aroused to a sense of duty." "Who is to provoke this agitation?" he asked. He was certain it would not be white Southerners or "the white men of the north," for they had already "buried the bloody shirt, have forgotten the crime of rebellion, and in the pursuit of commercial and political gain have allowed Henry W. Grady to declare . . . that the whites of the south would rule the south." "Under the circumstances, it is useless for us to look to white men to fight for black man's rights," he contended. "If we don't do it ourselves it will not be done."[40]

Yet, as many Black activists and publishers grew outraged at Washington, the U.S. Supreme Court again raised the stakes. In 1896, on the heels of its 1883 decision against the 1875 Civil Rights Act, the court decided in *Plessy v. Ferguson* that "separate but equal" facilities segregating Black and white people were legal under the Fourteenth Amendment. State-sanctioned racial discrimination, plaguing Black people mostly in the South, now became the sweeping law of the land. It was Southern policy cut from the New South writ large. For Black activists and journalists, the court ruling signaled a watershed moment—a clarion call for total Black resistance. And violent events in Wilmington, North Carolina, in 1898 only gave further confirmation. A reign of racial terror swept the majority-Black city during the November elections, the bloody culmination of an effective white supremacy campaign championed for about a year by Democrats to restore white political control of the city and state. The Democrats counted Josephus Daniels, publisher of the Raleigh *News and Observer*, among their ranks. Daniels led a wing of the Redemption campaign through his press, inveighing against Black political power and rights. In addition to overthrowing the interracial Fusionist government, expelling Black officeholders and Black municipal workers by force, and killing anyone who resisted, Black or white, the mob incinerated the headquarters of the local Black newspaper, the Wilmington *Daily Record*. Reportedly the only Black daily periodical in the country at the time, its publisher, Alexander Manly, had criticized lynching and the myth of the Black rapist. White papers across the South reported Manly's words in distorted form. Manly had already fled town before the mob struck. Droves of Black residents soon followed in a mass exodus from the city.[41]

By 1900 T. Thomas Fortune called for outright "revolution."[42] For now, at least, that revolution came through the militant Black press. Black newspapers not only exploded in number, but they also underwent consequential editorial changes that indicated a definitive shift to a resistant Black politics.[43] What Paul Laurence Dunbar had figured as the proverbial mask Black people wore to obfuscate their real thoughts and critiques in the presence of white people was obliterated as the pages of the Black press gave way to sharp and scathing social critique and political thought trained on dismantling white supremacy and raising public consciousness. Black journalists and writers increasingly moved away from discussing religious subjects concerning the character and respectability of Black people, as was the general tenor of many Black periodicals after the demise of Reconstruction, to hammering out matters of racial politics and citizenship rights. In 1900 Ida B. Wells published *Mob Rule in New Orleans*. Booker T. Washington, by contrast, published *A New Negro for a New Century* that same year. The book's title played up the watchword of the period couched in terms of Black uplift but centered on a positive narrative of Black progress shorn of virtually any social or political critique. Black journalists, on the other hand, began organizing like never before, and Fortune was certainly a model in this regard. A longtime journalist, writing for and editing a number of newspapers throughout the South and North, Fortune was easily considered the "most noted man in Afro-American journalism," who, as Penn observed in his *Afro-American Press and Its Editors*, "never writes unless he makes somebody wince."[44] His uncompromising journalistic approach deepened, especially as he became motivated, like members of the NACW had been, to stake out this crusade in rousing gendered terms reflecting the "newness" of the era. He demanded "a new man in black, a freeman every inch, standing erect and undaunted, an American from head to foot" to step forward and fight.[45] The first decade of the new century would be his most active, Fortune recalled. "It seems to me," he wrote to a colleague, "that I have entered upon a higher and stronger phase of my work as a journalist."[46] Many other Black newspaper men and women could relate.

Indeed, several Black editors called for Fortune to revive the Afro-American League, a group he originally organized in 1887 at the height of Grady's popularity, though other Black protest organizations began to emerge with force.[47] Altogether they built a chorus of critique alongside newly founded Black newspapers.[48] For instance, in 1901 William Monroe Trotter helped found the *Boston Guardian*, which was intended to "voice intelligently the needs and aspirations of the colored American" and "to protest forever against being proscribed or shut off in any caste from equal rights with other citizens." It would "remain forever on the firing line at any and all times in defense of such rights," the paper declared in martial terms meant to discursively counter racial injustice.[49] The popular monthly magazine the *Voice of the Negro* began reaching readers in Atlanta in 1904; Southern migrant Robert S. Abbott started the *Chicago Defender* in 1905.[50] W.E.B. Du Bois, a Harvard-trained historian and aspiring editor, for some time had freelanced for a number of papers, including T. Thomas Fortune's *New York Age*.[51] Like his cohorts, he saw how "all allusions to Negroes in the public press were chiefly confined to ridicule, caricature, gross invective, or maudlin pity."[52] In 1905 he launched the *Moon Illustrated Weekly: A Record of the Darker Races* in Memphis, Tennessee, and in 1907 the *Horizon: A Journal of the Color Line* in Washington, D.C.[53]

Emphasizing the deep connection between publishing and protest, a dialogic relationship in which one reinforced the other, Jesse Max Barber, editor of the *Voice of the Negro*; Trotter; Du Bois; and others launched the Niagara Movement in 1905. Named for the location of their inaugural meeting, which was held on the Canadian side of the river, members of the Niagara Movement demanded "every single right that belongs to a freeborn American" and promised to "protest and assail the ears of America" until "we get these rights." Barber, Trotter, and several Black activists also formed the Negro-American Political League in 1908.[54] Vigorous activism and vigorous journalism went hand in hand as Black activists and Black newspaper men and women took a decided stand in deed and in print. In addition to their concerted fight, Du Bois, for a time, especially appreciated the Niagara Movement for its "like-mindedness" or shared consciousness of Black resistance.[55] Collectively, members of the Niagara Movement appreciated that they had helped galvanize more Black activism while garnering a great deal of support from several Black papers across the country, which joined them in "advocating Niagara principles."[56] It was not uncommon for activist groups to carry some kind of publication, ranging from a newsletter, bulletin, journal, or newspaper. Neither was it uncommon for editors of one paper to write pieces for the presses of other editors, producing a robust cross-pollination in journalistic protest.[57] And even when organizing efforts and their publications waned or failed entirely, typically due to inadequate financial resources or ideological differences and personality struggles among members, they stood ready to organize again, start another periodical of some sort, and resume their roles as constant gadflies to the Jim Crow regime. Henry Grady would peg them all "Afro-American agitators." He meant it as an insult. They took it as a compliment.[58]

Carving out and constructing their own critical discursive space and expanding it with every publication and organized effort, the militant Black press engendered a Black counterpublic that flew directly in the face of the false logics of white supremacy. Increasingly, Black activists and journalists became one and the same, working to illuminate the realities of Black life, resist the erosion of Black people's rights, end racial violence, and challenge prevailing racist ideologies that figured Black people as simpletons content to be resigned from the weighty responsibilities of social equality and political engagement. Unmasked, the Black press transformed into a crucial site for Black people's critical political theorizing on questions of race, democracy, freedom, constitutional rights, citizenship, and justice—outlining a vision of America as it should be.

To be sure, the tenor of protest was not always uniform, as some journalists were more radical than others.[59] Furthermore, much of the phalanx of papers that constituted the militant Black press mobilized from cities mostly in the urban North. As the cases of Ida B. Wells and Alexander Manly demonstrated, the violence of the New South hampered the possibilities of a more widespread vocal Southern Black press.[60] Even Jesse Max Barber of the Atlanta-based *Voice of the Negro*, was eventually forced to take the paper to Chicago in 1906 after mob violence connected to the Atlanta Race Riot of that same year threatened his life. Barber had accused white politicians and white newspaper publishers of helping foment the riot.[61] Still, such life-threatening experiences did not deter Black journalists from continued publishing and activism. These violent episodes, rather, steeled their resolve to force the issues to the center of public thought. And even though mostly positioned in the North, a somewhat safer space for the era, many members of the Black press saw the North and South— two discrete regions of the country, according to popular representations—as deeply connected, if not merely differently marked versions of each other. In fact, their relentless efforts to build a critical discursive space made them so discerning of the value of certain literal and symbolic spaces in America that they were quick to recognize just how much the North was in league with the New South as a rigid "color line" ran through both. In fact, one white paper in the North tried to launch the "New North" to match Grady's "New South." The "New North" did not gain any traction, however.[62]

Indeed, the cadre of militant Black journalists construed both regions as culpable. "The present apathetic condition of public sentiment" concerning Black people was "North and South," Ida B. Wells trenchantly observed in an article in 1900.[63] Fannie Barrier Williams would put it more forcefully, collapsing the assumed spatial boundaries demarcating the country into distinct regions even further: "The wants, needs, limitations and aspirations of the Afro-American are about the same everywhere—North, South, East and West."[64] "The American Negro is a great deal of a foreigner to the average white American," Williams maintained in the *Voice of the Negro* in 1904. "As this average American sees but little of the Negro and knows but little of him, he is at liberty to form any kind of erroneous opinions concerning him." Williams spoke to Black people's popular positioning outside the American democratic project, which marked Black folk as something alien before the public and the law. She drew a direct line between misrepresentations of Black people, public opinion, and racial violence, affirming that "public opinion today seems to give sanction to these miserable fears of the proud and chivalrous Anglo-Saxon." "Public opinion is a good deal of a despot when it comes to showing favors or doing justice to those who are weak but deserve justice." "We must look to ourselves and not to the white race" to raise public consciousness and forge an influential counterpublic, she asserted, one that was not only disruptive to the racial politics of the country but also remained ideologically and discursively situated firmly inside the America that needed to be.[65]

This cadre of militant Black journalists constituted the "bumptious, irritated, young black intelligentsia of the day," Du Bois declared proudly, counting himself in the fold of these militants as he reflected on this challenging period years later.[66] Yet by 1910 Du Bois saw a way to sharpen their tactics by making a slight but strategic shift in the tenor of their protest and editorializing. Several developments moved him to make this shift. First, some of the organizing efforts in which he had been involved, particularly the Niagara Movement, had collapsed by this time as members splintered off to pursue organizing in other directions under different and often competing visions of Black protest.[67] Second, Booker T. Washington's influence had only peaked in these years. Testifying to how important Black newspapers had become in building a critical Black discursive space, Washington increasingly worked to influence, if not control, the Black press through patronage and financial subsidies to certain papers so that they would promote his approach over that of opponents.[68] This was a point that Du Bois openly criticized in his 1903 seminal publication, *The Souls of Black Folk*, a collection of essays based on several newspaper articles he had previously published. In no uncertain pejorative terms, Du Bois called Washington's efforts at control the "Tuskegee Machine." The book also criticized the New South. "For every social ill the panacea of Wealth has been urged," Du Bois wrote in protest, "wealth to overthrow the remains of the slave feudalism; wealth to raise the 'cracker' Third Estate; wealth to employ the black serfs, and the prospect of wealth to keep them working; wealth as the end and aim of politics, and as the legal tender for law and order." Moreover, *Souls* spoke to Black people's "two-ness," "double-consciousness," and "veil," or the collective alienation that Black people experienced being figured outside the American body politic and as a "problem" before the white public. But it was also this alienation that provided Black people with a "second-sight in this American world," a critical lens that revealed, Du Bois argued, that there were "no truer exponents of the pure human spirit of the Declaration of Independence than the American Negroes." With gripping prose and historical analysis, Du Bois eloquently named what he and other Black journalists had long identified as they endeavored to elevate a vision of America as it should be over the country as it was.[69]

Finally, as had long been the case for other Black journalists, Du Bois "sought publicity for a cause which was markedly unpopular with the white periodical press."[70] The failure of the Niagara Movement, the growth of Washington's influence, and the desire for a wider audience now shaped Du Bois's thinking in considering better strategies for reaching multiple publics. "We must have a vehicle for both opinion and fact," he reasoned, "a forum less radical than the *Guardian,* and yet more rational than the rank and file of Negro papers now so largely arrayed with Tuskegee." Du Bois called William Monroe Trotter's *Boston Guardian* "bitter, satirical, and personal," comments partly driven by disagreements the two men had with each other at different times.[71] Historians agree that Trotter's *Guardian* was indeed one of the most radical Black papers of its day largely because its editor was such an uncompromising but prickly activist. In 1903, for example, Trotter and several supporters confronted Booker T. Washington as he delivered a speech in Boston, a move that resulted in Trotter's arrest. The incident came to be called the "Boston Riot" and forever smeared Trotter's reputation in certain social and political circles.[72] It was this kind of approach and its adverse effects that Du Bois wanted to avoid.[73] That a Black newspaper should be "less radical" and "more rational" during this pivotal time of upsurge in Black protest and Black journalism is significant. For Du Bois, such an idea did not depart from the ethos of Black resistance in which he was situated as much as it was a deliberate re-presentation of the militant

Black press calculated to expand their critical discursive space and attract a mass audience and broader coalition to its cause.

When Du Bois, Mary Church Terrell, Ida B. Wells, and others joined with several white liberals in New York to found the integrationist National Association for the Advancement of Colored People (NAACP) in 1909, prompted by the Springfield Race Riot of 1908 and the ongoing erosion of Black people's citizenship rights, Du Bois got his chance to apply his new discursive strategy. The group dedicated itself to using agitation, litigation, and publications to attack racial injustice.[74] The organization appointed Du Bois director of publicity and research, and with this role he launched the *Crisis: A Record of the Darker Races* in November 1910, the group's "organ of propaganda," as he put it.[75] "The National Association for the Advancement of Colored People is organized to fight the wrong of prejudice," a monumental task that Du Bois argued would proceed first through "the printed word in a periodical like this, and in pamphlets and tracts."[76] True to the Black militant roots from which the paper and its editor had sprung, the *Crisis* was a "periodical of fact and agitation," but by deploying his new pragmatic approach, its content and spirit of protest would be "properly presented." That is, Du Bois planned to channel Black militancy through a carefully presented, scholarly approach of "studying the American Negro and making his accomplishment known," placing "consistently and continuously before the country a clear-cut statement of the legitimate aims of the American Negro and the facts concerning his condition."[77] Especially wary about being "misunderstood and misrepresented, as was the case with the Niagara Movement," he worked to appeal to "the general citizenship of the United States, in order that the cause for which [the NAACP] was fighting might be known," a posture that could do more to penetrate the white public sphere to win white allies.[78]

As he explained to readers in the inaugural issue of the *Crisis* in November 1910, "The object of this publication is to set forth those facts and arguments which show the danger of race prejudice." While the paper was so named because "the editors believe that this is a critical time in the history of the advancement of men," pointing to the realities of Black life, its editorial policy would be "simple and well defined." It would "record important happenings and movements in the world which bear on the great problem of interracial relations . . . review opinion and literature . . . and important expressions of opinion in the white press and colored press," and, finally, "stand for the rights of men, irrespective of color or race, for the highest ideals of American democracy, and for reasonable but earnest and persistent attempt to gain these rights and realize these ideals."

On the last point especially, Du Bois was pointing to the effort of his periodical to help instantiate the America that should be, as other Black journalists had also worked to do in pushing this vision to the center of the public sphere. And he promised to "avoid personal rancor of all sorts. In the absence of proof to the contrary it will assume honesty of purpose on the part of all men, North and South, white and Black."[79] Du Bois's strategic discursive moves proved successful. *Crisis* subscriptions increased "a thousand a month until by 1918.... We published and sold over a hundred thousand," circulating in "every state in the Union, beside Europe, Africa, and the South Seas." Exemplifying the nexus between protest and publishing, and the growth of Black people's critical discursive space into a strong Black counterpublic with widespread reach, Du Bois became, as he termed it, a "master of propaganda."[80]

But Du Bois's calculated re-presentation of the militant Black press anticipated other sophisticated discursive moves that other members of the Black press would also make to further raise public consciousness, elevate and substantiate Black people's rightful claims to citizenship, and engender concerted action. These moves generated a tremendous influence on the public that began to interest scholars by the 1920s and even some state authorities. Indeed, as oppressive racial conditions in the South continued apace, Robert S. Abbott's response was to urge Black people to leave the South altogether. Beginning around 1915, Abbott picked up on the spike in Black Southerners then migrating by the thousands from the South in what would become known as the "Great Migration." Abbott's *Chicago Defender* promoted the migration but did so by strategically appropriating the sensationalism deployed by major white newspapers of the time to launch an all-out editorial campaign laced in bold front-page headlines, striking images, and dramatic stories of racial injustice. Framed in thrilling, sensationalized language, the *Defender* couched the migration as a massive Black protest against the South. And state authorities in the South reacted, construing the *Defender* as a direct political challenge to the political economies and racial regimes of the region. Cities like Meridian, Mississippi, for instance, banned the *Defender*. In another direct challenge, Abbott circumvented these efforts by hiring Black railroad porters to secret the paper and sell it to readers in the South.[81]

During World War I, as the federal government grew concerned about alleged domestic subversives, it brought the Black press under surveillance for its sharp outspokenness on racial inequality.[82] Robert T. Kerlin, a white literary scholar, took notice of these significant shifts and developments in the Black press. In the vein of Irvine Garland Penn's 1891 book, Kerlin's *The Voice of the Negro 1919*, which was published in 1920, helped inaugurate a new wave of studies on Black newspapers. Kerlin was deeply intrigued by the powerful role Black newspapers played in protesting the race riots that had ripped through as many as twenty-five towns and cities across the country in 1919 in what became known as the "Red Summer." Exploding in many urban centers in the North, the open violence of the Red Summer heralded another watershed moment for Black people, much like the rise of Jim Crow had done toward the dawn of the twentieth century. This watershed was another bitter reminder that racial oppression and its attending violence were not confined to the South; they were indexes of a national problem that again exposed the continuities between the South and North, as Black journalists and activists had long argued. And not unlike the watershed before it, this one also invigorated yet another generation of Black activism mobilizing under a singular consciousness of militant Black resistance.[83]

In fact, many Black journalists announced this watershed as the dawning of a new era, still invoking the watchword of the age but again deploying it in the context of the exigencies of contemporary Black life and urgent Black protest. The "newness" of this moment signaled the emergence of the "New Negro," Black people's cultural and political signifier and trope for a militant Black resistance of the 1920s that would be expressed through a flowering of mass political organizing and robust critical intellectual and artistic productions.[84] Kerlin seemed a virtual newcomer to the critical role the Black press had long played for Black people, but he was still able to recognize, even in 1920, some of the core tenets that had animated the militant Black press from its inception. "We have too frequently heard foolish vaunts about 'knowing the Negro,'" he wrote, "the context of such boasting invariably convicting the speaker of dangerous conceit and the harsh spirit of suppression." But "here is the voice of the Negro, and his heart and mind." Unmasked, "here the Negro race speaks as it thinks on the question of questions for America—the race question," Kerlin affirmed. "Those who would honestly seek to know the Negro must read his papers."[85]

Indeed, the critical discursive space that Black journalists solidified in the face of Jim Crow, pervasive racial injustice and violence, and the so-called New South, had become more and more clear to outside observers by the 1920s, testifying that their influence and ethic of militancy had grown stronger than ever. Amid a large field of studies on Black newspapers in the 1940s, scholar Gunnar Myrdal dubbed the Black press a "fighting press" in his landmark study of Black life, *An American Dilemma*.[86] But what he correctly identified had its roots deep in the militant cadre of Black newspaper men and women that crystallized at the dawn of the twentieth century amid the consolidation of racial regimes and structures of white supremacy all disguised as a New South.

White elites promoted the New South under what they took to be an un-impeachable vision of unbridled economic promise and racial harmony. Such a vision, they imagined, could resolve the "race question," which really meant silencing Black people's demands for rights and respect. But Black journalists could well see the façade: the New South was no more than a marketing tool for white supremacy, masking the political economies of the South that hinged on labor exploitation, state-sanctioned racial discrimination, and racial terror. A militant Black press emerged to rip that mask off, along with the masks Black people had worn to dissemble and protect themselves before white publics. The Black press resisted. Though operating from different corners of the country, Black publishers, editors, and reporters converged in the critical discursive space they had to carve out to build a strong Black counterpublic. They essentially shared a singular objective and consciousness of Black resistance channeled pointedly through Black newspapers to illuminate the truth about racial conditions in the South as well as a transformational vision of the country. Against the promotional work buttressing the false logics of the New South, Black journalists promoted a far different vision, using Black newspapers to elevate a truth that exposed the South and country for what they actually were. And this is where their critical discursive space lay, right at the center of an ideal—not a New South but a "New America"—the full realization of which, however long it actually took, had to begin with them.

Notes

1. Henry Grady, "The New South," in *American Public Addresses, 1740–1952*, by A. Craig Baird, 183–86 (New York: McGraw-Hill, 1956); Harold E. Davis, *Henry Grady's New South: Atlanta, A Brave and Beautiful City* (Tuscaloosa: University of Alabama Press, 1990), 34.

2. See, for instance, George M. Frederickson, "The New South and New Paternalism, 1877–1890," chap. 7 in *The Black Image in the White Mind: The Debate on Afro-American Character and Destiny, 1817–1914* (Middletown, CT: Wesleyan University Press, 1971). Also see C. Vann Woodward's classic work, *Origins of the New South, 1877–1913* (Baton Rouge: Louisiana State University, 1971).

3. Davis, *Henry Grady's New South*, 178. Also see Rayford Logan, *The Negro in American Life and Thought* (New York: Dial Press, 1954), 178–87.

4. See Logan, *Negro in American Life and Thought*. Also see William Cohen, *At Freedom's Edge: Black Mobility and the Southern White Quest for Racial Control, 1861–1915* (Baton Rouge: Louisiana State University Press, 1991).

5. See Todd Vogel, ed., *The Black Press: New Literary Essays* (New Brunswick, NJ: Rutgers University Press, 2001). Also see Michael Huspek, "Transgressive Rhetoric in Deliberative Democracy: The Black Press," 159–177, in *Critical Rhetorics of Race*, ed. Michael G. Lacy and Kent A. Ono, 159–77 (New York: New York University Press, 2011); Catherine Squires, "The Black Press and the State," in *Counterpublics and the State*, ed. Robert Asen and Daniel C. Brouwer, 111–336 (Albany: State University of New York Press, 2001).

6. Peter Revell, *Paul Laurence Dunbar* (Boston: Twayne Publishers, 1979), 71.

7. See Kevin K. Gaines, *Uplifting the Race: Black Leadership, Politics, and Culture in the Twentieth Century* (Chapel Hill: University of North Carolina Press, 1996).

8. See, for instance, Robert Cassanello, *To Render Invisible: Jim Crow and Public Life in New South Jacksonville* (Gainesville: University Press of Florida, 2013). Also see the Black Public Sphere Collective, *The Black Public Sphere: A Public Culture Book* (Chicago: University of Chicago Press, 1995).

9. Woodward, *Origins of the New South*, ix. As Woodward stated, too, the term "New South" was "from the beginning . . . a slogan, a rallying cry . . . a popular slogan."

10. Quoted in Penelope L. Bullock, *The Afro-American Periodical Press, 1838–1909* (Baton Rouge: Louisiana State University Press, 1981), 101.

11. Shawn Leigh Alexander, ed., *T. Thomas Fortune, the Afro-American Agitator: A Collection of Writings, 1880–1928* (Gainesville: University Press of Florida, 2008), 118, 127; Fortune's emphasis.

12. I. Garland Penn, preface to *The Afro-American Press and Its Editors* (Springfield, MA: Willey, 1891), 13–14.

13. Ibid., preface, 431–32, 26, 510–13.

14. Alfreda M. Duster, ed., *Crusade for Justice: The Autobiography of Ida B. Wells* (Chicago: University of Chicago Press, 1970), 62.

15. See Logan, *Negro in American Life and Thought*.

16. Carol Anderson, "Reconstructing Reconstruction," in *White Rage: The Unspoken Truth of Our Racial Divide*, 7–38 (New York: Bloomsbury, 2016); Deborah Gray White, *Too Heavy a Load: Black Women in Defense of Themselves, 1894–1994* (New York: W. W. Norton, 1999), 25; Cohen, "Reinventing the Black Codes," 201–273.

17. Fredrickson, *Black Image in the White Mind*, 256–82.

18. Duster, *Crusade for Justice*, 71. Also see LeeAnn Whites, "Love, Hate, Rapes, Lynching: Rebecca Latimer Felton and the Gender Politics of Racial Violence," in *Democracy Betrayed: The Wilmington Race Riot of 1898 and Its Legacy*, ed. David Cecelski and Timothy Tyson, 132–48 (Chapel Hill: University of Chapel Hill Press, 1998); Estelle B. Freedman, "'Crimes Which Startle and Horrify': Gender, Age, and Racialization of Sexual Violence in White American Newspapers, 1870–1900," *Journal of the History of Sexuality*. 20, no. 3 (2011): 465–97.

19. Quoted in Paula Giddings, *When and Where I Enter: The Impact of Black Women on Race and Sex in America* (Toronto: Bantam Books, 1984), 93. Also see Beverly Washington Jones, *Quest for Equality: The Life and Writings of Amery Eliza Church Terrell, 1863–1954* (New York: Carlson Publishing, 1990).

20. Booker T. Washington, *A New Negro for a New Century* (Miami: Mnemosyne Publishing, 1969), 382, 397, 396, 390, 424–26. Also see Brittany C. Cooper, *Beyond Respectability: The Intellectual Thought of Race Women* (Urbana: University of Illinois Press, 2017).

21. Duster, *Crusade for Justice*, 69.

22. Ibid., 64, 71.

23. Mildred I. Thompson, *Ida B. Wells-Barnett: An Exploratory Study of an American Black Woman, 1893–1930* (New York: Carlson Publishing, 1990), 27. Also see Anne Field Alexander, "Lynch Law Must Go," in *Race Man: The Rise and Fall of the "Fighting Editor" John Mitchell Jr.*, 41–59 (Charlottesville: University of Virginia Press, 2002).

24. Duster, *Crusade for Justice*, 72.

25. Thompson, *Ida B. Wells-Barnett*, 30–33.

26. Ida B. Wells-Barnett, *On Lynchings* (New York: Arno Press, 1969), 16, 17, 20; original emphasis.

27. See, for example, Leon F. Litwack, *Trouble in Mind: Black Southerners in the Age of Jim Crow* (New York: Knopf, 1998).

28. Penn, *Afro-American Press*, 448.

29. Litwack, *Trouble in Mind*.

30. Quoted in Wood, *Lynching and Spectacle*, 105.

31. E. Davidson Washington, ed., *Selected Speeches of Booker T. Washington* (Garden City, NY: Doubleday, Doran, 1932), 32–35.

32. Hine, *Black Women in United States History*, 68.

33. Washington, *Selected Speeches of Booker T. Washington*, 35–36; Logan, *Negro in American Life and Thought*, 275.

34. See, for example, Kevern Verney, *The Art of the Possible: Booker T. Washington and Black Leadership in the United States, 1881–1925* (New York: Routledge, 2001).

35. Logan, *Negro in American Life and Thought*, 178.

36. See, for example, Gaines, *Uplifting the Race*, 37–66.

37. Logan, *Negro in American Life and Thought*, 276–82, 79.

38. Louis R. Harlan, "Dinner at the White House," in *Booker T. Washington: The Making of a Black Leader, 1856–1901*, 304–324 (New York: Oxford University Press, 1972).

39. For more on the differences between and nuances of Black people's political ideologies at this time, see, for instance, Gaines, *Uplifting the Race*.

40. Alexander, *T. Thomas Fortune*, 155–56. Also see Logan, *Negro in American Life and Thought*, 178, 275–313.

41. H. Leon Prather Sr., "We Have Taken a City: A Centennial Essay," in *Democracy Betrayed: The Wilmington Race Riot of 1898 and Its Legacy*, ed. David Cecelski and Timothy Tyson, 132–48 (Chapel Hill: University of Chapel Hill Press, 1998).

42. Quoted in Logan, *Negro in American Life and Thought*, 312.

43. Penelope L. Bullock, "After Reconstruction: General Periodicals," in *The Afro-American Periodical Press, 1838–1909*, 64–149 (Baton Rouge: Louisiana State University Press, 1981). Also see Henry Lewis Suggs, ed., *The Black Press in the South, 1865–1979* (Westport, CT: Greenwood Press, 1983).

44. Penn, *Afro-American Press*, 133, 137.

45. Quoted in Emma Lou Thornbrough, *T. Thomas Fortune: Militant Journalist* (Chicago: University of Chicago Press, 1972), 111.

46. Ibid., 178, 189.

47. Ibid., 178. Also see Alexander, *T. Thomas Fortune*, 127.

48. See Bullock, *Afro-American Periodical Press*.

49. Stephen R. Fox, *The Guardian of Boston: William Monroe Trotter* (New York: Atheneum, 1970), 29–30. Also see Kerri K. Greenidge, *Black Radical: The Life and Times of William Monroe Trotter* (New York: W. W. Norton, 2020).

50. D'Weston Haywood, "Go to It My Southern Brothers: The Rise of the Modern Black Press, the Great Migration, and the Construction of Urban Black Manhood," in *Let Us Make Men: The Twentieth-Century Black Press and a Manly Vision for Racial Advancement*, 20, 56 (Chapel Hill: University of North Carolina Press, 2018).

51. David Levering Lewis, *W.E.B. Du Bois: Biography of a Race, 1868–1919* (New York: Henry Holt, 1993), 230.

52. Herbert Aptheker, ed., *Writings by W.E.B. Du Bois in Periodicals* (New York: Millwood, 1982), 152.

53. Bullock, *Afro-American Periodical Press*, 143–49.

54. DuBois, *A Reader*, 367; Lewis, *W.E.B. DuBois*, 316; "Organization by Radicals: The Niagara Movement," in Fox, *Guardian of Boston*, 81–114.

55. Fox, *Guardian of Boston*, 112, 92.

56. Aptheker, *Writings by W.E.B. Du Bois*, 275.

57. See, for example, the works of Fannie Barrier Williams and W.E.B. Du Bois in the *Voice of the Negro*, 1:31, 79.

58. Quoted in William G. Jordan, *Black Newspapers and America's War for Democracy, 1914–1920* (Chapel Hill: University of North Carolina Press, 2001), 21.

59. See, for instance, Greenidge, *Black Radical*; Sharon Harley, "Mary Church Terrell: Genteel Militant," in *Black Leaders of the Nineteenth Century*, ed. Leon Litwack and August Meier, 307–322 (Urbana: University of Illinois Press, 1988).

60. See, for example, Suggs, *Black Press in the South*.

61. Gaines, *Uplifting the Race*, 60–66.

62. Logan, *Negro in American Life and Thought*, 215.

63. Ida. B. Wells, "The Negro's Case in Equity," in Thompson, *Ida B. Wells-Barnett*, 247–48.

64. Washington, *New Negro for a New Century*, 416.

65. Fannie Barrier Williams, "The Negro and Public Opinion," in *Voice of the Negro* 1, no. 1 (1904): 31–32.

66. W.E.B. Du Bois, *Du Bois: Writings*, ed. Nathan Irvin Huggins, 608–609 (New York: Literary Classics of the United States, 1986).

67. "Interracial Organization: The NAACP," in Fox, *Guardian of Boston*, 115–44.

68. See, for instance, Louis R. Harlan, "The Secret Life of Booker T. Washington," in *Booker T. Washington in Perspective*, ed. Raymond W. Smock, 110–32 (Jackson: University Press of Mississippi, 1988).

69. Du Bois, *Writings*, 612, 417, 364, 370; W.E.B. Du Bois, "The Souls of Black Folk," in *W. E. B. Du Bois: Biography of a Race*, by David Levering Lewis (New York: Henry Holt, 1993), 265–96.

70. Henry Lee Moon, *The Emerging Thought of W.E.B. Du Bois* (New York: Simon and Schuster, 1972), 404.

71. Du Bois, *Writings*, 613, 606.

72. Greenidge, *Black Radical*, 98, 106–109, 122–28.

73. Fox, *Guardian of Boston*, 114, 206. It should be noted that at this point Du Bois was also probably wary of Ida B. Wells's radicalism. Also see Duster, *Crusade for Justice*, 324–28.

74. David Levering Lewis, "NAACP: The Beginning," chap. 14 in Lewis, *W.E.B. Du Bois*.

75. Du Bois, *Writings*, 720.

76. Moon, *Emerging Thought of W.E.B. Du Bois*, 70.

77. Du Bois, *Writings*, 719–20, 760, 718, 721.

78. Moon, *Emerging Thought of W.E.B. Du Bois*, 404.

79. Daniel Walden, ed., *W.E.B. Du Bois: The Crisis Writings* (Greenwich, CT: Fawcett Publication), 54–55.

80. Du Bois, *Writings*, 719, 622. Also see David Levering Lewis, "Rise of the Crisis, Decline of the Wizard," chap. 15 in Lewis, *W.E.B. Du Bois*.

81. See Haywood, "Go to It My Southern Brothers," 20–56.

82. William G. Jordan, "Preparing America for War," chap. 2 in *Black Newspapers and America's War for Democracy, 1914–1920* (Chapel Hill: University of North Carolina Press, 2001). Also see Theodore Kornweibel Jr., *"Investigate Everything": Federal Efforts to Compel Black Loyalty during World War I* (Bloomington: Indiana University Press, 2002).

83. See, for instance, David F. Krugler, *1919, The Year of Racial Violence: How African Americans Fought Back* (New York: Cambridge University Press, 2015).

84. Henry Louis Gates Jr., "The Trope of a New Negro and the Reconstruction of the Image of the Black," *Representations* 24 (Autumn 1988): 129–55. See also

Barbara Foley, *Spectres of 1919: Class and Nation in the Making of the New Negro* (Urbana: University of Illinois Press, 2003).

85. Preface and introduction to Robert T. Kerlin, *The Voice of the Negro 1919* (New York: E. P. Dutton and Company, 1920), v, ix–xii.

86. Gunnar Myrdal, *An American Dilemma: The Negro Problem and Modern Democracy* (New York: Harper and Row, 1962), 908.

PART TWO

Racial Terror and Disenfranchisement

CHAPTER 3

The Press and Lynching

W. FITZHUGH BRUNDAGE

Newspaper reports in the nineteenth and early twentieth centuries literally defined American lynchings, both as discrete historical events and as a broader topic of national debate. Few historical sources other than published news accounts exist regarding most lynchings. Because lynchings were extralegal, and because most victims of lynch mobs were murdered before the completion of any formal legal prosecution, few if any official records were generated. When records were produced, they were often cursory and, just as often, were not preserved. Even coroners' reports of lynching victims are often lost. Oral history, an important resource, is inherently fragmentary. And now it is difficult to collect testimony about most lynchings that occurred a century or more ago. Consequently, any understanding of the phenomenon of lynching in the United States must begin with news accounts of lynchings.

The importance of both Black and white news accounts to the study of lynching has been recognized since the late nineteenth century when Ida B. Wells, John L. Mitchell, and other Black editors collected and analyzed them in order to discredit white justifications for lynchings. The earliest scholarship on lynching, beginning with James Cutler's *Lynch Law* (1903), similarly relied on news accounts to discern patterns in the ebb and flow of mob violence. Moreover, the vast majority of Americans learned about lynchings from their weekly and daily newspapers. On an almost daily basis between 1890 and 1920, when readers glanced at a newspaper, they encountered reports of threatened, thwarted, and "successful" lynchings. At a time when neither state nor federal officials displayed any urgency in addressing, let alone suppressing, lynching, newspapers and journals offered the most important forum in which Americans debated mob violence.[1]

Yet, surprisingly, scholars have given inadequate attention to the role of journalists and newspapers in the history of American discourse surrounding lynching. For instance, we know too little about how news accounts of lynching circulated on the wire services and how and when the tropes evident in many white lynching reports first emerged. In addition to sifting through the discourse about lynching produced by prominent editors and polemicists, scholars also need to study the work of those yeoman journalists whose accounts of lynchings provided the foundation for public understanding of the phenomenon to the present day.[2]

*   *   *

That lynchings were newsworthy during the late nineteenth and early twentieth centuries may appear self-evident from the vantage point of the twenty-first century. After all, between roughly 1890 and 1920, the nation experienced an epidemic of lynching. Beginning in the late 1880s, the number of lynchings began to climb, until the toll climaxed in 1892, when mobs executed more than 225 whites and Blacks, the largest total in the history of both the South and the nation. While mob violence had deep roots throughout the nation, it was especially prevalent in the South and along the border with Mexico, where African Americans, Native Americans, Mexicans, and Asians were favored targets of lynch mobs. With each succeeding decade, the proportion of lynchings that occurred in the South rose, increasing from 82 percent of all lynchings in the nation during the 1880s to more than 95 percent during the 1920s. The blatant connection between lynching and race in the South also became starker over time. Between 1880 and 1930, the proportion of lynching victims in the South who were white decreased from roughly a third to less than 10 percent.[3]

Yet, because the nation had a long tradition of vigilante violence before the end of the nineteenth century, contemporary observers only gradually came to attribute distinctive qualities to the lynchings at the turn of the twentieth century. Prior to the last decade of the nineteenth century, most reports of lynchings originated in weekly newspapers in the nation's heartland. Typically, lynchings happened in comparatively rural areas, where the county seat might be the only community graced with a newspaper. Only infrequently did lynchings happen in communities large enough to support daily newspapers.

In regional metropoles, daily newspapers served as news aggregators, collecting stories of interest from rural weeklies and republishing them. Occasionally, republished accounts of lynchings featured prominently, but others received only a brief note in a column of collected "jottings" from various weeklies. During the 1880s white journalists evidently had no preconception about the inherent significance of lynchings as "news."[4]

Reporting on lynchings prior to the 1890s also reflected the vagaries of the publication schedule of newspapers. If a lynching happened immediately before the publication of a rural weekly, the local editor might include only a brief note or even omit any discussion of the lynching until the subsequent issue. During the following week, he might decide that a recounting of the lynching was old news and instead might elect to offer only editorial commentary on the lynching. Daily newspapers, in turn, routinely carried summaries of reports of lynchings in the hinterland weeks after the event, raising the question of what significance readers might have attached to them.

Finally, during the 1880s the immediate proximity of lynchings to sites of news publication was important in shaping the extent and nature of the news coverage. A lynching in the immediate environs of a newspaper might receive extensive (even revealing) coverage in the local newspaper. A local editor might also feel duty-bound to offer substantive editorial commentary on the extra-legal violence in his community. Typically, white editors vigorously defended local lynchings as justifiable responses of an outraged populace, while Black editors, to the extent they deemed prudent, denounced vigilante acts. Lynchings that occurred elsewhere might provide an opening for a white editor to get ahead of a rival newspaper or community by assailing the lynch mob for defying the law and subverting civilization. Meanwhile, dailies tended to allocate space to lynchings on the basis either of geographical proximity of the events or the degree to which the lynchings were sensational. Thus, before the last decade of the nineteenth century, lynchings were treated in white newspapers as banal events unless they happened nearby or deviated from the norms of American violence in some noteworthy manner.

* * *

At the turn of the twentieth century, the newsworthiness of lynchings changed substantially. With the spread of telegraph lines, railroads, and wire services, the opportunities for timely reporting on lynchings increased markedly. The construction and consolidation of railroads during the 1880s and 1890s were especially pronounced in precisely those regions of the nation that were sites of most of the nation's lynchings. Simultaneously, daily newspapers with regional aspirations sought to exploit the increasingly dense transportation and communication networks to expand not only the territory about which they reported but also their circulation. Reliant more than ever on large circulations and advertising for revenue, newspapers hustled both to retain longtime subscribers and to appeal to impulse consumers who bought individual issues on the fly. To demonstrate their prowess and relevance, they competed to publish timely news from throughout their actual or aspirational circulation area. Meanwhile, stringers across the region could now contribute up-to-the-minute reports about anticipated lynchings. Indeed, an entire media cycle for lynching stories developed with headlines breathlessly reporting sensational crimes, to be followed by speculations about the prospects for extralegal action, and later yet by accounts of any attempted or accomplished lynching. The cycle ended with reports on local responses to the lynching and editorial assessments of the mob's actions.

The transformation of Tom Wilkes (aka Sam Hose), an otherwise obscure Georgia Black farmworker, into the embodiment of a "black beast rapist" and the victim of one of the most notorious lynchings of the 1890s illustrates the new symbiotic relationship between transportation, technology, and the reporting of lynching. Before the spring of 1899, little distinguished Wilkes from any other Black laborer in rural Georgia. Despite having to provide for his family while still a youth—his mother was a near invalid and his brother handicapped—Wilkes managed to learn how to read and write and gained the reputation of being a bright and capable man. After his sister married and his mother's health improved, he set out to find work in Atlanta, but various jobs kept him from reaching the city. Sometime in 1898 he arrived in Coweta County, located southwest of Atlanta, and began working for Alfred Cranford. Certainly nothing in his physical appearance fit the lurid image of a "burly black brute" that newspapers described; when lynched he weighed only 140 pounds and measured no more than five feet eight inches tall. If anything, he seemed bashful and reserved around whites.

Early in April 1899, Wilkes (who, for unknown reasons, had adopted the alias of Sam Hose) asked his employer to allow him to return to his home to visit his mother. He also asked Cranford for money. The planter refused to advance him any money, and the two men exchanged harsh words. On the following afternoon, while Hose chopped wood at Cranford's home, his employer resumed the previous day's argument. The planter grew increasingly angry, drew his pistol, and threatened to kill Hose. In self-defense, the Black man hurled his ax, which struck Cranford in the head and killed him instantly. Terror-stricken, Hose fled and began to make his way to his mother's home. Such is the account of events that white and Black private investigators offered after the lynching of Hose.

Within two days of Cranford's death, Atlanta newspapers began printing graphic accounts stating that on the evening of the crime, Cranford had been eating supper when Hose quietly crept up behind him and buried an ax in his skull. After delivering several more blows to the victim, Hose kicked Cranford repeatedly in the head. Then—so the accounts continued—the Black man, as though demented, grabbed Mrs. Cranford and, with a pistol to her head, compelled her to accompany him while he robbed the house. He dragged her to the room where her husband lay dying, snatched the eight-month-old baby from Mrs. Cranford's arm, and threw it to the floor. (The baby, papers noted, probably would not survive its injuries.) "Within arm's reach of where the brains were oozing out of her husband's head," Hose raped Mrs. Cranford twice. Still unsated, he "carried her helpless body to another room, and there *stripped* her person of every thread and vestige of clothing, there keeping her till time enough had passed to permit him to accomplish his fiendish offense twice more and again." The ultimate indignity of Hose's rumored brutality was that "he was inflicted with loathsome 'Sxxxxxxs' [syphilis] for which *Mr. Cranford was having him treated.*" Before leaving the house, Hose is supposed to have announced, "Now I am through with my work, let them kill me if they can."[5]

Newspapers, especially the *Atlanta Constitution*, printed extra editions that spread the story of Hose's crimes across the country, with cumulative embellishments. (It is important to note that Mrs. Cranford never publicly acknowledged that she had been sexually assaulted; indeed, she never gave an interview to any of the journalists who clamored to speak to her.) Clark Howell and William Hemphill, the editors of the *Constitution*, not only urged on the newspaper's frenzied reporting but also offered a five-hundred-dollar reward for the capture of Hose. For several weeks, column after column of the *Constitution* reported on efforts of self-appointed posses to track down the now-mythic African American desperado. Previously unexplained murders, rapes, and thefts from all corners of the state began to be identified as the work of Hose, and his inconspicuous life as a farmhand was recast as a life of brutal crimes and wandering. Courtesy of the telephone and telegraph, the *Constitution* gathered reports of alleged sightings of Hose from across the state and even neighboring states. Myriad innocent Black men were set upon by white vigilantes searching for the fugitive whose description in the *Constitution* seemed to vary from day to day. As the hunt continued, the *Constitution* used the tragedy at the Cranford farm as the pretext for a special edition focused on the safety of rural white Southern women and girls. In a collection of solicited commentaries, prominent white male and female civic leaders wrung their hands over worsening Black criminality, denounced the shortcomings of the criminal justice system, expressed skepticism that vigilantism could be suppressed, and, in a few cases, offered full-throated defenses of lynching.[6]

When Hose was finally tracked down at his mother's home, the *Constitution*'s rumination about the best means to ease the fears of rural whites quickly gave way to banner headlines about his likely fate in the hands of a lynch mob. Accompanying the news of his capture were predictions that Hose would be burned alive. Subsequent editions of the newspaper forecast the likely site and time of Hose's execution; such news was crucial to the newspaper's readership who wanted to catch specially scheduled trains to participate in the spectacle. When the mob of five hundred eventually tortured, mutilated, and burned Hose to death on April 25, 1899, the *Constitution* provided pages of coverage as well as countless editorial observations, letters to the editor regarding Hose's murder, and reprints of national commentary on the lynching.[7]

While the *Constitution* took smug satisfaction in its timely and comprehensive reporting on Sam Hose's alleged crimes and execution, African Americans set out to expose the falsehoods that permeated almost all accounts in white newspapers about the lynching. A group of Black anti-lynching activists in Chicago, led by Ida Wells-Barnett and Rev. Reverdy C. Ranson, hired Louis P. Le Vin, a white detective, to investigate Hose's murder. Le Vin spent more than seven days tracing Hose's final weeks and interviewing whites, many of whom feared reprisals if they spoke out publicly. He concluded that Hose had indeed killed his white employer but suggested that he might have done so in self-defense. Moreover, Le Vin's report refuted the charge that Hose had raped his employer's wife. Le Vin's report, which Wells-Barnett incorporated into her own extended article on the Hose lynching, was widely published in white newspapers in the North and Black newspapers in the South. The *Constitution*'s editors responded with a furious rebuttal, assailing the "unscrupulous" detective for his "mendacity" while chiding his employers for their "gullibility" in accepting the words of "strolling negroes and detectives." In a final burst of outrage, the *Constitution* concluded by accusing its Black and white critics of waging a "campaign for liberal assaults on [white] women."[8]

* * *

Narrative tropes were conspicuous throughout the extensive news reporting that preceded Sam Hose's execution. These tropes, which seemingly emerged without any identifiable site of origin during the 1890s, were the product of contemporary conventions for crime reporting, current racial dogma, and the broad influence of melodramatic forms in contemporary American culture. With the advent of wire services that quickly dispersed news accounts across the nation, journalists assimilated and replicated these emerging reporting conventions. White journalists relied on these narrative and interpretative tropes for at least another two decades to transform the otherwise disconnected, apparently random events of discrete lynchings into a simple moral narrative that could be understood, explained, and justified.

The narrative conventions that developed quickly during the 1890s were consonant with those of the so-called new journalism of the era. Every aspect of a news report, from headline to story structure and illustrations, aimed at capturing readers through, in the words of British commentator Matthew Arnold, appeals to "novelty, variety, sensation, [and] sympathy."[9] Conventions of crime reporting in particular were adapted to the task of translating the rudimentary details of lynchings into dramatic "news." Lynchings, of course, were crimes—but with a difference. Whereas newspaper reporting on murders typically dwelled on the character and behavior of murderers, the focus of lynching accounts in white newspapers was on the alleged transgressions that precipitated the lynchings. Whereas some murders were prosaic affairs sparked by petty jealousies or drunken rages, and therefore warranted little interest, lynchings were dramatic acts of collective vengeance that increasingly demanded some explanation.[10]

As the column space devoted to accounts of lynching grew during the 1890s, so too did the evocations of "sensation," especially pain and terror, in lynching coverage. Reports increasingly included graphic descriptions of the alleged crimes that precipitated lynchings and of the imagined agony of the crime victims. Recall, for example, the reporting on Sam Hose's alleged crimes, which lingered on descriptions of oozing brains, a sexual assault carried out in pools of blood, and a baby dashed against the floor. Illustrations of the crime scene and the crime victims magnified the power of the reports to titillate readers.

Lynching stories came to be populated by crime victims who were depicted as blameless archetypes. They were chaste young women, dutiful mothers and homemakers, or stalwart lawmen who were struck down by remorseless and inhuman villains. White crime victims were invariably described as exemplary residents of their communities; the white women were always pretty and popular while the white men were upstanding and respected. Contrasting the delicacy of white female victims of crime with the raw savagery of the alleged criminal played to public interest in both domestic and sexual crimes during the nineteenth century. With the appropriate narration, alleged crimes by Black employees like Sam Hose against white women could be transformed into terrifying tales of violated domesticity and ever-lurking danger.

Finally, the victim of the lynch mob was cast as irredeemably evil. White newspapers branded them as a "black brute," an "inhuman fiend," or an "imp of inferno." Such salacious language from the outset worked to exonerate the lynch mob. By contrasting the bestiality of the alleged Black criminal and the delicate or innocent nature of his alleged victim, reporters stoked the fury of their readers and encouraged them to identify with the lynchers.

White journalists typically heaped praise on lynchers for their decorum. If a sampling of news reports in Florida are to be believed, lynch mobs seldom displayed rash emotions or unseemly violence. For example, despite mounting evidence against Charlie Pittman of Greenville, Florida, for alleged rape and murder in 1908, the local newspaper applauded the "commendable patience [of] the outraged community that bided its time and would not be swayed by blind passion." The mob that subsequently lynched him apparently had displayed sufficient patience to escape condemnation from the same newspaper.[11] When a white mob in 1909 lynched Charles Scarborough in Polk County, Florida, for alleged attempted rape, the local newspaper vouched that "there was no excitement in the matter at all. The people were determined that the negro should pay the penalty for his attempted crime: that was all."[12] After the lynching of Amos Smith in 1909 for alleged attempted rape in Desoto County, Florida, the *Arcadia Champion* initially described the mob's enraged wrath against their victim's body. But a week later, the paper issued a correction: "Nothing could have been further from the truth. The people who punished the negro considered that they were doing their duty to their community, and they went about the business in the most orderly manner, and no unseemly passion or excitement was shown whatever."[13]

Lynchings, white newspapers insisted, were carried out by somber men who derived no pleasure from them. When whites in Marion County, Florida, lynched Robert Larkin for the alleged rape of eighteen-year-old Fannie Alexander in 1893, the Jacksonville *Florida Times-Union* lavished praise on the "quiet but determined men" of the mob, including "two of the most gentlemanly boys" that the community boasted. "Three hundred of the best citizens" overpowered law officers at the preliminary trial and "with the greatest forbearance" set about the lynching. There was neither excitement nor "a drop of whiskey in the crowd." A placard left by the corpse, which read, "Done by 300 of the best citizens of this county," attested to the mob's sterling character.[14]

When necessary, white newspapers readily reconfigured events to better conform to the familiar reporting tropes of Black criminality and white vengeance. Such was the case in the reporting of a murder in Polk County, Florida, in 1900. On June 25 a Black man was murdered following the death of a white man. The headline of the article on the affair in the local Bartow *Courier-Informant* described a "Bloody Scene at Kingsford." Neither in the headline nor the accompanying story did the newspaper describe the execution of the Black man as a lynching. Instead, the newspaper reported a minor dispute between Sam Smith (Black) and Joe Hendricks (white) that flared into lethal violence. The ruckus ended when Smith struck Hendricks fatally in the chest with an ax. Learning of the killing, the local sheriff formed a posse to apprehend Smith. By the time they tracked him down, the posse had evolved into a mob. The sheriff thwarted the mob's attempts to seize the prisoner for more than an hour, but the dead white man's friends eventually snatched Smith, dragged him off, and shot him to death. The reporter commented, "Thus, two men within the same twenty-four hours were sacrificed to what was, in its beginning, in all probability, a trifling." He concluded that "the killing may have been a violation of the law, the lynching certainly was, and it is hoped that at least the leaders of it may be brought to trial and made to answer for the violent deed."[15]

The *Tampa Tribune* reported a drastically different version of the event. Below the headline "BEHEADED BY NEGRO BRUTE," the *Tribune* recounted a lynching that followed a "peculiarly atrocious murder." In the *Tribune*'s version the perpetrator was Bob Davis, "a notorious negro," who "waylaid" Will Hendrix, a respected white citizen of nearby Brandon. First Davis struck Hendrix to the ground and then used an ax to chop off his head. When Hendrix's friends discovered his blood-drenched trunk and severed head, which had rolled down the road, they began to hunt for Davis. By the time they found him that night, their numbers had swelled to more than one hundred. After Davis confessed to the murder, the lynchers marched him back to the scene of the crime and riddled him with bullets.[16]

Only the broadest outlines of the events described in the local Bartow newspaper can be discerned in the tragic events reported in the Tampa newspaper. Instead of a quarrel that escalated into violence, the murder was a premeditated ambush and a vicious beheading. Now a briefly obscure Black man became an infamous desperado and his white victim a pillar of the local white community. The posse was not a lawless mob that overpowered the sheriff but instead a resolute group of grieving friends intent on meting out justice. And in this telling, Davis confessed to his crime, thereby granting legitimacy to his extralegal execution.

The *Tampa Tribune* reporter's liberties with the facts were neither surprising nor exceptional. Rendered as a conventional lynching story, featuring a desperate Black murderer and an innocent and respectable white man, the incident conformed to white Southerners' ideal of lynching as an honorable practice that upheld the defense of white civilization from the "black brute." By erasing any details that contradicted a tidy storyline, and by elevating the lynching victim's crime to an unprovoked and sadistic murder of a white man, the *Tribune*'s account reassured readers that the mob's actions were justifiable, indeed, even laudable.

Nor was the *Courier-Informant*'s comparatively candid report on the events in Bartow County unprecedented. Even white editors of rural weeklies sometimes expressed disapproval of what they deemed to be inappropriate mob violence. The discrepancies between the reports in the Tampa and Bartow newspapers signal no significant difference in the papers' attitudes toward lynching in general; on other occasions the *Courier-Informant* published crudely racist and sensational lynching reports. Rather, a comparison of the reports highlights the *Tribune*'s attempt to applaud one type of lynching and the *Courier-Informant*'s attempt to denounce another type. In these conflicting reports are displayed the ongoing efforts of white Southerners, especially white journalists, to define boundaries for mob violence and to distinguish between legitimate and illegitimate forms of lynching.[17]

The distinctions that white journalists drew rested largely on the perceived nature of the lynching itself. A justifiable lynching was, in the words of the *Courier-Informant*, "the spontaneous work of practically all the best citizenship of this place." Commenting on a different lynching, the newspaper applauded the virtue of the lynchers, noting that "there were no masks or attempts at disguise and it was done in the full light of day." "The men who did it," the newspaper explained, "are the same who are on our streets today doing the business of the community. Not a man of them would deny for a moment whatever share he took in the tragedy." In this instance, the *Courier-Informant* found the conviction of the lynchers to be ample proof of their righteousness, and the core of its defense was the simple assertion that "all that was done, was done decently and in order by sober and serious men, possessing the full average of kindly instincts, and on this we rest the case."[18]

Because of the way white Southerners liked, indeed needed, to conceive of the role of lynchers, we can imagine their distaste upon reading about lynchings that subverted their notion of "honorable" lynching. Lynchings for exceedingly petty crimes or lynch mobs that clearly acted out of personal interests seemed to cross the line of propriety. These lynchings were not merely unseemly; they also attracted unwanted attention to the problem of lynching, and to approve of such lynchings would be to allow a state of lawlessness that would call into question the legitimacy of lynching itself. Instead, white journalists attempted to regulate the practice by contributing to the gentle denunciation of "illegitimate" lynchings.

The murder of Charles Jones in Baker County in 1896 was a clear case of behavior that was indefensible to "upstanding" Southern whites. On the night of May 3, three Black men were returning from church when they stumbled across five white men sprawled out on the railroad tracks. Without provocation, the white men opened fire, killing Jones instantly. Jones's companions managed to escape into the swamp, and they made it into town the next morning and alerted the sheriff about the murder. Jones's body was found shot to death with a large gash on the head and "most mysterious of all[,] a piece of flesh about as large as a silver dollar was cut out of the top of his head as though the murderers had scalped him." The Jacksonville *Florida Times-Union* reported that the murderers were surely strangers to the community and that "the citizens are justly indignant over the affair as Jones, though a colored man, was regarded as an [*sic*] humble, peaceable negro." And in an editorial the next day, the *Times-Union* reasoned that "in the darkness it was difficult to see how the men who perpetrated the murder were known to be white men." In this wanton murder of an unassuming Black man, the newspaper apparently found no positive expression of Southern lynching values; thus it not only denounced the murder but also refused to call it a lynching and even implied that the murderers may not have been white.[19]

* * *

Even a cursory glance at turn-of-the-century reporting on lynching reveals that it was suffused with elements of melodrama. That journalists borrowed from the contemporary idiom of melodrama when crafting their reporting of lynching is hardly surprising. Melodrama's popularity, of course, predated both the dramatic increase of interest in and attention to lynching at the end of the nineteenth century. And it remains a pervasive cultural form to the present day. Yet, in fin de siècle United States, melodrama dominated American popular fiction while melodramatic spectacles reigned on the American stage and would soon dominate the American film screen.

The appeal of melodrama to turn-of-the-century Americans was its moral transparency and urgency. Melodrama acquires particular appeal at times when moral verities seem threatened by headlong change. When "traditional imperatives of truth and ethics have been violently thrown into question," writes Peter Brooks, melodrama "becomes the principal mode for uncovering, demonstrating, and making operative the essential moral universe."[20] The melodramatic tradition was profoundly, inescapably moral. "The melodrama," explains Robert Lang, "does not simply stage a battle between good and evil (with good triumphing) but rather tries to establish that clear notions of good and evil prevail, that there are moral imperatives."[21] At a time when the struggle to impose white supremacy was cresting, white Americans displayed a propensity for moral absolutism and moral binaries. Conventions of melodrama, whether in fiction, stage, film, or journalism, meshed easily with this Manichean predisposition. The binary opposition essential to melodrama—good versus evil—allowed little scope for consideration of the "human dividedness" that figures so prominently in tragedy.[22] Instead, familiar opposites—primitive versus civilized, rural versus urban, moral versus immoral—typified melodramas. Inevitably, stereotypes, especially ethnic and racial, gave human form to these binaries. Characters in melodrama necessarily were iconic figures with self-evident qualities and motivations. Heroic white fathers and brothers, virginal white mothers and daughters, bestial nihilistic Black men—these were the characters who populated the melodramatic landscape.

Well established in American literature and stage melodrama during the nineteenth century, these stereotypes quickly transferred into the ascendant cultural forms of the new century, including both journalism and early silent film. Perhaps no plot device was better suited to exploit the power of melodrama than an endangered white woman, especially a sexual assault against a virginal white girl. A brief survey of some of the films directed by D. W. Griffith, the most influential silent film director of the era, illustrates how central this trope was in contemporary culture. In Griffith's third film, *The Black Viper* (1908), a working-class "brute" stalks an innocent girl and attacks her. The climax of the movie involves the rescue of the girl and her sweetheart from the "viper" and his henchmen. In *The Fatal Hour* (1908), which depicts "a stirring incident in the Chinese White Slave Traffic," Griffith portrays the violent abductions of white women by a Chinese villain and his lackeys. In *The Chord of Life* (1909), a Sicilian "worthless good-for-nothing scoundrel" plots a devious revenge against a woman and her child. Finally, in *Birth of a Nation* (1915), Griffith's enormously successful multi-reel extravaganza, an animal-like Black rapist drives a young white girl to commit suicide before he suffers vengeance at the hands of white vigilantes.[23]

* * *

African Americans were acutely aware of the critical role that white newspapers played in legitimizing lynching between 1890 and 1920. Blacks encountered accounts of lynchings in white newspapers as well as wire service reports reprinted in Black newspapers. African American city dwellers removed from the immediate threat of lynch mobs suffered the humiliation of running the occasional gauntlet of newspaper sellers hawking special editions with lurid accounts of lynchings. Blacks understood that any campaign to delegitimize lynching had to begin with challenging the discourse about lynching in white newspapers. Consequently, a prominent feature of Black resistance to lynching was the sustained contestation of reporting, especially regarding lynching.

Black newspapers provided the essential forum for Black dissent. As Gunnar Myrdal observed in *An American Dilemma*, the Black press became a "safety-valve for the boiling black protest." While providing glimpses of furtive and spontaneous Black resistance across the South, African American newspapers simultaneously nurtured sustained protest that was couched in overtly political language. No translation or interpretation was needed for whites to understand Black journalists and editors when they denounced white violence and the values that sustained it. Although it is likely that few whites commonly read Black newspapers, white newspaper editors certainly did and periodically reprinted excerpts from them.[24]

Black journalists labored to connect their public discourse against lynching with grassroots forms of resistance to white violence. Thus, Black editors often endorsed Black self-defense and even condoned retaliation for white violence. Ida B. Wells, who herself had been threatened with lynching while she edited the *Free Speech* in Memphis, advised that "a Winchester rifle should have a place of honor in every black house" and praised Blacks who set fire to Georgetown, Kentucky, following a lynching.[25] "Not until the Negro rises in his might," she warned, "and takes a hand in resenting such cold-blooded murders, if he has to burn up whole towns, will a halt be called in wholesale lynchings."[26] John Mitchell Jr., who made a name for himself editing the *Richmond Planet* and vociferously denouncing lynching, proclaimed, "The best way to secure protection in the South is to own a repeating rifle and a shot-gun and know how and when to use it."[27] He and other editors encouraged organized local efforts to protect Blacks threatened by mob violence and on occasion even actively marshaled community outrage against white violence. After the lynching of three friends in 1892, for instance, Wells promoted acts of communal insubordination in Memphis, including a Black boycott of streetcars and organized emigration of Blacks from the city.[28]

Beyond coordinating opposition to lynching, Black newspapers enabled Blacks to compile their own collective history of white repression. The Black community, of course, had always maintained its own memory of white atrocities, but now Black newspapers brought that history into public view. The *Chicago Tribune* had published a list of lynchings in its annual almanac beginning in 1882. While a valuable resource for activists, the *Tribune*'s list presented lynchings alongside a hodgepodge of data on violent crimes and natural disasters. In contrast, the running list of lynchings that John Mitchell included in his newspaper gave added power and urgency to his searing critique of white public officials, ministers, and law officers who failed to take meaningful action to suppress lynching. It may be tempting to underestimate, or even dismiss, the radical character of this gesture. By straddling the threshold between news gathering and public protest, Black newspapers made public what otherwise might have escaped white notice. White leaders across the South, who feared the subversive implications of Black newspapers, predictably lashed out at them, hectoring Black editors, subverting their businesses, or driving them into exile. Ida B. Wells, Alexander Manly, and J. Max Barber were just a few of the Black journalists who experienced these tactics.

One conspicuous form of discursive resistance used by African Americans was the systematic inversion of the tropes of white lynching journalism. African American journalists used narrative techniques, rhetorical tropes, and morally drenched language no less than their white counterparts, but with a markedly different aim. African American accounts of lynchings displayed the same binaries of civilization and barbarism, lawlessness and public order, innocence and guilt, terror and compassion. But in Black renderings of lynchings, white vigilantes, rather than the mythic "black brute," threatened the nation's founding principles of democracy, justice, and laws. Indeed, white lawlessness posed the greatest threat to American civilization itself.

In Black news reports, the alleged crimes that prompted the fury of white lynchers bore little resemblance to those reported in white accounts. Beginning in the early 1890s, Ida B. Wells and other Black journalists exploded the claim that sexual assaults against white women were the principal cause of lynchings. Instead, Black journalists pointed out that a substantial portion of extralegal executions were for trivial offenses that often were not even crimes, let alone capital offenses. Evidence gleaned from white news accounts, moreover, demonstrated that altercations between white and Black men, and not alleged sexual assaults, precipitated the largest percentage of lynchings. And when white Southerners countered, as did Bishop Warren A. Candler, that "possible danger to [white] women is inherent in every offense against white men," Black journalists pointed to greed, petty resentments, and crude bigotry as the root cause of most white violence against Blacks.[29]

Similarly, white victims of alleged crimes by Blacks appeared strikingly different in Black accounts. Instead of describing innocent virginal white women, Black editors pointed to examples of white women who willingly engaged in biracial romances. How often, they asked, had the accusation of rape been leveled against a Black man to protect the reputation of a white woman caught in a consensual relationship with him? Instead of blameless white lawmen or white employers who were set upon by Black desperadoes, Black journalists depicted put-upon Black men forced into desperate acts of self-defense by wanton white violence. Black accounts, for instance, acknowledged that Sam Hose might have committed manslaughter after extreme provocation, but they repudiated the claims that he had committed premeditated murder and rape. Cranford, they insisted, had been a mean-spirited and exploitative employer whose mistreatment of Hose had triggered the fatal clash between the two men. Likewise, Anthony Crawford, a Black man lynched in Abbeville, South Carolina, in 1916 was not an "uppity bad negro" who hated whites (as reported in the white press) but instead an independent, hardworking, prosperous African American farmer whose success aroused white envy and resentment. Moreover, publicized instances of white malefactors apprehended while wearing blackface as a disguise prompted Black journalists to wonder how often crimes pinned on Blacks had actually been committed by disguised whites.[30]

In perhaps the most striking inversion of white lynching accounts, Black journalists encouraged their readers to view victims of lynch mobs as human beings worthy of pity. Far from the "beast" described in white accounts, Sam Hose, for instance, was a dutiful son who had attended to his younger siblings and infirm mother. John Mitchell similarly dwelled on the ordeal of Isaac Jenkins, a blameless Black man from near Norfolk, Virginia, who was lynched for allegedly poisoning his neighbor's horses and setting fire to his house. Left dangling from a noose, Jenkins miraculously managed to free himself and escape his would-be executioners. His near-death experience gave firsthand authenticity to his accounts of the harrowing physical anguish and mental torture he had experienced.[31]

Lynchings themselves, as rendered by Black journalists, were not somber rituals of civic self-defense carried out by well-mannered mobs but, rather, grisly fêtes of sadism and barbarism. Black accounts dwelled on the nauseating cruelty and violence of white lynchers, highlighting graphic descriptions of the techniques of torture employed by mobs, of whites collecting body parts from the corpses of lynching victims, and of the participation of white women and children in the mob's handiwork.

John Edward Bruce, a widely reprinted Black columnist, exploited all of these techniques of inversion in an acerbic column titled "A Southern Pastime." Perhaps in an effort to puncture the complacency of readers who had become immune to the horrors of lynching, his column exaggerated, if only slightly, commonplace elements in countless lynching stories. He proposed a number of improvements to the rituals surrounding the lynching of Blacks. White Southerners should insist that all "first class lynching parties" include their state's elected officials. Handbills should advertise the coming attraction as well as the ample supplies of the "best pitch pine and bush wood" and "95 proof oil" for saturating the mob's victim that were on hand in preparation for the festivities. Once the execution was completed, "choice cuts of darky meat" along with teeth, and parts of the heart and liver, should be sold. In keeping with the wholesome family atmosphere of the affair, "coon songs" and cakewalks should accompany the proceedings. Finally, a portion of the revenue raised by selling photographs of the lynching should be used to fund the evangelizing of heathens in foreign lands. Bruce's dark humor almost certainly offended the sensibilities of many white Americans, but for Black readers it likely was a devastating burlesque of white sanctimoniousness about lynching. As John Dollard, a white witness to similar humor during the 1930s, observed, "To take cheerfully a matter of such terrible moment [lynching] is really to turn the joke back on the white man; some fun is squeezed even out of his warning."[32]

Loath to rely solely on their wordsmithing to counter white renderings of lynching, Black journalists also sought ways to turn their opposition into spectacle. Perhaps no Black journalist was more adept at doing so than Ida B. Wells. She used her exile from Memphis as a pretext to mobilize international public sentiment against lynching in the United States. During two publicized and controversial tours of Great Britain, in 1893 and 1894, she recast the debate over lynchings in ways that compelled whites to address at least some of the social realities of white violence. Through her skillful melding of frank discussions of lynching, rape, and interracial sexual desire, she garnered unprecedented attention to her cause. She routinely used quotations from white news accounts to establish the "facts" of lynching and to give her critique credibility that, as she put it, "came from their own mouths." For instance, she pointed to white newspaper accounts of "white women of the South who love the Afro-Americans' company." She substantiated her claims about the causes of lynchings with copious statistics derived from published new accounts. Her own carefully modulated stage presence intensified the power of her appeal. Even while presenting melodramatic accounts of the lynching of a fifteen-year-old girl and other atrocities, she spoke with "singular refinement, dignity, and self-restraint." As one spectator explained, her exceptional composure enabled her "to move us all the more profoundly." While her white Southern critics dismissed her British tours as crass publicity stunts, they could not deny that she had deftly drawn international attention and censure to lynching in the United States.[33]

John Mitchell Jr. used the columns of the *Richmond Planet* to play an essential role in creating a climate conducive to important efforts to suppress mob violence in Virginia. His editorials tirelessly prodded elected officials and concerned whites to assume responsibility for the protection of Black prisoners and to use state authority to halt lynching. In perhaps his most audacious effort, he waged a year-and-a-half-long publicity campaign to defend three Black women accused of being accessories in the murder of a white woman in Lunenberg County. In Mitchell's eyes, the trio, who had barely escaped a lynch mob, were victims of both white prejudice and corrupt justice. They, he promised, were not only innocent but also of excellent reputation and spotless virtue. He filled the front page and editorial columns of his weekly newspaper with coverage and commentary on every aspect of the women's saga. Equally important, he organized support for the accused in the Black community—women's groups were especially active and effective—and hired a team of highly regarded white lawyers to represent them. Eventually the campaign secured the release of the three accused women. Throughout the struggle, Mitchell had made a point of highlighting his role in it. He was determined to embody resolute and dignified Black defiance of white violence and white supremacy. His self-aggrandizing publicity was no more conspicuous than that of the editors of the Atlanta *Constitution* in the weeks before the lynching of Sam Hose.[34]

Alex Manly, the editor of the *Wilmington Messenger*, similarly courted controversy by mocking the most-sacred shibboleths of white supremacy. In August 1898 his newspaper published an editorial that dismissed the rantings of white defenders of lynching, especially the insistence that no white woman would engage in a consensual sexual relationship with an African American man. The pressing issue of the day, the *Messenger* warned, was not the mythic Black rapists but the white men who violated Black women while ignoring the protection of white women. White women, the editorial explained, "are not any more particular in the matter of clandestine meetings with colored men than are the white men with colored women." Even more explosive was the editorial's insistence that white women found Black men alluring: "Every Negro lynched is called a 'big burly, black brute,' when in fact many of those who have thus been dealt with had white men for their fathers and were not only not 'black' and 'burly' but were sufficiently attractive for white girls of culture and refinement to fall in love with them as is very well known to all."[35]

Manly and his associate editor, William L. Jeffries, could not have been surprised by the controversy the editorial aroused. White newspapers across the South reprinted the editorial under headlines that denounced it as "Vile and Villainous" and "An Insult to the White Women of North Carolina." The *Wilmington Morning Star*, a local white journal, reprinted the text of the editorial in nearly every issue in the months leading up to North Carolina state elections. The Democratic Party likewise made Manly and his newspaper a specific target during its strident white supremacy electioneering campaign. After the publication of the editorial, the owner of the building that housed Manly's printing business evicted him. Concerned Black citizens surrounded the site to prevent a mob of whites from destroying his presses. Manly responded by advocating that Blacks boycott local white businesses. In the days after the Democratic Party carried the state's elections, a mob of white men searched throughout Wilmington for Manly and demolished his printing offices before destroying Black property and carrying out murderous attacks on Black residents.[36]

Beginning in 1899, Dr. Monroe Nathan Work of the Tuskegee Institute institutionalized the compilation of "objective" lynching data that Wells had informally initiated years before. As head of the institute's Department of Records and Research, Work gathered, organized, and disseminated all manner of information about African Americans. Beginning in 1899, he hired press clipping bureaus to collect and organize all published news accounts relating to lynchings, attempted lynchings, and prevented lynchings. Thereafter, once a year Work's office issued an annual tally of lynchings along with a concise summary of the historical trends relating to the phenomenon. Within a few years, even white newspapers pointed to the Tuskegee Institute's annual lynching report as a barometer of American race relations, and anti-lynching activists relied upon it to underscore the urgency of taking action to suppress lynchings.[37]

* * *

A casual survey of accounts of lynchings in white Southern newspapers during the 1910s and 1920s may prompt a reader to conclude that little had changed since the late nineteenth century. Inherited tropes of Black criminality, white innocence, and decorous lynch mobs continued to grace news and editorial columns. They would endure in some of the region's newspapers well into the twentieth century, surfacing, for example, as late as 1955 in regional coverage of the lynching of Emmett Till in Mississippi.

Yet an important if gradual transformation occurred in white news reporting on lynching, contributing in turn to the gradual delegitimation of lynching. In the early twentieth century, more and more journalists working for major regional dailies professed to adopt "objective" and "value neutral" stances in their reporting. This emergent orientation reflected various influences, including increasing professionalization of the craft of journalism as well as more available space on newspaper pages to devote to extended stories. Newspapers still periodically traded in "sensationalism," but equally often they pledged to shy away from reporting that pandered to "cheap" emotions.[38]

Although the editors of a few white urban papers across the South had long pleaded with their readers to refrain from taking the law into their own hands, most had argued that the stern enforcement of white supremacy would produce calmer, less-violent relations between Blacks and whites. But the persistence of lynching more than a decade after the passage of Jim Crow laws and elimination of Black voting, exposed the fallacy of their argument. So, too, continuing streams of African American migrants who fled the South beginning during World War I exposed the lie that Blacks were content with the conditions that prevailed in the region. Moreover, the persistence of lynching in the South after the crime had waned elsewhere in the nation placed Southern white journalists and editors on the defensive every time a Southern mob meted out violence. Grudgingly, an increasing number of white journalists began to challenge inherited attitudes about lynching.

Evidence of the changing presentation of lynching in the white press was evident in the coverage of the lynching of Leo Frank in Georgia in 1915 and that of Jesse Washington in Texas in 1916. These two extralegal murders shared few common traits, but both became causes célèbres and provoked devastatingly negative commentary. Although some white newspapers in Georgia and Texas resorted to time-honored defenses of lynching, others employed language and arguments that a decade earlier had been used almost exclusively by Black journalists.

White journalists needed only to survey the national and international response to the trial and eventual lynching of Leo Frank in Georgia to find ample evidence of the corrosive effects of mob violence on the region's reputation. Frank was a Jewish industrialist in Atlanta wrongly charged with the murder of a young white girl in 1913. His trial and conviction appalled citizens throughout the country and directed withering criticism at the state, criticism that was further exacerbated when a small mob, angered by Governor John M. Slaton's commutation of Frank's sentence, removed Frank from prison and lynched him in 1915.

Frank's trial and lynching received unprecedented coverage that far exceeded the quantity of reporting on any previous lynching.[39] Stung by editorials in prominent national journals suggesting that "a state that has bowed to the will of the mob . . . is no longer worthy to be called a state" and that the only hope for Georgia "was a heavy inoculation of civilization," the *Atlanta Constitution* dejectedly observed, "Not only are the people of Georgia being branded as barbarians at the North, but the attacks and criticisms of our own neighbors and friends here at home are little milder than those that come from a distance." The lynching of Frank was an unwelcome notice to newspaper editors that lynching and the outmoded traditional values that sustained it threatened the smooth, orderly progress of the region.[40]

In response, urban newspaper editors attempted to turn lynching into a political issue. During the 1916 election season, for instance, the *Atlanta Constitution* sent letters to the state's gubernatorial candidates requesting their opinions about lynching and the steps they would take as governor to combat mob violence. Two years later, Georgia's major urban dailies strongly supported a new anti-lynching law that would allow the governor to remove any sheriff who failed to prevent a lynching through incompetence or connivance with the mob. In August, however, the anti-lynching bill ran aground on the constitutional fundamentalism of legislators, who voted to table it by a vote of 122 to 39. In subsequent years, white editors of urban dailies in Georgia and elsewhere continued to call for states to take action against lynching while placing their greatest hope in campaigns of public education against mob violence.

The lynching of Jesse Washington in Waco, Texas, on May 15, 1916, was an uncommonly grisly mass spectacle that even local white journalists found difficult to defend. Washington was a seventeen-year-old Black farmhand who was convicted of raping and murdering the wife of his white employer. Moments after the conclusion of his trial, which was completed less than a week after his alleged crime, spectators in the court corralled him with a chain around his neck, dragged him out into the streets, and paraded him before a crowd of some fifteen thousand spectators. After being tortured, he was burned alive in front of Waco's city hall.

The sadism of the lynchers, which was captured in photographs, made a mockery of the idealized notion of a lynching as a solemn and orderly ritual of community justice. News accounts depicted a delirious mob outside the courtroom anxious to release its fury on Washington. Men and boys, "running with the speed of wolves or hounds" and with "straining eyes and faces growing more excited each minute," had been frantic that they might miss the opportunity to take "some part in the gruesome work ahead."[41] Another reporter pronounced the members of the mob as "veritable demons."[42] Nor did white journalists mask the mob's viciousness with euphemisms. One reporter characterized Washington as "the plaything of the mob" while another described his body as "a solid color of red, the blood of the many wounds inflicted covered him from head to foot."[43] The frenzy of the crowd to be the first to light the fire to immolate Washington and the "shouts of delight" from "the thousands of throats" when fire engulfed him prompted one reporter to conclude "such a demonstration of people gone mad was never heard before."[44] News accounts even called into question the purported civility of Waco's residents, who boasted of their city's schools, colleges, churches, and cultural institutions. Inherited notions of feminine refinement had been shattered when, for instance, a "well dressed woman clapped her hands when a way was cleared so that she could see the writhing, naked form of the fast dying black."[45]

After the lynching, editorialists across the country and world weighed in on the "Waco horror." Few assessments were more damning than that of the nearby *Houston Chronicle,* which anticipated the world's condemnation. "It is with gloomy forebodings," the editorialist confessed, "that we await the stinging lash of criticism and reproach—criticism thrice hard to bear because it is merited, reproach thrice difficult to endure because it is justified. Not a word of defense is there to offer; not an extenuating circumstance to plead." The *Chronicle* raged against the mob for its lawless savagery: "What could the mob hope to do that the state had not already done except to satiate that blood lust and morbid antipathy which have no place in civilized communities?" In a critique of lynching that paralleled that of Ida B. Wells two decades earlier, the newspaper fumed at the hypocrisy of Americans and their vaunted civilization:

> We have denounced the Germans for certain alleged atrocities in Belgium; we have called upon the world to ostracize Turkey for her treatment of the Armenians; we have worked ourselves into horrified repugnance at the French revolution for more than a century; we have pretended to be humane, Christian and tolerant and have called upon others to emulate us. . . . Now we stand before the world, confessedly involved in one of the most revolting tragedies of modern times; a tragedy which for sheer barbarism has seldom been paralleled in American history.[46]

Although the handwringing over the Waco lynching in the white press did not lead to the prosecution of the leaders of the lynch mob or of city officials who failed to prevent Washington's murder, it did signal an accelerating change in the discourse about lynching. With increasing energy and consistency, editors began marshaling a host of practical reasons why whites should halt lynchings. This nascent campaign against lynching posed no threat to the preservation of white supremacy; indeed, many editors believed that the eradication of lynching would strengthen the claims of white Southerners that Jim Crow was humane and in the interest of Blacks themselves. Nevertheless, the mounting opposition to lynching in white Southern newspapers helped to create an environment in which anti-lynching organizations could work without facing crippling white hostility or provoking charges of pandering to the North.

No organization was swifter or more diligent in exploiting the historical moment than the National Association for the Advancement of Colored People (NAACP). When Jesse Washington was lynched in 1916, the fledgling organization was less than a decade old. Until then the association had not directed its attentions specifically against lynching. The lynching in Waco, however, stirred the NAACP leadership to launch a full-scale investigation of Washington's murder. The organization contacted Elizabeth Freeman, a prominent activist who was attending a women's suffrage convention in Dallas, and requested that she visit Waco and collect firsthand information about the lynching there. A month later Freeman's findings, titled "The Waco Horror," were published in the *Crisis*, the association's monthly journal.[47]

Freeman's investigation and the publicity it provoked became a template for subsequent efforts by the NAACP. The following year, the association pledged to use its burgeoning influence to investigate and publicize lynchings in order to win public support for federal anti-lynching legislation. At the same time, the organization pressed local white authorities to prosecute lynchers and made sure that reports of racial violence were not suppressed by publicity-conscious local authorities.[48]

The expansion of the NAACP into the hinterlands of the South transformed the struggle against lynching. As long as rural Blacks had to rely upon their own limited resources, they could make little headway in their attempts to secure protection from white mobs. By waging a campaign for the passage of a federal anti-lynching law, the NAACP performed the vital task of whittling away at white justifications for extralegal violence. Of more immediate importance to Blacks in the most mob-prone regions, however, was the existence of an organization that investigated and exposed otherwise slighted or ignored instances of mob violence in their locales.

The NAACP exposé of the lynching of Berry Washington in 1919 illustrates the effects that the organization could have simply by providing a full accounting of a lynching. Washington, a seventy-two-year-old Black man in the town of Milan, in Telfair County, Georgia, aroused the fury of a white mob when he shot the town mayor's drunken son, who was attempting to rape a young Black woman. After Washington surrendered himself to the police, a mob seized and hanged him. County officials and the mayor convinced local editors to suppress the story of the lynching, but Rev. Judson Dinkins in the nearby town of Cordele contacted both the NAACP and the Tuskegee Institute about the lynching. After securing an affidavit from Dinkins, the NAACP released a full account to newspapers throughout the nation. The editorial protests of the *Atlanta Constitution* and the Macon *Telegraph*, which severely criticized the local authorities for their handling of the incident, provoked the superior court judge of Telfair County to issue a strong charge to the county grand jury to investigate the lynching. The grand jury promptly indicted the county sheriff for negligence and his deputy as ring leader of the lynch mob. The deputy sheriff, however, could not be prosecuted—he had been killed while attempting to arrest a criminal—and the sheriff, whose negligence could not easily be proven without the testimony of his dead deputy, was acquitted at trial.[49]

* * *

By the 1930s, lynching appeared to be on a trajectory to its eventual demise. During the decade, the continued efforts of anti-lynching activists and changes in Southern society eroded the legitimacy that the tradition of mob violence had enjoyed for at least three-quarters of a century. Nevertheless, few opponents of lynching were willing to wait idly for its disappearance. If anything, the diminishing incidence of lynching served to spur on their efforts.

The flurry of activity by anti-lynching activists during the 1930s represented the culmination of decades of activism. And now white Southern journalists assumed conspicuous roles in the campaign against lynching. Their methods were not new, but their forthright participation in anti-lynching activism, and their sustained opposition to it in their newspapers, was unprecedented. The Commission on Interracial Cooperation (CIC), a biracial organization committed to improving race relations in the South, proposed to carry out detailed investigations of all lynchings in 1930 in order to determine their precise causes. The CIC had already made it a practice to investigate lynchings, as had the NAACP. What distinguished the new campaign, which was labeled appropriately the Southern Commission on the Study of Lynching, was the prestige and influence of the participants. Among the members were George Fort Milton Jr., the editor of the *Chattanooga News*, and Pulitzer Prize–winning journalist Julian Harris of the *Atlanta Constitution*. The commission's findings appeared first in the report *Lynchings and What They Mean*, released in the fall of 1931, and then in fuller form in *The Tragedy of Lynching*, published in 1933.[50] Both served to codify the conclusions of Southern white liberals and anti-lynching activists about the causes of mob violence and the best way to suppress it. There was little that was strikingly new in the reports' findings; in fact, the NAACP had reached similar conclusions years before. But, by virtue of the reports' scientific tone and the influence of the commission's membership, the findings became the definitive contemporary analysis of lynching, at least in the eyes of concerned Southern whites. In the words of Milton of the *Chattanooga News*, everyone now had "all the necessary facts concerning the malady which has made the South a synonym for barbarity in other countries."[51]

Given the role of many of the region's most prominent liberal newspaper editors in the report, it was noteworthy that it emphasized the necessity of journalists in shaping white public sentiment while repeatedly chiding small-town white newspaper editors for failing to denounce lynchings in their communities and the local residents responsible for them. Arguably, of even greater significance was that many of the South's leading white newspapers now affiliated themselves with the campaign to suppress lynching. The *Atlanta Constitution*, for instance, which had actively incited the lynch mob that executed Sam Hose in 1899, was now announcing itself as a staunch opponent of mob violence.[52]

Of even greater importance to the evolution of national and regional reporting on lynching were the ongoing campaigns of the NAACP. If anything, the

NAACP's influence increased during the 1930s, when the organization's modest resources in the South could be used more effectively as the incidence of mob violence decreased. Branches of the organization throughout the South began again to defend the legal rights of alleged Black criminals both in and out of the courts. Simultaneously, the organization launched a relentless campaign to win passage of a federal anti-lynching law. To garner support for the bill, the NAACP intensified its campaign to publicize each instance of mob violence. For the most part, the efforts of the NAACP during the 1930s differed from the organization's earlier methods only in scale. For example, the extent of publicity that the NAACP generated following several notorious lynchings during the decade, including the exceptionally gruesome lynching of Claude Neal in Florida in 1934, was without precedent. No longer could Southern communities rest assured of the security of relative anonymity or of only a brief spasm of condemnation following a lynching; instead there was the certain prospect of a flood of hostile national publicity, much of it generated by the NAACP.[53]

Although no federal anti-lynching law passed during the 1930s, the publicity and public outrage generated by the disparate efforts of Black anti-lynching activists, their white allies, and Black and white journalists contributed to mounting demands for the federal Department of Justice to explore ways to combat lynching. Eager also to appease Black voters in the North who were outraged by lynchings, federal authorities took the unprecedented steps of investigating the lynchings and pressing charges against lynchers. After the lynching of Cleo Wright, a Black man accused of attacking a white woman in southwestern Missouri in 1942, the Federal Bureau of Investigation investigated the lynching, and, even more extraordinary, the Civil Rights Section of the Department of Justice brought charges against Wright's murderers. The failure of the prosecution of Wright's lynchers demonstrated that the newfound federal concern about lynching had clear limits. However, to countless Southern racists unlearned in the law, the meaning of the Department of Justice's investigations into the Wright lynching seemed clear: the federal government had thrown its support behind anti-lynching activists and against mob violence. Henceforth, even without a federal anti-lynching statute, federal administrators found legal pretexts for the expansion of federal authority to investigate and prosecute lynchers. And as they reinterpreted the obligation of the federal government to protect the civil rights of Blacks, they took a crucial, though admittedly tentative, step in placing federal power in opposition to lynching.[54]

* * *

The virtual disappearance of lynching in the South after World War II marked the passing of one of the most significant American rituals of Black degradation. The decline of lynching, of course, did not mean that white violence against Blacks stopped. But as the number of lynchings declined sharply during the 1940s, the tradition of murders by large mobs, like those that killed Sam Hose and Jesse Washington with exceptional cruelty, virtually came to an end. Lynching became the particular province of small, secretive mobs. There were no more assaults on jails, no more extended public rituals of torture and mutilation of mob victims, and no more carnival-like gatherings to witness the victim's corpse. Instead, when lynchings did occur, they were the actions either of law officers who exceeded even traditional standards of police violence against Black suspects or of a small number of mob members who displayed conspicuous concern for the concealment of their identities, like the mob who murdered Emmett Till in 1955.[55]

Of course, African Americans continued to encounter chronic injustice, especially in Southern courtrooms. But the injustices endured during court proceedings were exposed to the scrutiny of journalists and activists. At the same time, legal procedures imposed constraints, however limited, on whites that neither tradition nor community sentiment had imposed on lynch mobs. Blacks who had been victims of mock justice filled the dockets of Southern supreme court appeals for redress. Once the fight for color-blind justice moved from the streets to the courtroom, civil rights activists used the legal process itself to challenge racial discrimination in the courts. Beginning in the 1930s, when Black lawyers began to provide innovative representation for Black defendants, the courtroom became the setting for spectacles that caught the attention of reporters. However much the odds were stacked against Black defendants and their Black lawyers, the gathering momentum of the campaign to secure equal justice in the courtroom ensured that the odds were considerably better than those against Blacks caught in the clutches of lynch mobs. When Charles H. Houston, a brilliant Howard University law professor, skillfully defended a Black man charged with the murder of two white women in Virginia in 1936, his legal and intellectual prowess could not be ignored. The *Richmond News Leader* had to admit that "there are negro lawyers in the country who can be courageous without being obsequious, lawyers who can make a fight without arousing racial antagonisms." The newspaper concluded, "That of itself gave the trial a certain educational value."[56]

Throughout the history of lynching in the American South, the role of the press was of inestimable importance. The white and Black press created the only meaningful archival record of most lynchings, shaped the discourse through which Americans made sense of lynchings, and provided the most important forum in which Americans debated lynching. It is not an exaggeration to posit that between 1865 and 1945 the history of journalism is constitutive of the history of lynching and vice versa. Yet the inextricably bound histories of American journalism and lynching remain understudied and largely unacknowledged. It is altogether appropriate that the courageous journalism of Ida B. Wells, Alex Manly, and John Mitchell Jr. are celebrated. Nevertheless, we also need to acknowledge the roles of countless obscure editors and journalists in compiling the nation's record of lynching, transforming the mob's violence into sensational melodramas, and providing legitimacy to some of the most savage violence in the nation's history.

Notes

1. James Elbert Culter, *Lynch-Law: An Investigation into the History of Lynching in the United States* (New York: Longmans, Green, 1905).

2. A few important works have begun to fill this lacuna. See Estelle B. Freeman, "'Crimes Which Startle and Horrify': Gender, Age, and the Racialization of Sexual Violence in White American Newspapers, 1870–1900," *Journal of the History of Sexuality* 20 (September 2011): 465–67; Richard M. Perloff, "The Press and Lynchings of African Americans," *Journal of Black Studies* 30 (January 2000): 315–30; and especially Michael A. Trotti, *The Body in the Reservoir: Murder and Sensationalism in the South* (Chapel Hill: University of North Carolina Press, 2008).

3. For essential overviews of the toll of mob violence in the United States, see William D. Carrigan and Clive Webb, *Forgotten Dead: Mob Violence against Mexicans in the United States, 1848–1928* (New York: Oxford University Press, 2013); Stewart E. Tolnay and E. M. Beck, *A Festival of Violence: An Analysis of Southern Lynchings, 1882–1930* (Urbana: University of Illinois Press, 1995).

4. See, for example, "Georgia Gossip: Short Talks the Scribes of the County Press. The Fish Industry—A Colored Reform Society—A Runway Marriage—The East and West Narrow Gauge—A Burks County Lynching—Stephen Shell's Hunt for Gold," *Atlanta Constitution*, December 23, 1882, 2; "Georgia by Wire: The News of the State Briefly Chronicled. The Lynching of a Negro Fiend in Blakely," *Atlanta Constitution*, July 27, 1884, 4.

5. Wells B. Whitmore to Rebecca Lattimer Felton, April 25, 1900, Rebecca Lattimer Felton Papers, Special Collections, University of Georgia Library; emphasis in original.

6. A group of Black anti-lynching activists in Chicago, led by Rev. Reverdy C. Ranson, hired a private detective to investigate the circumstances surrounding

Hose's alleged crimes. The detective's report was widely published in white newspapers in the North and Black newspapers in the South. For two accounts of the detective's report, see *New York Age*, June 22, 1899, and the *Richmond Planet*, October 14, 1899. The campaign to challenge white accounts of Hose's crimes is discussed in Mary Church Terrell, "Lynching from a Negro's Point of View," *North American Review* 178 (June 1904): 859–60.

7. The lynching of Sam Hose has received considerable scholarly attention. The essential study is Donald G. Mathews, *At the Altar of Lynching: Burning Sam Hose in the American South* (Cambridge, UK: Cambridge University Press, 2017). See also Edwin T. Arnold, *"What Virtue There Is in Fire": Cultural Memory and the Lynching of Sam Hose* (Athens: University of Georgia Press, 2009)

8. Ida B. Wells-Barnett, *Lynch Law in Georgia* (Chicago: Anti-Lynching Bureau, 1899), 7–12; "Would Make Ananias Blush: Detective Levin's Version of the Sam Holt Lynching. Was Sent South by Chicago Negroes to Make a Report on the Lynching—And He Did It." *Atlanta Constitution*, June 5, 1899, 1; "That Chicago Detective," *Atlanta Constitution*, June 25, 1899, 4.

9. Matthew Arnold, "Up to Easter," *Nineteenth Century* 21 (May 1887): 638–39. See Kate Campbell, "W. E. Gladstone, W. T. Stead, Matthew Arnold, and a New Journalism: Cultural Politics in the 1880s," *Victorian Periodicals Review* 36 (Spring 2003): 20–40.

10. Valuable surveys of the developments in late nineteenth-century journalism include Richard D. Altick, *Deadly Encounters: Two Victorian Sensations* (Philadelphia: University of Pennsylvania Press, 1986); Karen Halttunen, *Murder Most Foul: The Killer and the American Gothic Imagination* (Cambridge, MA: Harvard University Press, 1998); Guy Reel, *The National Police Gazette and the Making of the Modern American Man, 1879–1906* (New York: Palgrave Macmillan, 2006); Karen Roggenkamp, *Narrating the News: New Journalism and Literary Genre in Late Nineteenth-Century American Newspapers and Fiction* (Kent, OH: Kent State University Press, 2005); Judith Rowbotham and Kim Stevenson, eds., *Criminal Conversations: Victorian Crimes, Social Panic, and Moral Outrage* (Columbus: Ohio State University Press, 2005); and Gretchen Soderlund, *Sex Trafficking, Scandal, and the Transformation of Journalism, 1885–1917* (Chicago: University of Chicago Press, 2013).

11. *Madison New Enterprise*, February 6, 1908.

12. *Bartow Courier-Informant*, April 29, 1909.

13. *Arcadia Champion* quoted in *Tampa Morning Tribune*, June 22, 1907.

14. *Florida Times-Union*, July 18, 1893.

15. *Courier-Informant*, June 27, 1900.

16. *Tampa Tribune*, June 28, 1900.

17. For a fuller discussion of the distinctions whites drew between "warranted" and "unwarranted" lynchings, see Susan Jean and W. Fitzhugh Brundage, "'Legiti-

mizing Justice': Lynching and the Boundaries of Informal Justice in the American South," in *Informal Criminal Justice*, ed. Dermot Feenan, 157–78 (Aldershot, England: Ashgate, 2002)8.

18. *Courier-Informant*, June 5, 1901.

19. *Florida Times-Union*, May 5–6, 1896.

20. Peter Brooks, *The Melodramatic Imagination: Balzac, Henry James, and the Mode of Excess* (New Haven, CT: Yale University Press, 1976), 14–15.

21. Robert Lang, *American Film Melodrama: Griffith, Vidor, Minnelli* (Princeton, NJ: Princeton University Press, 1989), 18.

22. Robert Bechtold Heilman, *The Iceman, the Arsonist, and the Troubled Agent: Tragedy and Melodrama on the Modern Stage* (Seattle: University of Washington Press, 1973), 9. Issues of race and racism were dealt with in the tragic form during the early twentieth century. The best example of a race tragedy is Edward Sheldon's play *The Nigger* (New York: Macmillan, 1910). Sheldon's protagonist, an icon of the highest Southern white culture, is trapped and destroyed by the racist stereotypes that he parrots after he learns that he is descended from a Black woman.

23. For a deft account of early film plot conventions, see Ben Singer, *Melodrama and Modernity: Early Sensational Cinema and Its Contexts* (New York: Columbia University Press, 2001), esp. chaps. 6–7. For a brilliant discussion of the transformation of lynchings into visual spectacle, see Amy L. Wood, *Lynching and Spectacle: Witnessing Racial Violence in America, 1890–1940* (Chapel Hill: University of North Carolina Press, 2008), 71–178.

24. Gunnar Myrdal, *An American Dilemma*, vol. 2, *The Negro Problem and Modern Democracy* (New York: Harper and Row, 1944), 910. For a convenient overview of Black newspapers, see Henry Lewis Suggs, ed., *The Black Press in the South, 1865–1979* (Westport, CT: Greenwood Press, 1983). Among the most valuable discussions of Black editors are Ann F. Alexander, *Race Man: The Rise and Fall of the "Fighting Editor," John Mitchell, Jr.* (Charlottesville: University of Virginia Press, 2002); Henry Lewis Suggs, *P. B. Young, Newspaperman: Race, Politics, Journalism in the New South, 1902–62* (Charlottesville: University Press of Virginia, 1988); Julius E. Thompson, *The Black Press in Mississippi, 1865–1985* (Gainesville: University Press of Florida, 1993); George Tindall, *South Carolina Negroes, 1877–1900* (Columbia: University of South Carolina Press, 1952), 149–52; John M. Matthews, "Black Newspapermen and the Black Community in Georgia, 1890–1930," *Georgia Historical Quarterly* 68 (Fall 1984): 356–81.

25. Ida Wells-Barnett, *Southern Horrors: Lynch Law in All Its Phases*, in *Selected Writings of Ida B. Wells-Barnett*, ed. Trudier Harris (New York: Oxford University Press, 1991), 42.

26. Quoted in the *Memphis Appeal-Avalanche*, September 6, 1891, 4.

27. *Richmond Planet*, September 7, 1895, 2. See also January 4, 1890, 2; May 21, 1892, 2; February 1, 1896, 2.

28. W. Fitzhugh Brundage, "'The Roar on the Other Side of Silence': Black Resistance and White Violence in the American South, 1880–1940," in *Under Sentence of Death: Lynching in the South*, ed. W. Fitzhugh Brundage, 280–81 (Chapel Hill: University of North Carolina Press, 1997), 280–81.

29. Candler quoted in *Forum* 76 (December 1926): 813.

30. *Abbeville Press and Banner*, October 25, 2916; Terence Finnegan, "'The Equal of Some White Men and the Superior of Others': Racial Hegemony and the 1916 Lynching of Anthony Crawford in Abbeville County, South Carolina," *Proceedings of the South Carolina Historical Association* (1994): 54–60.

31. The plight of Jenkins can be traced in the *Richmond Planet*, July 22, 29; August 5, 12; September 30; October 14; November 4, 18, 28, 1893.

32. Bruce Grit [John Edward Bruce], "A Southern Pastime," *Colored American*, February 13, 1900; John Dollard, *Caste and Class in a Southern Town* (New York: Doubleday, 1957), 310. For discussions of Black humor as resistance, see Raymond Gavins, "North Carolina Black Folklore and Song in the Age of Segregation: Toward Another Meaning of Survival," *North Carolina Historical Review* 66 (October 1989): 412–42; Trudier Harris, "Adventures in a Foreign Country: Humor and the South," *Southern Cultures* 1 (Summer 1995): esp. 459–60; and Lawrence W. Levine, *Black Culture and Black Consciousness: Afro-American Folk Thought from Slavery to Freedom* (New York: Oxford University Press, 1977), 342–43.

33. For a thoughtful and concise survey of Wells's British tours, see Teresa Zackodnik, "Ida B. Wells and 'American Atrocities' in Britain," *Women's Studies International Forum* 28 (2005): 259–72. Her tour is extensively discussed in Jodi Rightler-McDaniels and Lori Amber Roessner, eds., *Political Pioneer of the Press: Ida B. Wells-Barnett and Her Transnational Crusade for Social Justice* (Lanham, MD: Lexington Books, 2018); and Sarah L. Silkey, *Black Woman Reformer: Ida B. Wells, Lynching, and Transatlantic Activism* (Athens: University of Georgia Press, 2015). Other useful discussions include Mia Bay, *To Tell the Truth Freely: The Life of Ida B. Wells* (New York: Hill and Wang, 2009), 151–90; Crystal N. Feimster, *Southern Horrors: Women and the Politics of Rape and Lynching* (Cambridge, MA: Harvard University Press, 2009), esp. 87–125; Patricia Ann Schechter, *Ida B. Wells-Barnett and American Reform, 1880–1930* (Chapel Hill: University of North Carolina Press, 2001), 22–26, 91–104.

34. *Richmond Planet*, July 20, 27; August 3; August 10, 24; September 13, 21, 1895. The *Richmond Times* sent attorney William M. Justis to Lunenburg to investigate the case against the women. His reports in the *Times* substantiated the charges that Mitchell had already made in the *Planet*; *Richmond Times*, July 23, 1895; *Richmond Dispatch*, September 13–19, 1895. A concise and lucid summary of the complex legal battles of the case is Samuel N. Pincus, "The Virginia Supreme Court, Blacks and the Law, 1870–1902" (PhD diss., University of Virginia, 1978), 412–46. For fuller accounts of the case and Mitchell's role in it, see Suzanne Lebsock, *A Murder in*

Virginia: Southern Justice on Trial (New York: W. W. Norton, 2003), and Trotti, *Body in the Reservoir*, 118–26, 202–204.

35. *Wilmington Record*, August 18, 1898.

36. The best account of the attack on Manly, his press, and the subsequent violence in Wilmington is LeRae Umfleet, principal researcher, *1898 Wilmington Race Riot Report*, 1898 Wilmington Race Riot Commission (Research Branch, Office of Archives and History, North Carolina Department of Cultural Resources, May 31, 2006).

37. Linda E. McMurry, *Recorder of the Black Experience: A Biography of Monroe Nathan Work* (Baton Rouge: Louisiana State University Press, 1985).

38. These developments are traced in Kathy Roberts Forde and Katherine A. Foss, "'The Facts—the Color!—the Facts': The Idea of a Report in American Print Culture, 1885–1910," *Book History* 15 (2012): 123–51.

39. Charles Seguin, "Making a National Crime: The Transformation of US Lynching Politics 1883–1930" (PhD diss., University of North Carolina at Chapel Hill, 2016), 90–97.

40. *Outlook*, August 25, 1915, 946; "Lynching and Illiteracy," *World's Work*, October 1915, 637; *Atlanta Constitution*, January 23, 1916, 4.

41. "Swift Vengeance Wreaked on Negro," *Waco Morning News*, May 13, 1916, 5.

42. "Shocking Exhibition of Mob Rage," *Houston Post*, May 17, 1916, 6.

43. "Mob Takes Negro from Court House," *Waco Times Herald*, May 15, 1916, 1; "Negro Burned at Stake," *Waco Semi-Weekly Tribune*, May 17, 2016, 7.

44. "Mob Takes Negro from Court House," *Waco Times Herald*, May 15, 1916, 1.

45. "Swift Vengeance Wreaked on Negro," *Waco Morning News*, May 13, 1916, 5.

46. "Horror at Waco," *Houston Chronicle*, May 16, 1916, 8. For a thorough study of the lynching of Washington as well as valuable attention to the role of newspapers in it, see Patricia Bernstein, *The First Waco Horror: The Lynching of Jesse Washington and the Rise of the NAACP* (College Station: Texas A&M University Press, 2005), esp. 127–72. See also William D. Carrigan, *The Making of a Lynching Culture: Violence and Vigilantism in Central Texas, 1836–1916* (Urbana: University of Illinois Press, 2004), 162–88.

47. "The Waco Horror," supplement to the *Crisis* 12 (July 1916): 1–8.

48. The best extant account of the NAACP's national campaign against lynching remains Robert L. Zangrando, *The NAACP Crusade against Lynching* (Philadelphia: Temple University Press, 1980).

49. Rev. Judson Dinkins to the Tuskegee Institute, May 26, 1919, reel 221, Microfilm Tuskegee Lynching Records; "A Lynching Uncovered," group 1, series C, box C-354, Milan File, NAACP Papers, Library of Congress; *Atlanta Constitution*, July 25, 29; August 27; September 7, 1919; Macon *Telegraph*, August 11, 1919; *Eastman (GA) Times-Journal*, May 29; September 11; October 30, 1919.

50. *Lynchings and What They Mean: General Findings of the Southern Commission*

on the Study of Lynching (Atlanta: Commission on Interracial Cooperation, 1931); Arthur Raper, *The Tragedy of Lynching* (Chapel Hill: University of North Carolina Press, 1933).

51. *Chattanooga News*, November 12, 1931, 4.

52. For a brilliant treatment of the emergence of "liberal" white journalists in the South, see John T. Kneebone, *Southern Liberal Journalists and the Issue of Race, 1920–1944* (Chapel Hill: University of North Carolina Press, 1985), esp. 21–37.

53. On the Claude Neal lynching, see James R. McGovern, *Anatomy of a Lynching: The Killing of Claude Neal* (Baton Rouge: Louisiana State University Press, 1982), chap. 6; and Zangrando, *NAACP Crusade against Lynching*, esp. chaps. 5 and 6.

54. Dominic J. Capeci Jr, "The Lynching of Cleo Wright: Federal Protection of Constitutional Rights during World War II," *Journal of American History* 72 (March 1986): 886.

55. For a provocative account of the decline in lynching and the role of the NAACP, see Ashraf H. A. Rushdy, *The End of American Lynching* (New Brunswick, NJ: Rutgers University Press, 2012), 20–127.

56. Quoting Richard Kluger, *Simple Justice: The History of* Brown v. Board of Education *and Black America's Struggle for Equality*, rev. ed. (1974; repr., New York: Vintage Books, 2004), 153.

CHAPTER 4

Mississippi Plan

ROBERT GREENE II

"When I returned to my home after the adjournment of Congress in March, 1875, the political clouds were dark. The political outlook was discouraging. The prospect of Republican success was not at all bright."[1] John Roy Lynch's reflection on the politics of his home state of Mississippi, written in 1913 in his book *The Facts of Reconstruction*, represented the views of many African Americans about Southern politics at the end of the Reconstruction era. Lynch, an African American congressman, understood that Mississippi was at the center of a political maelstrom threatening to destroy the tenuous gains African Americans made during the post–Civil War years. His book reflects the importance of the written word in chronicling African American reaction to what came to be called the "Mississippi Plan," the successful efforts of white Democrats to exclude Black Mississippians from electoral politics through violence, suppression, and fraud—first in 1875 through a violent election year overthrow of the Republican Party and again in 1890 through a new state constitution meant to formally disenfranchise Black voters.

The Reconstruction era, the erection of Jim Crow, and the reaction to both changed the course of American political, social, and intellectual history for generations to come, reverberating into today's politics. The print media was part of this process, working to spread the ideas of the Mississippi Plan and foment white backlash to Reconstruction-era advances for African Americans. This chapter examines both the role of the white press in this process and the

Black *reaction to the reaction*, as it were: how African Americans, in various newspapers, periodicals, and books, attempted to craft a response to the white "redemption" of Southern states via political subterfuge, intimidation at the polling place, and outright violence.

The rise of the African American press during the nineteenth century is, of course, a story that has been well covered in African American political, social, and intellectual history. But the specific time period of the 1870s and 1880s bears closer examination, as it offers a window into the fierce and illuminating debates African Americans held about what to do next in the face of a concerted campaign to destroy their newly gained civil rights. The saga of the Mississippi Plan begins in 1875, when the plan was first promulgated and executed in the state, and ends in 1890, when debates about the federal Lodge Bill—what white Southern Democrats called the "Force Bill" and defeated in 1891—signaled the last attempt by the federal government to enforce the Fifteenth Amendment with legal and political remedies until the passage of the 1965 Voting Rights Act.[2] In 1890 the white leadership of Mississippi launched a second phase of the Mississippi Plan when the state's constitutional convention codified new laws eliminating Blacks from political and civic life and formally implementing Jim Crow rule in the New South.

In the fifteen years between the violent launch of the Mississippi Plan and its culmination with ratification of the state's new constitution, African Americans in the state, the South, and beyond attempted to rally for a renewed fight for their voting rights and political power, often encountering, at best, lukewarm support from allies and, at worst, outright condemnation and hostility. Newspaper editors, historians, and writers became the center of this story as they revitalized Black print culture and used it to rally opposition to those who would deny civil, political, and social rights to African Americans.

African American writers have often had two audiences in mind when crafting essays, editorials, long-form works, and books. One audience has been other African Americans, rallying them to the cause of civil rights and self-determination through the written word. The other audience has been white Americans, trying to help them understand the African American experience via moral suasion. Although African American efforts to rally white allies to their cause failed to stem the tide of white supremacist government throughout the American South, they did enrich a legacy of African American resistance through newspapers, periodicals, and books.

A robust array of work demonstrates that print media have been the chief method by which African Americans argued for their rights, their citizenship, and their very humanity. This chapter places print culture at the center of a tenacious but often overlooked struggle to protect Black citizenship in the South in the immediate post-Reconstruction period. It also emphasizes the unique political and social circumstances that Black editors, authors, and activists faced. The collapse of Reconstruction was not accepted peacefully by African Americans, neither in 1875, when the Mississippi Plan was first deployed; nor in 1883, when the *Civil Rights Cases* before the U.S. Supreme Court decimated civil rights progress for African Americans; nor in 1890, when a second phase of the Mississippi Plan led to codification of Jim Crow laws in new state constitutions across the South.[3]

The Mississippi Plan

The Mississippi Plan began as an organized effort to eliminate biracial democracy for good in the Deep South by suppressing the Black vote, crafted and perfected by Democratic Party leaders in the Magnolia State. By 1875, white Democrats opposed to Reconstruction had displaced Republican administrations in Virginia, North Carolina, Georgia, Alabama, Texas, and Arkansas. But Mississippi, South Carolina, Louisiana, and Florida remained under biracial governments. In the run-up to the 1875 elections, the white editor of Mississippi's Jackson *Clarion*, Ethelbert Barksdale, the head of the former Confederate planters and a leader of the state's Democratic Party, devised and helped execute a coordinated assault on the state's Republican administration and its African American supporters.

Working with James Z. George, a Confederate general who was elected Democratic Party chairman in 1875, Barksdale planned and carried out a campaign of propaganda, vote fraud, and merciless anti-Black violence. As the Democratic Party leadership, Barksdale and George wielded the *Clarion* as a political weapon, using its pages to promote a strategy to sow chaos at political rallies and at polling sites to disrupt the Black franchise. A fundamental tactic was the creation of a "white line" policy to systematically disrupt Republican meetings and prevent Black men from voting. The policy was enacted by white line rifle clubs—societies of white Democrats who would form, metaphorically and literally, an armed line that no Black person was permitted to cross. The *Clarion*, the most influential newspaper in the state, promoted the white line policy and clubs, instructing party members to "hold the line" at any cost, and smaller Democratic papers followed suit. The result was, as intended, widespread political violence against Black communities and citizens. Robert

Gleeds, a Black Republican in Mississippi, later observed that the 1875 election season was "the most violent time that ever we have seen." In 1868 Gleeds read an Alabama paper that said, "We must kill or drive away the leading Negroes and only let the humble and submissive remain." He was shocked. "The idea of a party being built up on the principle of the open slaughter of human beings," he said. "It was startling to me, the advocacy of such a principle." The white press in the South had been laying the groundwork for what happened in Mississippi for years.[4]

Democrats signaled their bloody intentions a year before the critical 1875 elections in the river town of Vicksburg, when white militia members opened fire on a crowd of largely African American Republicans who were marking the anniversary of the fall of Vicksburg to the Union Army eleven years earlier. In 1875 rampaging white mobs burned Black neighborhoods and assassinated community leaders, concentrating on heavily Republican counties. As thousands of African Americans fled their homes and sought refuge in the countryside, Barksdale, George, and their allies used the *Clarion* and other white newspapers to blame the chaos and bloodshed on the supposed fecklessness of Republican governor Adelbert Ames and his "Negro-dominated" administration. Ames pleaded with President Ulysses Grant to send federal troops to protect African Americans, but, fearing a political backlash in the North, Grant refused.[5]

Barksdale and George used the *Clarion* office, just 250 yards from the governor's mansion, to stockpile guns several weeks before the election. After the election, they used the pages of the *Clarion* to demand that all Black Mississippians vote for the Democratic candidate in the 1876 presidential election on pain of losing their employment.[6]

At the time of the 1875 elections, Mississippi's political apparatus included a substantial number of African Americans—55 in the state house (out of 115) and 9 in the state senate (out of 37). The Mississippi Plan had clear goals: suppress Black voting, end Republican rule in the state, and undermine popular support for Reconstruction in the North. On Election Day the threat of violence kept most African Americans away from the polls in Mississippi, and the Democratic Party swept Republicans out of office. The victory catalyzed Southern Democrats, and the Mississippi Plan became a model for white supremacist counterrevolution in South Carolina the following year. Its brutal mix of violent intimidation and sustained political pressure broke the last of the brittle and isolated Republican parties that had flourished briefly during Reconstruction.[7]

The inventors of the 1875 Mississippi Plan went on to powerful careers in the white supremacist Southern world they helped to build: James Z. George became a U.S. senator in 1881, serving until his death in 1897, and Ethelbert Barksdale became a two-term U.S. congressman from 1883 to 1887. They took their views and goals to the federal government, where they prepared the national ground for the state's 1890 plan to formally disenfranchise Black voters, a plan that became a template other Southern states followed. Senator George proposed and oversaw the amendment of Mississippi's constitution to empower county officials to impose poll taxes and subjective literacy requirements in order to prevent Blacks from even registering to vote. Meanwhile, Barksdale contributed the Mississippi chapter of *Why the Solid South?*—an 1890 book written mainly by Southern federal legislators, dedicated "to the business men of the North," and meant to persuade potential Northern investors that the South's industrial prosperity depended on the North leaving the "problem" of Black suffrage to the white South to solve. It was also meant to dissuade Northern support of the Lodge Bill. As 1890 drew to a close, George led Democratic Southern opposition in the U.S. Senate to the Lodge Bill, meant to enforce the Fifteenth Amendment and protect Black voting rights by providing oversight of federal elections in the South. In a filibustering Senate speech against the Lodge Bill, Senator George, known in Mississippi as "the Old Commoner," defended his state's amended constitution and contributed to the federal bill's ultimate demise. In a devasting repudiation of Black efforts to quell the tide of Jim Crow, the U.S. Supreme Court upheld the state's new constitution, and once again the Mississippi Plan spread to other states. Across the last decade of the nineteenth century and the first of the twentieth, Democratic Party leaders in one Southern state after another called constitutional conventions to codify Jim Crow's draconian restrictions on the political, economic, and social lives of African Americans.[8]

African American Print Culture and Resistance

In a cruel historical irony, 1875 should have been remembered—if not for a Supreme Court decision discussed later in this chapter—for a progressive bill passed by Congress designed to protect African American civil rights. The Civil Rights Act of 1875, considered by some to be "one of the last hurrahs of Reconstruction," outlawed segregation in public accommodations, transportation, and juries, going the furthest Congress would go in the nineteenth century to enforce equality under the Fourteenth Amendment throughout the land. As the bill was passed, however, African Americans already began to publicly discuss the need to protect their rights in the face of the problems being reported in Mississippi.[9]

The Black Mississippians who were most outspoken in the fight against the Mississippi Plan were often newspaper editors. As noted in *The Black Press in the South, 1865–1979*, "Six of the most outstanding Black leaders in Mississippi from 1860 to 1899 had significant experiences as working journalists, in addition to their other careers." Henry Mason, I. D. Shadd, James J. Spelman, Hiram Revels, Blanche K. Bruce, and James Lynch held political office in Mississippi during the Reconstruction era and were all either newspaper founders or editors. These editors were a decided minority among African Americans; the total number of African American newspaper editors in Mississippi between 1865 and 1900 did not reach above one hundred.[10]

African American newspaper editors, in Mississippi and across the nation, saw their duty to "the race" as using the power of the pen—and the printing press—to argue for their interests. The Reconstruction era witnessed a flowering of African American print culture as the demands of protecting civil and political rights, combined with a hunger among the African American populace for sources of information, led to the creation of many new African American newspapers and periodicals. As historian David Prior has argued, during Reconstruction there was a brief period of a "near-creation of a nationwide African American publishing network built around newspapers" for a newly freed people rapidly adapting themselves to electoral politics.[11]

In 1875 African American newspaper editors made use of an older tradition—that of African American conventions—to meet and debate how best to pool their resources. The "Convention of Colored Newspapermen" was held in Cincinnati as an attempt to find a way to make African American newspapers as independent and self-sustaining as possible. At this convention, the editors of African American newspapers across the nation came together to discuss some of the problems they saw plaguing the nascent Black press.[12]

The editors at the convention, at the outset, admitted that their mission would have to be different from that of most of their white counterparts. Former Louisiana governor P.B.S. Pinchback—the first African American governor in American history—began the proceedings by giving a brief address, designed to crystallize the hopes, fears, and understandings of the attending Black editors. "Our first object," said Pinchback, "is to make the colored people's newspapers self-sustaining—not that we expect to make money out of them." He went on to make an argument for, arguably, the biggest problem facing the growing African American press: "Our people, as a class, are not largely a reading class, but it is on them that we must rely for patronage." Time was both the greatest ally and biggest enemy of the Black press, argued Pinchback; slavery had robbed millions of African Americans of an opportunity to learn how to read and write and, for that matter, to pool resources and capital to create businesses that would purchase advertisements in newspapers. However, Pinchback also included a dose of optimism in his speech, stating, "We must look to their children as they grow up," referring to the generation of African American men and women born to once-enslaved mothers and fathers.[13]

Later at the convention, Peter Clark, editor of the moribund *Galveston Spectator*, laid forth the reasons why a Black-owned newspaper press was needed. As Clark put it, "We need papers for the discussion of a public policy, and for obtaining that unity of action that comes from a unity of views." The importance of Black newspapers as an organizing tool for the community, in Clark's view, could not be underestimated. For Clark, the newspaper was also a realm where African Americans could show "confidence in ourselves; confidence in our own intelligence; confidence in our own integrity; confidence in our own capacity." African American newspapers were not just sources of information or places of political organizing and agitation. They were, for Clark and the others in attendance at the convention, a way to forcefully uplift the African American race, at precisely a time when it appeared their staunchest white allies were in retreat.[14]

How, the editors at the convention asked, could they marshal their resources to live up to the lofty ideals laid out? The convention delegates planned to create a "press association" in order to pool resources and stories among the various African American newspapers. Already, during the Reconstruction period, African American newspapers, like other newspapers across the country, had continued the practice of sharing "guest editorials, correspondence from travelers, poems, and, although it was less common than today, letters from concerned readers."[15] Nonetheless, delegates wanted something with more structure—if not a press association, at the very least a "manufacturing house" that could provide African American newspapers with cheap and relevant content, or perhaps the formation of a periodical or newspaper that would be the formal "organ of the colored people" that could be supported by various African American organizations such as religious groups and other societies.[16]

Ultimately, the attempt by the Convention of Colored Newspaper Men to form a Colored Press Association did not get far. But it does show that newspaper editors were thinking hard about the challenges facing their community broadly and newspaper publishing in particular. The written word was a weapon against the rising tide of anti-Black sentiment across the United States. While newspapers were the primary place where these battles were being fought, historians enjoined the battle too.

In the nineteenth century, historians working in the new and emerging field of African American history saw their vocation as not only generating new knowledge but also telling the story of Black Americans through historical inquiry. In fact, their chief job was to show that African Americans actually *had* a history worthy of respect from other racial and ethnic groups. "Race histories," wrote Stephen G. Hall in his history of nineteenth-century African American historians, *A Faithful Account of the Race*, "not only mapped the racial past but instilled pride and provided a roadmap for how the race might adapt to freedom." History was a textual battlefield for African American historians, who were trying not only to understand the past but also to make sense of the present.[17]

By the post-Reconstruction period, historians such as George Washington Williams combined scholarly investigation with a zeal for using history—and the humanities in general—to push for civil and political rights for African Americans. Like most African American historians, Williams was what would be called a "scholar-activist" today, using his scholarship to fight for social equality. His book *History of the Negro Race in America*, released in 1882 in several volumes, attempted to give a complete history of African Americans— from their origins in West Africa through the then-recently completed Reconstruction era in American history. In two volumes Williams threaded a long history of, as he called it, "the saddest task ever committed to human hands!" In the introduction to the second volume of his history, he wrote, "Many pages of this history have been blistered with my tears; and, although having lived but a little more than a generation, my mind feels as if it were cycles old."[18]

The first volume of *History of the Negro Race in America* dealt with the history of the slave trade, the American Revolution, and the rise of the abolitionist movement in early Republic America. Volume 2 included a meditation on both the American Civil War and the Reconstruction period. It is in discussion of Reconstruction, especially, that Williams approaches the intersection of historical scholarship and the continuing need for political agitation about the place of African Americans in American society.

"The mistake of Reconstruction was two-fold," wrote Williams, "on the part of the Federal Government, in committing the destinies of the Southern

States to hands so feeble; and on the part of the South, in that its best men, instead of taking a lively interest in rebuilding the governments they had torn down, allowed them to be constructed with untempered mortar." Williams placed the blame for Reconstruction's collapse on both forces, ensuring that the reader understood that African Americans did their best during the era despite incredible odds. But he does not leave African American leaders completely unscathed in his analysis.[19]

One critical element of Williams's historical analysis was his focus on African Americans. Treating them not merely as victims but as flawed historical actors, reacting often to forces that threatened to overwhelm them, Williams wanted the reader to also know that they shared some responsibility for the collapse of Reconstruction. Williams described the mistakes of African Americans during the high tide of Reconstruction:

> The wine cup, the gaming-table, and the parlors of strange women charmed many of these men to the neglect of important public duties. The bonded indebtedness of these States began to increase, the State paper to deprecate, the burden of taxation to grow intolerable, bad laws to find their way into the statute-books, interest in education and industry to decline, the farm Negroes to grow idle and gravitate to the infection skirts of large cities, and the whole South went from bad to worse.[20]

For Williams, in other words, African American politicians lost their way during the Reconstruction period, and so did many African Americans in the rural South. The problems of government, he suggested, would have seemed familiar to any person reading about Reconstruction in the white press and in historical accounts by white academics from the 1880s through the mid-twentieth century. But this is merely part of Williams's objective historical analysis. He placed the greater part of the burden of the collapse of Reconstruction on the federal government and white Southerners.

As the Mississippi Plan was put to the test throughout the Southern United States, African American periodicals and newspapers became the primary places where African Americans concocted strategies to respond to the abrogation of their rights. By 1875 questions of the fitness of African Americans for the franchise permeated American society, and African American periodicals and newspapers were often the places where African Americans took their stand for their rights. "It is not a colored question," argued Colonel C. G. Baylor on the front page of the *Weekly Louisianan* in 1875. "It is not a question of African descent. . . . The question for America is to solve the negro question. It involves the negro. It involves the right of this man, *as a negro*, to abide under the shadow of the republic, and enjoy, *as a negro*, the same educational, civil and political rights enjoyed by any other law abiding citizen subject to taxation and military service."[21]

Baylor's essay was originally published in the *Boston Congregationalist*, but its reprinting in a Louisiana newspaper shows how African Americans saw the threat to their rights as a national issue. The essay was written as white Democrats in Mississippi were beginning their assault on democracy in the state. In the process, they provided a template for other Democrats across the South to push back the advance of African American rights.

The Pen as the Sword: T. Thomas Fortune and Resistance to Redemption

As the 1880s wore on, African Americans continued to press for their rights as citizens through the pages of their newspapers and periodicals. While Frederick Douglass continued to hold forth as the nation's best-known orator and writer for African American rights, a new generation of writers, intellectuals, and leaders was emerging in the aftermath of the Reconstruction period. Perhaps none was as well known as T. Thomas Fortune. Born before the Civil War, in 1856, Fortune had established a career in journalism, writing for multiple newspapers in New York City in the 1880s. A founder of the *New York Globe* in 1881, which later became the *New York Freeman* and the *New York Age*, Fortune built for himself not only a newspaper of record for African Americans but also a place where he could present his case for a more-militant civil rights campaign against injustices in the American South.[22]

Fortune often wrote editorials and columns lamenting the lack of federal response to the usurpation of African American civil rights across the South. A spate of columns in 1883 responding to the Supreme Court's *Civil Rights Cases* of that year provide an example of the kind of agitation Fortune sought to foment through his writing. The *Civil Rights Cases* were a death blow to the cause of African American civil rights for generations. Frederick Douglass, in the 1892 revised version of his 1883 autobiography, *The Life and Times of Frederick Douglass*, referred to it as the most blatant example of how the cause of equality "has lost ground ever since" the end of the American Civil War.[23]

The *Civil Rights Cases* overturned the 1875 Civil Rights Act, an ambitious attempt by Republicans in Congress to address the problem of unequal access to public accommodations for African Americans. The cases were a combination of several cases from across the nation—with only two coming from former slave states, thus suggesting, in the words of Eric Foner, the "national scope of the problem of racial exclusion." When the Supreme Court handed down its decision in 1883, outrage among African Americans was also national in scope, as reflected in the wide array of responses in African American–owned newspapers and periodicals.[24]

Fortune's thunderous reply to the *Civil Rights Cases* decision mirrored the reply of other African American journalists. Here, Fortune—like Douglass and others—argued that African American civil rights deserved protection due to the heroic actions of African Americans fighting for the Union cause during the American Civil War. "The man who dares to charge that we have ever been disloyal to the Union is either a knave or a blatant ignoramus," wrote Fortune. He later reminded his audience of readers that "the honor of citizenship was not conferred upon us because men loved us; it was conferred upon us because our conduct in the war, when men's nerves and souls were tired, earned it." Fortune not only uses history to buttress his argument for African American civil rights but also enters a long tradition of African Americans arguing for citizenship rights by pointing to valor on the battlefield and shedding blood for the American flag.[25]

Fortune also displayed his own frustration with the Republican Party, which had been the traditional political home of African Americans since the start of Reconstruction. By the 1880s, a growing segment of younger African Americans began calling for a more independent-minded philosophy of politics. They were willing to leave the Republican Party and, if necessary, vote for Democrats to express their displeasure over the halt in civil rights enforcement. Fortune placed the origins of this discontent with the Republican Party's behavior during the election of 1876, when the Reconstruction era ended due to the party agreeing to pull federal troops out of the South in exchange for the presidency. "The Republican party," he wrote, "sacrificed the Black vote of the South, and it has reaped disaster and infamy ever since." But this argument also led Fortune to embrace what seemed to many African Americans in the 1880s an even more radical idea: that of putting the African American race before loyalty to even the Republican Party or the states that fought for the Union (and emancipation) during the Civil War. Fortune proposed Black Americans "work out our own salvation; and, although we have in times past fought the battles of the North, we do not expect the North to fight our battles for us." Fortune's frustration with Republican weakness in the aftermath of the *Civil Rights Cases* mirrored a growing discontent among African Americans with American politics in general.[26]

Fortune used the pages of his newspaper to tease out ideas for political organizing that presaged the arguments African American activists leveraged throughout the twentieth century about using politics to agitate for civil rights. In an editorial written in April 1884, Fortune argued for the need for a new political party: "The colored people of the United States have a peculiar interest in the creation of a new party which shall champion the equal rights of all . . . and in the easement of the enormous burdens placed upon labor by onerous taxation and unjust laws enacted in the special interest of capital, to defraud labor of its just portion of its production wealth." He called for "the laboring men of the South, the North, and the West" to come together to form such a party. His analysis moved to capture the problems of both racism and economic exploitation that he saw as the biggest political challenges of the 1880s. In short, he was calling for the kind of national political movement that predicted the rise of the Populists in the 1890s.[27]

Finally, Fortune used books and pamphlets to continue his assault on the idea of staying loyal to the Republicans for the sake of history. His 1886 pamphlet, *The Negro in Politics*, was a lengthy version of the argument he had developed across the earlier years of the decade: that African Americans needed to put race first and shed any sense of loyalty to the Republican Party. The pamphlet also used other rhetorical tactics Fortune had perfected, such as the use of African American history, to bring home the idea of political independence. Fortune called on the memory of men "like Denmark Vesey and Nathaniel Turner" to fire up the spirits of African Americans in pursuit of freedom. This is a provocative argument from Fortune—invoking men who engaged in armed revolt to end slavery as a defense of his own ideas of political freedom—but it was in service of a greater argument: that, in the estimation of Fortune, "the race is sadly lacking in the quality of *esprit de corps* and proper race pride; because it is still permeated with the virus of jealousy, envy, and discord—produced by the odious contention of slavery." Fortune used the recent history of African Americans to make a case that if the race came together once more, they could forge a new and unique path in American politics, separate from the Gilded Age–era corruption of both major parties.[28]

Fortune used his pamphlet to launch into a sustained critique of the history of African American politics since 1865. For him, the Reconstruction era and its aftermath proved the lack of leadership from both the Republican Party and African American spokespersons for the race. Fortune called the loyalty of African Americans to the Republican Party a "political vassalage," going so far as to argue that the Republican Party was able to muster Black support only by looking back to "the Abolitionist sentiment before the war, or the honest sentiment of the Union after the collapse of the odious slave power." In Fortune's view, the Republican Party had done nothing about *current* attempts to deal with the fall of Reconstruction, the overturning of the 1875 Civil Rights Act, or the growing anti-Black sentiment across the nation.[29]

Referring to national African American leaders as "the so-called leaders of the race," Fortune lamented how little leadership was actually coming from those people. Pulling from his deepest reservoir of outrage, Fortune argued that these people were worse than even the Republican politicians who had turned their back on the antislavery and ostensibly pro–civil rights tradition of the party during and after the American Civil War. Fortune thundered that these "leaders" were "ever ready to use voice or pen to extenuate or apologize for the too manifest injustice of the masters they serve for a few pennies or a 'little brief authority.'" Fortune's problems were with leaders from a previous generation—most notably Frederick Douglass—who, it seemed to him, were too timid in their criticisms of the Republicans.[30]

In 1887 Fortune sought to turn his words into action through the creation of a national organization dedicated to the fight for Black civil rights. Using his *New York Freeman* newspaper as a bully pulpit, Fortune persuaded a group of independent and aggressive Black activists to form the Afro-American League. A forerunner of the NAACP, the league was conceived as a permanent organization with local chapters across the nation demanding citizenship rights and equal protection under the law for African Americans. To emphasize his commitment to political independence, Fortune fought to keep politicians out of the league to limit Republican Party influence. By 1890 the organization had changed its name to the National Afro-American League (NAAL) and had won an important segregation court case in New York. But as the Jim Crow regimes emerged in Southern states—and as Booker T. Washington's call for accommodation with white supremacy opened fissures within Black activism—the NAAL foundered and eventually collapsed. Yet as the work of Shawn Leigh Alexander and Blair LM Kelley has shown, the activism that spawned the league continued to grow, despite the failed efforts to halt the rise of anti-Black, anti-Democratic forces nationwide.[31]

The Second Mississippi Plan and
Black America's Newspaper Response

By 1890 political leaders in Mississippi were dissatisfied with their earlier attempts to suppress the African American vote. The last years of the 1880s saw a brief resurgence of African American political power in the state as Republicans slowly began to recover from the Democratic Party revolt of 1875–1876. C. Vann Woodward called it the "Second Mississippi Plan," one that was distinguished from the first Mississippi Plan by the lack of violence. Instead, this new plan was achieved entirely via electoral politics and a new constitutional convention in Mississippi.[32]

Concern about the potential of African American political power lay largely in the sheer numbers of African Americans living in the state. They were a sizable majority heading into the final decade of the nineteenth century. More importantly, however, the Republican Party had regained control of both houses of Congress as well as the White House by 1890 and appeared ready to use their power to investigate Mississippi's electoral rules. The Republican-controlled Congress prepared to contest the legality of three of Mississippi's seven congressional seats under section 2 of the Fifteenth Amendment, which gives Congress the power to enforce section 1 of the act—granting all men the right to vote, regardless of race or ethnicity—with "appropriate legislation."[33]

Within Mississippi, several factors pushed the need for a state constitution change to the forefront. The rise in power of the Agrarians, part of the broader rise of the Populist movement across the nation in the 1890s, gave them the political heft with which to push for a new constitutional convention. Second, the attention being focused on Mississippi's elections by Congress made it urgent that the state find new ways to restrict the franchise beyond violence.[34] Print media, especially newspapers, were a potent weapon for Democrats to use in their attempts to rile up support for anti-Black laws in their new constitution, disguised as attempts at voting reform. As historian Michael Perman has observed, "Of course, it could be argued that the Democrats and their newspapers had to emphasize race as the overriding objective because otherwise their white supporters would have felt betrayed."[35]

The attempts by Congress to overturn the results of the *first* Mississippi Plan reached their climax in 1890. That year it appeared there were enough Republican members of Congress who were ready to take up the federal election bill pushed by Massachusetts congressman Henry Cabot Lodge. This bill, derisively called the "Force Bill" by its Southern opponents, received tremendous support in the African American press. Black Mississippians sent clippings from the Jackson *Clarion-Ledger* to provide evidence for Senate Republicans supporting the Lodge Bill, including threats to potential federal electoral supervisors and accounts of violence against Black Mississippi voters. Yet as the editors of the *Washington Bee*, one of the most prominent African American–owned newspapers of the late nineteenth century, wondered, "What is the good of a law that cannot be enforced? What is the good of a republic that cannot protect its citizens?"[36]

The *Washington Bee* was a critical cog in the larger public sphere of African American thought and culture in the post-Reconstruction world. As both the home of a small but growing African American middle class and the nation's capital, Washington, D.C., was an important hub of national African American life. As such, the *Washington Bee* had the opportunity to shape national African American public opinion on a variety of topics. Founded by African American lawyer W. Calvin Chase, the paper was closely aligned with the Republican Party—an often-imperfect ally of African Americans but, for most, the only conceivable political home they had.[37]

The federal election bill was designed to weaken the onrush of laws across the Southern United States curtailing the voting rights of African Americans. Until the debates over the poll tax in Congress in the 1940s and the eventual passage of the Voting Rights Act in 1965, it was the last time a serious debate about African American voting rights occurred in Congress.[38] The bill would allow federal oversight if a small number of citizens in a voting district petitioned federal circuit courts for assistance.[39]

The *Washington Bee* continued to be one of the loudest national advocates for the Lodge Bill. Later in August 1890, the editors once again argued for the necessity of Congress passing the bill, drawing from a speech given by Chase on the plight of African Americans in society. "No wrong can prosper and neither can murder be concealed. So it is with legislation," Chase said. "If the declaration of independence had been wrong, the British flag would be floating on our public buildings; had the South been right the gray would have supplanted the blue and the American eagle would not only have been eliminated for the portraits of Jefferson Davis, but monuments of Robt. Lee would take the places of the brave comrades, who fell in defense of liberty."[40]

What the writers at the *Washington Bee* did is worth considering in terms of the broader history of African American appeals to American history for the cause of civil and human rights. First, they made an appeal to the broader concept of basic human rights—"no wrong can prosper"—as a way of alerting their audience to the basic rightness of their cause. But, arguably more importantly, the *Bee* also made an appeal to American history. By linking the Lodge

Bill to both the American War of Independence and the American Civil War, the *Bee*'s editors invoked a larger sense of national patriotism. Further, this appeal is an example of the kind of work African American editors and writers had to do as part of a larger civil sphere. It was a thunderous strike against what sociologist Jeffrey C. Alexander has identified as the "anticivil" society that African American intellectuals often found themselves battling against. The written word—and history—proved to be the tools that journalists, intellectuals, and historians used during and after Reconstruction.[41]

African American writers and editors during and after Reconstruction did their best to use the written word to communicate—among themselves and with other Americans—the problems they experienced with the collapse of the Reconstruction governments in the South. But their warnings went unheeded. In 1890, when Mississippi's constitutional convention approved new laws that evaded the Fifteenth Amendment to the U.S. Constitution and stripped African Americans of the right to vote, white Democrats took notice across the South. They used this pernicious second phase of the Mississippi Plan to implement Jim Crow regimes in their states. Eight years later, the justices of the U.S. Supreme Court upheld Mississippi's new suffrage laws, saying they "do not on their face discriminate." The statutes "have not been shown that their actual administration was evil," Justice Joseph McKenna wrote, "only that evil was possible under them."[42] With their unanimous decision, the justices blessed the rise of Jim Crow rule in the South and signaled the nation's acceptance of antidemocratic, anti-Black rule in a large swath of the nation.

Nonetheless, Black journalists, historians, and activists never stopped articulating their opposition. Whether it was through prominent newspapers or works of history, African American print culture shared a mission after 1875: to fight for "the race" in attempts to safeguard the freedoms that were rapidly disappearing in the late nineteenth century. While their protests against the Mississippi Plan and the Southern filibuster of the Lodge Bill fell on largely deaf ears, their efforts should not be regarded as failures. Instead, these editors, writers, and historians left behind a rhetorical and textual legacy built on by the editors, writers, and historians of the African American experience of the twentieth and twenty-first centuries.

Notes

1. John Roy Lynch, *The Facts of Reconstruction* (New York: Neale Publishing Co., 1913), 137.

2. Alexander Keyssar, *The Right to Vote: The Contested History of Democracy in the United States* (New York: Basic Books, 2000), 86.

3. Edward L. Ayers, *The Promise of the New South: Life after Reconstruction*, 15th anniversary ed. (1992; repr., New York: Oxford University Press, 2007), 146–47.

4. Ibid., 8; Nicholas Lemann, *Redemption: The Last Battle of the Civil War* (New York: Farrar, Straus and Giroux, 2006), 38–142; Timothy B. Smith, *James Z. George: Mississippi's Great Commoner* (Oxford: University Press of Mississippi, 2012), 99–101, 111–13; Ron Chernow, *Grant* (New York: Penguin Books, 2018), 788; David Oshinsky, *"Worse Than Slavery': Parchman Farm and the Ordeal of Jim Crow Justice* (New York: Simon and Schuster, 1996), 38; U.S. Congress, Senate, *Mississippi in 1875*, Report of the Select Committee to Inquire into the Mississippi Election of 1875, vol. 1, *1876*; Dorothy Sterling, ed., *The Trouble They Seen: The Story of Reconstruction in the Words of African Americans* (New York: Da Capo Press, 1994), 366, 448.

5. Lemann, *Redemption*, 71–75; U.S. Congress, Senate, *Mississippi in 1875*.

6. U.S. Congress, Senate, *Mississippi in 1875*, 1:163–64, 480.

7. Eric Foner, *Reconstruction: America's Unfinished Revolution* (1988; repr., New York: Harper Perennial, 2014), 573–75; Dorothy Overstreet Pratt, *Sowing the Wind: The Mississippi Constitutional Convention of 1890* (Oxford: University Press of Mississippi, 2018), 3–9.

8. U.S. Congress, Senate, *Mississippi in 1875*; Hilary A. Herbert, ed., *Why the Solid South? Or, Reconstruction and Its Results* (Baltimore: R. H. Woodward & Company, 1890); Bruce E. Baker, *What Reconstruction Meant: Historical Memory in the American South* (Charlottesville: University of Virginia Press, 2007), 23–25; Smith, *James Z. George*, 150–61; Michael Perman, *Struggle for Mastery: Disfranchisement in the South, 1888–1908* (Chapel Hill: University of North Carolina Press, 2001), 50; *Williams v. Mississippi* 170 U.S. 213 (1898); Foner, *Reconstruction*, 573–75; Pratt, *Sowing the Wind*, 3–9.

9. Chernow, *Grant*, 795.

10. Julius Eric Thompson, "Mississippi," in *The Black Press in the South, 1865–1979*, ed. Henry Lewis Suggs, 178–79 (Westport, CT: Greenwood Press, 1983).

11. David Prior, *Between Freedom and Progress: The Lost World of Reconstruction Politics* (Baton Rouge: Louisiana State University Press, 2019), 109.

12. Ibid., 129.

13. "Convention of Colored Newspaper Men," Cincinnati, August 4, 1875, https://omeka.coloredconventions.org/items/show/455, accessed April 21, 2020.

14. Ibid.

15. Prior, *Between Freedom*, 112.

16. "Convention of Colored Newspaper Men."

17. Stephen G. Hall, *A Faithful Account of the Race: African American Historical Writing in Nineteenth-Century America* (Chapel Hill: University of North Carolina Press, 2009), 2.

18. George Washington Williams, *A History of the Negro Race in America from 1619 to 1880* (New York: G. P. Putnam's Sons, 1883).

19. Ibid., 472.

20. Ibid., 471.

21. Colonel C. G. Baylor, "Louisiana and the Negro," *Weekly Louisianan*, October 30, 1874, 1.

22. Shawn Leigh Alexander, ed., *T. Thomas Fortune, The Afro-American Agitator: A Collection of Writings, 1880–1928* (Gainesville: University Press of Florida, 2008), xiv.

23. Frederick Douglass, *The Life and Times of Frederick Douglass* (Boston: De Wolff and Fiske Co., 1892), 652.

24. Eric Foner, *The Second Founding: How the Civil War and Reconstruction Remade the Constitution* (New York: W. W. Norton, 2019), 151.

25. Alexander, *T. Thomas Fortune*, 19.

26. Ibid., 22.

27. Ibid., 25.

28. Ibid., 28.

29. Ibid., 30.

30. Ibid., 31.

31. Shawn Leigh Alexander, *An Army of Lions: The Civil Rights Struggle before the NAACP* (Philadelphia: University of Pennsylvania Press, 2012), 23–65; Blair LM Kelley, *Right to Ride: Streetcar Boycotts and African American Citizenship in the Era of* Plessy v. Ferguson (Chapel Hill: University of North Carolina, 2010).

32. C. Vann Woodward, *The Origins of the New South, 1877–1913* (1988; repr., Baton Rouge: Louisiana State University Press, 1971), 321.

33. Ayers, *Promise of the New South*, 147.

34. Perman, *Struggle for Mastery*, 73–77.

35. Ibid., 28.

36. *Washington Bee*, August 16, 1890, 1; Pratt, *Sowing the Wind*, 8, 151

37. "About the Washington Bee," Library of Congress, Chronicling America, https://chroniclingamerica.loc.gov/lccn/sn84025891/

38. For more on the debate over the poll tax and broader voting rights issues during the 1940s, see Patricia Sullivan, *Days of Hope: Race and Democracy in the New Deal Era* (Chapel Hill: University of North Carolina Press, 1996).

39. Keyssar, *Right to Vote*, 86.

40. "W. Calvin Chase's Address on This and That or His Own Enemy," *Washington Bee*, August 23, 1890, 1.

41. For more on civil sphere theory and public discourse, see Jeffrey C. Alexander, *The Civil Sphere* (New York: Oxford University Press, 2006).

42. *Williams v. Mississippi*, 170 U.S. 213 (1898).

Building the
Solid South

CHAPTER 5

Populist Insurgency, Alabama

SID BEDINGFIELD

In the spring of 1888, Alabama's largest newspaper, the *Montgomery Daily Advertiser*, faced a crisis. The paper remained "the great central organ" of the state's Democratic Party, but it was losing money, and its longtime editor and publisher, William Wallace Screws, feared he would have to sell the paper or shut it down. He had hired a business manager in 1885 to improve the newspaper's finances, but three years later the *Advertiser* was still hemorrhaging cash.[1]

In a bid to save the paper, Screws reached out to Thomas Goode Jones, the speaker of the Alabama House of Representatives. Jones was a rising star in the Democratic Party who was preparing to run for governor. But that's not why the editor approached him. Screws had served as Alabama's secretary of state, and his party connections ran deeper than Jones's. During Reconstruction the *Advertiser* had been a ferocious supporter of the Democratic Party's campaign to restore white supremacy. After the Democrats overthrew the biracial Republican government and "redeemed" the state in 1874, the *Advertiser* and the *Mobile Daily Register* served as loyal mouthpieces for the so-called Bourbon Democrats who ran state government. When his paper faltered in 1888, however, Screws did not ask the Democratic Party for help. He turned to Jones because the house speaker had access to a new power center in Alabama society—the "Big Mules" who controlled the mining and railroad interests that were transforming the northern third of the state.[2]

Before running for office, Jones and his law partner, Jefferson Falkner, had been lead attorneys for the state's largest railroad, the Louisville and Nashville. Jones was close with the L&N's top brass, and at Screws's request, Jones encouraged the railroad to prop up the *Advertiser*. If Screws closed his newspaper or sold it to the wrong owner, Jones told an L&N executive, "it would do the railroads and conservative progress immense harm."[3]

The Louisville and Nashville had no intention of allowing the *Advertiser* to fold. The railroad had been subsidizing friendly newspapers and funneling cash to helpful politicians since it began rapid expansion in Alabama in 1879. The L&N's hard-charging boss, Milton Hannibal Smith, conceded as much in 1918 during an Interstate Commerce Commission investigation into the company's political donations. The railroad supported newspapers in Alabama and Tennessee that were "advocating certain views upon public questions in which the Louisville & Nashville concurred," Smith told investigators. The L&N made campaign contributions to defeat candidates "running on a platform of antagonism and injury to this company," he said.[4]

The *Advertiser* would earn its railroad subsidy in 1890 when the Democratic Party establishment in the state—led by the Big Mules of Birmingham and the big planters of the Black Belt—faced an existential challenge from a populist insurgency. Powered by the growing restiveness of the state's struggling small farmers, Reuben F. Kolb, a Barbour County farmer and the state's commissioner of agriculture, announced his candidacy for governor. The Democratic establishment had assumed that Jones or one of several other acceptable candidates would move into the governor's office and continue to pursue a New South vision for the state. That meant working hand in hand with the railroads and the industrialists to maintain white supremacy, limit taxes and regulations, and provide a steady stream of cheap labor. Since the late 1870s, the Bourbon Democrats had ensured delivery of low-cost workers through maintenance of a corrupt and unspeakably cruel convict leasing program that targeted formerly enslaved African Americans. Kolb's populist uprising, particularly its outreach to Black voters, appeared to threaten that arrangement.[5]

During the economic downturn of the late 1880s and 1890s, Alabama became a fertile recruiting ground for both the Southern Farmers' Alliance and its Black counterpart, the Colored Farmers' Alliance. The rapid rise of these two populist organizations reflected the harsh economic conditions farmers faced across the South. For conservatives like Screws, the emergence of a "radical" white farmers' movement was bad enough; the organizing of Black farmers and the new industrial workers in Alabama was unacceptable. If Black and white farmers and laborers saw their interests as the same and began to vote accordingly, they could create a majority coalition and defeat the Democratic Party establishment. It was a fear that dominated the thoughts of a new generation of white supremacist Democrats across the South, from James K. Vardaman in Mississippi to Benjamin Ryan Tillman in South Carolina and Josephus Daniels in North Carolina. A biracial coalition of Blacks and disaffected whites could overturn the political status quo in the South and pursue policies of economic and social justice in the region. They could end convict leasing and other measures that helped enforce the white supremacist social and economic order in the South.[6]

This chapter examines how Alabama's Democratic Party establishment—what historian Sheldon Hackney has called the "New South-Industrial-Railroad Complex"—used the press to help turn back a populist insurgency and preserve its grip on power. In three bitterly contested gubernatorial elections between 1890 and 1894, the *Advertiser* served as chief propaganda arm of the Bourbon Democrats, delivering a daily barrage of dirt and disinformation that questioned Kolb's character and his commitment to "white southern values." With frequent references to Reconstruction, the *Advertiser* and its chief ally, the *Mobile Daily Register*, stoked white working-class fears of Black competition in the labor market and domination at the ballot box. Under Kolb's leadership, the populist insurgency would inevitably become a "nigger party" controlled by "black Republicans," the newspaper claimed. Only the Democratic Party could prevent the "re-enslavement" of the white South.[7]

In response, a group of newspapers emerged to support the agrarian revolt in Alabama. Known collectively as "the reform press," most were published in rural towns and villages across the state's northern hill country and in some parts of its southern plain. In the pages of the *Choctaw Alliance* (Butler, AL), the *Randolph Toiler* (Wedowee, AL), the Greenville (AL) *Living Truth*, and dozens of other newspapers in the state, editors denounced the "banking, manufacturing, and mercantile interests" and the Democratic Party elites who supported them. The most prominent voice among the populist reformers belonged to Frank Baltzell, a combative editor from Troy who took over the *Montgomery Alliance Herald* in 1890. Baltzell turned the sleepy Farmers' Alliance organ into a fire-breathing proponent of agrarian revolt. He and his populist allies derided Democratic Party leaders as "tools of Wall Street" and "enemies of the people." They demanded transformational change to improve the agricultural economy, end convict leasing, regulate the railroad, and facilitate a "free vote and fair count" by eliminating election fraud.[8]

Dozens of Black newspapers joined the reform press in calling for change. The *Opelika Alliance State Banner*, in the state's southeastern wiregrass country, openly declared its support for the Farmers' Alliance and populist reform. But the most enduring and influential Black editorial voice in Alabama belonged to a Republican weekly based in Huntsville. Launched in 1879 by editor Charles Hendley Jr., the *Huntsville Gazette* survived until 1894—an unusually long life for a Black newspaper in the post-Reconstruction South. Contemporaries described Hendley as a "vivid and soul-stirring writer" who fought valiantly to "liberate the Negro."[9]

At first glance the battle over reform in 1890s Alabama appears clear-cut: a populist insurgent rallied a biracial coalition of farmers, industrial workers, and newspaper editors to challenge the entrenched power of the big planters, the new industrialists, and the Democratic Party elites. But the politicians who played the leading roles had trouble sticking to the script. For a populist, Kolb was surprisingly conservative; he had a cozy relationship with the railroads, and his support for Black voting rights and opposition to convict leasing were cynical and insincere. More-radical populist editors, such as Joseph C. Manning of the *Alabama Reformer*, questioned Kolb's commitment to transformational change. Jones, a former railroad company employee, was a model of the pro-business, antigovernment Bourbon Democrat of the era, yet he crossed his old bosses at the Louisville and Nashville at times, and his call to end convict leasing, while ineffectual, appeared more heartfelt than that of his opponent.[10]

If the politicians equivocated, the press remained fiercely committed. Across the 1890s, as the populist movement rose to national prominence and the People's Party emerged to challenge the two-party political system in the United States, the battle over reform in Alabama played out each day in the pages of the state's newspapers. The Democratic Party relied on the established journals in the state's largest towns: Montgomery, Mobile, and Birmingham, home of the *Age-Herald* and the more progressive *Birmingham News*. Backed by his patrons at the L&N railroad, Screws's newspaper was the most prominent of the group; as a central node in the state's communications network, the *Advertiser* played an outsized role in shaping public discourse, and even its fiercest critics conceded that the paper wielded influence. Kolb claimed that Screws had the power to "crush out all debate" and "prevent discussion of economic ideas." The irascible editor seemed to enjoy publishing harsh attacks from his enemies, and the populist editors were happy to oblige him. They called the *Advertiser* a "hireling of plutocrats" and encouraged readers to boycott it. One paper mocked "the little kite-tailed weeklies trotting along behind with their rehash of the *Advertiser's* falsehoods." Another populist editor described Screws and the Democratic Party press as "the worst enemy the people of Alabama have to contend with."[11]

Among the nearly one hundred populist-leaning papers in the state, Baltzell's *Alliance Herald* stood out. Backed by the Farmers' Alliance, the paper was distributed statewide, and its editor's attack-dog style of journalism fit the tenor of the times. Screws dubbed the *Alliance Herald* the "All-Liars Herald," and the Montgomery editors dueled mercilessly during campaign seasons. Even some populists thought Baltzell went too far. One disapproving paper chided the state's farmers for their seemingly blind allegiance to Kolb and the *Alliance Herald* editor. For years, the paper declared, farmers have "regarded Kolb as a new savior, Baltzell as his prophet, and *The Alliance Herald* as your Bible." Yet despite their popularity and influence, both the *Advertiser* and the *Alliance Herald* struggled financially. They were often on the verge of collapse.[12]

In the 1890s white newspapers in Alabama displayed many characteristics of the partisan press that had emerged a century earlier, when Jefferson and Hamilton were battling to shape the future of the new nation. Despite rapid growth in Alabama's mining district, the impoverished state generated precious little advertising. To survive, newspapers associated with political factions or business interests and received subsidies during campaign season, which came every two years in Alabama. Editors sometimes suspended publication after an election and resumed when the next campaign began. Baltzell had to shut down the *Alliance Herald* briefly in 1893 and again in 1894. When their side won, editors received patronage jobs and their newspapers won government printing contracts. In 1884, when Grover Cleveland became the first Democrat to win the presidency since the Civil War, Screws received a position at the Library of Congress and lived in Washington for a short time. When Cleveland won again in 1892, the editor was named postmaster of Montgomery, although he continued to publish the *Advertiser* as well. Editor/politicians launched and ran some of the most prominent newspapers in the state. Like Screws, they moved in and out of local and state offices while retaining control of their papers. A highly commercial and industrialized press, led by Joseph Pulitzer's *New York World*, may have been rising in the Northeast in the 1890s, but the trend had not penetrated the Deep South. Journalism in Alabama had more in common with the political press of the early republic—Benjamin Bache's *Philadelphia Aurora*, Phillip Freneau's *National Gazette*, and John Fenno's *Gazette of the United States*—than with the profitable "new journalism" of Pulitzer and Hearst newspapers in 1890s New York.[13]

The Black press in Alabama had always been a full-throated partisan on be-half of African American equality, but it faced a dangerous new environment after white Democrats regained control in 1874. As the scourge of lynching spread in the 1880s, journalist and activist Jesse Chisholm Duke emerged as a fearless opponent of white mob violence. But his story also revealed the new reality Black journalists faced in the emerging New South. When Duke founded the *Montgomery Herald* in 1886, it was one of four Black newspapers serving the Alabama capital's vibrant Black community. With a motto that demanded "Equal and Exact Justice for All Men," Duke's newspaper demanded the gov-ernment protect Black Americans and "not allow men to be shot down like mad dogs." In August 1887 Duke responded angrily to a barbaric act that he witnessed firsthand in his hometown. A white mob murdered a young Black man and dragged his body through the streets of Montgomery, claiming the man had raped a white woman. In the *Herald*, Duke dismissed the allegations of Black sexual assault as a fabricated excuse for anti-Black violence, and he wrote provocatively about interracial sex: "Why is it that white women at-tract Negro men now more than in former days? There was a time when such a thing was unheard of. There is a secret to this thing, and we greatly suspect it is the growing appreciation of the white Juliet for the colored Romeo, as he becomes more intelligent and refined." [14] White newspapers reprinted Duke's "outrageous and indecent" editorial, and a white citizens' group denounced him as a "vile and dangerous character." [15] Duke was forced to flee the city to save his life. Hendley and other Black editors continued the fight, but they had to tread carefully.

In the 1890s, as the farmers' revolt grew stronger in Alabama and the debate over reform escalated, the partisan nature of the state's press kicked into high gear. As historians have noted, politics was a major source of public enter-tainment in Alabama at the turn of the twentieth century. And editors on all sides of the debate were desperate to increase readership of their struggling newspapers. At a critical moment in the state's political and economic history, the state's press ratcheted up the rhetorical combat and turned the battle over populist reform in Alabama into a spectacle of partisan warfare. [16]

Big Mules, King Cotton, and the
Populist Movement in Alabama

Like its Southern neighbors, the state of Alabama emerged from the Civil War with a battered agrarian economy. Black and white farmers eked out a living growing cotton for cash and a few other crops for food. Some owned small plots of land, but most struggled as sharecroppers or wage laborers. By 1890, however, economic change had transformed the state in a way that would distinguish it from the rest of the Deep South. The rise of heavy industry in a mineral-rich swath of north-central Alabama turned the sleepy village of Elyton into a bustling boomtown. In the 1870s investors converged on the new city of Birmingham and placed their bets on start-ups hoping to strike it rich in railroad construction, coal mining, and pig iron production. Many returned home broke. For the winners, like Smith's L&N Railroad, the numbers tell a remarkable story of industrial growth in Alabama: between 1870 and the 1890s, railroad companies laid more than two thousand miles of new track, coal production jumped from thirteen thousand tons to more than five million, pig iron increased from eleven thousand tons to nearly a million, and the population of Birmingham and surrounding Jefferson County rose from twelve thousand to more than eighty-eight thousand.[17]

The rapid industrialization that transformed Alabama required an abundance of three ingredients: raw materials, transportation, and labor. Coal and iron ore had been discovered in North Alabama at the turn of the nineteenth century, and the beginnings of a railroad system emerged across the antebellum years. But mining the coal and iron ore and building out the railroads required workers. For that, Alabama turned to the same source of labor that had built the cotton economy before the war—African Americans.

The state's business and political leaders worked together to create an extensive and enduring convict leasing system designed to reassert administrative control over the formerly enslaved people of Alabama and to use coerced labor to build the state's new industrial economy. Officials did little to hide the racist intent of the leasing system. In 1896, to take one typical year, the state leased 1,710 convicts to the Tennessee Coal, Iron and Railroad Company (TCI). Of those, 1,496 were Black. To meet the state's labor demands—and to fill state and local coffers—police rounded up Black Alabamians, charging them with vagrancy, loitering, or simply of being unemployed. After a quick guilty verdict, the new convicts were funneled into the mines, quarries, and blast-furnace operations, where they worked twelve- to fourteen-hour days, slept two to a bunk in rough-hewn wooden barracks, and risked brutal floggings if they failed to meet assigned quotas. Convict leasing benefited the companies in two significant ways: it provided cheap labor that could literally be worked to death, and it suppressed the wages of free labor and undermined the bargaining power of an emerging union movement in Alabama. Workers who threatened to strike knew they could be replaced by Black convicts, which intensified racial animosity in the state. As historians have noted, the convict lease system was a source of corruption throughout society; the lure of easy money tempted police officers, judges, prison administrators, and state and county officials to bend rules and cut side deals with the industrial giants now operating in Alabama.[18]

Launched in the 1840s, the leasing system survived into the late 1920s despite a robust reform movement that emerged in the 1880s and appeared to have widespread political support, even among prominent Democratic Party lawmakers such as Thomas Goode Jones. Nonetheless, when the critical votes came, the business interests that exerted so much influence in Alabama managed to keep convict leasing alive. In 1927 the legislature finally abolished the practice. The vote came, historian Matthew J. Mancini points out, only after more white convicts were caught up in the lease system.[19]

As industrialization emerged in North Alabama in the 1880s, the state's cotton economy collapsed. Overproduction in the United States suppressed prices, and the opening of the Suez Canal in 1869 flooded the European market with cotton from India and Egypt. In Alabama prices cratered, falling from thirty cents a pound in 1866 to just seven cents during the economic downturn of 1893. For small farmers, the onerous crop-lien system exacerbated their woes. Without capital reserves, small farmers had to borrow money to plant a crop each spring and repay the loan with proceeds from the harvest in the fall. That required farmers to plant more cotton—the only reliable cash crop at the time—which increased the cotton supply and lowered prices further. Many lost their land and were forced into sharecropping or reduced to wage labor. In the late 1880s, when the national economy soured, angry farmers began to organize and demand change.[20]

The Southern Farmers' Alliance began in Texas in 1887 and spread across the South and the Midwest. By 1889 the reform group had an estimated fifty thousand white members nationwide. At the same time, an independent and aggressive Black populist movement emerged across the South. As Omar H. Ali has noted, Black populism grew out of the church and fraternal organizations that had built and sustained the Black community since the end of slavery. Black farmers, sharecroppers, and agrarian workers had joined associations like the Colored Agricultural Wheel in Alabama in the early 1870s. In the following decade, they began to coordinate their efforts with Black industrial workers. Organizers like W. J. Campbell, a barber from Warrior, Alabama, in the heart of the mining district, traveled the state seeking to build ties between

Black workers in the state's agrarian and industrial economies. Working with the Knights of Labor, Campbell and other Black organizers pursued an audacious goal: integrate the labor movement in Alabama and develop a biracial, statewide coalition of farmers and industrial workers.[21]

By 1889 the Colored Farmers' Alliance was coordinating efforts with the white National Farmers' Alliance, and in Georgia, North Carolina, and several other Southern states, white populists were reaching out to Black farmers to form biracial political coalitions. As Kolb would make clear in Alabama, white populists often proved to be untrustworthy allies in the African American quest for political equality. But the threat of a new, biracial political coalition spread fear in the Democratic Party. In the *Mongtomery Daily Advertiser*, Screws summarized the concern repeatedly: white farmers must not abandon the Democrats and launch a third party, the editor declared. If they did, all parties would be forced to seek the support of Black voters and thus grant African Americans the power to decide elections in Alabama. And they might use that political power to gain economic and social equality.[22]

Reuben Kolb, Thomas Goode Jones, and the Election of 1890

Reuben Kolb's background made him an unlikely challenger of white supremacy and the Democratic establishment in Alabama. He was born into a politically prominent family, served the Confederate cause with distinction, and had been a loyal supporter of the Democrats who "redeemed" Alabama from Reconstruction. After the war, he rebuilt his family's farm in Eufaula, near the Georgia border, and experienced firsthand the difficulties small farmers faced in the global cotton market. Kolb tried his hand at other careers, including running the Eufaula Opera House, but he never gave up on farming. He experimented with crops other than cotton, including pears, pecans, and cucumbers, before hitting on a winner: watermelons. He developed a hybrid melon called the "Kolb Gem" that retained its flavor and freshness longer than other varieties. The Kolb Gem revived his economic fortunes and launched his political career. In 1887 Kolb was appointed Alabama's commissioner of agriculture. The following year, he joined the Southern Farmers' Alliance and began planning a run for the governor's office.[23]

In the summer of 1889, Kolb attended the Farmers' Alliance national convention in St. Louis, but he remained wary of the group's politics. Earlier that year, Alliance leader C. W. Macune had launched a newspaper in Washington, the *National Economist,* and had been using it to demand Congress intervene on behalf of the struggling farmers. Macune and the Alliance eventually called for the creation of a "sub-treasury," a massive government program that would provide credit to small farmers at low interest rates and create state-run exchanges that would prop up cotton prices.[24] Alliance leaders also hinted at the need for a new political party to represent the farmers' interest in national politics. Macune's ideas infuriated Southern conservatives like Screws who associated federal government intervention with Reconstruction. The *Advertiser* denounced Macune's "St. Louis demands" and warned that a farmers' political party would damage the Democrats and undermine white supremacy in the South. Eyeing his run for the governor's office, Kolb refused to endorse Macune's sub-treasury proposal and rejected calls for creation of the People's Party, a populist third party.[25]

When Kolb launched his campaign for governor in early 1890, he tried to split the difference. He ran for the Democratic Party nomination, citing his "untarnished loyalty to the Democracy," but he also denounced party leaders who sided with the "plutocrats" and ignored struggling small farmers. Screws responded with his own declaration. In announcing its support for Jones, the *Advertiser* called on "true Democrats" to join the "grand and noble fight against Kolb and Kolbism." A few days later, the editor unveiled his first batch of opposition research designed to reshape public perception of the popular agriculture commissioner. "Kolb's Character," read an unusually large headline in the *Advertiser*. "What his Neighbors of Barbour Have Said About It." It was a classic hit piece, aimed directly at Kolb's credibility with the farmers' movement. Twenty years earlier, the *Advertiser* claimed, Kolb had cheated a small farmer. He had allegedly sold land to a farmer knowing that ownership of the property was in dispute. Six months after the sale, another owner emerged and demanded the farmer vacate the property. According to the newspaper, Kolb never returned the money, and the farmer had to pay enormous legal fees to fight the challenge to the sale. Further, the newspaper claimed, the disputed land had been inherited by Kolb's wife, and she and her husband had both acted dishonorably in the sale. Kolb denied anyone had been misled and dismissed the paper's attack as trivial. But Screws disagreed. "The private character of a man becomes a proper subject of investigation whenever he becomes a candidate for public office," the *Advertiser* said. "Is Mr. Kolb an honest man? Does he possess those lofty principles of personal integrity and honor that we are accustomed to find and should demand in our Chief Executive?" The newspaper said the people of Barbour County, the neighbors who know his "true character," did not think so. "Not even his own town newspaper supports him," the *Advertiser* reported. The editor of the Eufaula *Times and News*, William Dorsey Jelks, was a staunch Democrat who eventually became governor of Alabama. His opposition to Kolb was no surprise.[26]

Of the five major Democratic Party candidates running for governor in 1890, Jones had the strongest connections to the New South establishment emerging in Alabama. He had unimpeachable ties to the Confederacy and the Lost Cause. As a young officer, he had risen to the rank of captain in Robert E. Lee's Army of Northern Virginia and at age twenty had been selected to travel through Union lines at Appomattox Courthouse to inform U.S. general Ulysses S. Grant that Lee was ready to surrender. In 1874 Jones gained national recognition after delivering a Memorial Day speech in Montgomery calling for reconciliation between soldiers of the Confederate and Union armies. Like Kolb, Jones failed at farming after the war, but he pursued a successful career as a lawyer in Montgomery. Jones was elected to the state house of representatives in 1884 and named speaker of the house two years later. At the same time, he and his law partner, Jefferson Falkner, served as lead attorneys for Smith's L&N Railroad in Alabama. Yet during his time in the legislature, Jones twice appeared to side with reformers in the battle over the independence of the state railroad commission. He lost that battle but gained respect from surprised observers who assumed he was in the pocket of the L&N and the other railroads in the state. Yet others wondered if the wily Smith had not approved those small acts of independence in order to enhance Jones's stature and improve his future political prospects. In 1890, with the apparent blessing of the L&N president, Jones joined the race for governor.[27]

As the populist insurgent, Kolb's campaign called for lawmakers to support the struggling small farmers and rein in the power of the railroads, mine owners, and big planters of the Black Belt. At the time, the Alabama Railroad Commission exerted minimal control over the railroad companies, which used their money and lobbying power to ensure the regulatory body remained docile and toothless. To win friends around the state, the L&N and other railroads frequently provided free passes to key lawmakers and government officials. During the 1890 campaign, when Kolb called for lawmakers to strengthen the commission, Screws pounced with another well-timed hit. The *Advertiser* claimed the agricultural commissioner had often received free passes from the Louisville and National. And in a more damaging revelation, the newspaper said Kolb had submitted fraudulent expense reports and been reimbursed by the state for the free trips. Screws accused Kolb of "hypocrisy" and "fraud," and he called for lawmakers to conduct a full audit of the candidate's travel expenses. How did Screws discover that Kolb had been using free passes from the L&N? The editor would call it good reporting, but skeptics suggested Jones's former colleagues at the L&N, including its savvy president, leaked the information to the *Advertiser*.[28]

To defend himself, Kolb turned to friendlier newspapers. He granted a lengthy interview to the *Evergreen Star*, published in a small town about seventy-five miles south of Montgomery. Kolb told the *Star* that he had bought a ticket for the train trip in question but inadvertently used the L&N pass when he boarded the train. He said he had intended to reimburse the railroad once the state of Alabama paid his travel expense. Even the *Star* seemed skeptical. The newspaper called the explanation "more or less plausible," but it noted that Kolb could end the controversy if he produced the train ticket that he said he had purchased. Kolb said he had apparently thrown the ticket away. The *Advertiser* called Kolb's response "bunglesome" and declared in a nearby headline: "If Anything Was Needed to Put Him In His Political Grave, He Has Furnished It With His Own Hand."[29]

But the *Advertiser*'s headline was premature. Kolb's political career was far from dead. With the backing of the Farmers' Alliance, the agriculture commissioner arrived at the state's Democratic Party convention in May with more support than any other candidate. In the first roll call vote, Kolb won 235 delegates, just short of the 264 needed to win the party's nomination. Of his four opponents, Jones received the fewest votes, a mere 45. But all four opposing candidates were Democratic regulars who were loath to turn the party over to Kolb and the farmers' movement. They remained in the race, and through more than 30 roll call votes, Kolb never reached the magic number of 264.[30]

With the convention stalemated, the 1890 governor's race was decided in a classic smoke-filled room in Montgomery's Exchange Hotel. During an all-night negotiating session, representatives of the anti-Kolb candidates haggled over how to unite their support and defeat the Alliance candidate. The Democratic Party kingmakers included Falkner, the L&N Railroad lawyer who supported Jones; *Birmingham News* owner and editor Rufus N. Rhodes, representing banker and future governor Joseph F. Johnston; and J. J. Willet, an Anniston attorney supporting James F. Crook, a former state railroad commissioner. At 7:00 the following morning, the group emerged with a decision. Jones would be the state's next governor. The other anti-Kolb candidates were dropping out of the race.[31]

Why Jones? Because the party bosses in the hotel room realized Jones was the only candidate who could defeat Kolb on the convention floor. Delegates supporting the other three candidates were fiercely opposed to Kolb and would never support him for governor. But many of Jones's delegates considered Kolb to be their second choice. The remaining candidates realized that if Jones left the race, Kolb would pick up enough delegates to reach the 264 mark and win the nomination. Winning the Democratic nomination was tantamount to Kolb becoming the next governor in what was virtually a one-party state at the time. For the Democratic Party establishment, that outcome was unthinkable.[32]

At first Kolb accepted the party's decision graciously. He withdrew his name from consideration, allowing convention delegates to nominate Jones unanimously, and he agreed to campaign for the Democratic nominee against the Republican candidate in the August general election. Even Screws's *Advertiser* published a few nice words about the Farmers' Alliance candidate. It ran an editorial from a Georgia newspaper that praised Kolb's "magnificent fight" and his ability to rally "great strength" in the crowded field. But Jones's nomination was "the most natural and desirable end" to a campaign that had turned Alabama into a "political cauldron," the newspaper said. Jones is "a thoroughbred of Alabama's best type, a clean, brave, chivalrous gentleman, the soul of honor and the ideal of the young Democracy," the newspaper gushed. His nomination "will doubtless fall like oil upon Alabama's troubled waters."[33]

Just days after the editorial appeared, Kolb showed how wrong it was. In what was supposed to be a show of unity, Jones and Kolb appeared together at a campaign kickoff rally in Kolb's hometown of Eufaula. Shortly after taking the stage, Kolb stunned the crowd by declaring the Democratic establishment had "stolen" the nomination from him. His angry tirade infuriated the Jones campaign but thrilled supporters who were eager for him to run for governor again in 1892.[34]

Jones's controversial election in 1890 fueled the political mobilization of the populist farmers' revolt in Alabama. Kolb had distanced himself from the national Farmers' Alliance in his first race for governor. But in late 1890, after the national organization laid out a new set of "demands" for federal government aid, the state Farmers' Alliance formally endorsed the proposals. The state group stopped short of supporting the People's Party, a national third-party effort founded by populist farmers in Kansas. But Alliance members vented their anger and frustration at the state Democratic Party and the new governor. As Jones prepared for his inauguration, reform newspapers mocked him as "the fraudulent one" and "his distinguished accidency." The state Farmers' Alliance also passed a resolution denouncing the actions of the *Montgomery Daily Advertiser* and the *Mobile Daily Register* during the campaign. The farmers' organization called the two newspapers "dirty sheets." Perhaps hitting closest to home, they described the *Advertiser* and its Mobile ally as "subsidized enemies of the farmers and laboring people of Alabama."[35]

Even some Democratic Party papers, such as the *Birmingham Age-Herald*, thought Screws had gone too far in the 1890 race. Mocking the elderly editor, the *Age-Herald* said, "Our ancient and esteemed contemporary" had behaved with "rashness and desperation" during the campaign but was spared humiliation by events "over which he had no control." Nonetheless, the *Age-Herald* conceded the *Advertiser* had reason to celebrate. "The candidate against whom it so persistently trained its batteries is defeated, and the candidate of its choice is the nominee," the Birmingham paper said. "We congratulate it." Screws published the *Age-Herald* editorial and offered his own rebuttal. "Very few thinking people in Alabama will agree with our green-eyed Birmingham contemporary that the result was due to 'luck,'" he wrote. "Every right thinking man knows that the result was due to good conduct, not only on the part of the Press of Alabama, but of the forces that nominated Col. Jones, and eminently of the latter himself."[36]

Convict Leasing, African American Voters, and the 1892 Election

After the 1890 election, Kolb signaled his intention to challenge Jones's reelection before the new governor had even taken office. Jones returned the favor by replacing Kolb as commissioner of agriculture and sending state police to demand he vacate his office. Their battle for the governor's office would grow more contentious from there. One historian has called their 1892 rematch the "most scurrilous" political campaign in Alabama history. The candidates debated corporate power, political corruption, convict leasing, school funding, and the right to "free votes and fair counts." Kolb was actively seeking Black voters as part of a populist coalition, and Jones wanted to undermine that effort by pointing out the ways he had supported Black aspirations. But the *Advertiser* made sure neither candidate forgot the critical issue of white supremacy—"not for one minute."[37]

Jones had less than a year to position himself as a strong and successful incumbent before the 1892 race began, but he faced a daunting obstacle. Farmers' Alliance candidates had swept to victory in the statehouse, winning a majority of seats in the state house of representatives. When the new legislature convened in December 1891, lawmakers elected the president of the alliance, Samuel M. Adams, as speaker of the house. In his inaugural address, Jones took steps to appeal to the "Alliance Legislature" and to distance himself from the Big Mules and the Democratic Party establishment. While he emphasized his commitment to white supremacy, declaring African Americans "wholly unfit for political duties" and in need of "guidance and control" by whites, the governor struck a more moderate tone on major policy debates concerning Black Alabamians. The new governor rejected calls for Alabama to follow Mississippi's lead and write a new state constitution to disenfranchise Black voters, and he opposed legislation that would "segregate the taxes," a scheme that allowed local governments to allocate funds from white taxpayers to white schools only. Both proposals were gaining popularity among New South politicians at the time, and some Democratic newspapers in Alabama excoriated the new governor. Calling his stance on the educational tax issue a "gross injustice," one paper claimed, "The white children have been robbed by the kinky heads long enough."[38]

Jones's decision won praise from a rising force in the Black community, Booker T. Washington, principal at Alabama's Tuskegee Institute. Washington led a group of Black leaders to the capital city to discuss the education funding issue with the governor. According to the *Montgomery Daily Advertiser*, the "colored convention" left the capital "mightily pleased" with what they heard. Jones would develop a working relationship with Washington. After he rose to national prominence, the African American leader continued to praise Jones's opposition to lynching and white mob violence, and in 1901 the Tuskegee educator persuaded President Teddy Roosevelt to appoint Jones to a federal judgeship. But in 1890 the new governor misled the Black leader on the issues of school funding and disenfranchisement. Days after his meeting with Washington, Jones signed a revised bill that allowed municipalities to apportion property tax funds the way local white officials saw fit. And in 1896, two years after leaving office, Jones switched course and supported the push for a constitutional convention designed to restrict Black suffrage.[39]

Jones also denounced convict leasing in his 1890 inaugural address and appeared determined to abolish the practice in the new legislative session. State and local governments should never make revenue the "chief consideration" of the state's penal system, Jones said; in fact, revenue should not "be considered at all when it conflicts with the demands of humanity." The governor also noted the rising complaints of free laborers who were forced to compete with convicts in the state's coal-mining industry. With Kolb and the Farmers' Alliance publicly supporting abolition, the stage appeared set for the abolition of convict leasing in Alabama. It is time to "put an end to the lease system," Jones declared. But that turned out to be misleading as well.[40]

As the new legislature gathered in Montgomery, Jones sent a formal message to lawmakers declaring his intention to abolish leasing. He called the system "cruel and unusual punishment" and urged the legislature to fund construction of a new penitentiary to house inmates who would be returning from the mines and quarries. The pro-Alliance legislature was expected to support the governor's plan. Additionally, coal miners in Jefferson County went on strike briefly to protest working conditions and demand an end to convict labor. The new governor had met with the miners, and his assurances regarding convict leasing reform helped bring the strike to a peaceful conclusion. The momentum behind abolition appeared inexorable. Yet, in the end, the lawmakers failed to act. The legislature refused to fund the new prison; instead, lawmakers resorted to an old trick often used to address an issue without actually getting anything done: they established a special commission to investigate the leasing system and propose a solution.[41]

Jones played a role in this sham. He was a member of the commission, and he continued to declare his support for the abolition of convict leasing during his two terms as governor. In 1893 the legislature passed a law requiring the removal of all convicts from the mines by January 1, 1895. But the measure had an escape clause tacked on the end: "if it can be done without detriment to the financial interests of state." The governor and the Farmers' Alliance lawmakers never summoned the political will required to ignore that clause. They claimed the economic downturn of 1893 prevented the state from implementing the law and losing the revenue that leasing generated. However, pressure from the Big Mules also played a role in preserving convict leasing.[42]

The *Advertiser*'s shifting rhetoric reflected the Democratic Party's sleight of hand on convict leasing. In 1890, when Jones was battling Kolb for the votes of farmers and workers, the *Advertiser* agreed that convict leasing "must go." The system "will undoubtedly be ended," the newspaper said. "There seems to be a demand for it, which those in authority are justified in respecting." After Jones was elected governor, Screws's newspaper took a more cautious line. The lease system should be abolished, but the governor and legislature must act "with care and deliberation" to protect the state's finances. By the 1892 campaign, when Kolb demanded immediate abolition, the *Advertiser* called him "reckless" and said the state must abide by existing contracts with Tennessee Coal, Iron and Railroad, which did not expire for another five years. In 1894, when Kolb lost his third run for governor, this time to conservative Democrat William C. Oates, the legislature's effort to end leasing came to a halt. And Screws's *Advertiser* sounded relieved. "The [leasing] system must be made self-sustaining and in order to do that convicts must be dealt out to the highest bidder," the *Advertiser* declared. "All that sentiment about [convicts] not being made to perform any labor that free labor performs, has long since been exploded."[43]

When Kolb ran for governor in 1892, he broke with the Democratic Party, but he stopped short of joining the People's Party, which was gaining strength across the nation. The bitter disappointment of the 1890 loss had politicized the state farmers' movement and increased support for Macune's economic proposals and the national third-party movement. But Kolb was not ready to break with the party that had "redeemed" the state from Reconstruction. Instead, he created what he called the "true Democracy" in Alabama: the Jeffersonian Democrats. Backed by leaders of state Farmers' Alliance, Kolb still envisioned his campaign as an insurgency that would eventually take control of the Democratic Party, the defender of white supremacy in the South. But to achieve that goal, he needed Black voters. And in the 1892 campaign, he made an aggressive bid for them. But his efforts were also tentative and stumbling at times, revealing a deep sense of ambivalence. In addition, Kolb and his campaign would draw charges of "hypocrisy" and worse from Screws and the rest of the Democratic press.[44]

Kolb's problems began before the campaign got under way. The state convention delegates who would determine the nominee were selected in executive committee meetings in each county, and Kolb realized those committees were stacked with supporters of Jones and the Democratic establishment. In response, he called for Democratic Party voters to decide their party's nominee through a statewide primary. But he said the primary should be for white voters only. Kolb claimed his all-white primary plan was designed to stop vote fraud in the Black Belt, the rich agricultural region where Democratic Party officials routinely stuffed ballot boxes with nonexistent Black votes. But Screws and other Democratic editors would turn his "white primary" proposal against him, further undermining Kolb's credibility with Black voters.[45]

Kolb announced plans to seek Black votes in the platform of his new party. The Jeffersonian Democrats "favor the protection of the colored race in their political rights, and should afford them encouragement and aid in the attainment of a higher civilization and citizenship," the party declared. On the campaign trail, Kolb stressed the shared economic interests of Black and white farmers and workers, and his events often included African American speakers. In Talladega a Black man spoke on Kolb's behalf for more than an hour, much to the chagrin of a reporter for the *Birmingham News*. "Men of Alabama," he asked, "whither are we drifting?" Some of Kolb's most aggressive speakers were angry white populists who defended Black voting rights and threatened Democratic officials who stole votes. "I am in favor of killing them if they don't count it right," Birmingham lawyer Peyton G. Bowman told a crowd of more than eight thousand white and Black supporters in Opelika. "Let the colored man stand up for his race and vote for a free ballot and civil liberty."[46]

Jones hoped his occasional jabs at convict leasing, lynching, and the Mississippi Plan for Black disenfranchisement would attract some Black votes that might otherwise had gone to Kolb. So the governor avoided attacking Kolb's outreach to Black voters directly on the campaign trail. He left that job to Screws and the Democratic press. The *Advertiser* accused Kolb of "negro vote begging" and said the populist candidate was running under a "black flag of revolt." He frequently charged Kolb's campaign with buying African American votes. In one account, Screws said two Black "Kolbites" had been traveling through Black Belt counties handing out cash to prospective voters. These men "had what it took to make the mare go," Screws wrote, "and they flashed it openly." The editor claimed Kolb had obtained this "filthy lucre" on a trip to New York to meet key Republican senators and to commit his party's support for GOP presidential candidate Benjamin Harrison. The *New York Times* believed Kolb could win the state, but Screws told his white readers not to worry, because "Kolbism" would be defeated by the "invincible white supremacy Democrats."[47]

Screws had it right. Kolb was defeated in the August 1892 election, and he may well have lost to "invincible white supremacy Democrats." But those Democrats weren't the voters; they were the election supervisors in key counties in the Black Belt. Both contemporary observers and historians who have studied the race believe Kolb received more votes at the polls that day. But voting fraud on a massive scale swung the election to Jones. According to the official vote count, the incumbent received 11,435 more votes than the challenger, with Jones's margin of victory coming from Black Belt counties, where African Americans were in the vast majority. Kolb led Jones by 15,000 votes in the white-majority counties outside the Black Belt, but Jones outpolled Kolb by 26,000 votes in the Black Belt counties, where African Americans comprised an overwhelming majority. Did Jones benefit from a stunning wave of enthusiastic Black support for a white Democrat on that broiling August day? Historians and political analysts find it unlikely. Some note that African Americans had reasons to select Jones over Kolb—the insurgent candidate had made his white supremacist views crystal clear on the campaign trail—but only massive fraud could generate the vote totals required for the Democrat to overcome Kolb's lead outside the Black-majority counties.[48]

Populism, Progressivism, and Black Disenfranchisement

Kolb lost his last chance to take power in Alabama when he ran for governor a third time in 1894. Once again, votes stolen from African Americans in the Black Belt likely swayed the outcome, this time in favor of former U.S. congressman William C. Oates. Kolb initially declared himself the governor-elect, and he and two hundred supporters gathered in Montgomery the day Oates was inaugurated, but they retreated without violence. Instead, Kolb launched a newspaper in Birmingham, the *People's Tribune*, and continued to push for his moderate version of populism.[49]

Two years later, in the pivotal elections of 1896, Kolb decided against a fourth run for governor, and the competing wings of the agrarian movement—Kolb's Jeffersonian Democrats and Joseph Manning's more radical populists—tried to unite with the state's Republicans. In the Democratic Party, *Birmingham News* editor and publisher Rufus N. Rhodes pushed his candidate slightly toward the left and discovered the sweet spot in Alabama politics—at least among the state's white voters. Joseph F. Johnston, a loser in the 1890 and 1894 races for the Democratic nomination, broke with the party establishment and embraced key policies proposed by the farmers' movement. He supported stronger regulation of the railroads and mining companies, and he called for tax increases to improve infrastructure and help the state's dismal agricultural economy. If Johnston sounded like a populist on economic issues, he was fervently a Bourbon Democrat on the question of race. Johnston strongly emphasized his commitment to white supremacy, and he demanded the state hold a constitutional convention to curb Black voting rights.[50]

In a year when the populist orator William Jennings Bryan lead a Democratic–People's Party alliance to a crushing defeat in the presidential election, Johnston and the Democrats handily defeated populist candidate Albert T. Goodwyn in the Alabama governor's race. Johnston's marriage of reform and white supremacy did so well, in fact, that he would have won the election even if the usual ballot stuffing in the Black Belt had not occurred. Johnston had performed a neat political trick. He had appropriated key populist proposals and merged them seamlessly with the Democratic Party's zeal for white supremacy. One approving editor called the results "the death knell of Populism in Alabama and a glorious victory for the Democratic Party."[51]

Johnston made election fraud a key campaign issue, and he blamed the state's corrupt voting system on African Americans. Without Black suffrage, he argued, whites could compete against one another freely without granting

Black voters the power to determine the winner. Furthermore, Democratic Party leaders in the majority-Black counties of the Black Belt would no longer fear African American political control in their region. It was an argument laced with irony: if Blacks were denied their democratic rights, Johnston said, whites would stop the fraud that was damaging democracy in Alabama. To achieve this goal, Johnston and his new "reform" wing of the Democratic Party urged the state to follow the Mississippi Plan and rewrite the state's constitution to limit Black suffrage.[52]

Johnston's convention plan called for other reforms as well. Backed by emerging "progressives" from the state's larger cities, Johnston wanted an elected railroad commission, a crackdown on lynching, new limits on convict leasing, and abolition of a law that limited county and municipal taxing powers. His proposed constitution would empower the former populist farmers at the expense of the old Bourbon Democrats and their new industrial allies. In limiting Black suffrage, Johnston's plan avoided literacy and property requirements that would deny the vote to many poor white farmers too. By the time his convention proposal reached the floor of the legislature, however, Johnston had lost control of the process. His conservative opponents in the Democratic establishment eliminated the broader reform measures and pursued suffrage rules that would also remove many farmers from Alabama politics. The New South industrial railroad complex had emerged victorious once again. The great switch seemed to please Screws's *Advertiser* and the rest of the Democratic press. "The [constitutional] convention is now set to address the critical question that is so important to Alabamians, white supremacy," the newspaper said. The *Birmingham Age-Herald* declared, "The elimination of the negro from politics [is] at last a practical certainty." The new constitution "will lift the ballot box above fraud and manipulation, and the public business above corruption and general demoralization."[53]

African Americans protested the proposed new voting laws. As delegates gathered in the spring of 1901, Booker T. Washington and a group of middle-class Black professionals sent a conciliatory letter to convention leaders pleading for the state to retain at least some degree of African American voting rights. A more aggressive group of Black leaders gathered at their own convention. If Blacks are denied the vote, the group said in a statement, Black residents should flee Alabama and move to a state "where the rights of manhood will be respected." The group also warned poor whites in Alabama—farmers and industrial workers—that they were "being used as instruments to effect their own political destruction." Black journalists in the North lashed out as well.

In a new national journal, the *Voice of the Negro*, T. Thomas Fortune said a "voteless citizen" would be treated like a "pariah." He will be "victimized by individuals and mobs and by legislators," Fortune wrote. "A body of citizens so large as that of Afro-American people in the Southern states would never with the ballot in their hands be subject to separate car laws, separate school laws, separate penal institutional regulations—separate everything that arrogance and insolence, uncurbed by fear of retaliation at the ballot box, are disposed to heap upon the defenseless."[54]

These dissenting voices had little impact in Alabama. The convention delegates made their goal unequivocal. "And what is it we want to do?" one Democrat asked. "Why, it is in the limits imposed by the federal constitution, to establish white supremacy in Alabama." In 1898 the U.S. Supreme Court had upheld Mississippi's use of literacy, property, and other subjective measures to limit voting rights without violating the Fifteenth Amendment's prohibition against racial discrimination at the ballot box. Alabama added its own twist to the Mississippi Plan. It gave county election officials the right to waive those literacy and property-ownership requirements if those officials vouched for the "good civic character" of the applicant. It allowed white county officials free rein to reject and accept voters as they wished. In November 1901, after voters ratified the new constitution, Screws declared victory in a banner headline stripped across the *Advertiser*'s front page: "The Citizens of Alabama Declare for White Supremacy And Purity of the Ballot. The Putrid Sore of Negro Suffrage is Severed From the Body Politic of the Commonwealth."[55]

Conclusion

Thousands of white and African American farmers joined agrarian reform movements in Alabama during the economic struggles of the 1880s. By the early 1890s, ambitious organizers from both races worked to unite the farmers and the state's new industrial workers into a powerful coalition demanding social, economic, and political change. Buoyed by a rising national agrarian movement, the rebellion in Alabama showed signs of success. In response, industrialists, railroad executives, and Bourbon Democrats launched a campaign to undermine the growing populist uprising. Both sides turned to the state's partisan press to prosecute the fight. Led by Jack Baltzell's *Alliance Herald*, Joseph Manning's *Alabama Reformer*, and aggressive Black editors such as Charles Hendley Jr. at the *Huntsville Gazette*, the reform press rallied farmers and some workers to join the struggle. But the populists and African

American newspapers lacked the reach of the established conservative press, particularly the *Montgomery Daily Advertiser* in the state's capital city, which played an influential role in framing the debate over race and reform. In 1896 many white farmers who had supported populist candidates returned to the Democratic Party, lured by timid promises of economic reform wed to a full-throated commitment to white supremacy. By the fall of 1901, when the state's constitutional convention concluded its work, those economic reforms had been eliminated, and the new suffrage laws designed to end Black voting denied ballots to many poor white farmers too. After a decade of fierce journalistic battle with his populist foes, a thoroughly satisfied William Wallace Screws would declare the convention to be a "glorious victory" for white supremacy and the Democratic Party. It was a glorious victory for Screws's *Montgomery Daily Advertiser* as well.[56]

Screws, Baltzell, Hendley and their compatriots in Alabama's conservative, populist, and African American press were editors of partisan newspapers who reveled in the central role they played in Alabama politics. But they also struggled to keep their newspapers afloat. Founded in 1879, Hendley's *Huntsville Gazette* was one of the longest-running Black newspapers in the South. The *Gazette* survived the economic and political turmoil of the 1880s, but the newspaper collapsed after the 1894 elections. Baltzell's *Alliance Herald* also folded that year. Two years earlier, Baltzell had accused the state's sitting governor, Thomas Goode Jones, of cheating a minster and an elderly woman earlier in his legal career. Jones had Baltzell charged with four counts of criminal libel, and by 1894 the expensive legal battle forced the populist editor to shutter his newspaper. He emerged two years later to edit the *Alabama Monitor*, another paper with statewide distribution. He hoped it would jump-start a run for the U.S. Congress, but the decline in the populist movement after the 1896 election dashed Baltzell's political dreams.[57]

Screws took over the *Advertiser* in 1865 and remained its editor until just before his death in 1913. During those forty-eight years, the paper changed only marginally in style and tone. Screws was an editor/politician who saw the newspaper as an essential component of political life in his state. In 1893 he wrote a history of Alabama journalism that proudly noted the many white elected officials who had once been newspaper editors. The essay appeared in a book published just months after the brutal 1892 governor's race in which Screws and his newspaper had played such a critical role. With a touch of pride, Screws told his readers that Alabama journalism was "becoming more influential every day."[58] And he was right.

Notes

1. "Alabama Secretaries of State, William Wallace Screws," Alabama Department of Archives and History (henceforth, ADAH); Rhoda Coleman Ellison, *History and Bibliography of Alabama Newspapers in the Nineteenth Century* (Tuscaloosa: University of Alabama Press, 1954), 55.

2. Thomas Goode Jones to Eckstein Norton, December 31, 1888, Thomas Goode Jones Papers (henceforth, TGJ Papers), ADAH. Norton held the title of president of the L&N from 1886 to 1891, although Milton H. Smith retained day-to-day operational control of the railroad. See Maury Klein, *History of the Louisville & National Railroad* (Lexington: University Press of Kentucky, 2003), 375–80; Allen Johnston Going, *Bourbon Democracy in Alabama, 1874–1890* (1951; repr., Tuscaloosa: University of Alabama Press, 1992), 9–26.

3. Jones to Eckstein Norton, TGJ Papers, ADAH; Sheldon Hackney, *Populism to Progressivism in Alabama* (Tuscaloosa: University of Alabama Press, 2009), 10–14. Originally published by Princeton University Press, 1969.

4. James Fletcher Dorster, *Railroads in Alabama Politics, 1875–1914* (Tuscaloosa: University of Alabama Press, 1957), 56–57; "Milton H. Smith Testifies Regarding Political Contributions," *Railway Age* 64, March 1, 1918, 446.

5. Hackney, *Populism to Progressivism in Alabama*, 3–47; William Warren Rogers, Robert David Ward, Leah Rawls Atkins, and Wayne Flynt, *Alabama: The History of a Deep South State* (1994; Tuscaloosa: University of Alabama Press, 2018), 277–319; Gerald H. Gaither, *Blacks and the Populist Movement: Ballots and Bigotry in the New South* (Tuscaloosa: University of Alabama Press, 2005), 155–69; Omar H. Ali, *In the Lion's Mouth: Black Populism in the New South, 1886–1900* (Jackson: University of Mississippi Press, 2010), 116–19; Douglas A. Blackmon, *Slavery by Another Name: The Re-Enslavement of Black Americans from the Civil War to World War II* (New York: Random House, 2008); Brent J. Aucoin, *Thomas Goode Jones: Race, Politics, and Justice in the New South* (Tuscaloosa: University of Alabama Press, 2016).

6. Sid Bedingfield, "Tillman's Rebellion, South Carolina"; Robert Greene II, "Mississippi Plan"; and Kristen L. Gustafson, "Death of Democracy, North Carolina," all in *Journalism and Jim Crow*.

7. Hackney, *Populism to Progressivism*, 10. See, for example, "Kolbism," *Montgomery Daily Advertiser*, March 10, 1890, 4; "Kolb and the Democratic Party," *Mobile Daily Register*, March 1, 1890, 2.

8. William Warren Rogers Sr., *The One-Gallused Rebellion: Agrarianism in Alabama, 1865–1896* (1970; repr., Tuscaloosa: University of Alabama Press, 2001), 249–55; Rogers et al., *Alabama*, 307, 313. For example, see "The Advertiser's War, Evergreen Star," *Montgomery Daily Advertiser*, February 8, 1890, 4. Usage of "the reform press" spread in 1889 after the *National Economist*, the Washington newspa-

per of Farmers' Alliance leader C. W. Macune, began using the phrase to headline a daily roundup of editorials from populist newspapers across the country. Baltzell's *Montgomery Alliance Herald* used the headline over a roundup of editorials from populist newspapers in Alabama; *Montgomery Alliance Herald*, September 20, 1891.

9. Irvine Garland Penn, *The Afro-American Press and Its Editors* (Springfield, MA: Willey & Co., 1891), 286; Allen W. Jones, "The Black Press in the 'New South': Duke's Struggle for Justice and Equality," *Journal of Negro History* 64, no. 3 (1979): 215–28; James C. Wilder, "History of Alabama Negro Press, Post-Reconstruction to 1901 (Unpublished MA thesis, University of Alabama, 1964), 11–13. Also see Martin E. Dann, ed., *The Black Press, 1827–1890: The Quest for National Identity* (New York: Capricorn Books, 1971).

10. For more on populist organizer and editor Joseph C. Manning, see Paul W. Pruitt, "Joseph C. Manning, Alabama Populist: A Rebel against the Solid South" (Unpublished diss., College of William and Mary, Williamsburg, Virginia, 1980.

11. "Speaking of 'Partisan Newspapers,' Kolb Said at Birmingham," *Montgomery Daily Advertiser*, October 1, 1891, 1; *Choctaw Alliance*, May 10, 1890; *Troy Jeffersonian*, February 16, 1894, December 1, 1893, last two quoted in Rogers, *One-Gallused Rebellion*, 249–50.

12. "One hundred populist papers" is from Rogers, *One-Gallused Rebellion*, 250. Quotation about Kolb, Baltzell, and Alabama farmers comes from the *Alabama Pioneer* and is quoted in *Montgomery Daily Advertiser*, July 6, 1893, 4.

13. "Alabama Secretaries of State, William Wallace Screws," ADAH; "Baltzell's Papers Suspending Production," in Rogers, *One-Gallused Rebellion*, 254.

14. Jones, "Black Press in the 'New South,'" 221.

15. Ibid., 222.

16. On politics as entertainment, see Rogers et al., *Alabama*, 305.

17. Doster, *Railroads in Alabama Politics, 1875–1914*, 47; Rogers et al., *Alabama*, 277–394 (coal, pig iron, population numbers: 281); Hackney, *Populism to Progressivism*, 3–31; Matthew J. Mancini, *One Dies, Get Another: Convict Leasing in the American South, 1866–1928* (Columbia: University of South Carolina Press, 1996), 99–116; Blackmon, *Slavery by Another Name*, 39–57.

18. Mancini, *One Dies, Get Another*, 99–116; Blackmon, *Slavery by Another Name*.

19. Mancini, *One Dies, Get Another*, 115.

20. Rogers et al., *Alabama*, 277–394; John B. Clark, *Populism in Alabama* (Auburn, AL: Auburn University Press, 1927); Hackney, *Populism to Progressivism*, 3–31.

21. Robert C. McMath Jr., *Populist Vanguard: A History of the Southern Farmer's Alliance* (Chapel Hill: University of North Carolina, 1975; Ali, *In the Lion's Mouth*, 13–77.

22. See, for example, "The State and National Farmers Alliance," *Montgomery Daily Advertiser*, March 27, 1890, 4.

23. William Warren Rogers, "Reuben F. Kolb: Agricultural Leader of the New

South," *Agricultural History* 32 (April 1958): 112, 113; Leah R. Atkins, "Populism in Alabama: Reuben F. Kolb and the Appeals to Minority Groups," *Alabama Historical Quarterly* (Fall/Winter 1970); Hackney, *Populism to Progressivism*, 4–8.

24. McMath, *Populist Vanguard*, 62.

25. "The St. Louis Resolutions," *Montgomery Daily Advertiser*, December 20, 1889; Rogers, *One-Gallused Rebelion*, 171–73; Lewis Reece, "Creating a New South: The Political Culture of Deep South Populism," in *Populism in the South Revisited: New Interpretations and New Departures*, ed. James Beeby, 145–75 (Oxford: University Press of Mississippi, 2011).

26. "Kolb's Character," *Montgomery Daily Advertiser*, May 3, 1890, 3; "William Dorsey Jelks," in Rogers, *One-Gallused Rebellion*, 180; Aucoin, *Thomas Goode Jones*, 21–23.

27. Aucoin, *Thomas Goode Jones*, 16–19; Rogers et al., *Alabama*, 277–312.

28. "Kolb's Circular. His Long Promised Explanation of the Charges," *Montgomery Daily Advertiser*, March 23, 1890, 3.

29. "Kolb's Explanations," *Montgomery Daily Advertiser*, March 23, 1890, 3.

30. Hackney, *Populism to Progressivism*, 14–16; Aucoin, *Thomas Goode Jones*, 21–23.

31. Historians have written extensively about the 1890 election and the meeting in the Exchange Hotel. One of the most detailed versions can be found in Hackney, *Populism to Progressivism*, 16–18. Also see Aucoin, *Thomas Goode Jones*, 21–25, and Rogers et al., *Alabama*, 306–307.

32. Hackney, *Populism to Progressivism*, 16–18. Also see Aucoin, *Thomas Goode Jones*, 22–24, and Rogers et al., *Alabama*, 306–307.

33. "Alabama Politics: *The Tribune of Rome* [GA]," *Montgomery Advertiser*, June 3, 1890, 7.

34. Aucoin, *Thomas Goode Jones*, 24.

35. Ibid., 47; I. L. Brock, Secretary-Treasury, Alabama State Farmers' Alliance and Industrial Union, to Thomas Good Jones, August 21, 1891, TGJ Administrative Files, box 3, file 2, ADAH.

36. "The Advertiser in Luck," *Montgomery Daily Advertiser*, June 3, 1890, 4.

37. "Most scurrilous" campaign quote from Hackney, *Populism to Progressivism*, 18; "Alliance in Politics," *Montgomery Daily Advertiser*, October 13, 1889, 3.

38. *Moulton Advertiser*, quoted in *Montgomery Daily Advertiser*, December 2, 1890, 4. On white supremacy, Black disenfranchisement, and plan to segregate the taxes, see Aucoin, *Thomas Goode Jones*, 46–47; Booker T. Washington to Theodore Roosevelt, October 2, 1901, cited in Louis R. Harlan, *Booker T. Washington: The Making of a Black Leader, 1856–1901* (New York: Oxford University Press, 1972), 308.

39. "Many Gleanings by the Gossiper," *Montgomery Daily Advertiser*, February 8, 1891, 4.

40. "The Governor's Speech," *Montgomery Daily Advertiser*, December 2, 1890, 1, 2. Also see Aucoin, *Thomas Goode Jones*, 29; Robert David Ward and William

Warren Rogers, "Punishment Seven Times More: The Convict Lease System in Alabama," *Alabama Heritage* 12 (Spring 1989): 22; Robert David Ward and William Warren Rogers, *Convicts, Coal, and the Banner Mine Tragedy* (Tuscaloosa: University of Alabama Press, 1987), 37.

41. See Aucoin, *Thomas Goode Jones*, 33–36.

42. Ibid.; Mancini, *One Dies, Get Another*, 109–110.

43. "The Penitentiary," *Montgomery Daily Advertiser*, April 10, 1890, 4; "Kolb's Demand," *Montgomery Daily Advertiser*, May 18, 1892, 4; "Let the People Know," *Montgomery Daily Advertiser*, November 22, 1894.

44. Rogers et al., *Alabama*, 309–312.

45. Leah R. Atkins, "Populism in Alabama: Reuben F. Kolb and the Appeals to Minority Groups," *Alabama Historical Quarterly* (Fall/Winter 1970): 167–80.

46. *Choctaw Advocate*, July 13, 1892, quoted in Atkins, "Populism in Alabama," 173.

47. *Montgomery Daily Advertiser*, June 29, 1892, June 11, 1892.

48. Rogers, *One-Gallused Rebellion*, 221–28. For a detailed historiographical debate over African American voting in the 1892 Alabama governor's election, see Aucoin, *Thomas Goode Jones*, 60–65.

49. Rogers, *One-Gallused Rebellion*, 271–92.

50. Ibid., 293–317; Rogers et al., *Alabama*, 320–42.

51. *Prattville (AL) Progress*, August 7, 1896, quoted in Rogers, *One-Gallused Rebellion*, 317.

52. Michael Perman, *Struggle for Mastery: Disfranchisement in the South, 1888–1908* (Chapel Hill: University of North Carolina Press, 2001) 173–94.

53. "A Consitutional Convention," *Montgomery Daily Advertiser*, October 20, 1900; "The New Constitution," *Birmingham Age-Herald*, April 21, 26, 1901.

54. C. Vann Woodward, *Origins of the New South, 1877–1913* (1951; repr., Baton Rouge: Louisiana State University Press, 1971), 338; T. Thomas Fortune, "The Voteless Citizen," *Voice of the Negro* 1, no. 9 (1904): 397–402, republished in Shawn Leigh Alexander, ed., *T. Thomas Fortune, The Afro-American Agitator: A Collection of Writings, 1880–1928* (Gainesville: University Press of Florida, 2008), 103–112.

55. Perman, *Struggle for Mastery*, 173; *Williams v. Mississippi* 170 U.S. 213 (1898).

56. Rogers et al., *Alabama*, 343–54; "Citizens of Alabama Declare for White Supremacy and Purity of Ballot: Putrid Sore of Negro Suffrage Is Severed from the Politic of the Commonwealth," *Montgomery Advertiser*, November 12, 1901, 1.

57. Penn, *Afro-American Press and Its Editors*, 286; Rogers, *One-Gallused Rebellion*, 255.

58. W. W. Screws, "Alabama Journalism," in *Memorial Record of Alabama: A Concise Account of the State's Political, Military, Professional, and Industrial Progress, Together with the Personal Memories of Many of Its People* (Madison, WI: Brant & Fuller, 1893), 158–235.

CHAPTER 6

Tillman's Rebellion, South Carolina

SID BEDINGFIELD

The bloodshed began early on Election Day in 1898, outside a polling place at the Phoenix crossroads in rural Greenwood County, South Carolina. A prominent white Republican, Thomas P. Tolbert, placed a wooden box on the porch of Watson and Lake's General Store and began taking affidavits from African Americans who had been denied the vote under the state's new suffrage laws. A white man named J. I. "Bose" Etheridge kicked over the box and ordered Tolbert to leave. When Tolbert refused, Etheridge and his friend Robert Cheatham began beating him with a wagon axle and a piece of board. A Black man, Joe Circuit, rushed to Tolbert's aid and the four men crashed through the splintered porch railing. During the melee, both Circuit and Cheatham pulled guns and fired, spraying bullets wildly across the storefront. One of those shots hit Etheridge in the forehead, killing him instantly.[1]

According to the *Greenwood Journal*, witnesses could not say whether Circuit or Cheatham fired the fatal shot that morning, but the newspaper believed the real culprit was obvious. "It seems that for some time the negroes of this section, under the leadership of white Republicans, have been trying to come above their natural sphere," the *Journal* declared. At least eight African Americans died in a spasm of racial violence that swept across Greenwood County in the two days that followed. The *Journal*'s initial report, which appeared in newspapers across the state, described the first mass killing in detail. Late in the afternoon, about "two or three hundred" white men held eight African Americans at gunpoint near Rehoboth Church, where the Tolbert family worshiped, the *Journal* reported. The crowd stayed "commendably quiet" for a while, but after "loud talk and profane language" erupted, a Black man was yanked up from his seat on a log "and about one hundred shots were poured into his body." When four other prisoners "made a break for liberty" through a nearby swamp, the "infuriated mob" turned on three Black men "who remained rooted to the log from fear." The gunmen "poured a volley of at least two hundred shots into their bodies before they could move from their seats," the newspaper reported.[2]

The violent rampage in Greenwood County culminated a decade-long campaign to restore white supremacy as the political, social, and economic law of the land in South Carolina. It was a particular vision of white rule championed by the state's dominant political figure, Benjamin Ryan Tillman. Although a prosperous landowner himself, Tillman claimed to be a radical reformer defending white yeoman farmers from rapacious merchants, bankers, and Democratic Party elites who ran the state. In reality, Tillman was not a radical nor even much of a reformer. He was, however, a talented communicator who crafted an emotional narrative that valorized poor white males and activated their deepest fears regarding Black equality. His political success was not the product of a populist uprising born in the fields of the state's struggling white farmers. It was, as his biographer Stephen Kantrowitz argues, an example of political elites manipulating images and ideas *about* those farmers, stoking their resentments and demonizing perceived enemies during a time of immense social and economic upheaval.[3]

The white editors of the state's Democratic Party press helped Tillman propagate his vision of the New South, yet their role in the rise of Jim Crow rule in South Carolina has received only passing attention. They are usually portrayed as colorful bit players in the drama, not as main characters whose actions shaped outcomes. Like any successful demagogue, Tillman developed a symbiotic relationship with the press; he injected drama and excitement into the state's political culture, and the newspapers ensured Tillman remained front and center in the public's imagination. The state's rural weeklies dubbed him the "Agricultural Moses" and legitimized his claim to leadership of the farmers' revolt. Tillman heaped scorn on the state's largest dailies, mocking their editors as corrupt members of elite "rings" that misled the public to protect their power and privilege. The editors returned the fire. Tillman and his followers were "ignorant red necks" whose "uncouth" and "uncivilized" behavior threatened to deter business investment, undermine white Democratic Party rule, and lead the state to ruin.[4]

In the urban North in the 1890s, the age of popular mass politics was slowly giving ground to the less-partisan and more-restrained Progressive era, but in rural and impoverished South Carolina—where the state capital had twelve thousand residents, sixteen telephones, and no paved roads—politics remained a source of diversion and entertainment. Tillman split the state's Democratic Party into warring factions of "reformers" and "conservatives," and his running battles with opponents, particularly the newspaper editors, made for good political theater. Yet in the end, those fights were merely theater; they focused on style, not substance. Tillman's foes at major dailies—the *News and Courier* in Charleston and the *State* newspaper in Columbia—had no serious disagreements with Tillman's primary goals. They too supported the move to enshrine white supremacy in the state's legal code. But they preferred a more genteel and paternalistic version of white rule, one that placed as much emphasis on class as race. They despised the thought of poor white farmers displacing the old planter-class aristocracy in the state's political hierarchy, and they feared Tillman's rough ways would alienate Northern investors and derail their vision of a modernizing New South.[5]

Tillman rode the farmers' revolt to near-absolute political power in South Carolina in the 1890s, and he used his position to codify a Jim Crow social and political order that remained firmly in place for more than six decades. He was elected governor twice (1890, 1892) and to the U.S. Senate (1894), where he served until his death in 1918. In 1895 he oversaw a state constitutional convention called for the purpose of "ensuring white supremacy" through the passage of restrictive suffrage laws.[6] To enforce the new order, Tillman encouraged lynching and mob violence in the Carolinas, including the 1898 massacres in Greenwood County and across the border in Wilmington, North Carolina. Yet over the following two decades, the senator from South Carolina became something of a respected elder statesman who carried his gospel of white supremacy across the nation—and where even he was surprised by the warm welcome he received from white audiences and the white press.[7]

Rapid changes in economics, transportation, and culture in the postwar South helped fuel Tillman's rise. But the press played a significant role too. This chapter contends that Tillman's supporters and opponents at the state's newspapers warrant more attention as serious political actors during his long and influential career. Serving as both supplicants and foils, the state's newspaper editors elevated Tillman at key moments in the drama, and they helped ensure that his brand of white supremacy played an outsized role in shaping the future of South Carolina and the New South at the dawn of the twentieth century.

Reconstruction and "Redemption" in South Carolina

After the Civil War, emancipation and Reconstruction transformed civic life in South Carolina. The biracial Republican Party prospered as the state's majority-Black population gained citizenship rights and took its place in local and state government. In 1868 Blacks comprised two-thirds of the delegates at a convention that rewrote the state's constitution and expanded voting rights for South Carolina males. Between 1868 and 1876, a legislature dominated by Black and white Republicans pursued reforms that aided the impoverished state. Lawmakers introduced public education, rebuilt transportation infrastructure, initiated criminal justice reforms, and formed the South Carolina Land Commission to help small farmers purchase land. "We were eight years in power," Black lawmaker Thomas E. Miller recalled during Tillman's 1895 constitutional convention. "We had reconstructed the State and placed it upon the road to prosperity."[8]

The Republican government in South Carolina experienced its share of corruption too, including an embarrassing bond scandal that cost the state thousands of dollars. White opponents seized on the issue to declare Black South Carolinians unfit for citizenship. A shadowy campaign coordinated by former Confederate generals had been challenging the legitimacy of the Reconstruction government since its inception. Democratic Party lawmakers accused Black and white Republicans of incompetence and theft, while the Ku Klux Klan and other paramilitary groups—including one led by a young Ben Tillman—terrorized Black communities and baited Black state militia troops into violent confrontations. They created chaos in South Carolina and blamed it on the biracial Republican administration.[9]

Republican and Democratic Party newspapers flourished during Reconstruction, and prominent Black editor/politicians emerged to compete in the battle to shape the contentious public debate. The best known of these was Robert Smalls, the intrepid Civil War hero who hijacked a Confederate ammunitions ship in 1862 and evaded a rebel blockade to deliver it to the Union Navy. In 1872 Smalls launched the Beaufort *Southern Standard* and used it to fight for African American rights and further his own political career. Smalls served five terms in the U.S. House of Representatives between 1874 and 1887, despite a Democratic campaign of harassment that included trumped-up charges of corruption and threats on his life. In Charleston, Rev. Richard Cain, head of the African Methodist Episcopal (AME) Church, launched a secular newspaper, the *South Carolina Leader*, and also built a political career. Cain was elected to the state senate, served as a delegate to the 1868 state constitutional convention, and in 1872 became the first Black South Carolinian to serve in the U.S. Congress.

The state's most influential white newspaper also emerged during Reconstruction. The *Charleston News and Courier* was owned and edited by a talented Englishman named Austin John Reeks. Born in London to a downwardly mobile family of aristocratic lineage, Reeks fled to Southampton in 1861 and joined the crew of a Confederate Navy ship. He adopted the nom de guerre Francis Warrington Dawson and eventually rose to the rank of captain, a title he carried proudly the rest of his life. After the war, Dawson settled in Charleston and worked briefly for Robert Barnwell Rhett Jr., the fire-breathing secessionist editor of the *Charleston Mercury*. In 1867 Dawson and a partner purchased the *Charleston News*; six years later they added the *Courier*, and across the 1870s Dawson built the *News and Courier* into a journalistic powerhouse. Based in Charleston, the newspaper was distributed statewide and read closely by the state's white and Black political class.[10]

Dawson created a serious breach in the Democratic Party in early 1876 when the *News and Courier* called on white voters to support the reelection of the Republican governor, Daniel Chamberlain. By that point, Chamberlain had abandoned his African American allies and urged white Republicans to unite with white Democrats in a new conservative coalition. Dawson supported this "Fusionist" strategy as a means of ending Reconstruction and bringing peace to South Carolina. But so-called Straightout Democrats rejected any alliance with the Republicans. They demanded white voters support a straight Democratic ticket headed by Wade Hampton, one of the former Confederate generals leading the guerilla campaign against the Reconstruction government. Angered by Dawson's support for the Fusionists, several Hampton supporters turned to Dawson's old boss, Robert Barnwell Rhett, to launch a competing newspaper in Charleston.[11]

Rhett's incendiary paper, the *Journal of Commerce*, was designed to build resentment among white voters and undermine Chamberlain and the Fusionists in advance of the November election. To achieve his goal, Rhett hired two young journalists who would later launch important newspapers in the state—Alfred B. Williams, an early editor and co-owner of the *Greenville Daily News* in the Appalachian foothills, and Narciso Gener Gonzales, founder of the *State* in the capital city of Columbia. In the summer of 1876, as the campaign for governor heated up, Williams and Gonzales filed a series of hyped reports about a labor dispute in the rice fields of the state's lowcountry region along the Atlantic coast. Angered by pay cuts and poor work conditions, Black workers had organized an ad hoc union to bargain collectively with the white planters. But according to *Journal of Commerce* reporters, the laborers had threatened to riot if they failed to get their way. In one dispatch, Gonzales accused the Black farmworkers of menacing white families in the area, but he said the "negroes, being ephemeral, fled precipitately" when confronted by white men. The paper also renewed the focus on armed African Americans in the state militia, claiming they were intimidating white farmers to stop them from voting. Rhett's editorials encouraged white Democrats to stand up to the Black militias.[12]

In the upcountry counties of Edgefield and Aiken, across the river from Augusta, Georgia, Tillman's Sweetwater Sabres and other white paramilitary clubs had been harassing Black state militia regiments for months. On the Fourth of July, 1876, a confrontation in the small, mostly African American enclave of Hamburg ended in a massacre, and it further engendered the sense of violent chaos that Rhett and the Straightout Democrats wanted in South Carolina. The clash began when two young white men from prominent local families claimed that a Black militia company marching on the main street in Hamburg had blocked their buggy. After a brief standoff, the two white men passed without incident, but both the militia leader and the white men filed legal complaints. On the day the case was scheduled to be heard, hundreds of armed white men dressed in bright red shirts descended on Hamburg, eager for a confrontation. Their leader, former Confederate general Matthew Butler, demanded state militia members apologize for the Fourth of July incident and surrender their guns to the Red Shirts. When the militia leader refused, the white gunmen went on a rampage. At least six African Americans died, four of them murdered in public as they surrendered to the Red Shirts.[13]

Two months later, Red Shirt gunmen joined white allies from Georgia in an attack on African Americans in the nearby town of Ellenton. The assault began after a white farm wife claimed that a Black laborer had sexually assaulted her. In two days of violence, the South Carolina Red Shirts and their Georgia compatriots killed as many as thirty African Americans, including women and children.[14]

Initially, Dawson's *News and Courier* denounced the violence as "wholly unjustifiable" and called the Red Shirts "barbarous in the extreme." But the Charleston editor was out of step with the narrative running in the *Journal of Commerce* and in county-seat weeklies across the state. They blamed the violence on the Black militia units and the Republican governor, and they hailed the Red Shirts as defenders of law and order and protectors of the white race. The *Edgefield Advertiser* would later celebrate the Hamburg massacre with a special edition printed in red ink. When angry Democrats organized a boycott of the *News and Courier*, Dawson switched sides. He dropped his support for the Fusionist ticket and embraced Hampton and the Straightout Democrats with the passion of a convert.[15]

Backed by a Red Shirt campaign of voter intimidation and fraud, Hampton and the Straightout Democrats claimed a narrow victory in November, but South Carolina's Electoral College votes eventually helped Republican Rutherford B. Hayes defeat Democrat Samuel Tilden in that year's contested presidential election. As part of his settlement with Tilden and the Democratic Party, Hayes agreed to remove the remaining federal troops from South Carolina, Florida, and Louisiana, essentially bringing Reconstruction to an end. Its job complete, Rhett's *Journal of Commerce* shut down shortly after Hampton's inauguration in March 1877.[16]

Without federal troops in South Carolina, Republican Party influence declined and Black citizens began a slow but steady migration out of the state, although they would remain a majority of the population until 1930. Black males were still eligible to vote, but Hampton's Democratic administration moved quickly to limit their influence. Under a gerrymandered redistricting plan, the state created one majority-Black district along its southern coast, which meant a Black South Carolinian would continue to win a congressional seat every two years, and a small number of African Americans would still serve in the state legislature, but they were politically isolated and exerted little influence.[17]

Throughout his life, Tillman proudly recalled his part in the violence and voter fraud that elected Hampton and "redeemed" South Carolina from "Negro rule" in the 1876 election. But the two men had little in common. Hampton was a courtly and aristocratic plantation owner who had been one of the nation's richest men before the Civil War. A paternalist at heart, he had peppered his 1876 campaign with promises of fair treatment for the state's African Americans. They could continue to vote, to hold public office, and to pursue economic gain in South Carolina as long as they posed no threat to white, Democratic Party leadership. To assuage Northern public opinion and the new Republican administration in Washington, Hampton denounced mob violence and embraced the rule of law. Like Dawson, he even criticized the violence and intimidation of the Red Shirts. Hampton's high-minded rhetoric galled Tillman. He knew that voter fraud and intimidation had won the election. "Poor ol' Wade," Tillman told friends. "He thinks 18,000 niggers really voted for him."[18]

Hampton and his conservative allies were wealthy landowners with close ties to the bankers and merchants of the state's largest towns, Charleston and Columbia. They never championed New South ideology in the way Atlanta editor Henry W. Grady would, but South Carolina's Redeemers did pursue New South economic policies. They strove to build more railroads, lure more industry, and see the state's towns grow into cities. To attract investment, they promised stable government, cheap and compliant labor, and an end to lynching and other acts of vigilantism. To aid railroad construction, the governor authorized convict leasing in South Carolina. Three years earlier the Republican legislature there had outlawed the practice, the only Southern state to declare a permanent ban on leasing. But Hampton and the Redeemer government overturned that decision; the governor said the penal system should be self-supporting and convict labor "could be made profitable." It was clear the policy was designed to utilize Black labor. Tillman's older brother, George, a state lawmaker at the time, said African Americans have "a constitutional propensity" to commit crimes and taxpayers should not be compelled "to support them in idleness."[19]

South Carolina's convict leasing was minimal compared with other Southern states, but the suffering was extreme. Between 1878 and 1880, 247 prisoners died under lease. In 1887 the Blackville and Newberry Railroad mistreated prisoners so badly that the state canceled the company's contract.[20] Even Hampton's closest allies in the press were squeamish about leasing. In 1883 the *Charleston News and Courier* denounced the "horribly filthy condition" at a Georgetown and Land Railroad camp where ten "broken down" prisoners, some of them near death, had to be returned to the state penitentiary before their lease had expired. Dawson's newspaper called the ailing men "ten more counts in the long indictment against" the leasing of prisoners. It was "impossible to secure proper treatment for convicts out of sight of those who are officially responsible for their well-being," the newspaper argued.[21]

Otherwise, Hampton's vision of the New South had unstinting support from the newspaper that mattered most in South Carolina. After the brief boycott during the 1876 election, Dawson's *News and Courier* emerged stronger and more influential than ever. In 1880 Dawson hired Narciso Gonzales, one of the two young journalists who had contributed to the short-lived *Journal of Commerce*, and sent him to Columbia to cover political news. An aggressive reporter and lively writer, Gonzales's daily "Columbia Column" became a must-read for the state's political elite. Over the simple, concluding byline of "N. G.," Gonzales delivered news, gossip, humor, and a heavy dose of political opinion from across the capital city. The son of a dashing Cuban expatriate who had married the daughter of a wealthy lowcountry family, Gonzales idolized Hampton and defended the conservative government vigorously. Dawson also hired James C. Hemphill, another son of the lowcountry aristocracy and Hampton devotee. Hemphill would eventually succeed Dawson as editor.

The *News and Courier* faced little competition in the daily newspaper market in South Carolina in the 1880s. Only a handful of dailies were published in the state, and none could match the reach of Dawson's paper. In 1880 Alfred Williams, Gonzales's former coworker on the *Journal of Commerce*, launched the *Greenville Daily News* to compete with the *Greenville Enterprise and Mountaineer* in the northwestern corner of the state. A Virginian who traced his ancestry to John Marshall, the first chief justice of the U.S. Supreme Court, Williams was another son of Southern aristocracy, but his up-country newspaper would eventually support Tillman's challenge to Hampton's leadership. In the state capital, Charles A. Calvo's *Columbia Daily Register* had been in business since 1875. Although Calvo would eventually support Tillman, his editorial voice was timid, and the *Register* frequently complained that readers in the capital city preferred the *News and Courier* rather than their hometown daily.[22]

During the 1880s even Tillman admitted that Dawson and the *News and Courier* bestrode the state "like a colossus."[23] The Charleston newspaper controlled the flow of information, shaped political debate, and had the power to make or break politicians. Most of the smaller newspapers followed its lead. As one Republican lamented at the time: "Liberty of the press in South Carolina! There is none. The metropolitan Thunderer, the *News and Courier*, issues its Jovian mandate, and the country newspapers croak, 'Me, too; Me, too, Me, too.'" In the early 1880s that was an accurate assessment of the public sphere in South Carolina. By the end of the decade, it would no longer be true.[24]

Tillman, Populism, and the Farmers' Revolt

South Carolina's agricultural economy was changing rapidly in the postwar years. Railroads were pushing deeper into the state, opening new lines of transportation and communication with Northern and international markets. Merchants were the greatest beneficiaries; they received more goods at cheaper wholesale prices and could generate larger profits. Hampton and other planters who owned large plots of land also prospered. But yeoman farmers trying to eke out a living on small plots in the state's up-country struggled to survive.

They frequently found themselves at the mercy of a new and powerful force in Southern agriculture: merchant capital.[25]

In the antebellum era, yeoman farmers in South Carolina could feed their families and survive on what they grew. Merchants played a limited role in their lives. But the ravages of the war had undermined that self-sufficiency, and encroaching industrialization and modernization transformed their relationship with the larger world. After the war, most small farmers had to borrow money to get a crop into the ground and to pay living expenses for the year. Under the crop-lien system that emerged, ambitious merchants provided that credit, but they charged a high interest rate. And they demanded cash payments, not corn, peas, or other foodstuffs as barter. To generate the necessary cash, small farmers had to devote more acres to cotton—the only reliable cash crop—and fewer to growing food for the family. If the cash generated by the cotton harvest failed to cover the loan payment, farmers could lose ownership of their land. They could be forced to pay rent as a sharecropper or, worse, to serve as a common laborer. By the 1880s yeoman farmers in South Carolina had abandoned subsistence farming and joined an unforgiving global market economy.[26]

The timing was terrible. The global demand for cotton that had made slavery so lucrative in the antebellum South no longer seemed insatiable. India, Egypt, and other sources of cotton now competed with the American South, and prices fell. Between 1875 and 1894, the cost of a pound of cotton declined by more than half, dropping from eleven cents to less than a nickel. Yeoman farmers fell into a vicious cycle. They devoted more acres to cotton each year to pay off their loans, which helped saturate the global market and push down prices, forcing them to plant even more cotton the following year. In the South Carolina up-country, angry farmers began searching for relief.[27]

Tillman loathed the mercantile class that he saw emerging in the South in the postwar years. Although a relatively wealthy landowner, he espoused a version of "producerism," a philosophy that values those who produce goods with their own labor. In Tillman's view, only white men who worked their own fields were worthy of political leadership. Bankers, merchants, and other city dwellers were parasites feasting on the hard work of virtuous white male farmers. The crop-lien system treated white farmers no better than Black ones, he argued, and it allowed the "money men" to benefit from the misery of those whose labor had built the state. The forgotten white farmers were being humiliated and degraded by the emerging economic and social order, and according to Tillman, Hampton and his government were to blame.[28]

Yet despite his "producerist" views, Tillman's primary criticism of Hampton was not economic—it was racial. Allowing African Americans to vote, even in a limited way, created an existential threat to white supremacy, Tillman argued, because it raised the possibility of biracial political coalitions. If Blacks could vote, white unity would always be in jeopardy. One faction of whites could join forces with Black voters to defeat another white faction. Under such an arrangement, Blacks could exert tremendous political power. In the years after Hampton's election, the editor of Tillman's local newspaper, the *Edgefield Advertiser*, stressed this point repeatedly. Hampton and the rich landowners who controlled the Democratic Party were sowing the seeds of their own destruction by allowing African Americans to vote, the *Advertiser* argued in 1878. Hampton's "sentimentality about the negro on paper and in speeches is an exceedingly different thing from a practical application of the negro at the ballot box," the editor wrote. "The one is pretty; the other is the *devil*." The *Advertiser* was particularly concerned about the possibility of class overtaking race as a primary concern among poor farmers in South Carolina. "Seeing themselves without any voice in the State they helped to save," poor white farmers could abandon the Democratic Party and create a biracial "working-man's party," the editor said.[29]

Tillman would confront just such a threat in 1882 when a populist-tinged agrarian rebellion emerged briefly in South Carolina. Hendrix McLane, a white farmer from Fairfield County, encouraged white and Black farmers to unite under the political banner of the Greenback-Labor Party. Modeled after Virginia's Readjuster Party, which had rallied a biracial coalition to dethrone that state's Democratic Party three years earlier, the Greenbackers denounced Hampton's government as part of the "money power." McLane demanded fair elections and accused Democrats of shouting "white supremacy" to distract poor voters from the state's economic problems. Hampton and the Redeemer Democrats "foster prejudice between the two races" so that they can "run state government for their own benefit and to the injury of both white and colored taxpayers of the state," McLane declared.[30]

Tillman agreed with parts of McLane's economic critique, but he detested the Greenbackers' plea for Black support. Tillman supported Hampton's candidate in the 1882 election, and with the help of the press, he and his Red Shirt allies moved aggressively to ensure populism's brand of biracial politics failed to take hold in the state. Dawson set the tone in the *News and Courier* by raising the specter of Reconstruction. He called the Greenbackers "the Negro Party" and accused McLane of secretly working with the Republicans to "Africanize the state" and bring federal troops back to South Carolina.[31] The state's *Anderson Intelligencer* agreed, calling the Greenbackers "really nothing more (and nothing less) than Radical Republicans."[32] Some Democratic papers suggested that a Greenback-Labor Party victory would encourage Black men to rape white women. Most editors focused on the threat Black voting posed to white unity. The *Keowee Courier* editor warned farmers that "Negro rule" would make "all other reform impossible." He said after white supremacy is "securely won we will fight all our other grievances." The *Edgefield Chronicle* agreed. "If we have family quarrels, for heaven's sake let us fight among ourselves and not go to our enemies for comfort," the newspaper declared.[33]

The rhetorical assault from the newspapers combined with Red Shirt intimidation to turn back the Greenback-Labor Party threat in 1882. But for Tillman, the editors of the *Keowee Courier* and *Edgefield Chronicle* had identified the larger problem. He understood the economic roots of McLane's popularity with the farmers, but Tillman was more interested in preserving white supremacy than facilitating much-needed agricultural reform. A decade later, he saw populist figures such as Georgia's Tom Watson and North Carolina's Leonidas L. Polk and Marion Butler unite Black and white farmers to challenge Democratic Party establishments in their states. Tillman was determined to prevent that from happening in South Carolina. Like the *Edgefield Chronicle*, he believed racial unity superseded class divisions. In the political world that Tillman envisioned, white Democrats should be able "to divide with safety"—that is, to debate economic policies without one class of whites turning to Black voters to win the political battle. "Divide with safety" became his mantra as he entered the political arena on behalf of the struggling farmers in South Carolina.

Tillman launched his bid to stir a farmers' revolt in 1885 with a fiery attack on the conservative administration in Columbia. State government had facilitated the farmers' "descent into hell," Tillman told members of the Agricultural Society and Grange at its annual meeting in Bennettsville. He surprised the otherwise low-key gathering—and thrilled many of the state's newspapers—with the ferocity of his attack. "The people have been hoodwinked by demagogues and lawyers in the pay of finance," Tillman declared. Lawmakers in Columbia wasted money on pet projects and refused to support the agricultural industry, and the "polluted atmosphere" in the statehouse ruined any chance at reform. He called on the state to fund an experimental farm and convert South Carolina College—the future University of South Carolina—into "a real agricultural institution."[34]

To broaden his political profile after the Bennettsville speech, Tillman reached out to Dawson and the *News and Courier*. He understood the newspaper's power to spread his ideas statewide and grant him political legitimacy. Dawson agreed to print several letters from Tillman that continued his assault on state government and its lack of effort on behalf of the small farmers. Dawson remained a firm supporter of Hampton and the lowcountry establishment that ran the Democratic Party, but the editor shared Tillman's concerns about the restive farmers in the upcountry. A political "earthquake" would be coming if the Democratic leadership did not act soon, Tillman warned the editor, but he added, "I would never under any circumstance have anything to do with pulling down our Democratic temple."[35] Tillman wanted to reshape the party from within, and Dawson agreed that some reform was necessary. The two formed an alliance in the mid-1880s: The *News and Courier* publicized Tillman's speeches and referred to him in the newspaper as a prominent representative of the upcountry farmers. In return, Tillman dialed back some of his rhetoric about the lowcountry "aristocracy," particularly his complaints about state funding for the Citadel, a military school beloved by Charleston high society.[36]

When the 1888 election arrived, however, Tillman had no qualms about turning on Dawson and the *News and Courier*. The British-born editor was famous in South Carolina, and he served as a perfect foil for Tillman's assault on the wealthy, out-of-touch elites. Tillman was not on the ballot in 1888; he was supporting an insurgent campaign challenging a candidate selected by the Democratic Party's establishment. The state was run by a small "ring" of rich planters, Tillman declared on the campaign trial, "and that ring is on Dawson's little finger." Tillman also resumed his attacks on the Citadel, dismissing the Charleston college as a "dude factory" and demanding the state build an agricultural college to benefit the small farmers. The *News and Courier* responded in kind to Tillman's attacks. Dawson's paper called Tillman and his allies "red necks" who "carry pistols in their pockets, expectorate on the floor, have no toothbrushes, and comb their hair with their fingers."[37]

Dawson's establishment candidate won the 1888 gubernatorial race, but it would be the editor's last campaign in South Carolina. The following year, he was shot and killed in a titillating incident worthy of a tabloid front page. The editor suspected that one of his Charleston neighbors was having an affair with the Dawson family's twenty-two-year-old Swiss governess. The facts of the matter remain murky. Many Charlestonians assumed Dawson had fallen in love with the young woman and was jealous of the neighbor's interest. But

Dawson's friends say he was angry that "a disreputable person" was taking advantage of a naïve young woman whom Dawson was obligated to protect. For whatever reason, Dawson confronted the neighbor at his home on the afternoon of March 12, 1889. The two came to blows, and the neighbor pulled a pistol and shot the editor in the chest.[38]

Dawson's death stunned Charleston society and sent a tsunami of gossip rippling through the state's political class. But the *News and Courier* suffered surprisingly little damage to its statewide influence. In the months before his sudden death, Dawson had designated Hemphill as his chosen successor, and the new editor quickly assumed Dawson's role as champion of the conservative establishment within the state's Democratic Party. Hemphill would play a significant role in the coming battle with Tillman's "reformers" for control of the party and the government in South Carolina.

Governor Tillman, the "Mississippi Plan," and the Rise of Jim Crow Rule

In 1888 a new logo began to appear on some newspaper mastheads in the state—"An Alliance Newspaper." Editors at the *Anderson Intelligencer*, the *Barnwell People*, the *Columbia Daily Register*, and others were declaring their support for the Farmers' Alliance, a reform movement and political interest group that began in Texas in 1887 and spread quickly across the South and the Midwest. The Alliance brought organization and structure to the farmers' revolt in South Carolina, and it would help Tillman build a political machine that would dominate the state for more than a decade. But Tillman was wary of the national Farmers' Alliance. He and the Alliance both claimed to support small farmers, but their political priorities were far apart.[39]

In a foreshadowing of Progressive reforms and New Deal programs of the following century, the Farmers' Alliance urged the federal government to step in to help the farmers. To address the crop-lien issue and to deal with fluctuating cotton prices, the Alliance called on Washington to create a "subtreasury"—a government program that would provide credit to small farmers at low interest and set up a series of cooperative warehouse exchanges. For Tillman, federal government intervention in South Carolina evoked memories of the Civil War and Reconstruction. The Alliance might be fighting on behalf of small farmers, but if that help came from Washington, Tillman wanted no part of it. Tillman also despised the populist politics associated with the farmers' organization. A Colored Farmers' Alliance had emerged in parallel with the white organization, and in Georgia, North Carolina, Alabama, and other states, white populists were reaching out to Black farmers to form biracial political coalitions. Tillman wanted to move in the opposite direction; he wanted to use the farmers' revolt to protect white supremacy and eliminate Blacks from politics. To borrow Kantrowitz's colorful description, Tillman and his allies in the press presided over a "shotgun wedding" of white supremacy and agricultural reform.[40]

In 1888 Tillman began a delicate courtship of the state's Alliance members. He used his access to the press to identify and denounce the farmers' enemies—the "ring" of planters, merchants, and editors who allegedly ran the state—and he encouraged the farmers to "organize, organize, organize." But he shied away from supporting the national Farmers' Alliance itself. Instead, Tillman created a new state organization, the Farmers' Association, which gradually subsumed the Alliance chapters in each county in South Carolina. Tillman's new group also launched a stealth campaign to take control of the state Democratic Party. In each of the state's thirty-five counties, Farmers' Association members began attending the normally sleepy Democratic Party Executive Committee meetings. Over time, the Tillman supporters worked their way onto the committee. By the beginning of 1890, Tillman's Farmers' Association controlled a majority of the votes on the state Democratic Party Executive Committee. In March 1890 he and his allies held a "farmers' convention" and demanded the Democratic Party nominate a farmers' candidate to run for governor. At the *News and Courier*, Hemphill and Gonzales cried foul. Hemphill accused Tillman of "unfair" and "underhanded tactics," and the volatile Gonzales denounced Tillman as a demagogue unworthy of elective office. But it was too late. Before the conservatives realized what had happened, Tillman's reformers had taken control of the Democratic Party in South Carolina. With the rhetorical aid of the "alliance newspapers" to counter the influence of the *News and Courier*, the "Agricultural Moses" from Edgefield was ready to assume the governorship of South Carolina.[41]

When the executive committee named Tillman the Democratic nominee for governor, some members of Hampton's conservative faction split from the regular party and announced plans to nominate their own candidate to run in the November general election. They selected A. C. Haskell, a former party chairman who had been a close confidant of Hampton's. Hemphill was skeptical. He preferred Haskell and the conservatives, but he feared that a split in the Democratic Party vote, combined with a large Black turnout, could return a revived Republican Party to power in the statehouse. Tillman had gained the nomination "unfairly," Hemphill wrote in the *News and Courier*. "But the risk of dividing and allowing our enemies to take power is too great. We must support the party nominee."[42]

Tillman and the reformers won the election easily that November, and his supporters in the white press expressed relief. The *Anderson Intelligencer* praised the state's African Americans for "refraining" from voting. "It was a white man's quarrel," the *Intelligencer* said, "and [Blacks] showed good sense in keeping out of it."[43] In Greenville, where Williams had turned the *Daily News* into a strong Tillman supporter, the editor said the "fight is over," but he acknowledged that the "hatreds that have been created rankle on both sides." Williams encouraged white South Carolinians to put aside their grievances and focus on the real enemy: "Let the white flag of truce be raised on both sides, let us get together as sons of the same good old state, members of the same party, brethren whose veins hold the blood of the same splendid race. With mutual toleration, forbearance and forgiveness we will soon again be a compact mass of white South Carolina Democrats, keeping our soil against all foes, moving together for our common welfare and advancement, undismayed and invincible."[44]

Gonzales had a different reaction to the 1890 election. Infuriated by Tillman's victory—and miffed that he had not been selected as Dawson's successor—Gonzales and his two brothers raised thirty thousand dollars and launched a new paper in Columbia. Those investors included Haskell, former governor John Richardson, and other prominent members of the conservative, anti-Tillman wing of the Democratic Party. On February 18, 1891, the Columbia *State* rolled off the press and began hammering the "tyrant" in the governor's office. Once in office, the new governor pushed few initiatives to help the beleaguered farmers. Instead, he focused on the perceived threat of Black voting rights, launching a campaign to bring the "Mississippi Plan" to South Carolina.[45]

In 1890 Mississippi Democrats rewrote the state's constitution to severely limit Black suffrage. They evaded the Fifteenth Amendment granting African Americans the right to vote primarily through the creation of a subjective literacy requirement. The "understanding clause" required voters to be able to read and interpret sections of the U.S. Constitution. County election supervisors, overwhelmingly white, were empowered to determine if voters did indeed understand what they were reading. The plan had been first proposed in 1875, when white Democratic militias in Mississippi overthrew elected governments across that state. In 1890 Mississippi lawmakers were clear about the new constitution's goal. It was passed "for no other purpose than to eliminate the nigger from politics," said state representative James K. Vardaman.[46] The U.S. Supreme Court upheld the constitutionality of the understanding clause in 1898, two years after it promulgated *Plessy v. Ferguson*'s "separate but equal" doctrine that legalized racial segregation in public facilities. Along with additional poll taxes and a handful of other qualifications, the understanding clause would be used to block African Americans from registering to vote well into the 1960s.[47]

In 1892 populism emerged as a serious political force across the South. White reform candidates backed by a biracial coalition of farmers and workers were running surprisingly strong campaigns for governor and other state offices across the region. In South Carolina, however, Tillman embraced an alternative vision of the South's political future. He made the "Mississippi Plan" a signature of his successful reelection campaign that year. In 1894, the year he ascended to the U.S. Senate, Tillman managed to get a referendum on the state ballot giving voters the power to pursue the Mississippi Plan through a state constitutional convention.[48]

The *Charleston News and Courier* and the Columbia *State* initially opposed the convention, arguing that Tillman would pack the meeting with reformers and shape the new constitution to gain "partisan advantage" over the conservative faction. But Hemphill and Gonzales supported white supremacy, as long as it was enforced discreetly. "We would not do anything to oppress the colored people, but we would do anything that is honest and lawful to preserve for the white people of the South Carolina the right and power to rule South Carolina," Hemphill's *News and Courier* declared. Even Tillman's supporters in some county-seat weeklies worried that an understanding clause designed to eliminate Blacks from politics could restrict illiterate white farmers from voting too. But the Tillman press eventually got in line behind the "divide with safety" argument. "Good government requires virtue, patriotism, and sacrifice," the *Barnwell People* declared. "The white race must unite, without concern for partisan advantage, to ensure that these people are never again allowed to serve as arbiters of our fate."[49]

When the referendum passed narrowly, the conservatives in the press and in the Democratic Party turned to the fight over delegate selection. Tillman reformers clearly outnumbered conservatives on the Democratic Party Executive Committee. But Hemphill and Gonzales argued that writing a new state constitution should be above partisan politics. To ensure the legitimacy of the new charter, they argued, the convention should include an equal number of delegates from the Democratic Party's warring factions of reformers and conservatives. The dispute raged during the months after the 1894 referendum.

In February 1895 the editor of the *News and Courier* stepped forward to play a direct role in trying to settle the issue. Representing the party's conservative wing, Hemphill helped negotiate a "peace agreement" with Tillman. The two sides agreed that conservatives and reformers would comprise an equal number of delegates at the convention and that no white men would be disenfranchised under the new literacy requirement. Hemphill praised the deal he helped negotiate and said the time had come for a "cessation of strife and bitterness and misunderstanding."[50] Two months later, however, Tillman reneged on the agreement. He claimed that U.S. Senator John Irby, a reformer and early stalwart of the farmers' revolt, would not support it. In the *News and Courier*, Hemphill accused Tillman and the reformers of "treachery" and "bad faith." Nonetheless, Tillman moved forward with plans to seat an overwhelming majority of reform delegates at the convention.[51]

In the summer of 1895, as the convention approached, a group of Black ministers organized a last-ditch effort to fight Tillman's plan to eliminate Blacks from state politics. They created a statewide ministerial union and gathered in Columbia to map out the resistance. A government that "forces a class of people to contribute to its existence without a voice," and where power is held by "a privileged class" and used as an "engine of oppression," is worse than government "among the savages, where all men are at least equal," the group said in a statement released to the press.[52] In response, a white editor in Barnwell said granting Blacks the vote had been "a grievous wrong done to the civilization of the white man as well as to the well-being of the colored race." Foreshadowing arguments Booker T. Washington would make in his "Atlanta Compromise" speech later that fall, the *Barnwell People* encouraged the ministerial union to "teach their people that they are yet in the infancy of their freedom" and that they should pursue "an era of peace best calculated by the up building of their race." If they did, the editor said, "they would secure the full recognition of all rights before the law suited to them and receive kindly help from the older white civilization."[53]

Black newspapers in the North struggled to discredit such views. The editor of the *Washington Bee*, W. Calvin Chase, claimed Tillman represented a new generation of "prejudiced and avaricious" whites who had resented Black progress since the end of slavery and were determined to crush African American aspirations permanently. "With but thirty years of opportunity, the negro in education is nearly the equal of the white man," and soon "negroes will hold large property and business interests and in almost every respect be the equals of whites in culture and ability of all kinds of work," Chase wrote. The public is "beginning to feel the rise of the darker races in intelligence, social elevation, and business enterprises," the editor said, and this is "exciting jealousies and apprehensions."[54]

Six Black delegates from the majority-Black lowcountry district participated in the state's constitutional convention, including former U.S. congressmen Robert Smalls and Thomas E. Miller, but they had little impact on its outcome. At one point, they appealed to Northern public opinion to bring pressure on the federal government to halt Tillman's actions in South Carolina. In a letter to Joseph Pulitzer's *New York World*, a leading Democratic newspaper, the Black delegates argued that Tillman's suffrage plan violated the Fourteenth and Fifteenth Amendments to the Constitution and, if approved by the convention, would "legalize fraud" in South Carolina.[55] The following day, the New York newspaper sided with Tillman. In an editorial that was published prominently in South Carolina newspapers, the *World* said that despite the existence of "intelligent and patriotic Negroes in South Carolina," there is a "vast black population that is not yet intelligent enough to be patriotic," and that group should not be allowed to dominate the state politically. The *World* called Tillman's suffrage plan "a necessity to redeem [South Carolina] from the danger of a dominance by ignorance denser than any that is known in a Northern state."[56]

In their letter to the *World*, the Black delegates noted Tillman's frankness in defending the plan to eliminate Black voting. He had avoided being "politic" or "hypocritical," they said. In fact, Tillman seemed to revel in what would now be called political incorrectness. In the lead-up to the convention, for example, the *Greenville Daily News* published a remarkable interview with Tillman conducted by Richard Carroll, a Black minister from Orangeburg who would later become a leading proponent of Booker T. Washington's accommodationist views in the state. The governor recalled his past acts as a Red Shirt militia leader and explained why he had fallen out with Hampton, the former governor he had helped elect:

TILLMAN: "Wade Hampton is a hypocrite . . ."
CARROLL: "I don't believe Gen. Hampton ever killed a Negro or wanted
them killed."
TILLMAN: "He accepted the results . . . and held office, which was the fruit
of intimidation, fraud, and much violence. I did my share of it in 1876."

CARROLL: "Don't you feel that you have done wrong?"

TILLMAN: "No. We had it to do. We could stand it no longer. I confess I have never killed a nigger, but I shot at one in Hamburg and tried to kill him, but I missed."

CARROLL: "I have never voted but once in my life, and do not plan to vote now, but I would like to have the privilege to do so."

TILLMAN: "Do you know anything about the Mississippi plan?"

CARROLL: "Not intelligently, sir."

TILLMAN: "Well, you must pay a heavy poll tax and be able to read the constitution of the United States and understand it. . . . Let me tell you something. We will carry [this convention] even if all the angels in hell . . . all the niggers and conservatives combine against us. We are compelled to carry it, and if the negroes give us any trouble they will receive no consideration in the constitution whatsoever."[57]

Phoenix, Wilmington, and Beyond

Tillman's reformers did carry the convention, and his version of the "Mississippi Plan" became law in South Carolina. Blacks lost any hope of voting in large numbers, and whites gained the ability to "divide with safety" in the state. The 1895 convention also laid the groundwork for legal segregation in public accommodations, a form of apartheid that the U.S. Supreme Court would approve in *Plessy v. Ferguson* the following year.

The massacre in Greenwood County three years later revealed the cruel inhumanity of Tillman's version of white supremacy. But the violence that began in the Phoenix community had economic motives as well. The Tolberts—the white Republicans who supported Black voting rights—were major landowners in the county and had been renting valuable plots to Black sharecroppers whose farms were prospering on the land. The massacre was in part a response to the growing autonomy of these Black farmers. White farmers wanted to remove them from the Tolbert land and return black farmers to white control.

This struggle over Black economic advancement adds another layer of meaning to the *Greenwood Journal*'s complaint about African Americans "trying to come above their natural sphere." Without access to decent plots of land, Black farmers would be forced to leave the county or to work as common laborers. Under the contract labor system that had emerged in South Carolina, a Black laborer who signed an agreement to work for a white contractor was little more than a slave. When laborers left abusive or exploitive contracts, they were tracked down by local and state law enforcement, just as so-called fugitive slaves had been before the war. Local newspapers contributed to the hunt by running "NOTICES" of missing laborers. One example ran in an Anderson County newspaper the week of the Phoenix massacre. Next to the editorials, under a large headline, a contractor warned the public that anyone "who hires or harbors Jerry Whitmire, a young negro man who is under contract to me for five more years . . . will be prosecuted under the full extent of the law." Such newspaper notices were common in the state's white press.[58]

Two days after the Phoenix massacre, white Democrats in North Carolina stormed the Black community in the port city of Wilmington, about fifty miles from South Carolina's northern border. They destroyed the office and printing press of the local Black newspaper, killed dozens of Black residents, and deposed the city's duly elected government. Tillman had gone to North Carolina two weeks earlier to support white Democratic candidates challenging the biracial "Fusionist" ticket that controlled state government. At a rally in Fayetteville, Tillman ridiculed the white Democrats in North Carolina for refusing to apply the "shotgun policy" the Red Shirt militias had used so effectively in South Carolina.[59]

After Democrats swept the elections in North Carolina, pro- and anti-Tillman newspapers in South Carolina hailed the state's "redemption." Many credited Tillman's effort to rally North Carolina Democrats, and they lauded his "shotgun policy" comment prominently in their coverage. In the North, however, Black activists forced white newspaper readers to confront the atrocities in the Carolinas. T. Thomas Fortune, editor of the *New York Age*, organized a mass meeting at that city's Cooper Union and denounced the brutality as "mobocracy by the whites" in North and South Carolina.[60] Coverage appeared on front pages of the *New York Times* and other major newspapers, increasing pressure on the Republican administration in Washington. Fearing the threat of a federal probe, Tillman and the South Carolina press began to deny that Tillman ever uttered the phrase "shotgun policy."[61] In the end, the McKinley administration deferred to the states, and no serious criminal investigations were conducted in Wilmington or Greenwood County.

It is tempting to think of paths not taken in the South at the turn of the twentieth century. Could the populist push for biracial democracy have created a fair and equal society? Or, perhaps more plausibly, could the paternalism of Wade Hampton and other conservative Democrats have prevented the strict codification of disenfranchisement and segregation, thus providing space for the Black civil rights reform movement to succeed much earlier than it did? The *Charleston News and Courier*'s response to the 1898 massacres suggests such an outcome was unlikely. Under Dawson and Hemphill, the newspaper had maintained its opposition to Tillman's harsh policies on suffrage and segregation. But in the aftermath of the massacres in Wilmington and Greenwood County, the *News and Courier* revealed the limits of white paternalism. The "bloodshed and lawlessness" in Greenwood County brought "shame and disgrace" on South Carolina "and exposed the weakness and hollowness of our beloved civilization," Hemphill declared. But the editor excused the violence in Wilmington. There is a difference, he said, between "riot and revolution." The massacre in North Carolina was understandable because African Americans, led by "wicked and designing white men," were "taking over our neighboring state." This "intolerable condition"—where Blacks had been "worked into the management of public schools and set up as judges of white people"—warranted a revolutionary response, Hemphill wrote, even one as bloody as the Wilmington Massacre. In South Carolina, however, "the negroes have been forced out of every official place" and the "supremacy of the white man is secure." Under those circumstances, Hemphill concluded, the "riot" in Greenwood County was indefensible, but the "revolution" in Wilmington was a heroic act of self-defense.[62]

The journalistic opposition to Tillmanism in South Carolina was cultural more than political. Tillman crafted his image as a rebel fighting the elites, a simple rural farmer battling the sophisticates from the towns and cities. His unrepentant claims about stealing votes, shooting "niggers," and "leading the lynch party" played well with white readers of the state's many rural, county-seat weeklies.[63] The editors at the state's largest dailies in Charleston and Columbia were offended by Tillman's political incorrectness. They preferred a more genteel and civilized approach, one that emphasized reconciliation with the North and investment in industry. They despised lawlessness, but their support for white supremacy was as unshakable as Tillman's. And in the end, they used their newspapers to help impose a Jim Crow regime that required six decades of Black struggle to overcome.

Notes

1. "Bloody Riot, Highly Respected White Man Murdered at Phoenix, S.C., Greenwood Journal, November 11," *Anderson Intelligencer*, November 16, 1898, 1. The author also reviewed contemporaneous news coverage of the Phoenix violence in the *Columbia Daily Register*, the *State* (Columbia), the *Charleston News and Courier*, and the *New York Times*. A member of the Tolbert family, R. R. Tolbert, published an account of the Phoenix violence immediately after the event. R. R.

Tolbert, "The Election Tragedy at Phoenix," *The Independent*, November 14, 1898. Among secondary sources, the most vivid account comes from Daniel Levinson Wilk, "The Phoenix Riot and Memories of Greenwood County," *Southern Cultures* (Winter 2002): 29–55. Also see H. Leon Prather Sr., "The Origins of the Phoenix Racial Massacre," in *Developing Dixie: Modernization in a Traditional Society*, ed. Winfred B. Moore Jr., Joseph F. Tripp and Lyon G. Tyler Jr., 37–49 (Westport, CT: Greenwood Press 1988).

2. "Bloody Riot, Highly Resepcted White Man Murdered at Phoenix, S.C., Greenwood Journal, November 11," *Anderson Intelligencer*, November 16, 1898, 1; *Barnwell People*, November 16, 1898, 1; and the *Edgefield Advertiser*, November 16, 1898, 4.

3. Stephen Kantrowitz, *Ben Tillman and the Reconstruction of White Supremacy* (Chapel Hill: University of North Carolina Press, 2000), 6–7. For more on Tillman, see Walter Edgar, *South Carolina: A History*: (Columbia: University of South Carolina Press, 1999); Francis Butler Simkins, *Pitchfork Ben Tillman, South Carolinian* (1944; repr., Baton Rouge: Louisiana State University Press, 1967).

4. See, for example, "Tillmanism," Columbia *State*, March 3, 1891, 1; "Tillman and Reform," *Charleston News and Courier*, October 18, 1890, 4. Also see Lewis Pinckney Jones, *Stormy Petrel: N. G. Gonzalez and His State* (Columbia: University of South Carolina Press), 114–18; Kantrowitz, *Ben Tillman*, 133–34.

5. Michael McGerr, *The Decline of Popular Politics: The American North, 1865–1928* (New York: Oxford University Press, 1986), 107–110; *Historical Statistics of the United States: Colonial Times to 1970*, part 1, U.S. Dept. of Commerce, 1975; Jones, *Stormy Petrel*, 71.

6. The phrase "ensuring white supremacy" was used frequently by Tillman and South Carolina newspapers. See, for example, "Constitutional Convention," *Columbia Daily Register*, March 23, 1895, 1.

7. For more on Tillman's national tours and the warm receptions he received as a paid speaker on the Lyceum and Chautauqua circuits, see Kantrowitz, *Ben Tillman*, 243–68.

8. Thomas Holt, *Black over White: Negro Political Leadership in South Carolina during Reconstruction* (Urbana: University of Illinois Press, 1977); Joel Williamson, *After Slavery: The Negro in South Carolina during Reconstruction, 1861–1877* (1965; repr., Chapel Hill: University of North Carolina Press, 1975); Eric Foner, *Reconstruction: America's Unfinished Revolution* (New York: Harper and Row, 1988); Eric Foner, *Forever Free: The Story of Emancipation and Reconstruction* (New York: Knopf, 2005), 220.

9. Foner, *Reconstruction*, 384–86; Hyman S. Rubin III, "Reconstruction," *South Carolina Encyclopedia*, http://www.scencyclopedia.org/sce/entries/reconstruction/.

10. E. Culpepper Clark, *Francis Warrington Dawson and the Politics of Restoration: South Carolina, 1874–1889* (Tuscaloosa: University of Alabama Press, 2002), 9–33; Jones, *Stormy Petrel*, 67.

11. William J. Cooper Jr., *The Conservative Regime: South Carolina* (1968; repr., Baltimore: Johns Hopkins University Press, 1991), 2–3; Kantrowitz, *Ben Tillman*, 65; Jones, *Stormy Petrel*, 47–48; Clark, *Francis Warrington Dawson*, 53–69; Clark, *Francis Warrington Dawson*, 58–69.

12. Brian Kelly, "Black Laborers, the Republican Party, and the Crisis of Reconstruction in Lowcountry South Carolina," *International Review of Social History* 51, no. 3 (2006): 375–414; Brian Kelly, "Class, Factionalism, and the Radical Retreat: Black Laborers and the Republican Party in South Carolina," in *After Slavery: Race, Labor, and Citizenship in the Reconstruction South*, ed. Bruce E. Baker and Brian Kelly, 199–220 (Gainesville: University Press of Florida, 2013); *Journal of Commerce*, June 12, 1876, 1.

13. Kantrowitz, *Ben Tillman*, 64–69; Edgar, *South Carolina*, 403.

14. Kantrowitz, *Ben Tillman*, 73–74.

15. "Hamburg," *Charleston News and Courier*, July 10, 11, 1876; see Kantrowitz, *Ben Tillman*, 71–72; *Edgefield Advertiser*, August 4, 1878; see Alfred B. Williams, *Hampton and His Red Shirts: South Carolina's Deliverance in 1876* (Confederate Reprint, 1915, 2015), 98; Clark, *Francis Warrington Dawson*, 64–67; Kantrowitz, *Ben Tillman*, 71–73.

16. Jones, *Stormy Petrel*, 49; Clark, *Francis Warrington Dawson*, 64–69.

17. I. A. Newby, *Black Carolinians: A History of Blacks in South Carolina from 1895 to 1968* (Columbia: University of South Carolina Press, 1973), 2.

18. Kantrowitz, *Ben Tillman*, 77–78; George Tindall Brown, *South Carolina Negroes, 1877–1900* (1952; Columbia: University of South Carolina, 2003), 39.

19. Matthew J. Mancini, *One Dies, Get Another: Convict Leasing in the American South, 1866–1928* (Columbia: University of South Carolina Press, 1996), 203; Tindall, *South Carolina Negroes*, 267.

20. Mancini, *One Dies, Get Another*, 198.

21. "Convict Leasing," *Augusta (GA) Chronicle*, June 12, 1883, 2. (The *Charleston News and Courier* is quoted at length in the Augusta newspaper.)

22. See, for example, "Around Town," *Columbia Daily Register*, March 15, 1888, 4.

23. "B. R. Tillman," *Charleston News and Courier*, August 29, 1888, 4.

24. Clark, *Francis Warrington Dawson*, 11.

25. Steven Hahn, *The Roots of Southern Populism: Yeoman Farmers and the Transformation of the Georgia Upcountry, 1850–1890* (New York: Oxford University Press, 2006), 170–203; Kantrowitz, *Ben Tillman*, 80–99; Edgar, *South Carolina*, 430–33.

26. Hahn, *Roots of Southern Populism*, 170–76; Robert C. McMath, *Populist Vanguard: A History of the Southern Farmers' Alliance* (Chapel Hill: University of North Carolina Press, 1975), 17–20.

27. Hahn, *Roots of Southern Populism*, 186.

28. See Shelton Stromquist, "The Crisis of 1894 and the Legacies of Produce-

rism," in *The Pullman Strike and the Crisis of the 1890s: Essays on Labor and Politics*, ed. Richard Schneirov, Shelton Stromquist, and Nick Salvatore, 179–203 (Urbana, University of Illinois, 1999); Kantrowitiz, *Ben Tillman*, 4–5.

29. *Edgefield Advertiser*, July 18, 1878.

30. Kantrowitz, *Ben Tillman*, 99–105; For more on the Greenback-Labor Party in the South, see Matthew Hild, *Greenbackers, Knights of Labor, and Populists: Farmer-Labor Insurgency in the Late Nineteenth-Century South* (Athens: University of Georgia Press, 2007).

31. *Charleston News and Courier*, September October 10, 1882.

32. Greenbackers," *Anderson Intelligencer*, November 23, 1892.

33. *Keowee Courier*, July 27, 1882, 1; *Edgefield Chronicle*, October 16, 1882, as quoted in Kantrowitz, *Ben Tillman*, 101–102.

34. Grange Speech, Bennettsville, Ben Tillman Papers, Clemson University Library; Cooper, *Conservative Regime*, 144–45.

35. Kantrowitz, *Ben Tillman*, 124–25.

36. Clark, *Francis Warrington Dawson*, 176, Jones, *Stormy Petrel*, 116–20.

37. Jones, *Stormy Petrel*, 66–75; Clark, *Francis Warrington Dawson*, 168–81.

38. Clark, *Francis Warrington Dawson*, 206–220.

39. See, for example, 1888 editions of the *Anderson Intelligencer, Barnwell People*, and *Columbia Daily Register*. For more on the Farmers' Alliance and the Colored Farmers' Alliance, see McMath, *Populist Vanguard*; Omar H. Ali, *In the Lion's Mouth: Black Populism in the New South, 1886–1900* (Jackson: University of Mississippi Press, 2010).

40. McMath, *Populist Vanguard*, 62; Kantrowitz, *Ben Tillman*, 80–119.

41. "Tillman Letter," *Charleston News and Courier*, January 18, 1886; "B. R. Tillman," *Charleston News and Courier*, October 24, 1890.

42. "New Governor," *Charleston News and Courier*, November 1, 1890, 1.

43. Editorial, *Anderson Intelligencer*, November 13, 1890, 4.

44. "From Greenville News," *Anderson Intelligencer*, November 13, 1890, 1.

45. Jones, *Stormy Petrel*, 189; Edgar, *South Carolina*, 440–45.

46. Neil R. McMillen, *Dark Journey: Black Mississippians in the Age of Jim Crow* (Urbana: University of Illinois Press, 1990), 41–42.

47. Michael Perman, *Struggle for Mastery: Disfranchisement in the South, 1888–1908* (Chapel Hill: University of North Carolina Press, 2001), 70–90; Dorothy Overstreet Pratt, *Sowing the Wind: The Mississippi Constitutional Convention of 1890* (Jackson: University of Mississippi Press, 2018); *Williams v. Mississippi* 170 U.S. 213 (1898); *Plessy v. Ferguson* 163 U.S. 537.

48. For more on populism, see Steven Hahn, *The Roots of Southern Populism: Yeoman Farmers and the Transformation of the Georgia Upcountry, 1850–1890*, updated ed. (New York: Oxford University Press, 2006); Ali, *In the Lion's Mouth*; William Warren Rogers Sr., *The One-Gallused Rebellion: Agrarianism in Alabama, 1865–1896*

(1970; repr., Tuscaloosa: University of Alabama Press, 2001); Barton C. Shaw, *The Wool-Hat Boys: Georgia's Populist Party* (Baton Rouge: Louisiana State University Press, 1984); C. Vann Woodward, *Tom Watson, Agrarian Rebel* (1938, 1955; repr., Eastford, CT: Martino, 2014); C. Vann Woodward, "The Populist Heritage and the Intellectual," in *The Burden of Southern History* (Baton Rouge: Louisiana State University Press, 1993), 141–66.

49. "The Convention," *Charleston News and Courier*, October 15, 1894; Columbia *State*, October 12, 1895; "Tillman Interview," *Charleston News and Courier*, February 22, 1895; "The Convention," *Columbia Daily Register*, "The Only Issue," *Charleston News and Courier*, February 25, 1895; See, for example, *Barnwell People*, October 11, 1895; 1; *Barnwell People*, October 11, 1894.

50. *Charleston News and Courier*, February 22, 1895, 1.

51. "Peace Agreement," *Charleston News and Courier*, April. 13, 1895, 2. Also see Perman, *Struggle for Masstery*, 99–101.

52. Ministerial Union statement as reported in "Appeals to Uncle Sam. The Negroes Adopt an Address to the People," *Barnwell People*, July 18, 1895, 1.

53. Editorial, *Barnwell People*, June 13, 1895, 4.

54. "The Situation in South Carolina," *Washington Bee*, September 15, 1895, 4.

55. Letter from Negroes in New York World," *Charleston News and Courier*, October 2, 1895. 6.

56. "A Question of Civilization. The World Does Not Believe in Negro Rule Which Means Ruin and Destruction—Editorial in the New York World," *Charleston News and Courier*, October 3, 1895, 4.

57. Carroll's interview with Tillman appeared in in *Barnwell People*, June 13, 1895, under a "Greenville News" byline.

58. "Phoenix Riot," *Greenwood Journal*, November 13, 1898; "Notice," *Anderson Intelligencer*, November 16, 1898. For more on peonage and contract labor in the South, see Pete Daniel, *The Shadow of Slavery: Peonage in the South* (Urbana: University of Illinois Press, 1971).

59. Prather, "Origins of the Phoenix Racial Massacre," 37–49.

60. "To Suppress Race Wars," *New York Times*, November 18, 1898, 1.

61. For example, see "Tillman & Wilmington," *Barnwell People*, November 13, 1898; "Wilmington," *Anderson Intelligencer*, November 13, 1898; "Washington and Wilmington," *Columbia Daily Register*, November 12, 1898.

62. "Riot and Revolution," *Charleston News and Courier*, November 12, 1898.

63. Tillman made this claim in reference to sexual assault of white women in 1892; the pledge drew harsh criticism nationally. *Edgefield Advertiser*, June 16, 1892; see, Kantrowitz, *Ben Tillman*, 168.

Henry W. Grady, managing editor of the *Atlanta Constitution* across the 1880s and most prominent spokesperson for the New South. (Library of Congress)

T. Thomas Fortune, editor of the *New York Age*, a leading Black newspaper in the late nineteenth century, and founder of the Afro-American League. (New York Public Library Digital Collections, Schomburg Center)

Ida B. Wells-Barnett, editor of the Memphis *Free Speech and Headlight* and a fearless investigator of lynching in the New South; a founder of the National Association for the Advancement of Colored People. (Courtesy of the National Portrait Gallery, Smithsonian Institution, Washington, D.C.)

W.E.B. Du Bois, leader of the Niagara Movement; editor of *The Crisis*, the NAACP magazine; and a founder of the NAACP. Also a sociologist, historian, author, and civil rights activist. (Library of Congress)

Jesse Max Barber, editor of the *Voice of the Negro*, an ambitious periodical that challenged the accommodationist strategy of Booker T. Washington. Barber was forced to flee Atlanta after questioning the veracity of white press coverage of the city's 1906 riots. (Library of Congress)

Mary Church Terrell, a journalist and essayist who published widely in the Black press. Terrell challenged anti-Black propaganda spread by Thomas Dixon, Charles Carroll, and other white Southern writers. In 1896 she cofounded the National Association of Colored Women. (Library of Congress)

Booker T. Washington, principal of Alabama's Tuskegee Institute. His "Atlanta Compromise" speech at the 1895 Cotton States Exposition called for Black accommodation with the white supremacist ideology of the New South. (Library of Congress)

John Mitchell Jr., editor of the *Richmond Planet* and a ferocious opponent of lynching and the new segregation and Black suffrage laws in the New South. (From *History of the American Negro and His Institutions*, vol. 5, ed. Arthur Bunyan Caldwell.)

Ethelbert Barksdale, editor of the Jackson (MS) *Clarion* and an architect of the "Mississippi Plan," the Democratic Party's campaign to overthrow Reconstruction through militia violence and voter fraud. (Mississippi Department of Archives and History, Hinds County, Jackson, Mississippi)

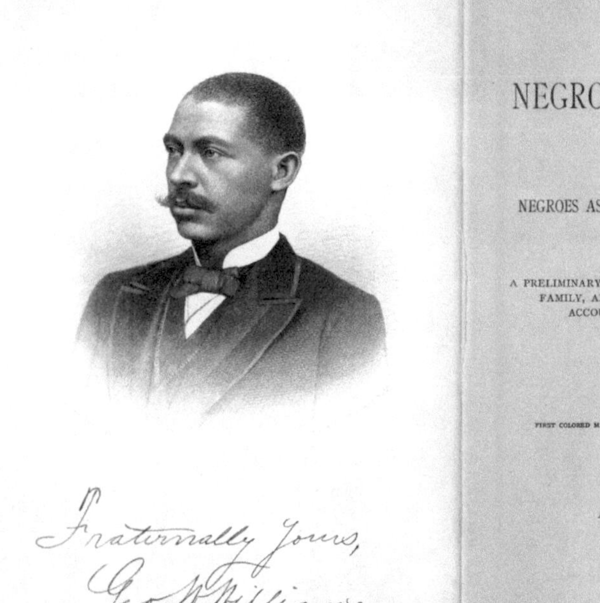

In 1882 historian George Washington Williams sought to counter white supremacist narratives of Black inferiority by publishing *History of the Negro Race in America*, a two-volume study that depicted the achievements of Black Americans. (David M. Rubenstein Rare Book and Manuscript Library, Duke University)

W. Calvin Chase, editor of the *Washington Bee*, a central cog in the Black public sphere that emerged in the 1880s to fight segregation and the suppression of Black voting in the Jim Crow South and to demand Black equality in the North. (New York Public Library Digital Collections, Schomburg Center)

William Wallace Screws, editor of the *Montgomery Daily Advertiser*, the leading Democratic Party organ in Alabama; Screws led the assault on Reconstruction and later aligned with the state's "Big Mule" industrialists to turn back a populist reform effort in the 1890s. (Alabama Department of Archives and History)

Francis Warrington Dawson, editor of the *Charleston News and Courier*. Born in England, Dawson boarded a Confederate ship in Portsmouth in 1862 and joined the Southern cause. After the war, he used his influential newspaper to shape Democratic Party politics in South Carolina. (David M. Rubenstein Rare Book and Manuscript Library, Duke University)

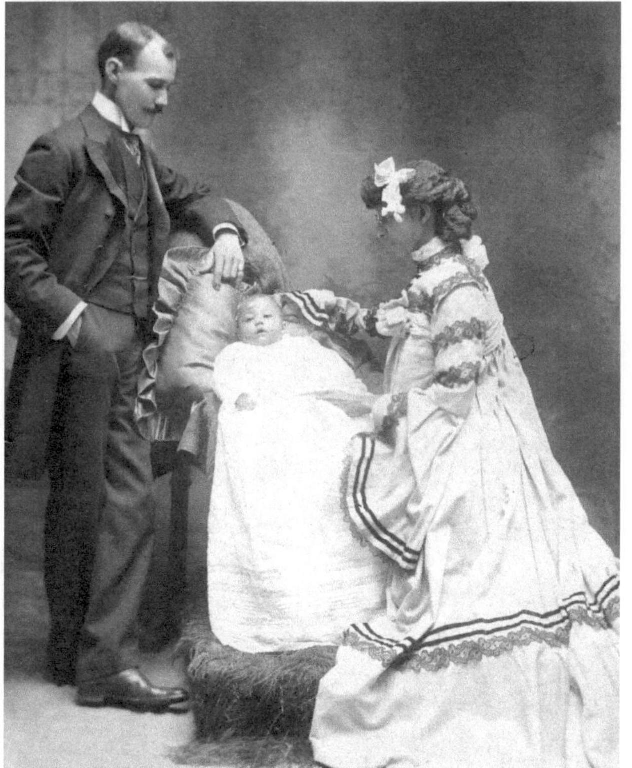

Alexander L. Manly, editor of the *Wilmington (NC) Daily Record*, with wife, Caroline Sadgwar Manly, and their infant son, Milo. Manly was forced to flee Wilmington during the massacre and coup in 1898. (East Carolina University Digital Collections).

Josephus Daniels, publisher and editor of the Raleigh *News and Observer*. Industrialist Julian S. Carr purchased the paper for Daniels, who used it to spearhead the Democratic Party's violent white supremacy campaign against the biracial Fusionist Party in 1898. (Library of Congress)

Organized white supremacists destroyed the *Daily Record* offices in Wilmington, believed to be the only daily Black newspaper of its era, during the Wilmington Massacre in North Carolina in 1898. (North Carolina Archives and History)

Arthur St. Clair Colyar, a lawyer, industrialist, and newspaper publisher, who used his newspapers and legal skills to support the white supremacist policies of the Democratic Party and to defend the use of convict labor in Tennessee. (Tennessee State Library and Archives)

Henry M. Flagler, industrialist and Standard Oil tycoon who purchased controlling interests in the Jacksonville *Times-Union* and other newspapers to shape press coverage of his railroad projects and to challenge federal investigations into his company's brutal treatment of peon labor. (State Library and Archives of Florida)

Workers on Henry M. Flagler's Key West Extension to the Florida East Coast Railway, filling in sand on Upper Matecumbe Key. (Keys History and Discovery Center, Jerry Wilkinson Collection, Islamorada, Florida)

A map of Henry Flagler's Florida East Coast Railway. The U.S. Justice Department charged Flagler's railroad company with peonage for its labor practices in building the fabled "Overseas Railroad." (FECR Annual Report 1917, State Library of Florida)

CHAPTER 7

Death of Democracy, North Carolina

KRISTIN L. GUSTAFSON

In March 1898, at the Chatawka Hotel in New Bern, North Carolina, Josephus Daniels, co-owner of the Raleigh *News and Observer*, met with two Democratic Party operatives to craft a statewide strategy to regain political control of North Carolina.[1] Several years earlier, finding common ground in shared economic interests, a biracial Fusionist coalition of Republicans and Populists had gained control of the governorship and the state general assembly and then redrew electoral districts, used patronage practices, and restructured local charters. And so it would be that in that hotel room, Furnifold Simmons, a longtime political strategist and then–Democratic Party campaign chairman; Charles Aycock, a prominent attorney and political operative; and Daniels took it upon themselves to direct the dismantlement and ruin of the Fusionist government. They would work closely with other white leaders in North Carolina, including businessmen and members of the younger wing of the Democratic Party. Democrats set their sights on several cities in particular, including Wilmington, the largest city in the state and majority Black, where the party's strategems of racial terror, voter fraud, and disinformation campaigns would be set in motion. Simmons devised a threefold Democratic campaign strategy with roles for men who could write, speak, and ride. The goal was to achieve electoral victory, as LeRae Umfleet writes, "through the unification of newspapers, traveling campaign speakers, and violent bands of men behind a singular argument—white supremacy."[2] These goals were ultimately realized in the destruction of the only statewide Black newspaper by arson; expulsion of its publisher, Alexander Manly, and other Black and white leaders from Wilmington; violent voter suppression; murder; and the installment of un-elected political leaders to rule Wilmington.

Four years earlier, in July 1894, Josephus Daniels and Julian Shakespeare Carr had purchased the bankrupt *News and Observer*; this was the second time in a decade Carr had loaned a portion of his tobacco manufacturing wealth to help Daniels purchase a Raleigh newspaper. A leading industrialist in the New South, Carr helped Daniels rise in status as co-owner of what biographer Lee A. Craig described as North Carolina's "best-known newspaper" and transform it into an immediate and enduring instrument of political and economic power.[3] The *News and Observer* would become, as Timothy B. Tyson put it, "a pivotal instrument of the white supremacy campaign."[4] Daniels used ideas and rhetoric from the *Democratic Party Hand Book* to persuade readers that "Negro rule" was a crisis to be resolved through white control and Black disenfranchisement.[5] The broad strategy was to sow division between the Republicans and Populists using race as a wedge and portraying North Carolina as in need of "redemption."[6] The *News and Observer* was used succesfully to inflame anti-Black prejudice by characterizing the Republican Party as taken over by Blacks and riddled with scandal, incompetence, and abuse, and by claiming, repeatedly and falsely, that Black men were sexually assaulting or threatening white women across the state. White supremacist propaganda under the thin guise of journalism was not limited to the eastern part of the state. Josephus Daniels influenced other white Democratic papers in North Carolina to foment racial terror; spread disinformation; publish anti-Black cartoons, public speeches, and special issues; announce secret political meetings; and provide free subscriptions to targeted voters as part of the Democratic Party's campaign in the election of 1898.

Political opponents, rival newspapers, and Black and white leaders—including the influential Black editor of the Wilmington *Daily Record*, Alexander Manly—countered the Democratic effort to strip power from the Fusionist movement. Manly, the acknowledged grandson of a former white governor in a city with a strong Black middle class, refuted one of white supremacy's central claims through his embodiment of miscegenation and through his stirring August 1898 editorial. In that editorial, he challenged the Democrats' politically motivated effort to rally around notions of white purity and drew attention to the hypocricy embedded in its arguments and its grotesque stereotypes. He argued that many rape accusations against Black men were built on lies that ignored clandestine liasons that emerged from a white woman's infatuation or love for a Black man. Manly said white men's rape of or intimacy with Black women should be held to the same standard. His editorial specifically criticized a speech by Rebecca Latimer Felton a year earlier and republished in August that advocated lynching a thousand Black men if they allegedly engaged sexually with white women. Historian Glenda Gilmore notes that Manly's "best-aimed blow was the suggestion that some white women freely chose black men as lovers, which shook the new construction of whiteness."[7] Manly skillfully built upon Felton's own patriarchial argument that white farmers were too soft on Black men's alleged rape of white women; in his editorial, Manly in turn chided poor white men for failing to guard "their women more closely" to protect them from "the human fiend, be he white or black."[8]

Democrats seized upon Manly's editorial swifly and reacted strategically. They held off on destroying the press and attacking Manly until after the election. Instead, white newspapers—including the *Wilmington Morning Star*, the *New Bern Journal*, the *News and Observer*, and the *Wilmington Messenger*—republished selected excerpts from it, some repeatedly and some as a preface to "other black 'outrages' against white women." They argued that Manly defamed poor white women and accused him of meeting clandestinely with wives of white men. Felton argued that Manly should fear being lynched as a result of his words.[9]

In November 1898 the strategic use of Manly's editorial and the deliberate three-prong strategy worked together to help the Democrats succeed in their manifold efforts. They won control of the state legislature through fraud and violence at the ballot box; defeated every Black candidate for statewide office; destroyed the state's most powerful Black newspaper; murdered anywhere from eleven to sixty Black citizens of Wilmington; exiled Black residents from this majority-Black city, where they had achieved notable political, civic, and economic success; forced Black and white Wilmington officials to resign and replaced them with handpicked white Democrats; occupied Wilmington to protect and maintain the newly installed government; persuaded state and national leaders not to intervene; spread a postelection news narrative that misdirected readers about the true cause of the events; and soon oversaw an amendment to the state constitution that effectively disenfranchised Black men in the state. In 1898 powerful white newspapers, following the lead of the Raleigh *News and Observer*, effectively destroyed a biracial democracy, supplanting it with a white supremacist political economy and social order that would stand in North Carolina for generations to come.

Newspapermen

Four years older than Manly, Josephus Daniels saw the newspaper business as a path to power unreachable in other ways. Daniels's father, a naval worker, died in 1865, when Josephus was two, and left his mother nearly destitute with three children to support. Within a year, she became the city of Wilson's postmistress, a Republican patronage appointment that she received despite being a Democrat. Republican leadership ousted her from the position in 1883 in response to her son's anti-Republican, anti-Black, and pro-Prohibition editorializing.[10]

Manly also found his way to the newspaper business. Born in 1866 two miles outside Raleigh, Manly's mixed-race father was a former slave who worked as a farmer and railroad fireman, and his mother was a mixed-race housekeeper. Manly's paternal grandfather, the former state governor Charles Manly, released from slavery his offspring birthed by a woman he had enslaved.[11] Manly moved to Wilmington to start a painting business after learning the trade at Hampton Normal and Agricultural Institute in Virgina. In Wilmington he became a political leader, taught Sunday school, and served as register of deeds before obtaining a Jonah Hoe printing press.[12]

The post office, located at the front of the Daniels' family home, served as a gathering spot and political hub for the town's leading residents. His biographer noted that Daniels, while sorting mail as a boy, observed the "dress, habits, demeanor, and transactions" of Wilson's professional men; learned the city's hierarchy; and noted "who had money to lend and who needed to borrow, who had cotton futures to buy or sell, and who had business or political connections beyond Wilson." Daniels saw how the men's interests "intersected on the pages of the local newspaper," and he often read newspapers from Raleigh—the capital, fifty miles west—before subscribers picked up their copies. It was through this experience that Daniels learned the critical differences between the two wings of the Democratic Party in North Carolina—the so-called unreconstructed or Bourbon wing, comprised of a planter aristocracy that profited from farmland and cheap labor, and the New South wing, comprised of progressives committed to industrial growth and Northern investment. Daniels felt "equal parts respect and animosity" for the first wing but clearly identified with the Democratic Party's younger progressive wing adhering to New South ideology.[13]

Without wealth, Daniels learned to leverage what he had to move up in the world. He began amassing experience in the newspaper business early and swiftly. He began working at a Wilson newspaper at age ten, and at eighteen he used his mother's house as leverage to finance his purchase of the weekly *Wilson Advance*. Daniels kept borrowing as his access to bank credit increased, and by age twenty-one he owned or held partial interest in three newspapers. Josephus Daniels, at age twenty-two, was elected president of the North Carolina Press Association. At age twenty-three, in 1885, and with no more than a thousand dollars' net worth, Daniels persuaded Julian Shakespeare Carr to help him purchase a newspaper in the state's capital in order to make it into a New South newspaper that competed with another Bourbon-friendly Raleigh newspaper. Carr agreed; he told Daniels to pay only if the venture proved financially successful and only the stock value without interest. Daniels's biographer argues that second to President Woodrow Wilson, Carr played the largest role in Daniels's life. Through the *State Chronicle*, he began to challenge his main Raleigh competitor, the daily *News and Observer*, and its owner, Samuel Ashe, a spokesman for the Democratic Party's older, conservative Bourbon faction. To make a profit, Daniels used his political contacts to become the state printer—a lucrative contract that gave his newspaper a financial advantage in addition to regular business operations.[14]

Although Daniels showed political ambitions early—serving as the state solicitor in eastern North Carolina before he was twenty—it soon became apparent when delivering press association speeches that his soft and breaking voice posed a challenge on the political stage. Daniels chose law school instead, a route that customarily helped advance the careers of ambitious young men who did not have land, railroad, or manufacturing ties, and was admitted to the bar in 1885. He held progressive Democrat political views on Prohibition, agricultural reform, public education, industrialization, the silver standard, railroad regulation, trusts, and the removal of racial conflict from politics. In 1888, when he married Addie Worth Bagley, a daughter of one of Raleigh's prominent families and granddaughter of a former governor, his social standing elevated. Daniels joined newspaper ownership and politics when he purchased the *North Carolinian* to help elect Grover Cleveland as president and Elias Carr as North Carolina governor in 1892. That decision propelled Daniels, Furnifold Simmons, and Charles Aycock to the top of the state's Democratic Party, displacing the Bourbons.[15] Cleveland then appointed Daniels to head the Department of the Interior, one of the most important of eight cabinet positions, and soon Daniels lead the Appointment Division, which functioned as the federal government's human resources office.

Daniels kept tabs on Raleigh and North Carolina throughout his federal service in D.C. between 1893 and 1895; he returned to the state in 1894 to purchase the *News and Observer* and respond to a political election when Fusionists defeated a Democratic Party riven by factions.[16] It was Carr, once again, who helped Daniels financially. They became co-owners before Daniels repaid Carr; Daniels would continue to pay off investors for decades to eventually take sole control. From the beginning, Daniels quickly modernized the newspaper operation, separated it financially from political patronage, and built its news value to attract subscriptions and advertisers. These financial and structural changes were designed to change an industry practice: instead of going to politicians for printing contacts or subsidies, something he had done for fifteen years, Daniels wanted politicians to come to him. This aligned with Daniels's political aspirations. By 1896 he represented North Carolina in the national Democratic Party and succeeded in getting the party to adopt the silver standard and to nominate William Jennings Bryan for president—only to watch as both lost on the national stage to the gold standard and Republican William McKinley. Closer to home, the Fusion Party in North Carolina continued its winning streak from two years earlier as Daniel Russell won the governorship in a landslide and Democrats lost seats in the state house.[17] As owner of the state's most influential newspaper and a North Carolinian with substantial political experience, Daniels was well situated to help change the state's trajectory. In 1898 he orchestrated Simmons's appointment to chair the North Carolina Democratic Party and immersed himself in the party's effort to reclaim political power.

Around the same year of the *News and Observer* purchase, 1895, Manly and his brothers purchased a used printing press from the *Wilmington Messenger*'s editor, Thomas Clawson, and began publishing the Wilmington *Daily Record*, which served "as a voice for the city's progressive African American community as he sought universal improvement of blacks throughout the city."[18] Like Daniels, Manly showed political ambition. Manly advocated for racial justice by arguing for better public services and against voting barriers. While he could pass as white, Manly proudly identified as a Black man with white blood, writes David Zucchino, and the editor "considered himself a spokesman for ambitious black men and sought a platform for his progressive ideals."[19] Fueled in part by growing advertising from white businesses, Manly's newspaper transitioned from a weekly to a daily in 1897, becoming the only Black daily in the United States at the time and one of very few in the South.[20]

The Fusionist Threat to the Democratic Party's Footing in North Carolina

As Populists peeled off poor white farmers from the Democratic Party and Republicans increased their number of Black voters, Fusionists became a formidable foe for Tar Heel Democrats during the 1890s. The Populist Party had emerged in 1892 out of the Farmers' Alliance, which began in the late 1880s. The Populists challenged both the Republicans and the Democrats but aligned more closely with Republicans. In 1892, when the Democratic Party won the governorship in a three-way race, it rejected Populist demands for increased funding for education and electoral and economic reforms, sending the Populists looking for allies elsewhere. While the two groups disagreed on certain positions and the best candidates, the Republicans and Populists came together on election reform and Black voting rights, empowering local governments, and increased support for public schools.[21]

Fusion politics, already a national phenomenon, became a well-organized campaign in North Carolina, spearheaded by white agricultural leader and newspaper publisher Marion Butler.[22] Fusionist victories in the 1894 and 1896 elections gave the coalition nearly complete control over North Carolina's political machinery, disrupting the Democratic Party's two-decade stronghold on political, economic, and social power.[23] The Fusionists won not only every open statewide office in 1894 but also the two U.S. Senate seats (Republican Jeter Connelly Pritchard and Populist Marion Butler, both white men). Republican Daniel Russell, also white, won the 1896 gubernatorial race in a landslide and became the state's first Republican governor since the national retreat from Radical Reconstruction. The *News and Observer* led Democratic opposition to the new governor.[24]

Republican George Henry White, a Black attorney and politician, won his race for U.S. Congress in 1896, and the fused Republican and Populist parties gained solid majorities in the legislature's two houses and the judiciary. With control of the state's general assembly, Fusionists enacted electoral reforms seen by some as the "fairest and most democratic in the post-Reconstruction South," expanding the vote for Black and poor white citizens.[25] Although most white Fusionists opposed equal rights for Black Fusionists, the coalition took "a practical approach to politics" and embarked on governmental reforms in 1895 that included equal voting rights and popular control of local government. After the 1896 statewide election, the largest number of Black legislators since the 1880s were elected to the state's general assembly. The political status of North Carolina's Blacks changed dramatically with Fusionism. A marker of this change was Home Rule, which meant that locally elected, three-person commissions could govern the mostly Black-majority unincorporated areas of counties between Raleigh and the Atlantic coast.[26] Fusion politics and its biracial solidarity also undermined the Ku Klux Klan and other vigilante terror groups, which found it harder to maintain a foothold there than in other states.

Forging Weapons with the
Democratic Party

However, in early 1898 there were fractures in North Carolina's Fusionist leadership, while in the background the Democratic Party was regaining strength. A few weeks after the assemblage at the Chatawka Hotel, Furnifold Simmons used his well-honed political skills to rally Democrats against the Republican Party, which he portrayed as corrupt and tainted by a large Black membership.[27] Historian H. Leon Prather Sr. says that Simmons made the terms "Negro rule" and "white supremacy" central to his efforts.[28] While the Democratic Party welcomed individual white Populists back into the fold, it firmly rejected a proposal to work with the Populist Party. The campaign began to attack any example of Black social, economic, or political power, including the appointment of Black postmasters.[29] One of U.S. congressman White's first actions in office had been to nominate more than 150 new postmasters in his largely rural district; before the end of his two years in Congress, he had appointed at least thirty-four Black postmasters.[30]

Democratic Party elites cloaked their class politics in racism by using white supremacy to "exploit black labor and marginalize white workers," writes historian Michael Honey, much in the same way they had during slavery.[31] Industry magnates and railroad financiers were less interested in the "hypothesis of Negro domination" and more worried that anti-corporation sentiments and state interference might hamper future industrialization efforts. To entice industrialists, Simmons asked for their political funding in exchange for the Democrats' promise not to increase taxes during the biennium, and to appease denominational colleges, the Democratic Executive Committee promised another secret deal: help us install a Democratic legislature and we will not increase the biennial appropriation for the University of North Carolina.[32] In his 1941 biography, Daniels recalled Simmons's "genius" in bringing "white men and white metal" together and putting three kinds of men to work to advance white supremacy and remove Black leadership: those who could write, speak, or ride.[33] The writing, speaking, and riding came together as newspapers published inflammatory speeches, announced gatherings of "violent bands of men" across the state, and hyped accounts of intimidation and activities.[34]

Ineffective at public speaking, Daniels found his place as a writer. One of his first tasks was to write a party speech about Fusion misgovernment that would be reprinted in newspapers. "My forte, if I had any, was to forge the weapons in *The News and Observer*," Daniels observed.[35] So he wrote party propaganda for Democratic Party circulars and newspapers across the state, with the *News and Observer, Charlotte Observer, Wilmington Messenger*, and Wilmington *Morning Star* leading the way. Prominent speakers like Charles B. Aycock traveled across the state to inflame white voters. Aycock had been one of Daniels's schoolmates at the Wilson Collegiate Institute and later became law partner with Daniels's older brother Frank. Other speakers included former governor Thomas J. Jarvis; two men who would become future governors, Robert B. Glenn and Cameron Morrison; and Wilmington native Alfred Moore Waddell, a Civil War veteran and former U.S. congressman.[36] Riders were recruited from clubs such as the White Government Union and the Red Shirts. The Fusionists had kept the Ku Klux Klan and other paramilitary groups at bay, but at the invitation of the Democratic Party, the Red Shirts, a popular force in neighboring South Carolina, were given a platform in North Carolina. Simmons invited Sen. Ben Tillman, a South Carolina orator known as "the brightest star in the firmament of Southern white supremacy," and three hundred of his fellow Red Shirts, "a terrorist wing of the Democratic Party," to ride at an October rally in Fayetteville.[37] These men intimidated Black citizens and pressured white Fusionists to vote for Democratic Party candidates. Speakers, parades, and shows of power were central to a strategy that needed to reach a broad audience including the illiterate and working-class who did not have newspaper subscriptions.[38]

Meanwhile Daniels helped stoke fear of federal intervention in the state—something reminiscent of Reconstruction. The *News and Observer* published the contents of an October 21 letter that Sen. Jeter C. Pritchard sent confidentially to President McKinley, asking for U.S. marshals to be sent to calm racial tensions and protect the innocent. On the eve of the election, the *News and Observer* encouraged every voter in the state to "put on his red shirt to wear it until old North Carolina has been redeemed."[39]

Daniels dispatched a reporter, Falc Arendell, to travel the state and gather anecdotal evidence of Fusionist corruption and Black criminality for publication in the *News and Observer*. Arendell visited small towns and local taverns to "hear, swap, and embellish news and gossip about the operation of the Fusionist machine in the area."[40] Daniels hired the illustrator Norman Ethre Jennett to create images supporting the Democratic Party's central argument: that Black political power was destroying the state, and only the restoration of white supremacy could save North Carolina.

Jennett would play a critical role in the campaign of 1898. The illustrator had been working for the Sampson *Democrat* earlier in the decade when he caught the attention of Gov. Elias Carr, who saw Jennett's depiction of Fusionist leader Marion Butler that the illustrator made using an imprint from wood carved with his pocket knife. The image "pleased" the governor, who suggested that Daniels hire Jennett. In 1897 Jennett left the *News and Observer* for New York to study at the William M. Chase School of Art after securing a one-hundred-dollar check from Julian Shakespeare Carr, a train ticket from Daniels, and biscuits and lunch from Daniels's wife. Jennett returned to the *News and Observer* for the campaigns of 1898 and 1900, and Simmons, Aycock, and others credited his cartoons as "one of the greatest factors in winning victories."[41] Between August and November of 1898, Jennett illustrated more than seventy-five editorial cartoons.[42] The illustrations criticized "negro rule," advocated for white supremacy, and, as the 1898 election neared, increasingly played upon familiar tropes of "sexualized images of black men and their supposedly uncontrollable lust for white women." It was not Jennett's drawing ability or wit that made his work significant; rather it was "the way they provided a visual element to the prevailing propaganda."[43]

Daniels said he used his newspaper to highlight race as an issue to divide Fusionists. For example, the *News and Observer* published the names of every Black person in office in North Carolina right before the Republican Party convention in July 1898, a list that U.S. congressman White in turn pointed to as a promise of more Black leaders in the future. A month later, the *News and Observer* portrayed Wilmington as a city controlled by Black people, which resulted in "unbridled lawlessness and rule of incompetent officials and the failure of an ignorant and worthless police force to protect the people."[44] Daniels's propaganda campaign had support from other Democratic papers. In Wilmington the *Messenger* and the *Morning Star* published articles criticizing local leaders that were then "picked up and expounded upon by the *News and Observer* and the *Charlotte Observer* to demonstrate to the rest of the state the perils of non–Democratic Party leadership."[45] The *Charlotte Observer* gave its readers "sensationalized and fabricated stories about black crime, corruption and atrocities against white women," including those by its star reporter, H.E.C. "Red Buck" Bryant, who sent dispatches from across the state supporting white supremacy and criticizing Fusion governance.[46]

The Democratic press benefited when Simmons got the Democratic Party and its funders, including Julian Shakespeare Carr, to support the purchase of twenty-five thousand to forty thousand subscriptions to newspapers such as the Raleigh *News and Observer* and the *Wilmington Messenger* for uncommitted voters. The party also produced "50,000 four-page supplements to regular editions that were sent out with weeklies for the last two months of the campaign."[47] Simmons organized the party's effort to blanket each county with five hundred copies of "a large campaign paper, fully illustrated, and containing a complete review of negro rule in North Carolina, and of the maladministration of public affairs under the present regime."[48]

Democratic leaders also worked to control the story told beyond the state's borders. The *News and Observer* described organized dinners held for visiting reporters from the *Washington Post*, the *Washington Star*, and the *Richmond Dispatch*. The out-of-state reporters "shared meals and drank whiskey with the city's leading white supremacists, absorbing their indignation and rage," writes journalist and historian David Zucchino, and the white hosts "made sure the correspondents did not interview black leaders."[49]

Strategic Use of Racial Animus

In the post–Civil War era, North Carolinians were adjusting to new social and class structures. Black men could vote, access public places, and serve on juries. The changes opened pathways for men like Abraham H. Galloway, a former slave who became one of three Black senators in the state.[50] Newspaper reports—possibly exaggerated to inflame white readers—provide potential evidence of Black people's political empowerment and social resistance. An 1898 news item from Tarboro republished in the *News and Observer* reported that U.S. congressman George White's daughter was "circulating a petition asking all colored women to refuse to work for white people" and that his wife had "received an express package containing rifles."[51] Another 1898 news item from Winston republished in the *News and Observer* told readers about a Black man who threw a brick at a police officer after the officer arrested a Black woman.[52]

As white women challenged their traditional position on a supposed pedestal and acted on new freedoms beyond their family's influence, sexual patterns changed as well. As a result, many of them began to choose partners they preferred, including both white and Black men.[53] Stereotypes and myths emerged to challenge this new power and frame social patterns. "In order to control these young women and their desires, southern white society developed the myth of the 'black beast rapist,'" which thrust women into the arms of white male protection, wrote historian J. Vincent Lowery.[54] According to Jacquelyn Dowd Hall, rape and lynching became inseparable acts of violence in the post-Reconstruction South. Together, the two acts were essential in a society that not only upheld both "men's control over women" and "white men's control over white and black women and black men" but also reinforced stereotypes of "the innocence of the white woman, the licentiousness of the black woman, [and] the lustfulness of the black man."[55] Those stereotypes found a home in newspapers. Reprinted in the *News and Observer*, "A Nameless Crime" describes a "highly respectable white girl" in Rich Square assaulted by "a fifteen-year-old negro" on a public road; the article made it clear that the indignant community would lynch the alleged attacker "in short order" if he was caught.[56] And during the 1898 political campaign, white newspapers republished a year-old speech by Georgia activist Rebecca Latimer Felton that declared if lynching would protect the "farmer's daughters," then "lynch; a thousand times a week if necessary."[57]

In her analysis of Jennett's cartoons, Rachel Marie-Crane Williams described how he used sexual and gender representations in his work. White women were "vulnerable"; Black men were "vampiric beasts, ignorant dandies, picaninnies, or children"; and the "masculinity, political motives, and honesty" of white Populists, Republicans, and Fusionists were challenged and antithetical to the white-Democratic norm.[58] One September 27 illustration portrays a menacing Black face on an oversized winged body with a tail, a foot connected to a ballot box, two outstretched arms, and two clawed hands reaching out as if to capture three small white women and two small white men running away from the winged being.[59] A month later, on October 28, another Jennett illustration combined the Democratic Party's opposition to any form of Black political power (including Black postmasters) and the strategic use of sexualized fear. In "Why the Whites Are United," Jennett shows a male postmaster caricatured as Black, using blackface, looking outward through the window of a post office. There are five male customers outside, facing toward the window, and at least four of them are portrayed as Black, also by using blackface.[60] In the center is a white woman in a dress. Her right hand is stretched forward toward the postmaster. One of the men represented as Black has his hand outstretched and placed on her back. The cutline reads, "McKinley has Filled

"The Vampire That Hovers Over North Carolina." Norman Jennett, Raleigh *News and Observer*, September 27, 1898.

the Postoffices With Negro Postmasters and in Some Instances Ladies do not find it Agreeable to Fall for Their Mail."[61]

There were voices that challenged these myths. Populist newspapers in the state, such as the *Progressive Farmer* and the *Union Republican*, defended the rights of Black men and challenged the images and stories that were rampant in the state's Democratic newspapers. And, of course, Alexander Manly, who published Wilmington's *Daily Record* with his brothers, discredited the myth of the Black beast preying on white women. Manly's famous editorial, published August 18, 1898, took aim at Felton's outrageous call for mass lynching "to protect woman's dearest possession from the ravening human beasts."[62] Manly challenged myths that he, through his mixed race, embodied. "Every Negro lynched is called a 'big, burly, black brute,' when in fact many of those who have thus been dealt with had white men for their fathers," Manly wrote, "and were not only 'black' and 'burly' but were sufficiently attractive for white girls of culture and refinement to fall in love with them as is very well known to all."[63] He confronted Felton and others like her for being "carping hypocrites" by defending virtuous white women while denouncing the morality of Black women. The editorial ended with this challenge: "Don't think ever that your women will remain pure while you are debauching ours. You sow the seed—the harvest will come in due time."[64]

Daniels reprinted three hundred thousand copies of Manly's editorial and distributed them across North Carolina.[65] Democratic Party chairman Simmons predicted that the editorial guaranteed "defeat of Fusion incumbents" statewide. Publicly he "fumed that Manly had 'dared openly and publicly to assail the virtue of our pure white womanhood'"; privately Simmons told a white Democrat from Wilmington that "the article would make an easy victory for us and urged us to try and prevent any riot until after the election."[66]

Two Wilmington newspapers, as well as others across the state, reprinted portions of Manly's argument. Editors capitalized the more salacious portions to capture readers' attention and inserted their own commentary, often directing their analysis at poor white readers. To anger poor white Populist men, the newspaper editors distorted Manly's focus on class differences, saying he argued that poor Black women were the moral equals of poor white women. They twisted Manly's mention of "clandestine meetings" to suggest he had met with poor white wives of white men. The *Morning Star* even cautioned male readers to use self-control amid growing tensions, adding, "The time may come in the near future when the white men of Wilmington will be called on to defend themselves and their homes."[67]

Wilmington as a Target

To win the 1898 election, Democratic leaders needed to convince Fusionist-leaning white counties in the western part of the state that "Negro domination" posed a problem in the east. However, Democrats needed to address white North Carolinian wariness about the party's message. The white western North Carolinians worried that Democrats would shift state control to the east and would disenfranchise white illiterate voters in the west through educational tests for voting, as had happened in other Southern states.[68]

To get its message out, the Democratic Party got help from the press to gain rural-white support, as depictions of "'Negro domination' and a promise of 'white supremacy' would induce them to vote unqualifiedly a racial rather than a party ticket."[69] One of Jennett's cartoons, "They Are Returning," published on September 16, 1898, and subtitled, "The Goddess of Democracy Welcomes Home All Honest White Men," captures the Democratic Party's portrayal of voting based on race rather than party. It shows an image of a white woman

"They Are Returning." Norman Jennett, Raleigh *News and Observer*, September 16, 1898.

in a Stars-and-Stripes dress and tiara that reads "White race" waving a wreath that reads "Welcome" at a crowd of white men with shirts that read "Honest Populist."[70] Jennett's cartoon "Behind the Bars," published on October 18, 1898, reminded readers from across the state about the dangers that "Negro domination" posed for all with capital letters and one word of "Negrorule" lettering in the foreground trapping "Eastern N.C." in the background.[71]

The visuals operated symbiotically with the content in the newspaper. For example, that same issue informed readers that a superior court clerk and Forsyth County Republican Executive Committee chairman said that Black people held offices in eastern North Carolina "because the white people there were no better than negroes."[72] Through a volley of words, illustrations, extra printing, and targeted distribution, Daniels's *News and Observer* "led in a campaign of prejudice, bitterness, vilification, misrepresentation, and exaggeration to influence the emotions of the whites against the Negro."[73]

Wilmington became a target and a test case for the Democratic Party's propaganda program. The eastern North Carolina city represented "a symbol of black hope in post–Civil War America."[74] It was the largest city in the state.[75]

Wilmington was led by Populists and Republicans "bolstered by a large black voting majority." The city had 11,324 Blacks and 8,731 whites, and it "boasted electric lights and streetcars when much of the state lumbered along in darkness." It was also the home city of Republican governor Daniel L. Russell, who became a target of Simmons's propaganda campaign. Newspapers outside the city picked up pro-Democratic Wilmington news stories that rested on the claim that Wilmington suffered under "the perils of non-Democratic Party leadership."[76] The *Democratic Party Hand Book* first mentioned Wilmington in its section "To rule Over White Men" as it described the city as an example of "negro domination" that could eventually endanger the entire state. The handbook said people of Wilmington would be unable to recognize the danger because "they see the negro policemen every day parading the streets in uniform and swinging the 'billy,' ready to let it fall upon the head of white and black alike."[77]

Jennett's cartoons in the *News and Observer* echoed the handbook's concern. On August 13, 1898, Jennett illustrated "A Serious Question—How Long Will This Last?" with a polished shoe of "The Negro" stepping on the body of "White man."[78] A week later, on August 30, his cartoon "A Warning. Get Back! We Will Not Stand It" shows a Black man in a suit and top hat that has the label "Negro rule" being hit over the head with a rolled-up piece of paper that reads "Ballot" held by the large, white hand of an "Honest white man."[79]

Government control of North Carolina and its cities had been contested since the Civil War ended. For nearly two decades of post-Reconstruction, from 1876 to 1894, Republicans had garnered many federal appointments made from Washington, D.C., while Democrats controlled most state and local governments.[80] In fact, by 1875–1876 North Carolina's general assembly had taken full control over local city ordinances, which gave it the power to institute racial gerrymandering.[81] For example, in Wilmington gerrymandering "ensured white Democrats at least seven of Wilmington['s] board of aldermen's seats and the mayorship," and the state's governor appointed the audit and finance board, which controlled the city's spending. Because of this, Black and white Wilmington citizens "had little power over their own political affairs beyond the extent to which they had allies among the Democratic leadership in Raleigh."[82]

Yet Wilmington also reflected improved social and economic conditions for Blacks, especially when compared to other Southern communities, and its political structures began to change with Fusionist leadership. During the Civil War, the port town had stayed open and profitable until federal troops occupied it in 1865. The Freedmen's Bureau and other organizations sent workers to the area to help with land, labor, education, and the political needs of newly

"A Serious Question." Norman Jennett, Raleigh *News and Observer*, August 13, 1898.

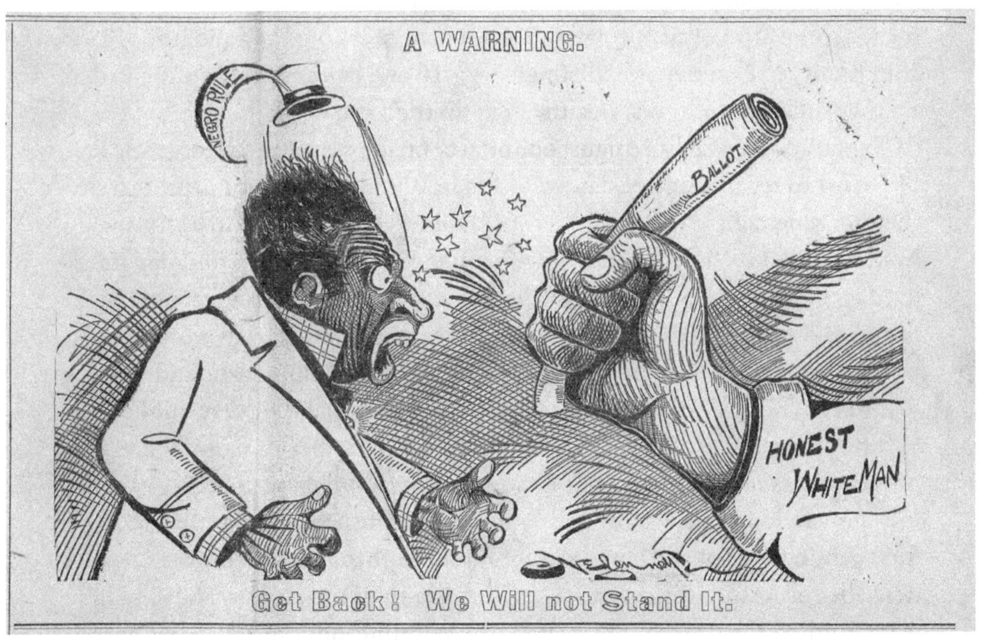

"A Warning." Norman Jennett, Raleigh *News and Observer*, August 30, 1898.

freed citizens. Thousands of white and Black refugees came to the financially ruined city after the war, and by the 1870s the city had rebounded. Its Black businesses grew faster than in any other city in the state, and it attracted Black workers who were able to share the same streets, neighborhoods, and shops with whites; to own businesses; and even to dominate some trades. When Fusionists beat Democrats in 1896, the new legislature changed Wilmington's city charter in such a way that made white Democrats and Black Republicans voice concerns about racism based on the alderman appointment process.[83] But the change also meant that Democratic appointees lost power and municipal elections became "more democratic." In the city elections of March 25, 1897, the mayor and six of Wilmington's ten aldermen were Fusionists. This included two Black men.[84]

In 1897 Blacks in Wilmington held political power through positions with the board of aldermen, board of audit and finance, public offices, Black fire departments, an all-Black health board, Black police officers, the mail clerk and mail carriers, and a collector of customs at the Port of Wilmington.[85] The city's Black community could choose from several schools, both public and private. And the community supported home ownership by developing the Peoples Perpetual Building and Loan Association in 1889 and the American Union Association in 1897. By 1897 more than one thousand Black residents owned some form of city property. These changes enabled Wilmington's Black community to experience a "distinctive social and cultural environment" that was "bolstered by schools, wealth, and inherited status."[86]

The attack on Manly's August editorial contributed to the Democratic Party's effort to regain control statewide and in Wilmington. "Home protection" rhetoric generated a "powerful psychosexual surge" that whipped up a growing hysteria based on a belief among white men that "their wives and daughters lived in danger."[87] In early autumn, Democratic Party organizers set up shop in the Wilmington offices of local lawyers and raised money from white-owned businesses, while two men—George Rountree of Wilmington and Francis Winston of Bertie County—organized a local club that the party dubbed the White Government Union. The Wilmington Chamber of Commerce supported the White Government Union and demanded "whites be given the jobs now held by Blacks, especially municipal positions." A central strategy for regaining legislative Democratic control was through what LeRae Umfleet describes as "clandestine operations."[88] A group of the city's white elite men were dubbed the "Secret Nine" by local Wilmington journalist and author Harry Hayden.[89] They "organized armed militias to take control of the streets and drew up lists of black and white Fusionists to be banished or killed."[90]

Manly's editorial continued to be fodder at white supremacist rallies. In Fayetteville, at the largest rally of the campaign, Tillman railed against the editorial and taunted the crowd to send Manly "to South Carolina and let him publish any such offensive stuff, and he will be killed.'" Tillman bragged how he and his terrorist militia "seized power in South Carolina by force and by fraud." He urged white North Carolinians "to adopt his 'shotgun policy' and shamed them for failure to use violence already." Wilmington's presence at that Fayetteville rally on October 10 was visible. A Wilmington delegation had traveled more than ninety miles to lead a parade that included "300 Red Shirts in military formation," "a float with 22 beautiful young white women dressed in white," cannons, and "a brass band from Wilmington."[91]

The *News and Observer*'s white supremacist editorials, news content, and illustrations persisted. On September 27 Jennett's cartoon, the one that identified the winged beast as a "vampire," reminded *News and Observer* audiences that a Fusion vote meant "Negro rule."[92] On September 30 the *News and Observer* invited readers to question Governor Russell's loyalties in an illustration captioned "The Source of the Governor's Inspiration," portraying Russell wearing an overcoat with caricatures of Black men, a pin reading "Negro Rule," and an image of James Young, a Black leader, *Gazette* editor, and anti-Democrat, on a ladder pulling Russell's ear and saying "Do This, Do That."[93] In his autobiography Daniels described the cartoon as "horrible looking, and Russell raved every time he saw it. I never blamed him. It advertised the fact that it was a white supremacy campaign which was being waged and that its main objective was the getting rid of the big Negro vote."[94]

The local Democratic Party worked to discredit and threaten six leading Populists and Republicans who were portrayed as contributing to Black political power. A speech and print campaign led by state newspapers made it clear that these men "were marked for death." The *Wilmington Messenger* published a boxed notice that read "Remember the Big 6" on October 15, followed by a boxed notice that read simply "5" on October 20.[95] The change in number came after the *News and Observer*, *Wilmington Messenger*, and *Wilmington Evening Star* obtained and published a September 26 letter from one of the "6," William Chadbourn, a wealthy Republican postmaster and business owner, to a Republican senator that said Wilmington was not dominated by Blacks. Under pressure from Democrats, Chadbourn retracted his statement and temporarily left the state. White men perceived to be Republican Party leaders were increasingly "targeted and vilified through speeches and newspaper articles."[96] By October 7 Chadbourn and the rest of the city's chamber of commerce declared in the *Wilmington Messenger* its opposition to "Negro Domination" and announced that their about-face was due to a political situation that was becoming "a menace to the peace and order of the community." They went on to claim that the "corrupt and incompetent men" in government led to "indignities to our white women which have cumulated in instances of personal violence to them on our streets, and in an attack on the virtue of the womanhood of our Southland by the negro editor of the infamous Daily Record."[97]

Toward the end of the month, white leaders met with Simmons at the Democratic headquarters to decide how to do "something more" that would bring home to all of North Carolina "the corruptions and the ills of Negro rule." They decided they would gather "the people of all Eastern North Carolina" for a White Supremacy Convention in Goldsboro and made Major William A. Guthrie of Durham, a former Populist gubernatorial candidate in 1896, a temporary chairman in order to mask the appearance of it as a Democratic rally.[98] An October 21 *News and Observer* article, "Looks for a Race Riot," described Guthrie as a military officer who left Wilmington after his Second North Carolina Regiment was ordered out and who insisted that his wife leave the city because "there may be a race riot if New Hanover politics does not cool down."[99] By October 24 Waddell gave a speech to an audience of prominent Wilmington citizens that included "Red Shirts and wives of leading businessmen." He promised to "'choke the current of the Cape Fear with carcasses' to end 'Negro domination'" in Wilmington. The *Wilmington Messenger* published the speech in its entirety the next day.[100] Potential violence in the state and Wilmington permeated newspaper pages. The Raleigh *News and Observer's* front page on October 25 said Senator Pritchard and Governor Russell had requested that the president send federal troops to control the state election.[101] Guthrie's response, published in the *News and Observer*, denounced the possibility of federal interference alongside an announcement that he would preside over the Goldsboro rally. In his autobiography, Daniels said his newspaper warned of "the white heat that dominated the white supremacy leaders" and that if federal troops came to the state, "it would have taken Grant's Army to have held them [white supremacists] back."[102]

On the eve of the 1898 election, Waddell delivered one more speech, this time at night, as he reminded his listeners of their Anglo-Saxon race, their duty to take action, and their armed preparedness for such action: "Go to the polls tomorrow, and if you find the Negro out voting, tell him to leave the polls and if he refuses kill, shoot him down in his tracks. We shall win tomorrow if we have to do it with guns."[103] Red Shirts went "hunting for" and were rumored to try to lynch the state's Republican governor, Daniel Russell, when he voted in Wilmington on November 8; his life was saved only after he hid in a railroad mail car. The rhetoric and threats of violence alarmed Republicans so much that they sent delegations to Raleigh and Washington, D.C., to warn the governor and the president "about the stresses created by the Democratic white supremacy campaign." In response, Governor Russell ultimately made a bargain with Wilmington's Democrats that Republicans would "not mount a slate of candidates in return for promises by Democrats that violence would be averted on election day."[104]

Destroying a Black Press and Implementing a Coup d état

Democrats swept North Carolina elections statewide on November 9. Armed white men patrolled every block in Wilmington on Election Day, intimidating Blacks and Republicans and escorting "less energetic Democrats to the polls to cast ballots under the watchful scrutiny of members of the White government Unions."[105] Gun sales in Wilmington had soared that year preceding the election, although sales to Blacks were often thwarted; it was said that there were almost enough guns, among the city's whites, for every man, woman, and child. Democrats replaced ballot watchers with those who would disrupt the process and stuffed ballot boxes to ensure victory. Despite threats of being fired from jobs or being harmed physically, and despite the Republican governor's deal with Wilmington Democrats not to mount a slate of Republican candidates, many of the city's Blacks did try to vote.[106] And despite the corruption and widespread intimidation, much of the Wilmington leadership would remain intact as Republican, because many municipal positions were not up for election. Democrats, however, had planned for this.

Before the election, the Secret Nine, in concert with the Citizens Vigilance Committee, the Red Shirts/Rough Riders, and White Government Union clubs, mapped two plans for Wilmington.[107] The first was to "retake control of the city after the election"; the second was "a citywide plan of action in case of violence."[108] On Election Day, November 8, the Red Shirts employed their intimidation campaign toward Black voters and threatened the governor's life. At 10 a.m. on November 9, the day after the election, eight hundred to one thousand white men rallied at the New Hanover County Courthouse to hear Waddell read the "White Declaration of Independence," a document previously crafted by the Secret Nine. The declaration contained eight resolutions, including that Manly would leave the city and stop printing his newspaper, that the mayor and chief of police would resign, and that the Committee of Twenty-five would implement the White Declaration of Independence.[109] (Despite the armed white gangs on the streets, Manly had already escaped.[110]) By 3:30 p.m. the Committee of Twenty-five summoned members of what it called the Committee of Colored Citizens (CCC) to a 6 p.m. meeting. The Committee of Twenty-five composed the new committee by selecting Black members they perceived to be Black community leaders and representatives.[111] These Black Wilmington politicians, attorneys, ministers, and business leaders arrived that evening and were told the Committee of Twenty-five's demands, to which the CCC was to consider and respond by 7:30 a.m. the next day. The CCC did not provide a reply by 7:30 a.m. directly to Waddell and instead reportedly placed a reply in a mailbox. On the premise that he did not receive the reply at his home, Waddell went to the Wilmington Light Infantry armory on the morning of November 10.[112]

That morning, two days after North Carolina's election, the Secret Nine implemented its plans: the armed overthrow of Wilmington's legitimately elected municipal government, the expulsion of more than twenty targeted Black and white political opponents, the mass exodus of more than twenty-one hundred other residents, the burning and destruction of the city's Black press, and an estimated fourteen to sixty murders. This was a conspiracy designed to seem impulsive and unintended, having lasting implications for the city and state. The campaign of expulsion targeted Manly and his *Daily Record*, Black leaders who openly opposed white supremacy, successful Black businessmen, and white Republicans or Populists who had benefited from Black votes. White Democratic leaders replaced aldermen who were forced to resign, paving the way for a new alderman board that would then elect Alfred Moore Waddell as the city's new mayor. And finally a preplanned paramilitary framework stepped in "to return the city to normal, peaceful, operations as quickly as possible."[113]

By 8 a.m. on November 10, Waddell led the men who had gathered at the courthouse to the *Daily Record*'s printing office, where as many as two thousand white men destroyed press materials and burned down the building. It was said that Waddell and other leaders were unhappy with the fire, "since they only wanted to damage the press and the ability of the black community to produce a newspaper." It would be nearly thirty years before Wilmington would have another regular Black newspaper.[114]

White men also boarded a streetcar and fired into homes and businesses in Black neighborhoods, and armed white patrols decided whether Black workers should return to work or leave for home amid threat of a white mob.[115] Reports differ on whether it was Blacks or whites who fired the first shots in a gun battle at a Wilmington store. Following a plan devised in advance, J. Allan Taylor (a member of the Secret Nine) alerted the Wilmington Light Infantry (WLI) and Naval Reserves using a riot alarm that notified Colonel Walker Taylor, the WLI's commander, and Colonel Roger Moore, leader of a militia organization in the city and one of the first Ku Klux Klan organizers in the city. Under the plan, Walker Taylor and Moore had been "conspicuously absent" during the morning mob and on alert. Once civilian block captains announced that shots were fired and violence had broken out, Moore contacted the army and Walker Taylor declared martial law and mobilized the WLI and Naval Reserves.[116] Governor Russell supported Walker Taylor's leadership through a telegram that instructed Taylor to quell the violence and restore peace. The men under Commander George Morton of the Naval Reserves used Lee magazine rifles and a Hotchkiss rapid-firing gun "to intimidate and terrorize both blacks and whites." Using a list of prominent Black and white Republicans provided to him by J. Alan Taylor of the Secret Nine, Walker Taylor acted to permanently banish the men from Wilmington. By dusk they were put in jail "for safekeeping," and many were soon forced on trains headed out of town.[117] Black men were killed and wounded throughout the city. The numbers of reported deaths range from the teens to more than one hundred, including reports that carts hauled Black bodies through the streets and that the "mouth of the Cape Fear [was] clotted with black bodies,"[118] recalling Waddell's threat two weeks before at the Goldsboro White Folks' Rally.

The replacement of Wilmington's government with white Democrats was both systematic and complete. While rioting continued in the streets, members of the Committee of Twenty-five implemented their coup d'etat to overthrow the city's elected leaders. The governor, "threatened with impeachment and death," was effectively silenced.[119] Waddell sent two committee members, Frank Stedman and Charles Worth, to find Mayor Silas Wright and Police Chief John Melton (a Populist who had been identified in the "Big 6" campaign) and to make them resign. By 4 p.m. George Rountree, John D. Bellamy, and others forced the Republican mayor and the police chief to resign. Outside the building, a mob supporting the Democrats swelled. Rountree and Bellamy with J. Allan Taylor assumed government authority. White Democrats also took over the police department after forcing every member to resign. Historian H. Leon Prather Sr., who wrote one of the first published book-length studies of the events in 1984 and then synthesized that work in a 1998 centennial essay, states, "The Secret Nine and their allies made of the riot a rather thin smokescreen for their violent and revolutionary seizure of power from the legally elected Fusionist government." Melton and others were rounded up and forced to leave the city. With Waddell "elected" as the city's mayor, the ousted Mayor Wright rode through town with James Sprunt, one of the city's wealthiest white businessmen and chamber of commerce member, in order to ease tensions, before leaving Wilmington by nightfall on November 11.[120]

Masterful Duplicity

The banishment of the city's Black newspaper editor, successful Black businessmen, Black leaders opposed to white supremacy, and white political allies from the city aligned with the Democratic Party plan to "save" cities like Wilmington from Black rule. The plan's success went beyond the replacement of political and law enforcement officials in Wilmington, however. The white press played a central and institutional role in the white supremacist reclamation of North Carolina through its symbiotic relationship with the Democratic Party and its strategic dissemination of political propaganda that continued well after the violent takeover of Wilmington. J. Allan Taylor—the Secret Nine member who helped oust Wilmington's government, who had sounded the alarm to activate military action, and who led the banishment campaign—reflected on the overthrow in the margins of his personal copy of one of the first white narratives of what happened in Wilmington, a booklet written by white newspaperman Harry Hayden titled *The Story of the Wilmington Rebellion*. Taylor wrote in the margins: "Masterful duplicity."[121] LeRae Umfleet, in the *1898 Wilmington Race Riot Report*, draws attention to Taylor's depiction and challenges the duplicitous narrative that the murders, banishments, and planned overthrow of the city's democratically elected officials was simply "a sudden break in peacefulness."[122] That report brought to light that what occurred was both planned and lasting. The coup d'etat "fully ended black participation in city and county government until the advent of the civil rights era," and the "campaign capped by violence in Wilmington proved to be a catalyst for the state—Jim Crow legislation and subjugation of blacks resulted statewide."[123]

White newspapers such as the Raleigh *News and Observer*, Wilmington's *Evening Dispatch*, and the *Wilmington Messenger* played along with the ruse and published propaganda that hid the real motives of white elites and silenced opposition to white supremacy. Reporters often crafted and then matched and reinforced the narrative developed by those who benefited from, watched, or participated in the 1898 campaign. This shaped how local historians told "the story of the riot and its causes as a response of white citizens to a corrupt municipal government unable to reduce crime or facilitate economic improvements for residents."[124] The *News and Observer*'s November 11 stacked headlines told readers that Black people precipitated the conflict by firing on white people. The paper presented the white government and military takeover as legal, saying the entire board of aldermen changed hands legally and that the mayor and police chief resigned. Articles assured citizens that a new Democratic government now controlled Wilmington and that the new mayor had put guards around the jail in order to "protect" Black prisoners. It reminded readers once again of Manly, framing his resistance to white supremacy and lynching as slanderous and defaming.[125] In the days following the takeover, white newspapers silenced opposition to white supremacy and made Black social, political, and economic power invisible. Wilmington's *Evening Dispatch* told its readers in a November 11 article how Black people were not allowed on the streets, guns were taken from people, Black leaders were removed from the city by train, Wilmington was "quiet," and the "patrol and guards will be kept up as long as it is deemed necessary though no further trouble of any kind is expected." Readers were assured that "no detailed account of the trouble" would ever be given. The newspaper attributed its silence to the impossibility of getting at or recollecting details due to "the excitement," adding that "the number of negroes killed or wounded will probably never be known."[126] The *Wilmington Messenger* told its readers that "there were no negroes to be seen" in one area of the city and that "quiet reigned, supreme." Readers of these newspapers would not find stories and counter-narratives of Black resistance in the Black press, because Manly was gone and his press was destroyed.[127] The news stories in white Democratic newspapers provided the first draft of history that would shape how the events in Wilmington would be retold and remembered.[128] It would be the kind of top-down, perpetrator-viewpoint history focused on party politics, economic jealousy, and racism that historian Glenda Gilmore says is often used to frame "the Wilmington slaughter" story "as a riot, a coup, or a massacre," and in the process, then, failing to recognize the essential truth "about how political rhetoric can license people to do evil in the name of good."[129]

Once in power, the Democratic Party and its supporters celebrated with parades and other gatherings in Wilmington and Raleigh. "White ministers on the Sunday following the violence voiced support for the coup and congratulated the leaders." Participation in the Wilmington 1898 campaign became "the irreplaceable political credential." Campaign leaders became "immortalized in statues, on buildings and street signs."[130]

In the days and years following the Wilmington destruction, Carr, Simmons, Aycock, and Daniels continued influencing the state. Outraged by the murders and overthrow of Wilmington's government, some North Carolinians sent letters or went in person to the U.S. capital asking President McKinley to respond and help. However, when two Wilmington newspapers published Carr's appeal to the president, Carr's opinion took precedence over those seeking government intervention.[131] Carr told the president that "men with white skins" would rule the state "ever hereafter. No need of troops now. Praise God!"[132] The wealthy businessman, by then one of the richest men in the state, reinforced his public statement with a private letter to the Republican president in which Carr leveraged his position as an employer of one thousand North Carolinian Black men, who, he said, were loyal to him. He repeated to the president, do not send troops.[133] Within a month, Carr reportedly described in a letter the Wilmington killings, coup d'état, and destruction as a "grand and glorious event."[134]

In the years that followed, Carr would continue to prosper through his investments in textiles, banking, railroads, public utilities, and newspapers.[135] Simmons defeated Carr in the race to become the Democratic Party's nominee for the U.S. Senate seat in 1900. Simmons won the general election over a Populist incumbent that year, Marion Butler, and he would hold the seat for three decades.[136] In 1901 Aycock became the state's fiftieth governor. Two years later, after a group of prominent Black scholars confronted social, economic, and political issues in "The Negro Problem," Aycock told an audience of three hundred that he was proud of how North Carolina had "solved the Negro problem." Aycock's three-part solution included disenfranchisement "as far as possible under the Fifteenth Amendment"; ignoring Black experiences by stopping all writing and talking about Black people ("let him alone, quit writing about him, quit talking about him, quit making him the white man's burden, quit coddling him"); and separating the races and preventing intermingling.[137] In the decades after the Wilmington Massacre, Daniels continued to use his newspaper to advocate for his political allies and "to persuade North Carolina citizens to support the disenfranchisement of black men and women," a position he later renounced, according to Jonathan Martin of the *North Carolina History Project*.[138] Daniels became President Woodrow Wilson's secretary of the navy in 1913, and President Franklin Roosevelt appointed him ambassador to Mexico in 1933. Daniels and his family continued to own the *News and Observer* for a century.

The Black U.S. representative from North Carolina, George White, won reelection in 1898 but did not run in 1900 for a third term. In 1901, during his

"This House Is Built Upon a Rock." Norman Jennett, Raleigh *News and Observer*, October 9, 1898.

final months, he spoke of his departure from Congress as "perhaps the negroes' temporary farewell" and spoke of a time when Black Americans—"outraged, heart-broken, bruised, and bleeding, but God-fearing people, faithful, industrious, loyal people" and "full of potential force"—would rise.[139] The U.S. Congress would have no other Black representatives serving until 1929; North Carolina would not elect another Black U.S. representative until a century later, in 1992. It was not until 1951 and 1964 that Black historians gained ground in writing the counter-narratives of the Wilmington Massacre.[140] The race riot and white supremacy campaign "slammed the door on democracy" and "cemented" racial segregation in the South, one historian argued.[141]

Among its calls to action, the *1898 Wilmington Race Riot Report* recommended that contemporary newspapers reconcile with their past, including looking further at who edited several of the newspapers—the *News and Observer*, the *Charlotte Observer*, the two Wilmington newspapers, and the *Washington Post*—and their political ties. This chapter takes up at least one of those newspapers in depth. In the *News and Observer*'s 2005 supplement "The Ghosts of 1898," Timothy B. Tyson argues that the Democratic Party could not have succeeded without the newspaper actions that placed Daniels at the center of the plan, saying, "He spearheaded a propaganda effort that made white partisans angry enough to commit electoral fraud and mass murder."[142]

One telling way that reveals how Daniels saw how his *News and Observer* was situated in this society can be seen in Jennett's front-page cartoon published on October 9, 1898, a month before the election and overthrow of Wilmington's government. At a time when Daniels and his newspaper furthered the Democratic Party agenda and white business interests by stoking racial hatred, the *News and Observer* is portrayed in the cartoon as a building under siege but with a strong base. Titled "This House Is Built Upon a Rock" and subtitled "The Waves and Rain and Hail and Missiles of Fusion Orators Are Hurled at it in Vain, Because It's Built Upon a Solid Foundation," the illustration portrays white supremacy as an under-the-surface base and the newspaper as the flag bearer for a set of white supremacist ideals. Placed on five stacked rocks that raise it high above the fierce waves, the newspaper building—identified by a flag that reads "The News and Observer"—becomes a central target of many smaller, hurled stones that read "Lies" and "Abuse." The top two rocks upon which the building rests are labeled "Facts" and "Truth." These two rocks rest on two more rocks that read "Principle" and "The White Metal." Finally, these two rocks rest on the most substantial rock of them all. Serving as the base for the rocks and building, this one reads: "White Supremacy."[143]

Notes

1. Glenda E. Gilmore, "Murder, Memory, and the Flight of the Incubus," in *Democracy Betrayed: The Wilmington Race Riot of 1898 and Its Legacy*, ed. David S. Cecelski and Timothy B. Tyson (Chapel Hill: University of North Carolina Press, 1998), 73–93, quote on 74.

2. LeRae Umfleet, *1898 Wilmington Race Riot Report* (Raleigh: North Carolina Office of Archives and History and North Carolina Department of Cultural Resources, 2006), 56.

3. Lee A. Craig, *Josephus Daniels: His Life and Times* (Chapel Hill: University of North Carolina Press, 2013), 77–78, quote on 134.

4. Timothy B. Tyson, "The Ghosts of 1898: Wilmington's Race Riot and the Rise of White Supremacy," Raleigh *News and Observer*, section H, November 17, 2006, 1–16, quote on 1.

5. Ibid., 1; State Democratic Executive Committee of North Carolina, *The Democratic Hand Book 1898* (Raleigh: Edwards and Broughton, 1898), transcribed by Apex Data Services Inc., University of North Carolina at Chapel Hill, "Documenting of the American South," https://docsouth.unc.edu/nc/dem1898/menu.html.

6. Tyson, "Ghosts of 1898," 6.

7. Glenda E. Gilmore, *Gender and Jim Crow: Women and the Politics of White Supremacy in North Carolina, 1896–1920* (Chapel Hill: University of North Carolina Press, 1996), 106.

8. Historian Stephen Kantrowitz argues that the Black-rapist myth made actions and desires of white men and Black women invisible. The white-male master-class violence became enfolded in the myth of paternalism. Stephen Kantrowitz, "The Two Faces of Domination in North Carolina, 1800–1898," in Cecelski and Tyson, *Democracy Betrayed*, 96–111.

9. Gilmore, "Murder, Memory, and the Flight of the Incubus," 91, 78. Gilmore identified it as the New Berne [*sic*] Journal.

10. Craig, *Josephus Daniels*, 1–80.

11. David Zucchino, *Wilmington's Lie: The Murderous Coup on 1898 and the Rise of White Supremacy* (New York: Atlantic Monthly Press, 2020), 46–47. Umfleet says Manly was either the governor's son or grandson. Umfleet, *1898 Wilmington Race Riot Report*.

12. H. Leon Prather Sr., "We Have Taken a City: A Centennial Essay," in Cecelski and Tyson, *Democracy Betrayed*, 24. Thomas Clawson, the *Wilmington Messenger's* editor, sold the press to Manly.

13. Craig, *Josephus Daniels*, 21, 41, 22. Craig noted how Daniels appreciated how business and politics came together on the pages of a newspaper: "The opinions of editors often offended subscribers and advertisers," while at the same time "an editorial approach that offended and angered no one also interested no one," which could hurt business. He solved this problem in his newspapers by separating news and opinion into distinct sections, a model established in bigger city newspapers. And he supplemented subscription and advertising revenue by printing government documents, such as election ballots and legal materials—a patronage doled out by the city's ruling Democratic Party to party loyalists like Daniels, who benefited financially and was in turn obligated to publish pro-Democratic content and maintain good terms with all party factions. Craig, *Josephus Daniels*, 41–80.

14. Craig, *Josephus Daniels*, 76–77, 78, 73, 81–122. Daniels was the first to inform Carr that he had become—unbeknownst to him—the owner of the Raleigh *State Chronicle* upon the death of its owner and fellow Confederate veteran, Captain Randolph Shotwell, to whom Carr had contributed financially when he was in need.

15. Ibid., 60, 41–122, 146.

16. Umfleet, *1898 Wilmington Race Riot*, 41.

17. Craig, *Josephus Daniels*, 138–40, 165–206; Ronnie W. Faulkner, "North Carolina Democrats and Silver Fusion Politics, 1892–1896," *North Carolina Historical Review* 59, no. 3 (1982): 230–51.

18. Umfleet, *1898 Wilmington Race Riot*, 95.

19. Zucchino, *Wilmington's Lie*, 47. The 1898 arson appears to have destroyed

the *Daily Record*'s archives; the earliest existing copies are from 1885. Alex Manly was editor, Frank Manly was general manager, Lewis Manly was a foreman, and Henry Manly was a compositor. Zucchino, *Wilmington's Lie*, 48.

20. Prather, "We Have Taken a City," 18, 30.

21. Umfleet, *1898 Wilmington Race Riot*, 34–55; Ronnie W. Faulkner, "Fusion Politics," North Carolina History Project, September 4, 2019, https://northcarolina history.org/encyclopedia/fusion-politics/.

22. Josephus Daniels, *Editor in Politics* (Chapel Hill: University of North Carolina Press, 1941). Daniels mentions Butler's role as *Caucasian* publisher at Goldsboro and says that after the 1892 election, Butler said his newspaper would become a daily and move to Raleigh to support the Fusionists.

23. Craig, *Josephus Daniels*, 165–206, quote on 173.

24. Tyson, "Ghosts of 1898," 5; Umfleet, *1898 Wilmington Race Riot*, 41.

25. Jeffrey J. Crow, "Cracking the Solid South: Populism and the Fusionist Interlude," in *The North Carolina Experience: An Interpretative and Documentary History*, ed. Lindley S. Butler and Alan D. Watson (Chapel Hill: University of North Carolina, 1984), 338, quoted in Joseph Campbell, "'One of the Fine Figures of American Journalism': A Closer Look at Josephus Daniels of the Raleigh *News and Observer*," *American Journalism* 16, no. 4 (1999): 37–55, quote on 41.

26. Tyson, "Ghosts of 1898," 4, 5; Prather, "We Have Taken a City," 15–41; Craig, *Josephus Daniels*, 165–206.

27. Umfleet, *1898 Wilmington Race Riot*, 59, 60.

28. Prather, "We Have Taken a City," 15–41, quotes on 20, 21.

29. Umfleet, *1898 Wilmington Race Riot*, 58.

30. Benjamin R. Justesen, "Black Tip, White Iceberg: Black Postmasters and the Rise of White Supremacy, 1897–1901," *North Carolina Historical Review*, 82, no. 2 (2005): 207–208. "Until 1897, fewer than two dozen black men and even fewer black women had served as postmasters in North Carolina" (197).

31. Michael Honey, "Class, Race, and Power in the New South: Racial Violence and the Delusions of White Supremacy," in Cecelski and Tyson, *Democracy Betrayed*, 163–84, quote on 165.

32. Fred Rippy, ed., *Funifold Simmons, Statesman of the New South*, 23–24, cited in Helen G. Edmonds, *The Negro and Fusion Politics in North Carolina, 1894-1901* (Chapel Hill: University of North Carolina Press, 1951), 139, 140. The secret arrangement was not revealed until 1936.

33. Daniels, *Editor in Politics*, 284.

34. Umfleet, *1898 Wilmington Race Riot*, 60.

35. Daniels, *Editor in Politics*, 284.

36. Craig, *Josephus Daniels*, 38; Tyson, "Ghosts of 1898," 6. Waddell served from 1870 to 1878.

37. Prather, "We Have Taken a City," 25.

38. Umfleet, *1898 Wilmington Race Riot*, 56, 64; Tyson, "Ghosts of 1898," 7.

39. Umfleet, *1898 Wilmington Race Riot*, 429–36; "Campaign's Glorious End, Rousing Democratic Rallies All Over the State. Concord, Roxboro, Reidsville, Tuckahoe and Other Towns the Scene of Remarkable Demonstrations of Enthusiasm and Determination to Win for White Supremacy," and "Sweeping Victory Ahead, Chairman Simmons Forecasts the Election Results from a Poll of the State," Raleigh *News and Observer*, November 6, 1898, 1.

40. Craig, *Josephus Daniels*, 182.

41. Daniels, *Editor in Politics*, 148, 150. There is no mention of why the print pleased Carr.

42. Rachel Marie-Crane Williams, "A War in Black and White: The Cartoons of Norman Ethre Jennett & the North Carolina Election of 1898," *Southern Cultures* 19, no. 2 (2013): 7–31.

43. Tyson, "Ghosts of 1898," 7; Williams, "War in Black and White," 9.

44. Daniels, *Editor in Politics*, 285.

45. Jeffrey J. Crow and Robert F. Durden, *Maverick Republican in the Old North State: A Political Biography of Daniel L. Russell* (Baton Rouge: Louisiana State University Press, 1977), 125, quoted in Umfleet, *1898 Wilmington Race Riot*, 60.

46. Tyson, "Ghosts of 1898," 7.

47. Umfleet, *1898 Wilmington Race Riot*, 62. Umfleet's citation is cut off in the original.

48. Furnifold Simmons, "Notice to County Chairmen and All Democrats," *Fayetteville Observer*, September 2, 1898, 1.

49. "Campaign's Glorious End" and "Sweeping Victory Ahead," Raleigh *News and Observer*, November 6, 1898, 1; Zucchino, *Wilmington's Lie*, 158.

50. David S. Cecelski, "Abraham H. Galloway," in Cecelski and Tyson, *Democracy Betrayed*. The Wilmington native had been a fugitive slave, a Union spy, a radical politician, and became an abolitionist leading fights for women's suffrage in 1868 and 1869 and for a bill against domestic violence.

51. "Negro Women Active: Congressman White's Wife Gets Rifles and His Daughter Asks Negro Women Not to Work for White People," Raleigh *News and Observer*, November 1, 1898, 1. Gilmore describes how black women "used their power to mount a campaign of nerves to counter the white supremacists." Gilmore, "Murder, Memory, and the Flight of the Incubus," 83.

52. "Outrages in Winston: Negro Pushes Two White Girls Off the Sidewalk—Negro Wounds an Officer," Raleigh *News and Observer*, October 20, 1898, 2. The cities of Winston and Salem were in the process of being known as Winston-Salem.

53. J. Vincent Lowery, "'Ever Threatened . . . Ever in Need': Alexander Manly's Confrontation with the Democratic Campaign in 1898 North Carolina," 347–52, in Umfleet, *1898 Wilmington Race Riot*.

54. Ibid., 347. Lowery cites the work of Jacquelyn Dowd Hall for discussion on the image and its consequences. Jacquelyn Dowd Hall, "'The Mind That Burns in

Each Body': Women, Rape, and Racial Violence," in *Powers of Desire: The Politics of Sexuality*, ed. Ann Snitow, Christine Stansell, and Sharon Thompson, 328–49 (New York: Monthly Review Press, 1983), quote on 339.

55. Hall, "'Mind That Burns in Each Body,'" 328.

56. "A Nameless Crime," Raleigh *News and Observer*, October 18, 1898, 1.

57. J. A. Holman, "Mrs. Felton Speaks. She Makes a Sensational Speech before Agricultural Society. Believes Lynching Should Prevail as Long as Defenseless Woman Is Not Better Protected," special to *Atlanta Journal* and reprinted in the *Wilmington Morning Star*, August 18 and 26, 1898, republished in Umfleet, *1898 Wilmington Race Riot*, 97.

58. Williams, "War in Black and White," n.p.

59. Jennett, "The Vampire That Hovers Over North Carolina," Raleigh *News and Observer*, September 27, 1898. The foot is connected to what was labeled "Fusion Ballot Box." Image available at *UNC Libraries*, https://exhibits.lib.unc.edu/items/show/2215.

60. One of the five men facing the window can be seen only from the back.

61. Jennett, "Why the Whites Are United," Raleigh *News and Observer*, October 28, 1898, 1. Image available at *UNC Libraries*, https://exhibits.lib.unc.edu/items/show/2240.

62. Holman, "Mrs. Felton Speaks," republished in Umfleet, *1898 Wilmington Race Riot*, 97.

63. "Alex Manly's Editorial," quoted in Umfleet, *1898 Wilmington Race Riot*, 98. Umfleet notes that few copies of Manly's newspaper survive and that the article can be found in partial and full transcriptions. Umfleet cites as her sources Jerome A. McDuffie, "Politics in Wilmington and New Hanover County, North Carolina, 1865–1900: The Genesis of a Race Riot," 588–89, and Thomas Clawson, "Recollections and Memories," Louis T. Moore Papers, Private Collections, State Archives, North Carolina Office of Archives and History, Raleigh.

64. "Alex Manly's Editorial," quoted in Umfleet, *1898 Wilmington Race Riot*, 98; Tyson, "Ghosts of 1898," 8.

65. Prather, "We Have Taken a City," 80; Joel Williamson, *The Crucible of Race: Black-White Relations in the American South Since Emancipation* (New York: Oxford University Press, 1984), 197, both cited in Umfleet, *1898 Wilmington Race Riot*, 350.

66. Tyson, "Ghosts of 1898," 8. Tyson said it was Walker Taylor who wrote that Senator Simmons told them this when he was in Wilmington.

67. Gilmore, *Gender and Jim Crow*, 105, and *Wilmington Morning Star*, August 24, 1898, both cited in Umfleet, *1898 Wilmington Race Riot*, 350.

68. Edmonds, "'White Supremacy' Campaign," 140.

69. Ibid., 141.

70. Jennett, "They Are Returning," Raleigh *News and Observer*, September 16,

1898. Image available at *UNC Libraries*, https://exhibits.lib.unc.edu/exhibits/show/1898/item/2204.

71. Jennett, "Behind the Bars," Raleigh *News and Observer*, October 18, 1898, 1. Image available at *UNC Libraries*, https://exhibits.lib.unc.edu/items/show/2231.

72. "No Better Than Negroes. That Is What a Republican Leader Says of Eastern White Men," Raleigh *News and Observer*, October 18, 1898, 1.

73. Edmonds, "'White Supremacy' Campaign," 141.

74. Umfleet, *1898 Wilmington Race Riot*, 60; Tyson, "Ghosts of 1898," 4.

75. In the 1900 census, Wilmington's population was 20,976; it had been 20,056 a decade earlier. Charlotte's population was 18,091 in 1900, up from 11,557 in 1890; Asheville was 14,694 in 1900, up from 10,235 in 1890; and Raleigh's population in 1900 was 13,643, up from 12,678 in 1890. U.S. Census, "Statistics of Population," table 8, "Population of Incorporated Cities, Towns, Villages, and Boroughs in 1900, with Population for 1890," in *1900 Census*, vol. 1, *Population*, part 1, "Cities, Towns, and Boroughs," tables 6–8 (1901), 467.

76. Umfleet, *1898 Wilmington Race Riot*, 60; Tyson, "Ghosts of 1898," 4.

77. *Democratic Hand Book*, 39.

78. Jennett, "A Serious Question—How Long Will This Last?," Raleigh *News and Observer*, August 13, 1898. Image available at *UNC Libraries*, https://exhibits.lib.unc.edu/items/show/2178. The pant leg above the polished shoe identifies "The Negro" and the writing on the back of the pants indicates "White man."

79. Jennett, "A Warning. Get Back! We Will Not Stand It," Raleigh *News and Observer*, August 30, 1898. Image available at *UNC Libraries*, https://exhibits.lib.unc.edu/items/show/2191. The sleeve above the white hand reads "Honest White Man."

80. Tyson, "Ghosts of 1898," 5.

81. Constitution of the State of North Carolina, 1875–76, art. 7, sec. 14, in Prather, "We Have Taken a City," 18.

82. Prather, "We Have Taken a City," 18–19.

83. Umfleet, *1898 Wilmington Race Riot*, 2–33, 34; Prather, "We Have Taken a City," 15–41.

84. Prather, "We Have Taken a City," 19.

85. Ibid., 15–41.

86. Umfleet, *1898 Wilmington Race Riot*, 328–29, 34.

87. Gilmore, "Murder, Memory, and the Flight of the Incubus," 76–77.

88. Tyson, "Ghosts of 1898," 8; Umfleet, *1898 Wilmington Race Riot*, 34.

89. Prather, "We Have Taken a City," citing Harry Hayden Papers, 7, Special Collections Library, Duke University, Durham, N.C. Umfleet and others identified these men as J. Allan Taylor, Hardy Fennell, W. A. Johnson, L. B. Sasser, William Gilchrist, Pierre B. Manning, Edward S. Lathrop, Walter Parsely, and Hugh Mac-

Rae. Some of them were members of other groups, such as the Citizens Vigilance Committee, the Red Shirts/Rough Riders, and the White Government Unions.

90. Tyson, "Ghosts of 1898," 8.

91. Ibid.

92. Jennett, "The Vampire That Hovers Over North Carolina."

93. Jennett, "The Source of the Governor's Inspiration," Raleigh *News and Observer*, September 30, 1898. Image available at *UNC Libraries*, https://exhibits.lib .unc.edu/items/show/2218. For further discussion of Young's opposition and his being a target of Daniels and the Democratic Party, see Umfleet *1898 Wilmington Race Riot*, 69–70. Edmonds describes Young's Fusion organizing, legislative actions, and interest in education on pp. 98–99. Daniels describes Young as a "Negro editor of the *Gazette*" in *Editor in Politics*, 122.

94. Daniels, *Editor in Politics*, 303.

95. Umfleet, *1898 Wilmington Race Riot*, 72, 75. Zucchino points out that the handbills did not list the six men, but the *Wilmington Messenger* made public the names "Mayor Silas Wright, Police Chief John Melton, Deputy Sheriff George Z. French, businessmen William H. Chadbourn, Flavel W. Foster, and a lawyer, Caleb B. Lockey." Zucchino, *Wilmington's Lie*, 114.

96. Umfleet, *1898 Wilmington Race Riot*, 72–75.

97. "The Chamber of Commerce Declares against Negro Domination," *Wilmington Messenger*, October 21, 1898, 5.

98. Daniels, *Editor in Politics*, 299, 300.

99. "Looks for a Race Riot," Raleigh *News and Observer*, October 21, 1898, 1.

100. Umfleet, *1898 Wilmington Race Riot*, 79; Tyson, "Ghosts of 1898," 6.

101. "To Invoke Bayonet Rule. Russell and Pritchard Want Federal Troops to Control the Election in North Carolina. Matter Discussed in the Cabinet Yesterday. Hot Words of Attorney-General Griggs," Raleigh *News and Observer*, October 25, 1898, 1.

102. "Rings like a Bell. Maj. Guthrie, Populist Candidate for Governor in 1896, Denounces Federal Interference—Will Preside Over White Man's Convention," Raleigh *News and Observer*, October 26, 1898, 1; Daniels, *Editor in Politics*, 302.

103. Waddell quoted in *Outlook*, November 19, 1898, and *Wilmington Messenger*, November 8, 1898, in Umfleet, *1898 Wilmington Race Riot*, 92. Umfleet does not provide a city name for the *Outlook* publication.

104. Tyson, "Ghosts of 1898," 6; Umfleet, *1898 Wilmington Race Riot*, 95.

105. Umfleet, *1898 Wilmington Race Riot*, 107.

106. Zucchino, *Wilmington's Lie*, xvi; Umfleet, *1898 Wilmington Race Riot*, 94, 108.

107. Prather, "We Have Taken a City," 15–41, citing Harry Hayden Papers, 7, Special Collections Library, Duke University, Durham, N.C. Also see Umfleet, *1898 Wilmington Race Riot*, 53n70, which describes the Secret Nine as J. Allan Taylor,

Hardy Fennell, W. A. Johnson, L. B. Sasser, William Gilchrist, P. B. Manning, E. S. Lathrop, Walter Parsley, and Hugh MacRae, though some men belonged to multiple groups—including the Group of Six, the Campaign Committee of the Democratic Party, and the Wilmington Chamber of Commerce—"all working toward the common goal of Democratic Party victory." The Group of Six members were William L. Smith, John Berry, Henry Fennell, Thomas Meares, William F. Robertson, and Walker Taylor. The Campaign Committee of the Democratic Party members were Frank Stedman, Edgar Parmele, Walker Taylor, and George Rountree. The chamber of commerce members were James H. Chadbourn Jr., George Rountree, Thomas Strange, William R. Kenan, Thomas C. James, Walker Taylor, S. H. Fishblate, Frank Stedman, William E. Worth, Thomas Clawson, Walter Parsley, J. Allan Taylor, Hugh MacRae, John L. Cantwell, and Samuel Northrop.

108. Umfleet, *1898 Wilmington Race Riot*, 56. J. Peder Zane, editor of "Ghosts of 1898," characterizes it instead as a four-pronged strategy, which was to steal the election, riot, stage a coup, and banish the opposition. Tyson, "Ghosts of 1898," 3.

109. Umfleet, *1898 Wilmington Race Riot*, 432.

110. Thomas Clawson, editor of the *Wilmington Messenger* and member of the Wilmington Chamber of Commerce, had sold Manly his printing press years earlier. In the days preceding the election, Clawson allegedly warned Manly of threats to his life and property and gave him the codes and money to help him pass through the Red Shirt picket lines. Umfleet, *1898 Wilmington Race Riot*, 55, 126, 159.

111. Umfleet, *1898 Wilmington Race Riot*, 433, 116. The names of people on the Committee of Colored Citizens were Dr. J. H. Alston, Richard Ashe, Salem J. Bell, Henry Brown, John H. Brown, John Carroll, John Goins, Elijah Green, Henry C. Green, Henry Green, James P. Green, Josh Green, William Everett Henderson, John Holloway, Daniel Howard, John Harriss Howe, John T. Howe, David Jacobs, David Jones, Rev. Lee (of St. Stephen's), J. W. Lee, Alex Mallett, Dr. T. R. Mask, Thomas C. Miller, William A. Moore, Carter Peamon, James Pearson, Robert B. Pickens, Isham Quick, Robert Reardon, Thomas Rivera, Frederick Sadgwar, Armond Scott, and Rev. James W. Telfair. Umfleet's report notes that federal appointees such as John C. Dancy and John E. Taylor "were not among those called to the meeting because of the fear of federal intervention."

112. Umfleet, *1898 Wilmington Race Riot*, 121.

113. Ibid., 1, 158, 156.

114. Ibid., 121, 127, Introduction (n.p.). The regular Black newspaper was the *Cape Fear Journal*.

115. Ibid., 121–55; Prather, "We Have Taken a City," 15–41.

116. Umfleet, *1898 Wilmington Race Riot*, 124. Umfleet's report draws upon historian Jerome A. McDuffie's interviews of Wilmington residents. McDuffie, "Politics

in Wilmington and New Hanover County, North Carolina, 1865–1900: The Genesis of a Race Riot" (PhD diss., Kent State University, 1979).

117. Umfleet, *1898 Wilmington Race Riot*, 121, 137, 435, 156.

118. Prather, "We Have Taken a City," 35, citing Harry Hayden Papers, Special Collections Library, Duke University, Durham, N.C., 22; June Nash, "The Cost of Violence," *Journal of Black Studies* 4 (December 1973): 164–65.

119. Umfleet, *1898 Wilmington Race Riot*, 121, 152. Umfleet notes that while Russell hid in the rail car during the election, Red Shirts taunted his family at the governor's mansion (108).

120. Ibid., 121, 131, 152, 166; Prather, "We Have Taken a City," 15–41, essay quote on 36. Prather wrote Taylor's first name with one *l*, "Alan."

121. Umfleet, *1898 Wilmington Race Riot*, Introduction, n.p., 136, 155. Umfleet cites McDuffie, "Politics in Wilmington," 719–20, regarding the banishment campaign leadership. Taylor later became an alderman in the city. Umfleet, *1898 Wilmington Race Riot*, 183–84.

122. Umfleet, *1898 Wilmington Race Riot*, Introduction, n.p. Umfleet addresses the duplicitous nature of the planned overthrow further: "The ultimate goal for Taylor and other leaders was the resurgence of white rule of the city and state for a handful of men through whatever means necessary. Many familiar with the history of the city and the events of November 10 will be quick to tell you that the coup d'etat—the overthrow of democratically elected officials—of the afternoon of November 10 is just as important to understand as are the murders and banishment campaign. The change in government on November 10th fully ended black participation in city and county government until the advent of the civil rights era. Furthermore, the 1898 campaign capped by violence in Wilmington proved to be a catalyst for the state—Jim Crow legislation and subjugation of African Americans resulted statewide. Because Wilmington rioters were able to murder blacks in daylight and overthrow a legitimately elected Republican government without penalty or federal intervention, everyone in the state, regardless of race, knew that the white supremacy campaign was victorious on all fronts."

123. Umfleet, *1898 Wilmington Race Riot*, Introduction, n.p.

124. Ibid.

125. Raleigh *News and Observer*, November 11, 1898, 1. The four stacked headlines for this front-page story were placed next to an illustration of Waddell with the caption "Hon. Alfred Moore Waddell, The New Mayor of Wilmington Who Was Elected Yesterday."

126. "A Summary of the Situation," *Wilmington Evening Dispatch*, November 11, 1898, 1. This reflected rhetoric of white political leaders in the following years.

127. "After the Battle," *Wilmington Messenger*, November 12, 1898, 2; Umfleet, *1898 Wilmington Race Riot*, 94.

128. Kantrowitz, "Two Faces of Domination," 95–111. Waddell's version is one

example. The former lawyer, newspaper publisher, Confederate lieutenant colonel, and three-term congressman (who lost his seat to Daniel Russell, who went on to win the governor's office), penned his version of the Wilmington Massacre in the days that followed and from his position as the coup's newly appointed mayor.

129. Gilmore, "Sex and Violence in Procrustes's Bed," 92.

130. Umfleet, *1898 Wilmington Race Riot*, 156; Tyson, "Ghosts of 1898," 14, 6. Tyson noted that at least five of the state's next six governors were drawn from the ranks of white participants in the 1898 campaign and overthrow. The immortalized names included Aycock and Daniels.

131. Umfleet, *1898 Wilmington Race Riot*, 194–221, quote on 195n7.

132. "Home Folks," *Wilmington Messenger*, November 12, 1898, 2.

133. Umfleet, *1898 Wilmington Race Riot*, 195; Craig, *Josephus Daniels*, 41–80.

134. William Sturkey, "Carr Was Indeed Much More Than Silent Sam," *The Herald-Sun*, Durham, North Carolina, October 31, 2017, https://www.heraldsun.com/opinion/article181567401.html.

135. "Julian Shakespeare Carr," History Beneath Our Feet, A Project of the Museum of Durham History, http://museumofdurhamhistory.org/beneathourfeet/people/CarrSJulian; Samuel A. Ashe, "Julian Shakespeare Carr," in the *Biographical History of North Carolina from Colonial Times to the Present*, vol. 2, 1840–1938, ed. Samuel A. Ashe, Stephen B. Weeks, Charles L. Van Noppen, HathiTrust Digital Library, http://hdl.handle.net/2027/nyp.33433067286686.

136. Richard L. Watson Jr., "Simmons, Furnifold McLendel," *NCpedia*, 1994, https://www.ncpedia.org/biography/simmons-furnifold.

137. "The 'Negro Problem' Perplexing and Portentous," January 14, 1904, National and International Notes, *Christian Advocate* 79, no. 2, available at ProQuest, https://www-proquest-com.offcampus.lib.washington.edu/docview/125809230/740ACD0069F54571PQ/1?accountid=14784. The article does not mention "the Negro problem" explicitly but does place "Negro Problem" in quotes in the headline.

138. Jonathan Martin, "Raleigh News and Observer," *North Carolina History Project*, https://northcarolinahistory.org/encyclopedia/raleigh-news-and-observer/.

139. U.S. House Congressional Record, 34, part 2, 56th Congress, 2nd Session (1901): 1591–1658, quoted text on 1638, available at HeinOnline, https://heinonline.org/HOL/P?h=hein.congrec/cro340002&i=650. White also provided evidence of voter fraud in the state's 1898 election. In Scotland Neck, for example, White said that 395 white voters were registered and 534 black voters were registered, but the count was announced that 831 Democrats won over 75 Republicans, and in Halifax the count of 990 Democrats (to 41 Republicans) exceeded the number of registered voters in the entire township by 492. Ibid., 1635.

140. Prather, "We Have Taken a City," 15–41, quote on 16. In 1951 historian and professor Helen Grey Edmond produced *The Negro and Fusion Politics in North*

Carolina: 1894–1901, a counter-narrative that received scholarly attention. In 1984 H. Leon Prather Sr., a history professor and recipient of the American Historical Association's Distinguished Scholar Award, told the story in his centennial essay, "We Have Taken a City: Wilmington Massacre and Coup of 1898." Since then, scholars have explained the event in ways that address class, gender, race, politics, and more. Yet despite feeling proud to have led this process, Prather said in words that preceded the essay's reprint in Cecelski and Tyson's 1998 *Democracy Betrayed*, "I cannot help but conclude that we have all failed in a certain way: most Americans remember nothing of these events despite the enormous impact that they continue to have on racial politics in the United States." In 2006 the Wilmington Race Riot Commission and the North Carolina Department of Cultural Resources' Office of Archives and History, with the principal researcher and author LeRae Umfleet, published findings and recommendations in its *1898 Wilmington Race Riot Report*. At the same time, the Raleigh *News and Observer* produced "The Ghosts of 1898: Wilmington's Race Riot and the Rise of White Supremacy," a sixteen-page section by Timothy B. Tyson that introduced and described the history through narrative, quotes, photographs, maps, and illustrations, and then summarized the Wilmington Race Riot Commission's recommendations. Tyson notes that history textbooks for children in 1901, 1903, and 1906 appear to have completely ignored the white supremacy campaign and later shifts to justifying the overthrow, such as with W[illiam]. C. Allen's descriptions of "incompetent negro and white officers" forced to resign and Alex Mathews [Arnett] with Walter Clinton Jackson's characterization of black office-holders in eastern North Carolina as "some of whom were poorly fitted for their tasks." Tyson does not include Allen's first name or Arnett's last name. William C. Allen, *A Child's History of North Carolina: A Text-Book for North Carolina Schools* (New York: Authors Co-operative Pub. Co), available at HathiTrust, https://babel.hathitrust.org/cgi/pt?id=loc.ark:/13960/t7pn9cd4r&view=1up&seq=13; and Alex Mathews Arnett and Walter Clinton Jackson, *The Story of North Carolina* (Chapel Hill: University of North Carolina Press, 1933), available at HathiTrust, https://babel.hathitrust.org/cgi/pt?id=uva.x000605926&view=1up&seq=7 and cited in Tyson, "Ghosts of 1898," 16.

141. Tyson, "Ghosts of 1898," 13.

142. Ibid., 6.

143. Jennett, "This House Is Built Upon a Rock," Raleigh *News and Observer*, October 9, 1898, 1. Available at *UNC Libraries*, https://exhibits.lib.unc.edu/items/show/2224.

CHAPTER 8

Convict Wars, Tennessee

RAZVAN SIBII

In the fall of 1891, miners from Briceville, a small Appalachian settlement in East Tennessee, smuggled a justice of the peace into a coal pit where the company had replaced free labor with convicts leased from the state. The magistrate interviewed a convict and convinced him to sign an application for habeas corpus proceedings, which the free miners' lawyers subsequently introduced in the Criminal Court of Knox County. The case, known as *State* ex rel. *Warren v. Jack*, hinged on the legality of subleasing convicts, a state-sanctioned system that passed the control of convicts from the state to a lessee (typically a private industrial company) and then on to another sublessee.

The attorney representing the coal companies' interests was Arthur S. Colyar, a former newspaper editor and owner and the founder and former president of the Tennessee Coal, Iron and Railroad Company, the premier lessee of convicts in Tennessee and Alabama.[1] The circuit court judge decided for the free miners, remarking on the strong resemblances between subleasing and slavery. Colyar appealed to the Supreme Court of Tennessee, where a Democratic judge reversed the decision, giving management the final victory.[2]

Not for the first time, Colyar put his prodigious lawyerly skills in the service of a cause—in this instance, convict labor—that was part and parcel of a vision of the New South he advanced in his journalism, included in his political platforms, and profited from in his own businesses. As an owner and editor of two different Democratic newspapers in Nashville, Tennessee, throughout the 1880s (the *Nashville American*, which he edited on two separate occasions and later folded into what eventually became the *Tennessean*, and the *Union*, which he founded), Colyar relentlessly promoted schemes that ensured his preeminence as a businessman and a politician within an unapologetically white supremacist social order. A former slaver, he was one of the first Southerners to advocate for, and then benefit from, the system of convict labor that targeted, terrorized, and oppressed the newly emancipated African American population. His propensity for writing long, persuasive editorials and letters to the editor, coupled with his ready access to the state's most established newspapers, ensured that his views on race relations and labor-management relations had a strong influence on Tennessee's public policy in the emerging Jim Crow era.

A Life in the Spotlight

Arthur St. Clair Colyar was born in 1818 in East Tennessee. His father was a river pilot, and Colyar grew up on a farm alongside twelve siblings, with scant opportunity for formal education. Nevertheless, in his early twenties he ended up teaching school while studying law. He began practicing in 1846, first in the town of Manchester, then in Winchester. His professional success led to financial prosperity. With that came prestige, as Colyar acquired the honorific "Colonel," by which he would be known for the rest of his long life, despite never having served a day in the military. According to his 1907 obituary in the *Nashville American*, "With the money made in the practice of law and in sound business ventures he bought a farm of 1,000 acres of the best land in Coffee County, and with twenty-nine slaves in his retinue he became one of the leading men in the section."[3] The most consequential of Colyar's "sound business ventures" in the first half of his long life was acquiring stock in, and then control over, the Sewanee Mining Company, which had initially been organized in 1852 in Grundy County. Upon assuming company management in 1861, he replaced the troublesome Irish miners already employed in the mines with forty slaves.[4] He would later declare that "in a few months, they [the slaves] were doing good service, and not one of the party failed in the effort to learn to dig coal."[5] He managed the company until 1863 when Union forces swept over the region. After the Civil War, in 1866 he sold much of his property, including his plantation, and, through a series of lawyerly machinations,[6] he became the principal owner and operator of the company, renamed the Tennessee Coal and Railroad Company.[7] Once again, his solution to the instability of the labor market was to put Black men to work in the mines[8]—that is, his former slaves, who, like the four million other African Americans living in the South at the time, were desperate to find jobs and could be drastically underpaid and mistreated.

By the late 1860s, A. S. Colyar had become known across the South as not only an eloquent attorney and able business manager but also a colorful politician who marched to his own drum as he refreshed alliances and, much less frequently, his convictions. Before the war, he had been a member of the Whig Party. He opposed Tennessee's secession from the Union, but in 1861, when the state joined the Confederacy, he served in the Confederate Congress. After the war, he embarked on a strange political trajectory characterized by a mix of persistence, as he repeatedly sought to get elected to statewide office, and abandonment, as he repeatedly withdrew from races, earning himself the moniker the "Great American Withdrawer."[9]

His business reputation, aggressive practice of the law, and loyalty to the state during the war had earned him enough credibility that, upon relocating to Nashville, he was able to quickly become a leading voice in the industrialist wing of the Democratic-Conservatives. He pushed relentlessly for policies that advanced his New South ideas and was an implacable foe of Radicals, Bourbon Democrats,[10] revolutionaries of all stripes, and corrupt government officials. His crusades against the latter reached their high point in 1868 when, employing a characteristic blend of legal action, public address, and letters to the editor, he was able to successfully instigate the placing of the municipality of Nashville into receivership—a feat for which no precedent existed in the United States at the time.[11]

Colyar ran for governor three times and for a seat in the Tennessee legislature twice, always facing considerable resistance not only from his natural political enemies but also from a considerable slice of the Democratic establishment that was deeply suspicious of his constant flirtation with third-party movements.[12] Only one of those races was successful, as he represented Davidson County in the legislature in the late 1870s. Colyar's biographers agree that he always perceived the pursuit of elected office not as a goal in itself but rather as just one way of influencing policy that would be favorable to his ideological and business interests.[13] In 1869 those interests would converge in the one issue Colyar would later declare to be "the great work of the times for Tennessee": convict labor.[14]

Advocating for the Convict Lease

The Tennessee state penitentiary was built in 1829 and, in the decades before the Civil War, had imprisoned primarily poor white men, as African American bodies were under the absolute control of slaveholders. From the beginning, the prison was run like a workshop in an attempt to make the prison financially self-sustaining.[15] That had long infuriated the state's so-called mechanics (that is, craftsmen), who had denounced the competition as unfair and had put constant pressure on the authorities to rethink the system. After the war, heavily in debt and receiving increasing numbers of African Americans arrested and convicted for serious and trifling reasons alike,[16] the penitentiary sought to alleviate its financial distress by leasing its prisoners to a furniture manufacturing company. The experiment ended three years later amid recriminations from both sides, and the state started looking for an alternative arrangement.[17] A solution was then suggested to them by two of the most powerful outfits in the state: the *Republican Banner*, a former Whiggish publication and one of only two Nashville newspapers to have survived the Civil War and subsequent political and economic turmoil,[18] and Colyar's Tennessee Coal and Railroad Company.

For a man who had put his slaves and then his freedmen to work in the mines, the notion of doing the same with the state's convicts must not have seemed too much of a stretch to Colyar.[19] Indeed, it must have seemed like an idea whose time had come, as many of his business peers had also begun considering the scheme. In December 1869 a group of some twenty-five railroad officers, manufacturers, coal mine owners, and coal dealers met in Atlanta, Georgia, for a so-called Coal Convention, with the goal of persuading the railroad men to make more train cars available, at a lower price, to the coal operators for the transportation of coal to market. Colyar was one of the leaders of the meeting, and he delivered a series of speeches stressing the need for closer collaboration between the two industries for the benefit of Tennessee's economy and the pockets of everyone in attendance. In *One Dies, Get Another*, Matthew Mancini argues that the gathering was also the site where the participants discussed Tennessee's eventual convict lease system.[20] Mancini apparently uses Rebecca Hunt Moulder as a source, who, writing in 1976, says that Colyar had also impressed on his audience "the absolute necessity for the southern states to provide convict labor."[21] According to Moulder, the Coal Convention "may have been a catalytic gathering for the future leasing of the [Tennessee] penitentiary system" to Thomas O'Conner (a railroad builder and business partner of Colyar's),[22] who knew the value of convict labor from having witnessed prisoners work on Atlanta's streets under the supervision of private operators. Mancini adds a layer of nefariousness to the conclave, concluding that "the meeting was an event worthy of the pens of Samuel Clemens, Charles Dudley Warner, or Henry Demarest Lloyd, but it has received little attention from historians, perhaps because, although it was a classic Gilded Age scene of industrialists in collusion, it took place in the agrarian South."[23] The newspapers of the era (the *Atlanta Constitution*, the *Nashville Republican Banner*, the *Montgomery Advertiser*, the *Georgia Weekly Telegraph and Journal & Messenger*) provided coverage of the convention, quoting at some length the main speakers, including Colyar, as they called for cheap transportation for their coal. The newspapers did not, however, make any mention of convict leasing.

While the Atlanta meeting might have had a secret side to it, there was nothing hidden or even subtle about the *Republican Banner*'s editorializing in support of convict labor just a few months later, in the summer of 1870. More than a decade before Georgia's Henry Grady would popularize the idea of a New South built on industry rather than agriculture, the *Republican Banner*'s editor felt comfortable prefacing his convict labor argument with the assertion that "it is now a pretty generally recognized theory among Tennesseans that the future commercial greatness of their State depends on her success as a manufacturer" for the other Southern states and that, in turn, manufacturing depended on the availability of "cheap fuel." That fuel would naturally be coal, which was abundant in Tennessee, and its cheapness would be ensured by the state buying up mines and forcing its prisoners to extract the coal—an idea that the *Republican Banner* called "at once novel and original, brilliant and practical." Besides providing the state with a plentiful labor force to kick-start its economy, this proposal would also provide a solution to two other vexing problems: the competition that workshop-trained inmates presented to the "mechanics" of Tennessee, and the expenses incurred by the nearly bankrupt state for the penitentiary. While the editorialist allowed that some of the inmates, who had already been trained as mechanics, would have to stay in their present jobs, he argued, "The common laborers, including the majority of the colored convicts, may be most profitably employed in the mines." The argument ended with a call for "the ablest minds in the State Senate and House of Representatives" to consider this proposal as they amended the laws regulating the functioning of the penitentiary.[24]

Two months later, another "able mind," A. S. Colyar, entered the canvass for governor of Tennessee and delivered a speech in Nashville dedicated in part to the same idea. The *Republican Banner* printed the entirety of the speech in eight columns covering an entire page. Colyar's ability to seamlessly integrate his political, commercial, and ideological interests was on full display. He observed that the state was not capable of running a workshop in the penitentiary without hemorrhaging money, and he attributed that failure not to corruption or incompetence but to what he saw as the state's fundamental inability to operate complex enterprises. "Business under the direction of Government does not pay," Colyar asserted, and the job of training and supervising workers, as well as producing and selling goods, was best left to private entrepreneurs such as himself.[25]

While the *Republican Banner*'s editorialist had focused earlier on the rapid industrialization element of the New South constellation of proposed reforms, Colyar chose to emphasize the need for workers—farmers, miners, railroad men, artisans and merchants alike.[26] He then proposed two ways to make up for the state's labor force deficit: encouraging immigration and putting the state's convicts to work in the mines and on the railroads. The arguments he marshaled for the latter proposal echoed those put forward earlier by the *Republican Banner* (that is, rescuing the state's mechanics from unfair competition, the financial advantages of the scheme, and the economic benefits to be gained from the mining and selling of large quantities of coal), but his long tenure as a slaveholder and business owner allowed him to add a crucial point: convict labor was superior to free labor in that prisoners could not go on strike. Having "absolute control of the labor," Colyar argued, "make[s] it a certainty that the labor can be profitably used."[27]

Colyar's insistence on the brilliance of the convict lease system did not secure him the governorship. But in 1870 his company formally requested convict labor from the state and was granted a contract for one hundred convicts who would work in its Tracy City mines on an experimental basis.[28] In a speech delivered to a "large assemblage" of citizens in Knoxville, Colyar, now in his second tenure as the president of the Tennessee Coal and Railroad Company, declared the arrangement a win-win-win: for the state, the company, and the convicts themselves, who, by his observation, were "much pleased with the change."[29] For its part, the *Republican Banner* expressed "great faith" in the experiment and bragged about being the first to editorialize for the convict lease system.[30] In March 1871 the newspaper followed up with a detailed exposition on the conditions in which the prisoners, all of whom were Black men, worked in the Sewanee coal mines:

They eat breakfast early and enter the mines about sunrise every morning in a body, taking with them their dinners. The guard consists of two or three men, who stand at the mouth of the mines. The convicts are brought out about sundown and marched to their quarters. They are rapidly learning to dig coal, and are already doing fair work. . . . The company employ[s] about one man to every twenty convicts, who instructs them and overlook[s] their work.

The mine is dry and comfortable, and the convicts are much pleased with the change. As a general thing, they do their work cheerfully, and but for their striped clothes, one would suppose they were working for pay.[31]

The state authorities agreed with Colyar's and the *Republican Banner's* positive evaluations of the convict leasing program, and that same year they followed up by leasing the entire state penitentiary to an enterprise headed by Colyar's fellow businessman Thomas O'Conner. Within a few months, the Tennessee Coal and Railroad Company had contracted with O'Conner for more than one hundred additional convicts to be worked in its mines.[32] Despite hitting many rough patches,[33] the company would eventually ride the competitive advantage this cheap labor gave to it to near supremacy in the South. In 1882 Colyar presided over a newly formed Alabama and Tennessee Coal and Iron Company.[34] Four years later, Colyar's outfit, now known as Tennessee Coal, Iron and Railroad Company (TCI) bought the Pratt Coal and Iron Company, Alabama's most important lessee of state convicts.[35] The terms of its ensuing contracts with Alabama were so favorable and the money-making potential so great that in the last years of the 1890s, TCI moved its entire center of operations to Alabama.[36] By now TCI had become "the largest and most formidable iron and coal enterprise in the South."[37]

The Haselton Debate

In 1870 the writer who penned the *Republican Banner* editorial declared that he had yet to meet "the first practical man" who had considered the convict lease system and was not impressed by its efficiency.[38] That was certainly true of Tennessee Coal and Railroad Company's shareholders, much of the political establishment (including the Conservative Republican governor under which the arrangement had been perfected), and the "mechanics" of Tennessee. However, throughout the late 1870s and the 1880s, while the company established its dominance in two states, an increasingly powerful array of forces began to gather in opposition to the convict lease system, some motivated by ethical and humanitarian concerns and others by business considerations. The backlash came from numerous newspapers; some of Colyar's business rivals; the prisoners themselves, who engaged repeatedly in escapes, sabotage, shutdowns, and arson; and, most importantly, the free miners employed by the Tennessee Coal and Railroad Company in both Tennessee and Alabama, who unleashed multiple strikes, some of them escalating into violence and even downright warfare.

As always with Colyar, much of this strife was chronicled in numerous newspaper articles, some authored by himself, some by his detractors, and some by various editors. Perhaps the most visible such media event took place from mid-December 1872 to the end of January 1873 in the *Republican Banner*, whose pages hosted a debate between Colyar and J. C. Haselton of Aetna Mining Company.[39] The latter had been a rival of the old Sewanee Mining Company, and he too had attended the Coal Convention in Atlanta three years earlier. In more than a half dozen published letters to the editor, Haselton and Colyar managed to not only impugn each other's business practices and politely ridicule each other but to also tease out some of the main arguments of the era both in favor of and against convict labor.

The debate was ignited by a brief, innocuous, unsigned piece the newspaper published on December 12 that quoted the *St. Louis Times* as saying that "first-class quality" Tennessee coal had begun making its way into St. Louis.[40] The next day, the *Republican Banner* carried a letter from Colyar complaining that his outfit, the Tennessee Coal and Railroad Company, had not been explicitly credited with supplying the coal in question. As important as the *who*, Colyar noted, was the reason *why* the company was able to ship coal over to Missouri—namely, the coerced working of convicts, which he described as "a steady and uniform system of labor."[41] A few days later, Haselton registered his own objection to Colyar's objection, and the battle was joined. In his opening salvo, Haselton accused Colyar's company of monopoly and warned that no businessman would open up shop in Tennessee (his own efforts notwithstanding) as long as the authorities granted "a few favorites" the use of hundreds of convicts "with power to set them down in any part of the State, to work against whoever they may wish to ruin, or to build up their own fortunes."[42] In his response, Colyar did not deny that his company enjoyed an advantage that others did not but argued that "a monopoly that makes the consumer laugh and the coal vender [*sic*] squeal is a healthy monopoly."[43] The back-and-forth over the question of monopoly continued to feature prominently in every letter written by the two opponents.

The combatants' opening arguments also contained a relevant clue with regard to the wider public opinion environment in which the businessmen operated. In his letter, Haselton alleged that the use of convict labor was "now happily being generally condemned."[44] Colyar did not immediately react to that statement but felt the need to address "the question of health and safety" of the convicts his company employed, even though his opponent had not actually brought up the issue in his initial indictment: "There is perhaps nothing in prison life surpassing the branch prison at the mines. The prison was built without cost to the State, and in all of its departments and arrangements is a first-class prison. The mine is a perfect prison while the convict is at work, and coal digging itself is well nigh a protection from disease."[45] The day after it published Colyar's answer, the *Republican Banner* carried an editorial in which it saluted Colyar's arguments and went even further in its endorsement of the convict lease system than he previously had:

> We are particularly impressed with the advantages of employing the convicts in the mines. The mine is certainly a prison, and if, as Mr. Colyar assures us, coal-digging is itself a sort of protection against disease, we know of no better place to keep a convict than under ground, and no better use for him than the development of the mineral wealth of the country. . . . We think it would be a real benefit to the State if the State prison was removed from the capital of the State to the vicinage of the Tennessee coal bed, and every convict in the State employed in digging out coal.[46]

In reality, of course, coal digging was no protection against disease, which was in fact rampant in the mines and added to the mistreatment of the miners, free and convict alike, at the hands of the guards and supervisors.[47]

Haselton's December 18 piece also forwarded an additional anti–convict labor argument: the probability that the free miners would strongly object to working next to convicts. Predictably enough, Colyar dismissed this concern as a joke.[48] Haselton subsequently presented proof for his assertion: his most skilled miners had left Tennessee because of the convict competition.[49] In a letter published on the first day of the new year, he elaborated, painting an idyllic image of paradise lost:

> When the convicts were introduced at Sewanee, we were working from 150 to 160 men and were supplying near all the coal used south of this point. . . . We had brought from England from thirty to forty families, as well as young men, all experienced miners. Our little settlement consisted of fifty (50) miners' cabins, each with a garden attached, and great was the competition

among those English miners to bring to perfection the finest fruits and flowers, and their cabins had to them all the attractions of *"Home."* . . . Although no default has been made in payments, nor any dissatisfaction expressed towards the management, not one of those English families remain in the State, some having returned to England and the remainder gone to other States. Some of the young men remained, but the places of the skilled miners are imperfectly supplied by the common labor of the country.[50]

Colyar was not impressed. "The working of convicts with us," he wrote, "has not had the effect upon our other miners which it seems to have had on Mr. Haselton's miners."[51] Once again, however, the reality appears to have been otherwise: the free miners employed by the companies controlled by Colyar strenuously objected to the convict lease arrangement from the day it was first implemented in 1870 until the day the state renounced the system altogether in the mid-1890s.

The owner of Aetna Mining was far from finished with his indictment of the Tennessee Coal and Railroad Company's convict lease arrangement, as his focus now broadened to include not just the issues of business fair play and the welfare of the free miner but also concerns about penal philosophy and, indeed, even racism. It is doubtful that Haselton sincerely believed in the righteousness of each one of the many arguments he marshaled in his letters against this system of unfree labor.[52] Nevertheless, the fact that he did open up such a wide front on the topic makes it evident that his contemporaries were indeed able to perceive most of the racial and systemic problems that have afflicted the prison labor system from the abolition of slavery to the present day.

The drudgery of digging for coal, which to Colyar's mind was an argument in favor of employing convict labor in the mines, constituted, in Haselton's opinion, a reason *not* to put prisoners to work underground. "Why not be philanthropic indeed," he asked, "and learn them mechanical trades, by which they may be able to get an honest living when discharged."[53] Prisoners are people too, his argument went, and they still retain some rights, chief among them being the right to be protected by the state from any harm that might come to them while being lawfully deprived of their liberty.[54] Besides, Haselton continued, why should the work of the state's convicts benefit private persons rather than the public at large?

> Many centuries ago this question was debated in the Roman Senate, and it was decreed that prisoner's labor should be used for the benefit of the State, not for private gain. The rock-paved highways of that metropolis remain to this day as a monument of the prisoners' labor and the wisdom of the Rulers.

> Are the highways of Tennessee which are alike enjoyed by poor and rich, so
> good that convict labor could not improve them?[55]

Of course, Haselton was well aware that the State of Tennessee received a
certain sum of money in exchange for leasing out the convicts. Colyar, for his
part, never tired of explaining to him, and to the *Republican Banner*'s readers,
precisely how much money the state received from the lease.[56] But Haselton
was ready to question the moral foundations of the entire system, and he did
so with scathing words:

> Was the penitentiary established as a matter of speculation, and is it the in-
> terest or wish of the State to make money out of it, anymore than to make
> money out of the lunatic asylum, alms house or asylum for deaf and dumb,
> or any other necessary public institution of the State? Why not as well let the
> State House for a pork packing establishment when the General Assembly
> is not in session, or for some other purpose that would command a good
> price, say for an opera troupe, circus or some other show?[57]

For his grand finale, Colyar's rival had prepared two more charges that might
well suit a twenty-first-century manifesto denouncing the use of convict labor.
First, Haselton argued, the overwhelming efficacy of mining coal with people
who can be underpaid, underfed, overworked, and punished violently when
failing to meet their productivity quota might exert so much pressure on future
judges as to induce them to hand out longer sentences to more people than
they would otherwise, thus corrupting the justice system. "The population
of the State has not increased rapidly since 1860," Haselton noted, "but the
number of convicts has."

Second, Haselton asked, "Why is the prison so full, and how does it happen
that nine-tenths, or a very large proportion of them, are colored men"?[58] Alas,
by mid-January 1873, when Haselton was formulating these important questions in his letters to the editor, Colyar had lost interest in debating his rival.
Despite continuing to publish countless opinions for another two decades,
Colyar never got around to addressing the issue Haselton had raised: Why *did*
Tennessee's prisons disproportionally incarcerate Black men, and why did his
mines disproportionally work Black prisoners?

Colyar's "Hierarchy of Labor"

Colyar's prolific output of editorials and letters to the editor over the years
does, however, allow us to discern his vision of a social order that was organized

strictly along class and racial lines. To begin with, his opinions were clearly informed by a basic "hierarchy of labor," to quote Karin Shapiro, whereby "the cities' white artisans deserv[ed] greater consideration than rural, upcountry whites and southern blacks."[59] As exemplified above, virtually every article he ever wrote in defense of the convict lease system opened with a stern reminder to the reader that the state's "mechanics"—that is, the generally white, skilled millworkers, shoemakers, cabinet makers, stonemasons, weavers, and the like—were in danger of being put out of business by the unfair competition presented by the penitentiary workshops. In the first years of his advocacy, Colyar did not care to acknowledge that moving the convicts from the penitentiary shops to the mines was simply moving the problem from one corner of the state's economy to another. Indeed, in his 1870 gubernatorial statement of intention, he stated unequivocally that "this convict labor can be employed at digging coal *without the slightest conflict*," because the "skilled miners which we have in Tennessee, would all be needed in opening mines and instructing the new labor."[60] Later, when public opinion began to turn against the convict lease system, Colyar would acknowledge that the scheme threatened the livelihood of free miners (white and Black alike[61]) but would argue that Tennessee had few such workers (in contrast to coal-rich Pennsylvania) and that those who did live in the state simply needed to see the bigger economic picture.

As far as the newly emancipated African Americans were concerned, Colyar reflected the general attitudes of his station. He had lived a good part of his adult life before the Civil War and was a sworn enemy of Republicanism, so he was not inclined to regard Black people as his potential equals in anything.[62] Having accepted the irreversible demise of the institution of slavery, however, he did grant African Americans a place in Tennessee's new economy. Indeed, he even remarked at one point that the abolition of slavery had benefited the South more than the North because it had freed up a considerable workforce that could transform an agrarian economy into a manufacturing one.[63] The problem, of course, was that white employers across the South, being accustomed to taking a dim view of African Americans' work ethic and intelligence, were hesitant to employ former slaves in their factories.[64] It was not at all surprising, then, that rich white Southerners like Colyar embraced the institution of convict labor, for, in the words of Douglas Blackmon, they "were true slavers, raised in the old traditions of bondage, but also men who believed that African Americans *under the lash* were the key to building an industrial sector in the South to fend off the growing influence of northern capitalists."[65]

While his role as a coal mine owner and operator had forced him to engage publicly with the questions raised by the Thirteenth, Fourteenth, and Fifteenth Amendments to the Constitution, as well as by the emerging "Black Codes," so did his parallel activities as a politician and newspaper editor. In February 1867, when the Radical Republicans who controlled Tennessee passed a first-in-the-nation bill giving African Americans the suffrage, Colyar did not join his fellow Conservative Democrats in their vocal opposition to the legislation. Instead, he set about to convince African Americans to vote for his party over the Republicans.[66] He did so, however, by invoking a vision of interracial harmony that was unlikely to be recognizable to any Black Tennessean who had suffered in bondage because of men like Colyar: "Fortunately, notwithstanding the late war, in which it was confidently predicted there would be a war of races, there is the best possible feeling between the two races. They [the Negroes] know very well that slavery was established, not by us, but by the people from whom we are descended; that we did not make them slaves, and that we were their best friends when they were slaves, and that we have been by no means unmindful of their interest since they were freed."[67] The South's African Americans, of course, did not perceive the Conservative Democrats to be "their best friends" and voted overwhelmingly for the Republicans. Colyar attributed this to carpetbagger deviousness, populism, and outright dishonesty, and expressed his hope that the Black man would eventually come to remember "the kindly treatment of the white at the South; that they gave him work when he wanted it, and assistance when he needed it, and never made him feel that he was an undesirable citizen, and that they did not want him to live with them."[68]

In her thorough examination of Colyar's journalism, Sarah Howell identifies two distinct phases in Colyar's public take on the African American's place in the South. The first phase, roughly lasting until the mid-1880s, is characterized by a relatively gentle tone, as Colyar dispensed paternal advice to the Black Tennessean and assured him of the white man's fundamental fairness and friendliness.[69] In the second phase, Colyar's tone changed noticeably as the advice turned to warnings: African Americans "would do well to have less politics," and should not follow the provocateurs who try to force, in the courts or in the streets, "social equality" between the races.[70] According to Howell, this transformation came as the Southern states began establishing the Jim Crow regime spurred by "the increasing influence of the poor whites in Southern politics."[71] Indeed, Tennessee's political stage was severely shaken up at the beginning of the 1890s, when members of the Farmers' Alliance movement, primarily representing poor whites, formed a third party, the Populist Party, which quickly became a political kingmaker.[72]

A. S. Colyar, Editor

At the beginning of 1882, with the public dispute over convict labor swirling all around him, Colyar decided to replace his impassioned letters to the editor with an even more powerful tool: editorials. At the age of sixty-four, at the height of his business prowess, he took over the Union and American Publishing Company and became owner and editor of *Nashville American*, a newspaper that had resulted from an 1875 merger between the Colyar-friendly *Republican Banner* and the Democratic loyalist *Union and American*.[73] With Colyar in charge, the *American* carried numerous editorials about Tennessee's debt, manufacturing, tariffs, immigration, the American merchant marine, monetary policies, corruption, the standing of the African American citizen, education, and, of course, convict labor. Despite initially assuring his readers that the *American* would remain faithful to the Democratic vision, Colyar vigorously pushed for tariff protections in his editorials, a position that the free-trade Democrats abhorred. In an echo of the legal struggles he engaged in the mid-1860s over the Sewanee Mining Company's fortunes, Colyar was forced to wage a continuous battle with other businessmen who claimed ownership over some of the *American*'s stock. In need of money, in April 1884 Colyar's *American* received a ten-thousand-dollar loan from the Louisville and Nashville Railroad. The loan was part of a wider campaign by the L&N to buy newspaper influence and support against an unfriendly railroad commission, and it was secured with the help of Edward B. Stahlman, a former L&N executive and soon to be a bitter rival in the publishing business.[74] However, in 1884, after just three years at the helm of the *American*, Colyar was muscled out of the editorship by his Democratic rivals. Undaunted, he incorporated a new publishing company and put out a new publication, the *Nashville Union*, which steered an even more independent course than the *American* had. Once again he received financial backing from the railroads.[75]

Colyar would own and edit the *Union* for less than two years, but during that time he was forced to withstand a journalistic assault on his convict labor track record that dwarfed the treatment he had received at Haselton's hands a decade before. The *Union*'s rival, Stahlman's *Nashville Banner*,[76] abhorred convict labor, and in 1885 its pages offered a steady diet of denunciations of both the inhumanity of the system and of Colyar's personal association with it.[77] The paper had plenty of ammunition to work with. TCI's treatment of the prisoners who worked for it had come under repeated investigation by the state government. Spurred to action by Colyar's critics, successive legislative committees had examined the conditions in which the convicts lived and labored in 1871 and 1873, but no wrongdoing had been found.[78] In February 1885, however, yet another investigation was unearthing evidence that TCI had colluded in 1883 with the Cherry, Morrow, O'Conner Company, an outfit that had been set up to manage the penitentiary lease, when they had both filed supposedly competitive bids for the convict lease, only to have TCI win the auction and then promptly sublease 40 percent of the convicts to the rival company.[79] The *Nashville Banner* pulled out all the stops. It named Colyar as the head of the "penitentiary ring" that had perpetrated fraud on the Tennessee taxpayers, and it published harrowing accounts of serious prisoner mistreatment at the hands of TCI guards. Enraged by the accusations, the penitentiary authorities sued the newspaper for libel. Colyar, the former TCI owner and director and the editor of one of the *Banner*'s most prominent Nashville rival newspapers, agreed to represent the penitentiary in court. He eventually won the suit, but the *Nashville Banner* did not relent in its virulent criticism.[80] Not content with denouncing Colyar for fraudulent management practices and inhuman treatment of his former workers, the paper also took him to task for his trademark combination of business, politics, law, and journalism:

> Fact upon fact has been brought out in proof already taken that the wardens and assistant wardens lash and larrup, beat and bruise the convicts not only without authority of law, but in direct violation of express provisions on our statute books. . . . Colonel, was not one little word due from you as an ambitious and aspiring, if not an earnest and patriotic journalist to uphold the majesty of the law by censuring its wanton and reckless violation—one small word, colonel, before you "closed the proof" and declared that the evidence overwhelmingly vindicated the penitentiary officials? . . .
>
> Dear colonel, attorney for the prosecution, lessee of the penitentiary and editor for the lease system, please explain to your readers why all these things were not given to them before you "closed the proof!"
>
> Explain quick, colonel, or a justice-loving people will look upon your new venture in newspaper property as they hold the concern over which you now preside, simply a ring organ for boosting individual interests through the operation of private journalism.[81]

On April 2 the investigating committee presented its findings, which came in two flavors: a majority report that identified some inadequacies in the way

TCI managed its Tracy City branch prison but cleared the company of all serious charges, and a minority report that spoke of brutality, lack of food, and high death rates among the convict workers. Colyar and the *Nashville Union* naturally declared themselves vindicated by the majority report and the favorable ruling in the libel suit. The *Nashville Banner* embraced the minority report and declared itself happy with having contributed to an investigation that had led to resignations among penal officers and much talk about reforming the system. Thomas Woodrow Davis, Colyar's biographer, points out that neither side was likely to have been animated by particularly high-minded concerns: the authors of the majority report merely hewed to the industrialist line promoted by the TCI and its friendly politicians; the minority report "probably reflected the viewpoints of several opposition groups, including states' rights Democrats, labor organizations, agrarians, and the Louisville and Nashville railroad"; and the business interests of the *Nashville Banner*'s owner and editor clashed with those of Colyar.[82]

While Colyar's political and economic power had once again carried the day, public opinion was increasingly breaking against him. Undoubtedly sensing the direction of the prevailing winds, he began to nuance his previously full-throated defense of the convict lease system. At one point during his back-and-forth with Haselton in 1873, he had rather casually made a distinction between putting prisoners to work in the mines (that is, convict *labor*) and assuming responsibility for operating branch prisons and guarding prisoners (that is, convict *lease*). The decision to lease the convicts belonged to the state authorities, he said, not to him, so he was not to be held responsible for the many evils Haselton had identified as natural by-products of the system.[83] Now, in the wake of the highly contentious dual report of the investigative committee, Colyar admitted that the convicts constituted an unfair competition to free labor, and that citizens and legislators alike were dissatisfied with the system.[84] On April 3, 1885, the *Union* published a letter from the president of TCI to the governor of Tennessee in which the official recognized that "the policy of renting and attempting to realize as much money as possible out of all convicts indiscriminately—both well and sick, women and children—does not work out the best results to be realized from penal convictions, and to a large extent abandons the idea of reform, and of separation and classification according to condition of life and grade of offenses."[85] A year later, Colyar nevertheless still took pride in having grappled with the question of "what shall be done with the criminals," seeing as how this has always been "a question of such a delicate public nature that the public man looking for office is afraid to express his real convictions."[86]

In May 1887 Colyar made a triumphant return at the helm of the *Nashville American*, which had been bought by a group of local businessmen, many of whom were affiliated with TCI.[87] Colyar had sold the *Union* to the company that published the *American* and had received some stock.[88] The new arrangement would last a little more than a year, as the main owners chose to quickly unload the paper onto a representative of a states' rights faction of the Democratic Party.[89] Nevertheless, Colyar did find enough time in his second tenure at the newspaper to carry on his battles with his rivals in journalism, notably E. B. Stahlman of the *Nashville Banner* and Henry Watterson of the *Louisville Courier-Journal*. In May 1887 Watterson, who advocated free trade and thus bitterly opposed Colyar's rather un-Democratic protectionist views, told an interviewer that he knew of six or seven Southern newspapers that "supported every Republican and opposed every Democratic policy."[90] Among the papers he listed were Henry Grady's *Atlanta Constitution* and Colyar's *Nashville American*. The latter, Watterson contended, was the ringleader. Regardless of the veracity of that accusation, by October 1888 Colyar had ended his editorial career for good, returning instead to his earlier habit of sending long letters to multiple newspapers in the region.

The "Convict Wars"

Whenever something threatened Colyar's business or ideological priorities, or simply just his sense of order, he tended to point his finger at Populist politicians or irresponsible journalists who allegedly spent most of their time poisoning the minds of simple people. By the last decade of the 1800s, many individuals belonging to those two categories of professional rhetoricians denounced the leasing of convicts to TCI and other mining companies. And the demise of the system was significantly hastened by the direct action of a group of people Colyar had repeatedly dismissed as too sparse in numbers to matter politically: the free miners.[91]

In his editorials and letters, Colyar had always made it clear that an important reason he favored convict labor was its inability to go on strike. His point had been inadvertently illustrated as soon as the Tennessee Coal and Railroad Company had put the first batch of prisoners to work in its mines in 1871, as the free miners already working in Tracy City immediately protested the new arrangement.[92] Their action had ultimately failed, as over the ensuing years, the company continued to add more and more convicts to its labor force. Two decades later, however, the free miners were both more desperate and more determined. In addition to the festering problem of the convicts, the miners were now incensed at several concomitant developments: the practice of paying them in scrip that had to be used in company stores,[93] the firing of their checkweigher, the temporary closing of the Briceville mine, and the imposition of an "iron-clad" contract that removed much of the miners' negotiation leverage. On July 14, 1891, three hundred armed miners entered the branch prison at Briceville, overwhelmed the guards, and put the convicts they found there on a train to Knoxville. The prisoners did not get far, for the state militia soon returned them to the stockade. A few days later, no fewer than fifteen hundred armed miners approached the mine. The commander of the militiamen wisely surrendered, and the convicts were released again. From Briceville the free miners marched to the Coal Creek mine and repeated their feat.

Colyar had seen enough. Although by this time he no longer held any management position in TCI, he was still the company's chief counsel and felt compelled to act. So he did what he had always done: he delivered impassionate public addresses and wrote letters to the editor. On November 3, 1891, the Nashville *Daily American* printed what it called "a vigorous communication from Col. A. S. Colyar."[94] The long missive began with a familiar review of the advantages of the convict lease system (especially the rescuing of the state's "mechanics" from unfair competition) and then segued into an unequivocal condemnation of "the indignity offered the State by this armed mob." There could be no compromise with the miners, Colyar wrote, for they were engaged in "an open, deliberate, premeditated, armed rebellion against the State." Their actions had dishonored Tennessee and "every man in the State," and a truly "chivalrous people" would not suffer such an outrage. He did not spell out exactly what he proposed state authorities do with the antagonistic free miners in this letter to the editor. He did so, however, in a speech he delivered in front of more than one thousand citizens the next summer: "There is but one course, and any man who has enough sense to get in out of the rain would know it—that is to get guns and shoot them!"[95] As to whether the law permitted the state to actually shoot the miners for releasing convicts and setting fire to stockades, the order-loving "Colonel" offered a simple solution: "Our Governor sits up here at the Capitol day by day, with his hands idly folded. I advised him to go and do something. He said he couldn't find it on the statute. I said, do something and then look up the statutes."[96]

Caught between a public opinion that was decidedly unfriendly to the convict labor system and his perceived duty to enforce the law and punish insurrection, Governor John P. Buchanan vacillated. He, in turn, negotiated with the free miners, sent hundreds of militiamen to confront them, negotiated with them again, and then sent for more armed men. During one period of negotiation, Buchanan promised the miners he would ask the state legislature to abolish the convict lease system. He kept his word, but the Democrat-dominated general assembly not only refused to do away with the lease but also gave the governor extra powers to deal harshly with the insurrectionists. It was at this point in the fall of 1891 that the Briceville free miners switched tactics and attempted to fight the coal companies in the courts, as detailed in this chapter's opening paragraph. Their efforts once again ended in failure, and TCI retained its ability to lease convicts and then sublease them to other outfits. More stockade attacks followed, more convicts were released, and more militiamen arrived. In the summer of 1892, the tensions exploded into violence, and loss of life occurred on both sides. In total, the free miners of Tennessee had mounted four major insurrections in two years and, at the end of their strife, had accomplished little.

TCI and the other coal companies, however, did not get to savor their victory. The gubernatorial election of 1892 saw every single major political faction advocate for an end to the convict lease system. In an ironic twist of history, the incoming governor who would eventually sign the bill abolishing the convict lease system was Peter Turney, the former Tennessee Supreme Court judge who had ruled in favor of the mining companies represented by Colyar in the 1891 *State* ex rel. *Warren v. Jack* case described at the opening of this chapter.

In 1895 Tennessee did away with the lease, the first state in the South to do so.[97] The convicts left the mines owned by private companies and moved to the Brushy Mountain state-owned mine. In Mancini's words, "Tennessee's experiment with convict leasing was a Hobbesian one—and was fittingly nasty, brutish, and short."[98] Colyar died in the winter of 1907 at the age of ninety, leaving behind a reputation as a pillar of the Tennessean white establishment but also as a man "who was so contrary that his corpse would float upstream."[99]

Conclusion

Perhaps more than any other man profiled in this book, Arthur S. Colyar managed to productively integrate his multiple roles as a well-respected attorney, an editor of prominent newspapers, an influential maverick Democratic politician, and an owner of and investor in multiple commercial enterprises. Many of the issues that his contemporaries most identified him with—the need for the South to develop homegrown mineral extraction and manufacturing; the need for Tennessee to welcome immigrants; the protection of artisans and tradesmen to the detriment of unskilled, strike-prone miners; the fickle Redeemer patronization of the newly freed Black Tennesseans; and, of course, the leasing of state convicts to mine and railway operators—were advanced through a combination of journalistic crusades, letter-writing campaigns, political initiatives, high-profile court cases, and closed-door meetings with various captains of Southern and Northern industry. Unlike the case of Henry Grady, whose name adorns several high-profile institutions in Atlanta, Colyar's name has not been enshrined on school or hospital frontispieces.[100] But the political economy and social order that he so skillfully advocated for in the public sphere for the entire second half of the nineteenth century undoubtedly carried the day both in the South and across the rest of the country.

In the 1891 *State* ex rel. *Warren v. Jack* case, "Colonel" Colyar brought to bear his prodigious lawyerly skills and his preeminent social standing in Tennessee to secure a win for the coal companies who relied on neo-slaves to increase their profits. But the consequences of his handiwork extended beyond the convict lease system. Almost a century later, the Tennessee Supreme Court's decision in favor of Colyar's clients was instrumental to the state giving the green light to the privatization of a portion of its correctional system.[101] The first private-prison management company in the United States, the Corrections Corporation of America (CCA), was founded in Nashville in 1983, and two years later it offered to lease the state's entire prison system for ninety-nine years. The attorney general of Tennessee scrutinized the proposal and concluded that while the state could not simply offload its correctional duties to a private company, *State* ex rel. *Warren v. Jack* did allow it to contract away the day-to-day management of correctional facilities. After much debate and intense lobbying from the CCA, the Tennessee legislature passed the Private Prison Contracting Act of 1986, one of the first pieces of legislation anywhere in the country to make the new convict lease system official.

To this day, CCA, now known as CoreCivic, remains the largest private prison company in the United States. The industry they helped grow currently incarcerates more than 120,000 people across the country. In her blockbuster book *The New Jim Crow*, Michelle Alexander draws a straight line between the profit motive that animates influential outfits like CCA and the maintenance of the nation's bankrupt criminal justice practices, quoting a 2005 CCA annual report in which the company warns, "The demand for our facilities and services could be adversely affected by the relaxation of enforcement efforts, leniency in conviction and sentencing practices or through the decriminalization of certain activities that are currently proscribed by our criminal laws."[102]

Tennessee now has the fifth-largest population of inmates in facilities managed by private companies whose business model is a direct outgrowth of the late nineteenth-century convict lease system.[103]

The transitions between the three phases of "racialized social control" that Alexander speaks of in her book (i.e., slavery, Jim Crow, and the war on drugs/mass incarceration system) have always been facilitated by prominent white Americans who worked to reassure their peers that they would never lose their economic and political dominance.[104] As Douglas Blackmon shows in *Slavery by Another Name*, for his part, Colyar was a man who "bridged the era of slavery and the distinct new economic opportunities of the region at the end of the nineteenth century."[105] He did that through his work as a political kingmaker in Tennessee, as an attorney, and as an owner and operator of a mining company utilizing convict labor. Most spectacularly, however, he did it through his indefatigable engagement with the press of his time.

He wrote countless letters to the editor to various newspapers in the South, gave numerous interviews to national newspapers (including the *New York Times*), and, of course, also published his own newspapers for a few years. In every one of his missives that dealt with the issue of convict labor, he wielded his considerable rhetorical skills to present the forced labor of Black bodies as a sensible economic measure rather than a continuation of slavery. He was one of the earliest captains of industry to advocate for convict labor. When that system was finally put into practice, he denied its obvious inhumanity. When public opinion turned sharply against neo-slavery, he admitted that the system had some flaws but challenged its detractors to find a better alternative for punishing criminals. The widespread denial surrounding America's current mass incarceration system is owed, in significant part, to pressmen like A. S. Colyar who have often used their control of information to both instigate and conceal racism.

Notes

1. Justin Fuller, "History of the Tennessee Coal, Iron and Railroad Company, 1852–1907" (hereafter, "History of the TCI") (PhD diss., University of North Carolina at Chapel Hill, 1966), 286.

2. Karin A. Shapiro, *A New South Rebellion: The Battle against Convict Labor in the Tennessee Coalfields, 1871–1896* (Chapel Hill: University of North Carolina Press, 1998), 134–37; A. C. Hutson Jr., "The Overthrow of the Convict Lease System in Tennessee," *East Tennessee Historical Society's Publications* 8 (1936): 82–103; Thomas Woodrow Davis, "Arthur S. Colyar and the New South, 1860–1905" (PhD diss.,

University of Missouri, 1962), 307–311; Pete Daniel, "The Tennessee Convict War," *Tennessee Historical Quarterly* 34, no. 3 (1975): 284.

3. "Colonel Arthur St. Colyar Goes to Reward," *Nashville American*, December 14, 1907, 4. According to Karin Shapiro, Colyar inherited his slaves from his first wife. Shapiro, *New South Rebellion*, 22.

4. Fuller, "History of the TCI," 23, 280.

5. "Speech of Colonel A. S. Colyar at Masonic Hall, Last Night," *Republican Banner*, August 14, 1870, 3. See also Douglas A. Blackmon, *Slavery by Another Name: The Re-Enslavement of Black People in America from the Civil War to World War II* (New York: Doubleday, 2008), 51; Fuller, "History of the TCI," 280–81.

6. Fuller, "History of the TCI," 25–28.

7. In 1859 Colyar was retained as legal counsel by one of two groups of creditors fighting over control of a financially distraught Sewanee Mining Company. In 1860 the opposing group created a new corporation, the Tennessee Coal and Railroad Company, with the intention of moving the Sewanee Company's property and operations under its purview. In 1861 Tennessee seceded from the Union, and a Tennessee court awarded Colyar and his partners control of the Sewanee Mining Company. The Civil War briefly halted the legal battles, which then recommenced in earnest in 1865. Intense negotiations between the two groups of creditors eventually led to an agreement in June 1866 that saw Colyar's group buy out its rivals' interest in the company. With its legal situation now clarified, the company became unequivocally known as the Tennessee Coal and Railroad Company. In 1881, having undergone yet another reorganization, it was renamed the Tennessee Coal, Iron and Railroad Company (TCI). Fuller, "History of the TCI," 16–28.

8. Neal Shirley and Saralee Stafford, *Dixie Be Damned: 300 Years of Insurrection in the American South* (Oakland, CA: AK Press, 2015), 125; Fuller, "History of the TCI," 31.

9. Clyde L. Ball, "The Public Career of Colonel A. S. Colyar, 1870–1877," *Tennessee Historical Quarterly* 12, no. 1 (1953): 23–47, 29; Sarah Hardcastle McCanless Howell, "The Editorial Career of Arthur S. Colyar: 1882–1888" (Master's thesis, Vanderbilt University, 1967), 8–10.

10. In 1870, as the newly re-enfranchised former Confederates prepared to contest the gubernatorial election, two political blocs formed in Tennessee: the Radicals, who had dominated the state since the Civil War, and the Conservatives. In turn, the latter were comprised of three subgroups: the Old Line Whigs, the Democrats, and the Conservative Republicans. Colyar ran for the Democratic nomination but soon withdrew his name from the race. He would spend the rest of his career loosely affiliated with the Democrat Party, as the informal leader of its New South industrialist Redeemer faction. That position was never strong enough for Colyar to dominate Democratic politics, but it did occasionally afford him the power to influence the Democrats' economic policies. A staunch advocate of protectionism,

tariffs, low taxes, currency inflation, and the repudiation of the public debt, Colyar fought heavy battles with the "Bourbon Democrats." Davis, "Arthur S. Colyar and the New South," 134–51. During the late 1870s and 1880s, the Bourbons, whom Davis characterizes as a "planter-military" alliance of interests, represented the strongest of three Democrat factions (the others were the New South faction and the Farmers' Alliance/Populist faction) and advocated for laissez-faire capitalism and states' rights. Roger L. Hart notes, however, that the compositions of these factions were "related less to the opposition of economic interests than to traditional group loyalties" that had formed before the war around political campaigns and the all-consuming issue of secession: "Race was not often a divisive issue in politics, because all significant white groups were racist and because blacks were almost inarticulate and powerless." Roger L. Hart, *Redeemers, Bourbons, and Populists: Tennessee 1870–1896* (Baton Rouge: Louisiana State University Press, 1975), xv-xvi.

11. Ball, "Public Career of Colonel A. S. Colyar," 38; Davis, "Arthur S. Colyar and the New South," 37–41; William Waller, *Nashville in the 1890s* (Nashville: Vanderbilt University Press, 1970), 238.

12. Clyde L. Ball, "The Public Career of Colonel A. S. Colyar, 1870–1877 (Continued)," *Tennessee Historical Quarterly* 3, no. 1 (1953): 230.

13. Davis, "Arthur S. Colyar and the New South," 4, 168, 225–26; Ball, "Public Career of Colonel A. S. Colyar," 39; Ball, "Public Career of Colonel A. S. Colyar (Continued)," 217.

14. "Address by Colonel A. S. Colyar on the Resources of Tennessee," *Republican Banner*, May 27, 1871, 1.

15. W. J. Michael Cody and Andy D. Bennett, "Privatization of Correctional Institutions: The Tennessee Experience," *Vanderbilt Law Review*, no. 40 (1987): 829–30; Rebecca Hunt Moulder, "Convicts as Capital: Thomas O'Conner and the Leases of the Tennessee Penitentiary System, 1871–1883," *East Tennessee Historical Society's Publications* 48 (1976): 44.

16. Shirley and Stafford, *Dixie Be Damned*, 123; Perry C. Cotham, *Toil, Turmoil, and Triumph: A Portrait of the Tennessee Labor Movement* (Franklin, TN: Hillsboro Press, 1995), 58; Ronald L. Lewis, *Black Coal Miners in America: Race, Class, and Community Conflict, 1780–1980* (Lexington: University Press of Kentucky, 2015), 21; Milfred C. Fierce, *Slavery Revisited: Blacks and the Southern Convict Lease System, 1865–1933* (New York: Africana Studies Research Center, Brooklyn College, City University of New York, 1994), 75.

17. Matthew J. Mancini, *One Dies, Get Another: Convict Leasing in the American South, 1866–1928* (Columbia: University of South Carolina Press, 1996), 154–55, Moulder, "Convicts as Capital," 46.

18. James Summerville, "Albert Roberts, Journalist of the New South: Part II," *Tennessee Historical Quarterly* 42, no. 2 (1983): 179.

19. Shapiro, *New South Rebellion*, 52.

20. Mancini, *One Dies, Get Another*, 155.

21. Moulder, "Convicts as Capital," 51.

22. Ibid., 50.

23. Mancini, *One Dies, Get Another*, 155.

24. "The Convict Labor of the State," *Republican Banner*, June 10, 1870, 2.

25. When it suited his purposes, Colyar did not hesitate to propose expanding government responsibilities as he did when he agitated for the creation of a state immigration office. Davis, "Arthur S. Colyar and the New South," 140. Moreover, according to Ball, the notion of "running the government as a business enterprise was a favorite one with Colyar." Ball, "Public Career of Colonel A. S. Colyar," 38.

26. For a discussion of the dearth of industrial workers in the South at the time, see Fuller, "History of the TCI," 272–336.

27. "Speech of Colonel A. S. Colyar at Masonic Hall, Last Night," *Republican Banner*, August 14, 1870, 3.

28. Alex Lichtenstein, *Twice the Work of Free Labor: The Political Economy of Convict Labor in the New South* (New York: Verso, 1996), 88; David Oshinsky, *Worse Than Slavery: Parchman Farm and the Ordeal of Jim Crow Justice* (New York: Simon and Schuster, 1996).

29. "Address by Colonel A. S. Colyar on the Resources of Tennessee," *Republican Banner*, May 27, 1871, 1.

30. "Undeveloped Wealth and Power," *Republican Banner*, February 7, 1871, 2.

31. "Convicts as Coal Diggers," *Republican Banner*, March 8, 1871, 4. In the opening paragraph of the article, the *Republican Banner*'s writer tells readers that his exposition is based on "information communicated to us." The exact source is not specified, but the article repeats Colyar's "much pleased with the change" assertion verbatim.

32. Fuller, "History of the TCI," 35; Mancini, *One Dies, Get Another*, 155–56.

33. Colyar lost control of the company temporarily in the Panic of 1873, because he was not able to pay for the convict labor lease. Lichtenstein, *Twice the Work of Free Labor*, 107; Fuller, "History of the TCI," 35.

34. Howell, "Editorial Career of Arthur S. Colyar," 47.

35. Fuller, "History of the TCI," 60; Lichtenstein, *Twice the Work of Free Labor*, 93.

36. For information about Alabama's convict leasing system and TCI's involvement in that state, see Fuller, "History of the TCI"; Blackmon, *Slavery by Another Name*; Mancini, *One Dies, Get Another*; Lichtenstein, *Twice the Work of Free Labor*; Robert David Ward and William Warren Rogers, *Convicts, Coal, and the Banner Mine Tragedy* (Tuscaloosa: University of Alabama Press, 2015).

37. Fuller, "History of the TCI," 78.

38. "The Convict Labor of the State," *Republican Banner*, June 10, 1870, 2.

39. Davis, "Arthur S. Colyar and the New South," 125–26; Fuller, "History of the TCI," 310–311.

40. "Tennessee Coal in Demand," *Republican Banner*, December 12, 1872, 4.

41. "The St. Louis Coal Trade Again—Is this Enterprise?" *Republican Banner*, December 13, 1872, 4.

42. "Ibid. Haselton's professed fears proved true, as in 1880 his company went bankrupt. Fuller, "History of the TCI," 310–11.

43. "Cheap Coal. Something More about This Vexed Question," *Republican Banner*, December 19, 1872, 4.

44. "Tennessee Coal—The St. Louis Coal Trade—Convict Labor, Etc.," *Republican Banner*, December 18, 1872, 4.

45. "Cheap Coal. Something More about This Vexed Question," *Republican Banner*, December 19, 1872, 4.

46. "Convict Labor Utilized," *Republican Banner*, December 20, 1872, 2. On December 28 the *Banner*'s editor reiterated his support for putting "the whole convict force at work in Tennessee coal mines, and the prison building in Nashville sold to individual manufacturers for a factory of some kind." "Utilization of Convict Labor," *Republican Banner*, December 28, 1872, 2.

47. Mancini, *One Dies, Get Another*, 160–61; Fuller, "History of the TCI," 301–306.

48. "Cheap Coal. Something More about This Vexed Question," *Republican Banner*, December 19, 1872, 4.

49. "Value of Convict Labor," *Republican Banner*, December 25, 1872, 4.

50. "Coal and Convict Labor Again," *Republican Banner*, January 1, 1873, 4.

51. "Coal and Convict Labor. Mr. Colyar to Mr. Haselton, of the Aetna Mines," *Republican Banner*, December 27, 1872, 4.

52. When answering Haselton's accusations, Colyar diagnosed his opponent with a chronic case of sour grapes, claiming that the latter had at one time shown an interest in leasing convicts for his mines. "Practical Benefits of Mining with Convict Labor," *Republican Banner*, December 29, 1872, 4. Moulder writes that Haselton had been so intent on obtaining the first convict lease that he had come to blows with the eventual grantee, Thomas O'Conner. Moulder, "Convicts as Capital," 53. For his part, Haselton denied having applied for the lease. "Value of Convict Labor," *Republican Banner*, December 25, 1872, 4. Finally, as far as Haselton's concern for the welfare of the Black man is concerned, while expressing his suspicions regarding the preponderance of African Americans in the penitentiary, the industrialist did not hesitate to assert that Black men have always "pilfered," for stealing is a "characteristic" of "this class." "Do Convicts Worked in Mines Pay the State Handsomely," *Republican Banner*, January 19, 1873, 3.

53. "Coal and Convict Labor Again," *Republican Banner*, January 1, 1873.

54. "Do Convicts Worked in Mines Pay the State Handsomely," *Republican Banner*, January 19, 1873, 3.

55. "Value of Convict Labor," *Republican Banner*, December 25, 1872, 4.

56. It's worth noting, however, that in 1897, after the convict lease system had been abolished by the Tennessee legislature, Governor Peter Turney wrote, "The state really made no money but rather lost by leasing of convicts on account of riots, outbreaks and invasions." Hutson, "Overthrow of the Convict Lease System," 103.

57. "Do Convicts Worked in Mines Pay the State Handsomely," *Republican Banner*, January 19, 1873, 3.

58. Ibid. Between 1867 and 1896, the percentage of African American prisoners in the penitentiary was about 60 percent. Lewis, *Black Coal Miners in America*, 20. In 1891, out of the 746 convicts working in Tennessee mines, nearly 75 percent were Black. More than 94 percent of the free miners were white. Daniel, "Tennessee Convict War," 274. Between 1892 and 1894, of the 1,587 male prisoners in the state penitentiary, more than 1,200 were Black. Fierce, *Slavery Revisited*, 89.

59. Shapiro, *New South Rebellion*, 51.

60. "Speech of Colonel A. S. Colyar at Masonic Hall, Last Night," *Republican Banner*, August 14, 1870, 3; my emphasis.

61. From the very beginning, the company's white workers held the better jobs. Fuller, "History of the TCI," 275. In the 1880s the vast majority (300) of the company's convict miners were Black. When hiring free Black miners, the company favored nonunion workers (332).

62. Ball, "Public Career of Colonel A. S. Colyar," 37; Davis, "Arthur S. Colyar and the New South," 29, 329. On the other hand, as Fierce notes, "conservative middle- and upper-class White Democrats" like Colyar "did not feel as threatened by Blacks as did other Whites." Fierce, *Slavery Revisited*, 19.

63. Howell, "Editorial Career of Arthur S. Colyar," 78. During the Civil War, Colyar had also been in favor of enlisting Black men into the Confederate Army. Ball, "Public Career of Colonel A. S. Colyar," 31–32.

64. Howell, "Editorial Career of Arthur S. Colyar," 16; Davis, "Arthur S. Colyar and the New South," 105.

65. Blackmon, *Slavery by Another Name*, 55; my emphasis. Fuller emphasizes the role that Black miners played as strikebreakers used by management to fight the striking white miners. Fuller, "History of the TCI," 283.

66. Ball, "Public Career of Colonel A. S. Colyar," 36.

67. *Nashville Daily Press and Times*, March 11, 1867, quoted in Ball, "Public Career of Colonel A. S. Colyar," 36.

68. "The Colored Voter," Nashville *Daily American*, April 15, 1883.

69. Howell, "Editorial Career of Arthur S. Colyar," 62.

70. "The Colored People," *Nashville Union*, April 18, 1885, 2 (unsigned editorial); "Democracy and the Rights of the Negro," *Nashville Union*, August 2, 1885, 4 (unsigned editorial). Perhaps a bit surprisingly, Ida B. Wells praised Colyar in

her now-famous *Southern Horrors: Lynch Law in All Its Phases* pamphlet, noting that he had written a letter to the editor of the *Nashville American* denouncing "the awful criminal depravity" of lynching in Tennessee. (Text of pamphlet available at http://www.curtisamerica.com/documents/lynching1892.html.) Colyar's body of editorials and letters, however, suggests that he was not as much bothered by the injustices visited on the victims of lynching as by the fact that the killing was done by mobs instead of the proper state authorities. Colyar abhorred all insurrectionist movements, from the KKK, to anarchists, to striking miners, for their activities outside the law.

71. Howell, "Editorial Career of Arthur S. Colyar," 89.

72. Paul H. Bergeron, Stephen V. Ash, and Jeanette Keith, *Tennesseans and Their History* (Knoxville: University of Tennessee Press, 1999).

73. Summerville, "Albert Roberts, Journalist of the New South, Part II," 179.

74. Maury Klein, *History of the Louisville and Nashville Railroad* (Lexington: University Press of Kentucky, 1972), 377.

75. The railroads' investment into Colyar's publishing endeavors does not seem to have paid off. Klein writes, "The mercurial and opportunistic Colyar proved no friend to the L&N despite the financial help he received from the company." Klein, *History of the Louisville and Nashville Railroad*, 377. Between 1881 and 1887, Colyar was a director and stockholder (and a counsel on retainer) of the Nashville, Chattanooga, and St. Louis Railroad Company. Davis, "Arthur S. Colyar and the New South," 2, 141, 225. He was also an attorney on retainer for the Memphis and Charleston Railroad. Davis, "Arthur S. Colyar and the New South," 392, 225. In 1887, at the time of his return at the helm of the *Nashville American*, Colyar was also a director of the Baltimore, Nashville, and Memphis Railroad and of the Alabama-based Sheffield Coal, Iron, and Railroad Company. Davis, "Arthur S. Colyar and the New South," 233–34.

76. Not to be confused with the defunct *Republican Banner*, the *Nashville Banner* was founded in April 1876 and was controlled by Edward Bushrod Stahlman. According to Davis, at this time the *Banner* claimed to be independent but harbored Republican sympathies. Davis, "Arthur S. Colyar and the New South," 227n3. When his railroad interests had aligned with Stahlman's, Colyar had praised his colleague, but when their interests began to diverge, the *American*'s editorial bullets flew hard and fast toward the *Banner*'s owner. Howell, "Editorial Career of Arthur S. Colyar," 83–84, 110–11.

77. Howell, "Editorial Career of Arthur S. Colyar," 92–95.

78. Davis, "Arthur S. Colyar and the New South," 120, 126.

79. The business careers of Colyar and O'Conner were deeply intertwined. In 1871 Colyar's company leased its convict laborers from O'Conner's outfit. Five years later the "O'Conner syndicate" actually acquired control of the TCI for five years—one of the many changes in ownership that the company went through

during those tumultuous decades. Davis, "Arthur S. Colyar and the New South," 236. Shortly afterward, O'Conner received a second lease to the penitentiary, which expired in 1883. The new lease was won directly by TCI amid strong suspicions that O'Conner and TCI had colluded to exclude everyone else from the auction. See Fuller, "History of the TCI," 290–92.

80. Howell, "Editorial Career of Arthur S. Colyar," 92; Davis, "Arthur S. Colyar and the New South," 293.

81. "Tewksbury Outdone. A Glimpse at Proof as Developed from the Inside," *Nashville Banner*, February 23, 1885, 2.

82. Davis, "Arthur S. Colyar and the New South," 297.

83. "Practical Benefits of Mining with Convict Labor," *Republican Banner*, December 29, 1872, 4.

84. "The State Prisons. Report of the Legislative Committee on Their Condition and Management," *Nashville Union*, April 3, 1885, 2.

85. Ibid.

86. "The Penitentiary Lease," *Nashville Union*, July 29, 1886, 2.

87. Davis, "Arthur S. Colyar and the New South," 232–33.

88. Waller, *Nashville in the 1890s*, 79.

89. Davis, "Arthur S. Colyar and the New South," 235.

90. Howell, "Editorial Career of Arthur S. Colyar," 110. See also Davis, "Arthur S. Colyar and the New South," 350.

91. For narratives about the 1891–1892 "convict wars," see Mancini, *One Dies, Get Another*, 162–66; Daniel, "Tennessee Convict War," 273–92; A. C. Hutson Jr., "The Coal Miners' Insurrections of 1891 in Anderson County, Tennessee," *East Tennessee Historical Society's Publications*, no. 7 (1935): 103–121; Hutson, "Overthrow of the Convict Lease System," 82–103; Lichtenstein, *Twice the Work of Free Labor*, 99–101; Shirley and Stafford, *Dixie Be Damned*, 121–43; Cotham, *Toil, Turmoil, and Triumph*; 55–79; Fuller, "History of the TCI," 294–96; Lewis, *Black Coal Miners in America*, 23–25; Fierce, *Slavery Revisited*, 196–99; Davis, "Arthur S. Colyar and the New South," 307–318.

92. Shapiro, *New South Rebellion*, 75; Mancini, *One Dies, Get Another*, 159; Cotham, *Toil, Turmoil, and Triumph*, 60; Fuller, "History of the TCI," 289–90; Lewis, *Black Coal Miners in America*, 21.

93. In 1885, replying to the *Banner*'s denunciation of the scrip system, Colyar had breezily dismissed the concern: "If the *Banner* desires to test the popularity of its position on this question [of the scrip], let it suggest to employes [*sic*] of the Tennessee Coal, Iron & Railroad company that they have a meeting and take action on the matter by vote, and we think we can guarantee that the company will act in accordance with the wishes of its labor." "The 'Scrip' System," *Nashville Union*, November 19, 1885, 2.

94. "The Late Outrage. A Vigorous Communication from Col. A. S. Colyar," Nashville *Daily American*, November 3, 1891, 3.

95. "Aroused Citizens. The Tabernacle the Scene of a Mass Meeting. The State's Humiliation and Disgrace Set Forth. Able Speeches by Col. A. S. Colyar, Mayor Guild and Others," Nashville *Daily American*, August 19, 1892, 4.

96. Ibid.

97. Shirley and Stafford, *Dixie Be Damned*, 138.

98. Mancini, *One Dies, Get Another*, 153.

99. Ball, "Public Career of Colonel A. S. Colyar (Continued)," 238.

100. Howell, "Editorial Career of Arthur S. Colyar," iii.

101. Cody and Bennett, "Privatization of Correctional Institutions," 829–49.

102. Qtd. in Michelle Alexander, *The New Jim Crow: Mass Incarceration in the Age of Colorblindness*, rev. ed. (New York: The New Press, 2012), 231.

103. "Private Prisons in the United States," The Sentencing Project, accessed June 8, 2020, https://www.sentencingproject.org/publications/private-prisons -united-states/.

104. Alexander, *New Jim Crow*, 4.

105. Blackmon, *Slavery by Another Name*, 55.

CHAPTER 9

Tourist Empires, Florida

KATHY ROBERTS FORDE
AND BRYAN BOWMAN

In the late nineteenth century, two Northern industrialists focused their entrepreneurial energy on Florida: Henry M. Flagler, Standard Oil partner of John D. Rockefeller, and Henry B. Plant, president of the Southern Express Company. They spent several decades building expansive railroad, steamship, hotel, resort, and land enterprises throughout the state, Flagler on the east coast and Plant on the west. Working in quiet cooperation while cultivating a public image as business competitors, they developed the modern state of Florida out of frontier swampland. Along the way, they crafted Florida's version of the New South: a tourist wonderland propped up by a white supremacist political economy and social order.

Flagler and Plant built their business empires, along with much of the early civic and industrial infrastructure of modern Florida, on the backs of Black and immigrant coerced labor. To do so, they took advantage of convict leasing and debt peonage, two brutal systems of unfree labor in the post–Civil War South underwritten by white supremacist ideology. When Northern muckraking journalists, prominent Black leaders and journalists, Justice Department investigators, and even a former convict camp captain exposed their exploitation of workers, Flagler attempted to whitewash public knowledge and opinion about their business and labor practices through his controlling interests in influential Florida newspapers. He was wildly successful, ultimately silencing critics and gaining favorable public opinion in Florida that endures today. Flagler's white-wash was so successful, in fact, that historians have yet to tell this story in full.

When Plant died in 1899, his heirs sold his Florida holdings. But Flagler continued developing his Florida businesses until his own death in 1913, just one year after he completed construction of his fabled Overseas Railroad across the Keys. As a Standard Oil partner, Flagler was more prominent than Plant in both Florida and the nation during their lifetimes and after. His greater longevity, reputational stature, and developmental exploits in Florida, plus his leadership in controlling press coverage of his and other railroad interests in the state, make him the primary actor in the story we tell.

While others have documented Flagler's and Plant's business activities, labor practices, and development of Florida, and the role of convict leasing and debt peonage in creating the New South, we are the first to explore these subjects collectively as constituent parts of Florida's modernization project. And while others have briefly noted Flagler's efforts to influence public opinion about his railroad's peonage controversy through his newspaper interests, we are the first to demonstrate in detail how Flagler, in cooperation with white supremacist business and political interests, co-opted influential Florida newspapers to successfully challenge exposés in the Northern press, combat a massive Justice Department investigation, and control public information and opinion in Florida about his and Plant's business and labor practices. As commercial enterprises tied to party politics, Florida newspapers were critical players in the political economy Flagler helped build in the state as he single-mindedly pursued his business interests and bent the political machinery to his needs.

Flagler and the Press

In the late nineteenth century, mass political parties dominated the U.S. public sphere, and despite the rise of independent commercial newspapers in big cities, many newspapers, keeping with past practices, remained editorially partisan. In Florida most white newspapers were closely allied with the Democratic Party, which was committed to white supremacy and nearly monolithic in the state. These newspapers supported one-party rule and tended to suppress information about election improprieties often aimed at blocking the Black vote. What's more, many Florida newspapers were owned or otherwise controlled by business interests, primarily the railroad and turpentine industries. Flagler was the master builder of this arrangement.[1]

In 1886 Flagler heard *Atlanta Constitution* editor Henry W. Grady deliver what became his famous New South speech at Delmonico's restaurant in New York City before the New England Society of New York. Flagler was just beginning his Florida business ventures in St. Augustine, and Grady's vision of a South open to and ready for Northern industrial investment must have been encouraging. Leaving nothing to chance, Flagler moved to control as many actors and forces as he could in Florida and bend them to his will, including newspaper editors and content—and thus public opinion.[2]

Flagler was the mastermind and primary mover in building a network of newspapers controlled by the Flagler System that served not only his business interests but also those of Florida railroads at large. Wherever his railroads traveled, he bought controlling interests in existing newspapers or started new ones, including the Jacksonville *Times-Union, St. Augustine Record, Palm Beach Daily News, Miami Metropolis* (eventually renamed *Miami News*), *Miami Herald*, and a newspaper in Key West. Controlling these newspapers was a means to control public knowledge about business activities, including unsavory labor practices, and to influence public policy.[3]

It was, in fact, common in the late nineteenth century for railroad interests to own newspapers. For a time, railroad magnate Jay Gould owned the *New York World* and held a controlling interest in the *New York Tribune*. The Southern Railway Security Company, for which Plant served on the board of directors, held interests in the *Raleigh News*, the *Richmond Dispatch*, the *Richmond Enquirer*, the Memphis *Commercial Appeal*, and the *Atlanta Constitution* for at least brief periods. The vertical integration was advantageous to both railroads and newspapers. After all, railroads had the capital resources to subsidize newspapers, including the means to provide paper at a lower freight rate and to distribute at reduced costs. While the railroads extended the reach of the newspaper, the newspaper offered positive publicity for the railroad and editorial influence. Newspapers also allowed railroad capitalists the means to manipulate markets in the interests of their railroads and bank accounts through the dissemination of fraudulent financial information. Of course, nothing about these arrangements benefited those who fell victim to the brutal labor systems railroads in the South that were often used to increase their profits.[4]

Flagler purchased the loyalty of the editor of the *Times-Union* and influenced the newspaper's editorial content, often using coded or indirect communication to soften his approach.[5] He loaned Wilson money when the newspaper's and his own personal finances floundered. He asked Wilson to republish items from other newspapers and publish original items favorable to Flagler and his interests. He donated twenty thousand dollars to finance the construction of a gymnasium at Florida Agricultural College, where Wilson was president of the board of trustees. This donation, ten thousand dollars more than the ten thousand dollars architects had proposed was necessary to build the gym, seems to have been an attempt to purchase editorial influence through both largesse to the college and lining Wilson's personal pockets. As always, Flagler was careful to keep his string-pulling cloaked in secrecy: "I have only one request to make in this connection, and that is that just as little publicity be given this letter as is possible."[6]

Along the way, Wilson—who was president of the Florida Press Association from 1905 to 1906—arranged to have the college pass a resolution testifying to Flagler's beneficent business and civic investments in Florida, all publicized in his newspaper. Wilson also published *Times-Union* editorials and content favorable to Flagler and complained that New York newspapers circulated in Florida negatively affected the circulation of Flagler's paper. Flagler suggested they "ought to do everything" possible "to suppress such a vile sheet as the [New York] *Journal*," which Flagler deemed to have the largest circulation in Florida of any New York paper.[7] The *New York Journal* was the principal holding of William Randolph Hearst's publishing empire and was often denigrated as a sensation-seeking yellow journal. Even more offensive to Flagler, the *Journal* was editorially committed to the Populist wing of the Democratic Party, while Flagler, though a Republican, was aligned with the Bourbon Democrats who controlled Florida. What's more, Hearst's newspapers and magazines often attacked government collusion with trusts, including Standard Oil.[8]

Railroad Empires

Stagnating under the burden of wartime debt, decimated infrastructure, and low population, Florida welcomed Northern investment and industrial innovation after the Civil War. The state, newly established in 1845, offered a generous land-grant program for railroads to encourage the development of transportation systems. Land grants continued in the postwar years as railroads, with many lines destroyed or damaged, rebuilt and extended their reach. In the 1880s and 1890s, railroad companies consolidated, with Flagler and Plant leading the way, making land grabs as they bought and built railway systems on the east and west coasts of Florida.[9]

From 1885 until his death in 1913, Henry Flagler spent a considerable part of his Standard Oil fortune and the better part of his time developing Florida's east coast from the northern city of Jacksonville to the southernmost point of Key West. He built hotels, resorts, and cities, including Palm Beach and Miami, investing heavily in civic infrastructure and connecting the state's entire east coast through his ever-expanding Florida East Coast Railway (FECR, Flagler's consolidated railroad system), eventually building his famous extension across the Keys. Flagler's extensive business interests in Florida became known as the "Flagler System." In 1898, two years after the first FECR passenger train pulled into what became the new city of Miami, Flagler invited President William McKinley to visit. "My domain begins at Jacksonville," he wrote. "If the East Coast of Florida belonged to anyone else, I should venture to say that it possesses very great attractions."[10]

Before Flagler moved to Florida in 1885 and became a visible investor and developer, he collaborated behind the scenes with Henry Plant, who had begun building his own Florida railroad enterprise in 1879. Plant created the Plant Investment Company (PICO) in 1882 to manage his various business enterprises, which came to extend well beyond railroads, and Flagler joined him as a principal investor. The two men quietly agreed to develop Florida cooperatively but separately along the two coasts. PICO eventually became the "Plant System," which included railroads, hotels, steamships, real estate interests, and even telegraph lines. By 1891 Flagler served on the board of directors of Plant's Savannah, Florida, and Western Railway Company (Plant's consolidated railroad system), and the two men began planning the jointly owned Union Station in Jacksonville in order to bankrupt competing railroads. In 1892 they planned a connection in Sanford between their respective railway lines and an expedition through the Everglades to explore the feasibility of laying railroad track from Florida's west coast to Miami. Viewed by the public as competitors, the men took pains to cloak their close collaboration.[11]

When Flagler and Plant began building their business empires in Florida, it was clear that labor shortages would be a constant challenge. It was also clear they could take advantage of Florida's poorly regulated state and county convict lease systems and widespread practice of debt peonage to remedy the problem. Before the Civil War, the South had a limited prison system that rarely involved the enslaved, whose social worlds were controlled by their enslavers. After the war, only a few prisons and jails remained to handle what soon became a flood of newly freed Black men, women, and children convicted of a range of crimes enumerated in new state laws that basically criminalized Blackness. Florida's Black Codes, passed in 1865, provided that anyone unable to pay the fine after arrest and conviction would be hired out to anyone willing to cover it. The most widespread offense was vagrancy, the so-called crime of being unemployed—which brought a large fine few Black people could afford to pay. Florida built its one state penitentiary in 1868 and instituted a dual system of prisoner control, housing some prisoners while leasing out others to private companies to use as labor for the railroad, turpentine, lumber, and cotton industries. By 1877 Florida closed the state prison and made convict leasing the primary vehicle of penal control. A bipartite system developed, with both the state and counties practicing convict lease. The county system was especially barbaric.[12]

A seemingly endless supply of prisoners and not enough jails was a problem that white sheriffs, government officials, businessmen, and industrialists in Florida concocted and then solved to their mutual benefit through convict lease. The opportunities made available through this system, for both the government and private business, were enormous. For the government, the convict lease system provided a powerful tool to subjugate Black Americans and intimidate them into behaving in accordance with the new social order. It also eliminated government expenses in housing and caring for convicts and generated revenue for a cash-strapped government. For the private businesses, the government provided cheap labor that undercut free labor and maximized profit—and proved to be disturbingly disposable.[13]

In addition to convict lease, another form of labor control emerged in Florida and across the South: debt peonage, a form of coerced labor based on a worker's debt to his employer, which primarily targeted Black people while sometimes ensnaring immigrants and poor white Southerners. In practice, convict leasing often led to debt peonage. Convicts were often kept by lessees after the lease or sublease had expired, acquiring debt and thus becoming peons. Conversely, peons who had escaped from abusive employers were often arrested by local sheriffs on charges of vagrancy and shifted into the convict lease system. In addition, the Florida legislature passed contract labor laws making it a crime to leave a job while owing money to the employer. Labor contractors, knowing the law was on their side, often rounded up indebted workers at gunpoint and forced them back to the labor camps to save time they would lose through engaging the judicial system.[14]

The Southern Democratic movement known as Redemption emerged in the early 1870s with the goal of rebuilding a racial caste system and reversing Black advances made during Reconstruction. Marked by waves of vicious racial violence and state legislation aimed at suppressing Black citizenship and equality promised under the Fourteenth and Fifteenth Amendments, Redemption seeded the ground for the expansion of convict lease and peonage. In the 1880s, the decade Flagler and Plant began building their Florida business empires, Black Floridians struggled to hold on to the ballot against the threat of white violence and lynching. They viewed the Democratic Party, Paul Ortiz writes, as "the party of privilege, railroads, and white supremacy." The white elite's efforts to "keep labor 'the weakest of all the factors' in society provided the engine for disfranchisement. Racial oppression and economic progress—as it was defined by Florida's elite—were two sides of the same coin." Redemption's racial caste system was not merely political and social. It was thoroughly economic. And Flagler and Plant benefited tremendously from it.[15]

By 1901 nearly every Southern state had barred Black citizens from voting and from serving in public office, on juries, and in the administration of the justice system. Florida's frontier culture and low population, coupled with virulent white supremacy and eager industrialists, produced a convict lease system with "an especially intense, violent quality," according to Matthew Mancini. In 1901, for example, a Jacksonville newspaper reported a white ex-convict's testimony of "barbarous treatment" at a Hillsboro County convict camp. He told of camp overseers mercilessly lashing the bare backs of their charges—including a Black woman and a fifteen-year-old Black boy—with a four-inch-wide leather strap up to seventy-five times and rubbing pine gum or sulfur into the wounds.[16] In a 1906 letter to the governor, a state prison physician reported that convicts were made to wear flesh-cutting "pick shackles" at all times at an Escambia County camp. He described them as "instruments of torture."[17]

Like convict leasing, Florida's peonage system targeted Black citizens—and was widespread and violent. In 1906 a special agent in Florida informed the Justice Department that the more he investigated, "the more convinced I am that peonage exists in every section of this State." That same year, the Justice Department twice prosecuted F. J. O'Hara, a prominent Floridian who owned sawmill and naval stores operations, for peonage; the jury acquitted him both times in less than half an hour after hearing massive evidence against him. Charles W. Russell, the assistant attorney general prosecuting the case, told the U.S. attorney general that the jury had been unduly influenced by biased, inaccurate reports in favor of O'Hara that they had read in the *Times-Union* during the trial. Russell complained about the news reports to George W. Wilson, the editor of the Jacksonville paper that Flagler partially owned and seemed to entirely control. Russell expected little to change. "The paper belongs to a corporation," he informed the attorney general, "and Wilson is a poor man and dependent on his salary." Soon the Justice Department was investigating Flagler himself for peonage.[18]

The corporation Russell mentioned was the Florida Publishing Company, which Flagler had bought along with Plant and another railroad owner in 1891. As a Standard Oil executive, Flagler had long endured state and federal government investigations into the growth of monopolies and the attendant press coverage; he understood from bitter experience the power of the press to expose unsavory business practices and shape public opinion.[19] He despised the press and was determined to control it, at least in Florida. The Jacksonville *Times-Union* was the most powerful newspaper in the state, and Flagler veiled the identities of its owners behind the entity of the Florida Publishing Company. As Flagler biographer Edward N. Akin writes, his "purpose was to establish a powerful 'Standard' newspaper in Florida."[20]

Henry Plant and Convict Labor:
American Siberia

In the spring of 1891, J. C. Powell published *American Siberia*, a book detailing his experiences as captain of various convict camps in Florida. The dispassionate and unrepentant chronicle laid bare the barbarism of Florida's convict lease system and exposed Henry Plant's role in it. At almost the same time that Powell's memoir was published, Flagler and Plant joined forces to purchase the powerful *Times-Union*, likely as a means, in part, to keep news of Powell's exposé from circulating in Florida's most influential newspaper. When the *Atlanta Constitution* reported on Powell's book in 1893, it neglected to note the connection to Plant. (The historical record has been silent on this critical point until recently.)[21]

Ten years before Powell published his memoirs, Plant's East Florida Railroad Company had bought the state convict lease contract for a period of two years, from 1881 to 1882, paying fifteen dollars a year for each convict. On receiving the lease, the railroad moved the state convicts, many of whom "were sick or maimed," according to Powell, to a new camp six miles outside Jacksonville. The immediate task was to build a new line from Jacksonville, Florida, to connect with another line being built simultaneously from Waycross, Georgia, to the Florida state line.[22]

Before Plant's railroad received the lease, Florida newspapers had reported horrific abuse in the convict lease system at Lake Eustace, where convicts were being used to build other railroads. Shelter and food were limited and crude; no medical attention was provided for rampant dysentery, scurvy, and pneumonia; and the punishments were inhumane. One prisoner was strung up by his thumbs and left to die. In response to public outcry about this abuse, the

Florida Senate sent a committee to investigate Plant's new East Florida Railroad camp. It found the food and housing "decent," recommended warmer clothing for the prisoners, and suggested the adjutant general should visit state convict camps unannounced five times a year, with his reports to be published "in a capital newspaper" (presumably the *Times-Union*). This last recommendation was never heeded, and the report itself was a whitewash. While Powell reported in *American Siberia* that food was plentiful at Plant's camp, brutal whippings were commonplace, workdays long and dangerous, and escape attempts frequent. Prisoners slept at night in stockades with one long chain running through their ankle irons. Every Sunday naked prisoners were blasted with icy water from a hose as a bath, even in winter. Soon an epidemic of spinal meningitis raged through the camp, killing twenty-seven in just one week. "Man after man was stricken down," Powell wrote, "and while many recovered, the deaths predominated, and their appalling suddenness and the uselessness of any precautions invested the visitation with a superstitious horror impossible to describe."[23]

Somehow the work on the railroad continued. The Waycross Short Line was completed on April 25, 1881, with the driving of a silver spike where the two lines met at the twenty-seventh milepost. Florida now had its most direct route to the North. State convicts moved on to build the Live Oak and Rowlands Bluff Railroad before Plant's lease ended. Plant continued to use convict labor as he built his empire along Florida's west coast. In 1897, just two years before his death, he used county convicts to grade and build roads and driveways to service his opulent Tampa Bay Hotel.[24]

Exposés of Convict Lease in the Press

In the last two decades of the nineteenth century, Southern newspapers, including Florida outlets, reported occasional public outcries against the convict lease system, but the issue garnered significant attention in the Northern press. Well-known white Southerners Rebecca Felton and George Washington Cable penned prominent magazine exposés.[25] Black leaders spoke out forcefully and often against convict leasing. In 1893 Ida B. Wells, along with Frederick Douglass, Garland Penn, and Ferdinand L. Barnett, laid bare the techniques of racial terror and control exercised across the South—"the 'twin infamies' of convict leasing and lynching," as Wells put it in the pamphlet *The Reason Why the Colored American Is Not in the World's Columbian Exposition*.[26] Thomas Fortune, a Florida native who became one of the most prominent Black leaders and editors of the era, testified about convict leasing before the U.S. Senate in 1883 and published his *Status of the Race* report in his newspaper the *New York Globe*.[27] In the pages of his popular Black newspapers in New York City, he repeatedly exposed and opposed convict leasing and debt peonage in the South.[28] Mary Church Terrell, a founder and former president of the National Association of Colored Women, published a magazine essay in 1907 exposing convict leasing and debt peonage, highlighting the plight of Black and white women and girls who were especially vulnerable to sexual violence in these systems.[29]

While these labor systems were widely criticized and disapproved outside the South, white supremacist political and business interests in the South quickly snuffed out periodic expressions of public concern. When it came to convict leasing and debt peonage, the Northern press and the Southern press operated in distinctly different public spheres. In 1899 a Florida state prison investigating committee issued a report about conditions at convict camps. At one camp, six convicts had been shot and killed by guards and two had killed themselves in despair. In another, eighty men and women were held in filthy conditions and provided scant food and no beds; they lived in fear of the whipping bosses and received no medical care. A 1913 state prison physician report showed that convicts with missing limbs, gunshot wounds, and diseases such as malaria and syphilis were systematically compelled to work. Kid Wright, convict #5083, had his "heel chopped off" and was "graded" by the physician as "1/3," meaning he was deemed capable of doing a third of the work of a healthy convict.[30] "Yet the public seemed ignorant of these brutalities," historian Gordon Carper notes. "No incident . . . occurred which stimulated action."[31]

Henry Flagler, Convict Labor, and Debt Peonage: The Land Where It Never Snows

When Henry Flagler began building hotels in St. Augustine in the 1880s, he quickly became frustrated with the lack of dependable railway services to deliver the necessary building materials. To solve the problem, he purchased existing railroads and consolidated them into a new entity, the Florida East Coast Railway Company. He made the line from Georgia to Jacksonville and into St. Augustine dependable. Once he discovered the unspoiled beauty of Palm Beach, he began extending the FECR southward so he could build more luxury hotels, create Palm Beach, and erect his Gilded Age marble mansion known as Whitehall.

By 1896 Flagler had extended the FECR into what became known as Miami (the city's early leaders wanted to call the new city "Flagler," but he demurred), and a great American city was founded. At the turn of the new century, he began publishing the *Florida East Coast Homeseeker*, a promotional magazine circulated outside of Florida seeking settlers, and he offered Northern newspaper editors free train trips to Florida. In 1905 Flagler announced he would extend the FECR from Miami across the open waters to the Florida Keys, with the idea that a port in Key West would open profitable trade lines with Cuba and Latin America. The "Overseas Railroad" came to be known as "Flagler's Folly" by contemporaries who believed the project impossible. It may have been foolhardy—the engineering feat cost untold numbers of lives in its construction and was ultimately destroyed by a hurricane in 1935—but it was not impossible. In 1912, one year before his death, Flagler rode the first passenger train into the Key West station at the end of his extension across the Keys.[32]

From the beginning, the Overseas Railroad project faced labor shortages, so Flagler hired managers with the will and wherewithal to gather workforces and ensure the work would be completed. Flagler's men used both convict and peon labor as a supplement to free labor to build his empire of hotels and railways. The extension of FECR south from West Palm Beach to Miami—a distance of approximately sixty-five miles—used convict labor. The FECR leased each convict for $2.50 a month and provided meals and lodging; given that free labor could receive up to $2.00 for a day's work (although the FECR typically paid $1.25 to $1.50 per day), the FECR made a considerable profit margin through leasing convicts.[33] In Miami, Flagler's builder for his Royal Palm Hotel, John Sewell, used convict labor to clear the land.[34] Foremen used long, notched whips to control the laborers. (Sewell later became mayor of Miami and arranged to have shackles placed on the ankles of convict laborers working on the streets in order to prevent escape.) Laying tracks into Miami was particularly dangerous work given the rocky terrain; between Lemon City and Miami, a distance of about five miles, about twenty convict laborers died while working and were buried in ditches along the train tracks. The rail lines leading to the Key West Extension, historian Paul Ortiz writes, "were first graded by Black convict laborers and then, at the turn of the century, by individuals held against their will by agents working for Flagler's railroad."[35] In 1898 guests at Flagler's hotel in Palm Beach witnessed the public auction of four hundred Black convicts, including many women and teenage boys. Many were emaciated from poor care and sickness, and all were led off by their new "masters" with bound hands and shackled feet. Some were destined to work on the southward extension of the FECR south of Miami.[36]

By the early twentieth century, the lucrative turpentine and phosphate industries had claimed most of Florida's state and county convict leases, and labor shortages were severe. Many Florida companies began recruiting labor from the North—in particular, recent immigrants from southern and eastern Europe, who were understood to be nonwhite in the late nineteenth and early twentieth centuries—and often used debt peonage to exploit workers. When J. C. Meredith, Flagler's chief engineer for the extension across the Keys, began work in May 1905, he had only a small force of Black workers. He quickly turned to labor recruiters in the North. Edward J. Triay, Meredith's labor agent for the FECR, built a particularly productive relationship with Francesco Sabbia, who ran the German-Italian Exchange, a labor recruiting agency in New York City that targeted recent immigrants. Triay agreed that the FECR would pay Sabbia three dollars for each immigrant he persuaded to sign a labor contract and delivered to Miami to work on the extension (the FECR tacked this three dollars onto each recruit's transportation debt). Sabbia sent his first labor recruits to Flagler in late 1905, and within seven weeks he had earned ten thousand dollars and the FECR had gained more than four thousand workers. Triay came out of the deal a thousand dollars richer too, having accepted a bribe from Sabbia to use his agency instead of another.[37]

Within a few months, workers began returning to New York with harrowing accounts of their experiences working on Flagler's extension in the Keys. Nineteen-year-old Harry Hermanson's experience illustrates the dirty tricks Sabbia and the FECR employed to obtain workers and compel labor. In New York a recruiting agent for Sabbia bought drinks for Hermanson and his friend while talking up the glories of working in Florida, "the land where it never snows" as recruitment flyers posted around the city claimed. Sabbia and his agents herded a crowd of boozy young men to a ferry that transported them to a train headed south; from that point, they were captives, locked in train cars until they reached Jacksonville, where they were moved to another train and eventually transported by boat to FECR work camps in the Keys. There, Hermanson was threatened at gunpoint, forced to work in waist-high water, made to sleep on coral rock with no bedding, poorly fed, and sickened with a poisonous rash. His mother traveled from New York to collect him after the FECR guards stole the money she had sent to secure her son's release, a sum meant to cover his debt to the company for transportation to Florida. He had been led to believe transportation was free. He told Justice Department investigators he had been "shanghaied."[38]

Voluminous evidence in the Justice Department peonage files, including worker and employee affidavits and reports from federal investigations, paints a vivid and damning portrait of FECR labor recruitment and peonage practices. Sabbia told recruits they would be working near Miami, so most had no idea they would be stranded on remote islands with no means of leaving except company boats. He also told recruits the FECR would provide transportation, room, and board as part of their payment, but they learned in the work camps that they were in debt to the company for transportation from New York to Florida and that room and board would be deducted from their paychecks. The prices of clothing, shoes, blankets, and food in the company commissary were unusually high, a ploy to increase worker debt. Several foremen required workers to give them a cut of their pay. Some walking bosses and foremen were brutal, threatening workers at gunpoint and beating them with axes. Many of them forced laborers to work even when sick. The men in charge lived on houseboats moored at camp docks and thus prevented common laborers from stowing away with passing fishermen. Workers could not leave the island without a pass from the FECR, and they could not get a pass if they owed the company money. They were even charged for the boat ride from the Keys to Miami when they were released. Several workers testified that boys, many in their teens and some as young as eleven, also worked in the FECR labor camps. (The Flagler Papers include a trove of "release of claims" contracts for minors, with parents required to sign away their right of claim against the FECR should their child be injured or killed while working for the railroad. Parents received one dollar for signing the release. Children worked as quartermasters, diver's tenders, deckhands, axmen, waiters, messengers, and common laborers.) Fresh water, not available in the Keys, was transported by barge; in the early days, shortages of drinking water sometimes occurred and workers reported being charged for it.[39]

Local sheriffs cooperated with J. C. Meredith in a system that lined both government and FECR pockets and kept laborers rotating through a corrupt system that was difficult to escape. Sheriffs and their officers guarded FECR laborers after they arrived in Miami and waited on docks for boats to take them to the Keys. They forced workers who had escaped to the mainland back to the Keys, receiving monthly payments from the FECR and additional fees for each returned worker. If the FECR released workers who had paid their debt to the company but had not saved additional funds, sheriffs arrested the workers on charges of vagrancy or other minor offenses and put them to labor on chain gangs or in the convict lease system. Once these workers had worked off their fines, they were forced to leave town by foot with no money. Many hopped trains and found themselves arrested and forced into convict labor again. As they made their way north and escaped the reach of the Southern convict lease system, they worked odd jobs until they made enough money for train fare home. Most returned penniless. In contrast, Meredith's contract with Flagler reportedly promised an additional fifty thousand dollars if he could complete the extension in five years.[40]

A young FECR foreman, E. T. Clyatt, was troubled by the company's treatment of its laborers. He left after only two months in the Keys and gave detailed testimony to Justice Department officials investigating peonage on the extension. FECR policy regarding the care and keeping of workers was largely unwritten but clearly understood: workers were not allowed to leave the island if they owed a debt; they were forced to work at 5:00 in the morning, even if sick; and they were not allowed food if they were not able to work. Amid the brutality, a few FECR officers were kind to the workers and helped them get released against company's orders. Nonetheless, Clyatt reported that many sick men nearly starved in the labor camps and that several Black women with restaurants in the Keys secretly provided food to keep the men alive. Many Black men died from fever or mistreatment, he said, and were buried on the islands. One FECR laborer, John Pinder, was able to sneak a desperate plea out to the world. In a letter addressed to U.S. senator William B. Allison, Pinder wrote, "In the name of God and humanity . . . for are [*sic*] children and wives and sisters and sweetheart's sake save us."[41]

The Flagler Peonage Investigation
and Muckraking Exposés

As long as industrialists exploited mainly Black Americans in their labor regimes, as was the case with convict labor, it was difficult for reformers to raise a sustained public outcry. But when thousands of putatively white immigrants from southern and eastern Europe became ensnared in the FECR's peonage scheme, and the Justice Department launched a massive investigation of peonage complaints against Flagler and his Florida East Coast Railway in late 1906, the Northern press machinery of exposure clicked into high gear. That same year, inspired in part by Ida Tarbell's serialized profile of Standard Oil published in *McClure's Magazine* across 1902–1904, the Justice Department initiated a Sherman Antitrust Act case against Standard Oil.[42] Flagler was in the Justice Department's crosshairs from two different angles.

The Justice Department's peonage investigation of Flagler's Florida East Coast Railway began in the fall of 1906, after Mary Grace Quackenbos, a New

York City lawyer whose practice was devoted to the protection of poor immigrants, informed both the attorney general and President Theodore Roosevelt that she was headed to Florida to investigate peonage on behalf of her clients. Assistant Attorney General Charles W. Russell was leading the Justice Department's peonage investigations in the South. He found Quackenbos's ability to gain the trust of immigrant witnesses so valuable that the Justice Department hired her as a special assistant U.S. attorney in October 1906.[43]

From 1906 to 1908, Russell and Quackenbos vigorously investigated peonage in the South, with the Flagler case given pride of place.[44] The expansive material on the Flagler peonage investigation in the Justice Department files—correspondence, memoranda, affidavits, depositions, case documents, press clippings, government reports, and more—presents a clear and convincing case that the FECR practiced peonage. It also documents dramatic backstories. As the government's case grew stronger, the FECR employed strongmen to intimidate government agents and bribe witnesses. Russell and Quackenbos suspected John Moses Cheney, the U.S. attorney in Florida, of sympathy with the Flagler interests, leading the attorney general to issue a stern warning to Cheney against "lukewarmness" in prosecuting peonage cases. For his part, Cheney informed the attorney general of his suspicions that Russell and Quackenbos were sharing information about the Flagler case with muckraking journalists. Government attorneys filled their correspondence, memoranda, and reports with worries that press exposure would inspire backlash in Florida and prejudice juries against the government's case.[45]

The press appears practically everywhere in the Flagler peonage episode. In New York, foreign-language newspapers serving immigrant communities carried stories about the FECR's mistreatment of immigrant workers, leading consulates to raise the alarm with the U.S. federal government. Magazine publisher S. S. McClure helped finance Quackenbos's initial trip to investigate peonage in the South before she was employed by the Justice Department. When prominent Floridian reformer Emma Stirling asked President Roosevelt in October 1906 to investigate peonage in her home state, newspapermen in the White House published her statements, prompting editorial blowback from Florida newspapers. When Flagler's engineers in charge of the extension across the Keys, Meredith and William J. Krome, were indicted for peonage in February 1907, the *Florida Times-Union* and newspapers across the state launched a sustained attack on the federal government's prosecutions of peonage cases in Florida.[46]

Shortly after Meredith and Krome were indicted, Russell sent the attorney general a report naming Flagler as the conductor of orchestrated resistance among the business and government elites of Florida:

> We have henceforth a fight in the open with those who have combined to thwart our purposes through the ownership of the principal Florida newspaper, the Jacksonville Times-Union, which has suppressed and misrepresented the truth, and sought, by the most extraordinary methods to influence juries and public opinion and to drive us out of the State. Flagler, the millionaire lord of the East Coast, to whom everything there good or bad is attributed, the turpentine association, the United groceries concern, the newspapers which take their cues largely and their news from the Times-Union, and whatever else can be organized, all these are organizing for this principal struggle, so far as Florida is concerned.[47]

For once, at least, Russell and his subordinate Cheney agreed. "Everything is in a ferment here in regard to peonage matters," Cheney reported to the attorney general, enclosing a *Times-Union* article as evidence. The Florida State Board of Trade, citing "grossly erroneous and flagrantly unjust" reports in Northern papers, demanded that U.S. senators and representatives from Florida introduce resolutions in Congress calling for an investigation of the Justice Department's peonage investigations in the South.[48] The *Times-Union* and other Florida newspapers reported it all and joined the attack against the Justice Department.[49] The Florida Press Association passed a resolution to "unite in a vigorous effort to refute the published conditions in Florida."[50] S. A. Rawls, president of the State Board of Trade, Cheney explained to the attorney general, was "the very head and font of the convict system in Florida and is, in fact, the lessee of the State convicts and the very foundation of the political graft connected with the convict system." Rawls was also "one of the moving spirits in the political 'ring' that control[led] the Democratic politics of Florida." The FECR indictments, Cheney wrote, have "concentrate[d] the tremendous influences that are thus aroused against us."[51]

Cheney also sent the attorney general a muckraking exposé published in March 1907 in *Cosmopolitan* magazine, part of the Hearst media empire. In "Slavery in the United States Today," muckraker Richard Barry described the enslavement of Black and white workers "under trust domination" across the South. His article detailed the vast symbiotic systems of convict leasing and debt peonage and featured a prominent portrait of Flagler with the caption "Henry M. Flagler, of the Standard Oil Clique, Whose Florida East Coast Railway Is Largely Responsible for Slavery Conditions in Florida." What's more, Barry accused Flagler of masterminding a "whitewashing process" involving "prominent citizens, the machinery of journalism and politics." The *New York Evening Journal,* a Hearst paper, republished a large part of the *Cosmopolitan* article.[52] As Barry noted ironically, "The monumental error made by the employers of Florida was going beyond the Black man with their slavery."[53]

The *Cosmopolitan* exposé was not the first news report to shine light on debt peonage in Florida and across the South. Several years earlier, Fred Cubberly, U.S. commissioner for the Northern District of Florida, successfully prosecuted the first peonage case in the United States and generated intense interest across Florida and the entire country. Newspaper coverage was expansive, and Cubberly himself published an anonymous article on the case in the *Independent,* a muckraking journal in New York. The Clyatt case, as it was known, traveled all the way to the U.S. Supreme Court, which upheld the constitutionality of the 1867 federal peonage statute under which Clyatt was prosecuted.[54] Armed with a constitutionally protected peonage law, progressives focused their reform energies on peonage in the South, and even before the *Cosmopolitan* exposé, Flagler found his name and railroad connected to peonage charges in New York newspapers and the most widely read Socialist newspaper in the United States, *Appeal to Reason.*[55] While these previous exposés inflamed passions in Florida, the *Cosmopolitan* article lit a raging fire of outrage.

In short order, Frank Clark, a prominent Florida representative in the U.S. Congress, rumored to have received his position through Flagler's patronage, attacked the Justice Department and the press from the House floor and called for a congressional investigation of the department's conduct. He called reports of peonage in Florida "sensational rot"; Northern newspapers and magazines were "slimy publications"; the attorney general, whose last name was Bonaparte, was "this transplanted bud of alleged French nobility"; Quackenbos was a "slum worker"; and Russell, both a Southerner and a Democrat, was a "dirty bird that fouls its own nest."[56] Responding to the *Washington Post's* ongoing coverage of the Justice Department's FECR peonage investigation, Clark had dismissed the veracity of witnesses weeks before the *Cosmopolitan* exposé appeared, saying, "The Government witnesses in these so-called peonage cases are, as a rule, riff-raff scum from the large cities and loafing negroes, and neither class will work."[57] The *Times-Union* carried a front-page story about Clark's attack on the Justice Department and a few days later the front-page story "Mr. Flagler's Wonderful Work in the Development of Florida." Newspapers across the state denounced the *Cosmopolitan* story as "lies," "false reports," and "slander" and praised Representative Clark for defending Florida's honor.[58] The editor of the Tallahassee *Morning Sun* summarized the *Times-Union*'s response: "The concern of the Times-Union is chiefly aroused because the name of Henry M. Flagler has been connected with the charge of peonage."[59] Cheney wrote again to the attorney general to warn him that "the press of the State has fallen into line almost unanimously" with the Flagler interests and that the Justice Department should make efforts to prevent jury tampering. The exposés published in the Northern press, he wrote, "are very burdensome to me," and "justice will be more or less thwarted on account of them. . . . Every such article renders it more and more difficult to obtain an unprejudiced jury."[60]

The government prosecuted FECR engineers in Florida and labor agents in New York. In summer 1908 a federal judge in Jacksonville, James W. Locke, dismissed the peonage charges against the engineers, finding lack of evidence.[61] The labor agents were tried in New York in November 1908 under an 1866 slave-kidnapping law. An organized campaign by the FECR to tamper with and bribe Justice Department witnesses during the lead-up to the trial damaged the government's case. An attorney representing Sabbia and Triay paid witnesses to sign statements contradicting prior depositions given to the Justice Department. Other witnesses were offered large payouts if they would leave New York and not testify at trial. The FECR even attempted to bribe a government official to hand over classified documents, and an employee of an FECR attorney was charged with assaulting a Justice Department agent. By the time the Justice Department learned what was happening, the credibility of many of their firsthand witnesses had been undermined. Quackenbos was forced to gather evidence to discredit her own witnesses in case Sabbia and Triay attempted to call them on their own behalf. "It is very annoying to have one's work count for naught," she wrote with rare candor in a report to the attorney general.[62]

In a trial that amounted to theater of the absurd, the defendants admitted to peonage but denied enslavement and kidnapping. Judge Charles M. Hough told the prosecution that if it proved peonage "up to the hilt, I will dismiss the indictment." Sympathetic with the defense from the beginning, the judge dismissed the case within a few days, stating the government had failed to establish conspiracy.[63] Flagler's efforts to thwart the Justice Department had succeeded, and his whitewash was complete when the Immigration Commission of the U.S. Congress published its follow-up report maligning the Justice Department, clearing Flagler and the Florida East Coast Railway and cleansing Florida's reputation of barbaric labor practices.[64] As Russell had predicted in his report to Attorney General Bonaparte, at the center of it all was Flagler's network of newspapers throughout Florida.

Conclusion

Brutal penal and labor systems blanketed the South for at least fifty years following the Civil War and were central to New South modernization projects. They disproportionately targeted Black Americans and, for a brief period during the first decade of the twentieth century, immigrants who occupied a liminal space between whiteness and Blackness in the racial hierarchy of the period. In Florida the white press played a constitutive role in protecting these labor systems and the white supremacist regimes of economic and political power that produced and profited from them. Henry Flagler, with his network of newspapers and immense influence in the state, made sure of it. Journalism was a blunt instrument Flagler could purchase and use to thwart justice and corrupt the democratic process.

Florida abolished the state convict lease in 1919 but the barbarous county system lived on. After five decades of state-sanctioned racial terror, this system ironically came to an end when a sixteen-year-old white boy from North Dakota named Martin Tabert was brutally murdered in a Putnam Lumber Company convict camp by a sadistic whipping boss. A reporter for the *New York World*, Samuel D. McCoy, relentlessly covered the case for two months in 1923, forcing Florida officials to investigate what they initially claimed was a death from malaria. McCoy's reporting, fifty articles that typically appeared on the front page of the influential Pulitzer newspaper, shone a bright light in the darkest corners of the Florida convict lease system, raising an editorial outcry across the country, even in Florida, to abolish the convict lease. Florida was forced to abolish the convict lease for good, and McCoy won a Pulitzer Prize for Public Service. But other forms of forced labor, including the chain gang, lived on.[65]

The role of convict leasing and peonage in building the Sunshine State—and the role of Flagler and Plant in both—barely registers in popular historical narratives of Florida. Historians have almost entirely missed Plant's critical appearance in *American Siberia*, J. C. Powell's memoirs of serving as captain of convict camps throughout Florida.[66] Two prominent histories of Flagler's Overseas Railroad—both sold in the Flagler Museum store—gloss Flagler's use of convict labor and thoroughly misrepresent the government's peonage case against Flagler's Florida East Coast Railway. Les Standiford erroneously claimed the U.S. government dropped its charges against the FECR because witnesses were unreliable; many, he wrote, "had criminal backgrounds, most were uneducated, others were alcoholic." He consulted neither the historical literature on convict lease and debt peonage nor the Justice Department's voluminous records in its peonage investigation of Flagler's operations.[67] Seth Bramson also did not consult these critical secondary and primary sources. Instead, he blamed the workers themselves for raising false peonage charges: "Trouble arose from the 'United Nations' of people employed in the construction."[68] Flagler's whitewash worked during his lifetime, and it continues to work in our own era.

Flagler's name appears today across the Florida landscape: Flagler College, Flagler County, Flagler Memorial Bridge, Flagler Beach. The Flagler Museum celebrates Flagler as the inventor of modern Florida: "The transportation infrastructure and the tourist and agricultural industries he established remain, even today, the very foundation of Florida's economy."[69] This much is true. It's also true that Flagler co-opted the communication network of Florida through his financial and political control of powerful newspapers across the state. In this way, he controlled public knowledge and opinion about his and other industrialists' exploitation of convict and peon labor in the service of ambition, empire, and white supremacy.

Notes

1. Richard L. Kaplan, "From Partisanship to Professionalism: The Transformation of the Daily Press," in *A History of the Book in America*, vol. 4, *Print in Motion: The Expansion of Publishing and Reading in the United States, 1880–1940*, ed. Carl F. Kaestle and Janice A. Radway (Chapel Hill: University of North Carolina Press, 2009), 133–35; Paul Ortiz, *Emancipation Betrayed: The Hidden History of Black Organizing and White Violence in Florida from Reconstruction to the Bloody Election of 1920* (Berkeley: University of California Press, 2005), 37–39, 53; R. Pope Reese to William R. Harr, Assistant Attorney General, December 20, 1910, in Pete Daniel, ed., *The Peonage Files of the U.S. Department of Justice, 1901–1945* (microfilm, 26 reels, University Publications of America, 1989; hereafter, *Peonage Files*), reel 15, describing industry control of newspapers and effects on attempted peonage prosecutions.

2. Raymond B. Nixon, *Henry W. Grady: Spokesman of the New South* (1969; New York: Russell and Russell, 1943), 242.

3. Henry Flagler to J. R. Parrot, Vice President FECR, November 18, 1899, letter book vol. 99c, p. 452, Henry Morrison Flagler Papers, Flagler Museum, Palm Beach (hereafter, Flagler Papers); Henry Flagler to J. R. Parrot, Vice President FECR,

November 20, 1899, letter book vol. 99c, p. 459, Flagler Papers; David Leon Chandler, *Henry Flagler: The Astonishing Life and Times of the Visionary Robber Baron Who Founded Florida* (New York: Macmillan, 1986),141–42, 268–69; Jim Cox, *Rails across Dixie: A History of Passenger Trains in the American South* (Jefferson, NC: McFarland, 2011), 85; Sidney Walter Martin, *Florida's Flagler* (1949; Athens: University of Georgia Press, 2010), 244; David L. Willing, "Florida's Overseas Railroad," *Florida Historical Quarterly* 35, no. 4 (1957): 287–302.

4. Edward J. Renehan Jr., *Dark Genius of Wall Street: The Misunderstood Life of Jay Gould, King of the Robber Barons* (New York: Basic Books, 2006), 217–18; Scott Reynolds Nelson, *Iron Confederacies: Southern Railways, Klan Violence, and Reconstruction* (Chapel Hill: University of North Carolina Press, 1999), 153–56; H. David Stone, *Vital Rails: The Charleston and Savannah Railroad and the Civil War in Coastal South Carolina* (Columbia: University of South Carolina Press, 2008), 310; Richard White, "Information, Markets, and Corruption: Transcontinental Railroads in the Gilded Age," *Journal of American History* 90, no. 1 (2003): 36.

5. George West Wilson became editor in chief of the Jacksonville *Times-Union* in 1897 and served in this position until his death in 1908. F. P. Fleming, "George West Wilson," *Publications of the Florida Historical Society* 1, no. 2 (1908): 40–42.

6. Henry Flagler to Wilson, January 11, 1902, letter book vol. 132, p. 472, Flagler Papers.

7. Correspondence Henry Flagler to Wilson acknowledging Wilson's letters, August 5, 1901, letter book vol. 131, p. 13; August 12, 1901, letter book vol. 13, p. 65; August 27, 1901, letter book 131, p. 90; January 3, 1902, letter book 132, p. 416; September 23, 1901, letter book 131, p. 231, Flagler Papers; Fleming, "George West Wilson," 41.

8. Fleming, "George West Wilson," 40–42; "Meeting of the State Press Association," *Ocala (FL) Banner*, June 1, 1906; Ben Procter, *William Randolph Hearst: The Early Years, 1863–1910* (New York: Oxford University Press, 1998), 164–65.

9. Gregg Turner, *A Short History of Florida Railroads* (Charleston, SC: Arcadia, 2003), 22, 47–49; William E. Brown Jr. and Karen Hudson, "Henry Flagler and the Model Land Company," *Tequesta* 56 (1996): 46–78; Dudley S. Johnson, "Henry Bradley Plant and Florida," *Florida Historical Quarterly* 45, no. 2 (1966): 118–31. Florida gave Flagler more than two million acres of public land to encourage his railroad building and even passed a land-grant law to give him eight thousand acres per mile to extend his line below Daytona. See Brown and Hudson, "Model Land Company," 47.

10. Edward N. Akin, *Flagler: Rockefeller Partner and Florida Baron* (Kent, OH: Kent State University Press, 1988), 190, quoting Flagler to John Addison Porter, McKinley's private secretary, February 15, 1898 (microfilm), William McKinley Papers, Library of Congress (Research Library, University of Florida).

11. Herbert J. Doherty Jr., "Jacksonville as a Nineteenth-Century Railroad Cen-

ter," *Florida Historical Quarterly* 58 (April 1980): 376–83; Jesus Mendez, "1892—A Year of Crucial Decisions in Florida," *Florida Historical Quarterly* 88 (Summer 2009): 85–99; George W. Pettengill Jr. and B. F. Simmons, "The Story of the Florida Railroads 1834–1903," *Railway and Locomotive Historical Society Bulletin* 86 (July 1952): 9.

12. Noel Gordon Carper, "Slavery Revisited: Peonage in the South," *Phylon* 37 (1976): 85–86; Noel Gordon Carper, "Martin Tabert, Martyr of an Era," *Florida Historical Quarterly* 52 (October 1973): 115; Pete Daniel, *The Shadow of Slavery: Peonage in the South, 1901–1969* (1972; repr., Urbana: University of Illinois Press, 1990), 25; Matthew J. Mancini, *One Dies, Get Another: Convict Leasing in the American South, 1866–1928* (Columbia: University of South Carolina Press, 1996), 183–85; Ortiz, *Emancipation Betrayed*, 14–15.

13. For a thorough discussion of state convict leasing in Florida, see Mancini, *One Dies, Get Another*, 183–97.

14. Carper, "Slavery Revisited," 85–87; Daniel, *Shadow of Slavery*, 20–25; Mancini, *One Dies, Get Another*, 195–96.

15. Eric Foner, *Forever Free: The Story of Emancipation and Reconstruction* (New York: Vintage Books, 2005), 201–205; Ortiz, *Emancipation Betrayed*, 37–39, 53–54.

16. Mancini, *One Dies, Get Another*, 183–84, quote on 183; Ortiz, *Emancipation Betrayed*, 53–54; "Horrible Cruelty in Convict Camp Alleged by a White Ex-Convict," Jacksonville *Times-Union*, April 5, 1901.

17. State Prison Physician Reports on Escambia County Prison Camp, September 24 and November 13, 1906, box 6, folders a5 and a6, Convict Lease Program Subject Files, 1890–1916 (S 42), State Archives of Florida.

18. Daniel, *Shadow of Slavery*, 33, 38, citing A. J. Hoyt to Attorney General, September 26, 1906, file 50-162, Dept. of Justice, National Archives, Record Group 60; "Verdict of Acquittal Ends First of the Peonage Cases," Jacksonville *Times-Union*, December 25, 1906; C. W. Russell to Attorney General C. J. Bonaparte, December 27, 1906, *Peonage Files*, reel 13.

19. See, for example, H. D. Lloyd, "The Story of a Great Monopoly," *Atlantic Magazine*, March 1881, 317–34.

20. Martin, *Florida's Flagler*, 244; Cox, *Rails across* Dixie, 85; Seth H. Bramson, *Speedway to Sunshine: The Story of the Florida East Coast Railway* (Ontario: Boston Mills Press, 1984), 53; Akin, *Flagler*, 104–106.

21. "Some New Books: Two Recent Publications about Prison and Prison Reforms," *Atlanta Constitution*, March 19, 1893. As far as we know, only two scholarly works to date have noted that Plant appears in Powell's memoir: Canter Brown Jr., *Henry Bradley Plant: Gilded Age Dreams for Florida and a New South* (Tuscaloosa: University of Alabama Press, 2019), and Eric Musgrove, *Lost Suwanee County* (Charleston, SC: History Press, 2017). Scholars of convict labor in the U.S. South, while often citing Powell's *American Siberia*, have curiously neglected to note that

Powell worked for Henry Plant for at least two years. Paul Ortiz misidentifies Plant's state convict labor lease as belonging to Flagler, an understandable error given the similarity in the names of their respective railroads (Plant's was East Florida Railroad Company and Flagler's was Florida East Coast Railway). See Ortiz, *Emancipation Betrayed*, chap. 2, 268n157.

22. Akin, *Flagler*, 204; J. C. Powell, *The American Siberia; or, Fourteen Years' Experience in a Southern Convict Camp* (Chicago: Homewood Publishing, 1891), 12–13; State Prison Report for 1881–1884, Report of the Adjutant-General, *Journal of the Florida House of Representatives*, 1885, 25; State Prison and State Convicts, Reports of the Special Joint Committee appointed to Examine the Books and Records of the Office of the Commissioner of Agriculture, *Journal of the Florida House of Representatives*, 1893, 1314.

23. The State Prison Report for 1881–1884 suggests that in 1881 the East Florida Railway Company received 230 convicts with fourteen deaths and thirteen escapes, and in 1882 the company received 208 convicts with ten deaths and five escapes. For these two years, 88 percent of the convicts were Black. The number of convict deaths reported for 1881 is considerably smaller than the twenty-seven deaths Powell reports from the spinal meningitis epidemic. It is impossible to adjudicate this difference, although scholars agree that records during this early period of the convict lease in Florida were haphazardly kept. Powell, *American Siberia*, 12–13, 138, 148–51; Johnson, "Henry Bradley Plant and Florida," 120; Doherty, "Jacksonville as a Nineteenth-Century Railroad Center," 376; Joint Committee on State Convicts Report, *Journal of the Proceedings of the Senate of the General Assembly* 11 (1881): 342–44; State Prison Report for 1881–1884, Report of the Adjutant-General, *Journal of the Florida House of Representatives*, 1885, 25.

24. Johnson, "Henry Bradley Plant and Florida," 120; Doherty, "Jacksonville as a Nineteenth-Century Railroad Center," 376; "Grading Grand Central Avenue and Six Mile Creek Road," *Tampa Weekly Tribune*, April 15, 1897.

25. Rebecca Felton, "The Convict System of Georgia," *Forum* 2 (January 1887): 484–90; George Washington Cable, "The Convict Lease System in the Southern States," *Century Magazine* 27 (February 1884), 582–99.

26. Ida B. Wells, ed. *The Reason Why the Colored American Is Not in the World's Columbian Exposition* (Chicago, 1893).

27. T. Thomas Fortune, *Status of the Race*, in *T. Thomas Fortune, the Afro-American Agitator: A Collection of Writings, 1880–1928*, ed. Shawn Leigh Alexander (Gainesville: University Press of Florida, 2008), 6–14.

28. Susan D. Carle, *Defining the Struggle: National Organizing for Racial Justice, 1880–1915* (New York: Oxford University Press, 2013), 48n64, citing "Rambles in the South: Industrial Slavery in South Carolina, *New York Freeman*, May 16, 1885; "Infamies of the Southern Convict Lease System," *New York Globe*, February 2, 1884.

29. Mary Church Terrell, "Peonage in the United States: The Convict Lease System and the Chain Gangs," *Nineteenth Century and After* 52 (August 1907): 306–322.

30. State Prison Physician Report to Commissioner of Agriculture, April 1, 1913, box 6, folder a12, Convict Lease Program Subject Files, 1890–1916 (S 42), State Archives of Florida.

31. Clarissa Olds Keeler, *The Crime of Crimes; or, the Convict System Unmasked* (Washington, DC: Pentecostal Era Co., 1907), 13; Carper, "Martin Tabert," 116.

32. Chandler, *Henry Flagler*, 165–66; Akin, *Flagler*, 184; Aaron Kyle Reynolds, "A Long Quavering Chant: Peonage Labor Camps in the Rural-industrial South 1905–1965" (diss., University of Texas–Austin, 2013), 55–56, https://repositories.lib.utexas.edu/handle/2152/41771; Les Standiford, *Last Train to Paradise: Henry Flagler and the Spectacular Rise and Fall of the Railroad That Crossed an Ocean* (New York: Crown Publishers, 2002), 93; Willing, "Florida's Overseas Railroad," 287–302.

33. Standiford, *Last Train to Paradise*, 66; Turner, *Short History of Florida Railroads*, 70; Gregg M. Turner, *A Journey into Florida Railroad History* (Gainesville: University Press of Florida, 2008), 135; Christian Wolmar, *The Great Railroad Revolution: The History of Trains in America* (New York: Public Affairs, 2012), 225.

34. Jack E. Davis, *An Everglades Providence: Marjory Stoneman Douglas and the American Environmental Century* (Athens: University of Georgia Press, 2009), 107–108; Benjamin Reilly, *Tropical Surge: A History of Ambition and Disaster on the Florida Shore* (Sarasota, FL: Pineapple Press, 2005), 127; John Sewell, *Miami Memoirs: A New Pictorial Edition of John Sewell's Own Story*, ed. Arva Moore Parks (Miami: Arva Parks, 1987), 53.

35. E. T. Clyatt (FECR foreman) deposition, n.d., *Peonage Files*, reel 14; Joseph Faus, "Lemon City: Miami's Predecessor," *Miami News* (Sunday Magazine), September 19, 1948, 14; Standiford, *Last Train to Paradise*, 66; Ortiz, *Emancipation Betrayed*, 54.

36. "Slavery Days Revived," *Springville (NY) Journal*, January 13, 1898.

37. David R. Roediger, *The Wages of Whiteness: Race and the Making of the American Working Class*, rev. ed. (1991; London: Verso, 1999), 180; Akin, *Flagler*, 214–17; Daniel, *Shadow of Slavery*, 96–97; Carper, "Slavery Revisited," 86; Oscar S. Straus (Secretary, Department of Commerce and Labor) to Attorney General, February 12, 1907, including "Report on Labor Conditions on the Florida East Coast Railway Extension," *Peonage Files*, reel 13; Michele Berardinelli deposition, n.d., *Peonage Files*, reel 14.

38. Harry Hermanson deposition, n.d., *Peonage Files*, reel 14; Amanda Hermanson deposition, n.d., *Peonage Files*, reel 14, telling of being repeatedly turned out of the offices of Sabbia and FECR in her efforts to reclaim her son.

39. Laborer depositions, Gulio Gimmella, Albert Grant, John Kane, John J. Ke-

gan, Edward Maher, Robert Martin, Frank Meany, George Morris, Robert Murray, Vincent Paradise, John Reiss, Winifield Ronald, Sam Rosen, James Toomey, Percy White, Thomas Wilson, Charles Zinke, Jake Anderson, n.d., *Peonage Files*, reel 14. Men employed by Sabbia and FECR also gave depositions confirming the laborers' testimony, e.g., Giocomo Lapiparo and E. T. Clyatt, n.d., *Peonage Files*, reel 14; Oscar S. Straus (Secretary, Department of Commerce and Labor) to Attorney General, February 12, 1907, including "Report on Labor Conditions on the Florida East Coast Railway Extension," *Peonage Files*, reel 13; Release of Claim Forms, Florida East Coast Railway, General Business Records, Personnel & Work Force Records, box 20, Flagler Papers.

40. See FECR laborer and employee depositions cited in previous note. The Department of Commerce and Labor's Report on Labor Conditions on the Florida East Coast Railway documents that 209 workers were convicted at Key West and 858 at Miami during the five months from November 1, 1905, to March 31, 1906. See also "Florida Resents Charge That Peonage Is Slavery," Jacksonville *Times-Union*, April 21, 1907.

41. E. T. Clyatt depositions, n.d., and John Pinder to Senator William B. Allison, January 16, 1908, *Peonage Files*, reel 14.

42. Ron Chernow, *Titan: The Life of John D. Rockefeller, Sr.* (New York: Knopf Doubleday, 2007), 439, 538.

43. Daniel, *Shadow of Slavery*, 83–84.

44. Russell and Quackenbos also gathered evidence from two independent investigations, one by the U.S. Department of Commerce and Labor conducted in March 1906 and one by a Florida investigator appointed by Governor Napoleon B. Broward at Flagler's request. While both reports attempted general exculpatory narratives, both also contained multiple examples of peonage practices, including workers being held against their will because of debt. See Oscar S. Straus (Secretary, Department of Commerce and Labor) to Attorney General, February 12, 1907, including "Report on Labor Conditions on the Florida East Coast Railway Extension," *Peonage Files*, reel 13. Two important secondary sources on the Flagler peonage investigations—Daniel's *Shadow of Slavery* and Reynolds's dissertation, "Long Quavering Chant"—misidentify part of the "Report on Labor Conditions" as being authored by the FECR. This error is likely due to the separation of the report into two sections—the summary report and the complete report—that appear in different places in the Justice Department files. Mary Grace Quackenbos to Charles W. Russell, September 3, 1908, *Peonage Files*, reel 14, referencing S. J. Triplett's report detailing his investigation of FECR labor camps in the Keys in September 1906.

45. Attorney General to John M. Cheney, January 16, 1907, *Peonage Files*, reel 13; John M. Cheney to Attorney General, April 4, 1907, *Peonage Files*, reel 14; John M. Cheney to Attorney General, April 3, 1907, *Peonage Files*, reel 14; Mary Grace

Quackenbos to Attorney General, April 8, 1907, *Peonage Files*, reel 14. In fact, Cheney's assistant attorney, Richard P. Marks, was disqualified from prosecuting the Flagler peonage case because he also served as counsel to the FECR. Attorney General to John J. Jenkins (Chairman, Committee on the Judiciary, House of Representatives), February 27, 1907, *Peonage Files*, reel 13.

46. Mary Grace Quackenbos to Charles W. Russell, September 3, 1908, *Peonage Files*, reel 14; Quackenbos to Attorney General, April 8, 1907, *Peonage Files*, reel 14; Charles W. Russell to Attorney General, February 14, 1907, *Peonage Files*, reel 13; John Cheney to Attorney General, February 23, 1907, *Peonage Files*, reel 13; Jacksonville *Times-Union*, February 21, 1907.

47. Charles W. Russell to Attorney General, February 14, 1907, *Peonage Files*, reel 13.

48. John Cheney to Attorney General, February 23, 1907, *Peonage Files*, reel 13.

49. "Ask Congress for Peonage Investigation," Jacksonville *Times-Union*, February 21, 1907; "Frank Clark's Denunciation of Untrue Peonage Stories," Jacksonville *Times-Union*, March 5, 1907; "Peonage Stories Reeking with Evident Falsehoods," *Tampa Tribune*, March 14, 1907; "The State Lawmakers," *Live Oak Daily Democrat*, April 4, 1907; "Frank Clark Wants Some Information," *Pensacola News Journal*, February 27, 1907; "Denies Charge of Peonage," *Gainesville Daily Sun*, January 22, 1907.

50. "Florida Press Peonage Resolution," *Ocala (FL) Banner*, March 22, 1907.

51. John Cheney to Attorney General, February 23, 1907, *Peonage Files*, reel 13.

52. Richard Barry, "Slavery in the South To-day," *Cosmopolitan Magazine* 152, no. 5 (1907), 481–91; "Strong Resolutions Adopted Condemning Barry and Hearst," Jacksonville *Times-Union*, April 4, 1907.

53. Barry, "Slavery in the South," 483.

54. Carper, "Slavery Revisited," 88, citing "Peonage in the South," New York *Independent* 55 (July 9, 1903), 1616–18; Daniel, *Shadow of Slavery*, 4–18; *Clyatt v. United States*, 197 U.S. 207 (1905).

55. Seymour Martin Lipset and Gary Marks, *It Didn't Happen Here: Why Socialism Failed in the United States* (New York: W. W. Norton, 2001), 151. In 1913 *Appeal to Reason* had a national circulation of more than 750,000. In March 1907 it had almost 285,000 subscribers, with 3,265 in Florida (see *Appeal to Reason*, subscription figures, March 16, 1907, p. 1). From December 1906 through January 1907, the *Appeal* published stories each week purporting to be from a "special correspondent" working in one of Flagler's FECR labor camps in the Keys. The reports detail harsh living conditions and brutal treatment that align closely with Justice Department affidavits of immigrants who had escaped Flagler's camps. It is likely the "special correspondent" was an invention, a technique of sensational reporting, rather than an actual person. On December 1, 1906, the *Appeal* published the deposition of escaped peon Benjamin Wilenski, taken by Mary Grace

Quackenbos, the New York City lawyer for the poor whom the Justice Department appointed as a special assistant in the peonage investigations. In a related article, the editor said he had information about hundreds of peonage cases and intended to publish information about "the 'white slavery' proposition" in the next several issues. The editor also noted he would share correspondence from an undercover reporter for the *Appeal* in future issues. The following week, in its December 8 issue, the *Appeal* published its first installment from its "special correspondent" purportedly held in a Flagler labor camp in the Keys. In a monthlong series, this "correspondent" reported brutal conditions and treatment, including being held captive, in the camp. On January 12, 1907, the *Appeal* reported that its correspondent was missing and was "probably murdered." On March 2, 1907, the *Appeal* provided details from a report filed by Florida governor Napoleon B. Broward's representative, S. J. Triplett, who surveyed FECR camps in September 1906. The Triplett report found that peonage existed the previous winter and was expected again in winter 1906.

56. "Hon. Frank Clark with Vigor Answers Charges of Peonage," Jacksonville *Times-Union*, March 3, 1907; "Attack on Bonaparte: Floridian Denounces His Methods in Peonage Cases," *Washington Post*, March 3, 1907.

57. "Denies Charge of Peonage," *Washington Post*, January 18, 1907.

58. "Asks for Information," *Ocala (FL) Evening Star*, February 22, 1907; "A Standard Oil Peon in Congress," *Ocala (FL) Banner*, March 15, 1907; "Congressman Clark's Defense of Florida," *Pensacola Journal*, March 13, 1907; "The State Lawmakers," *Live Oak Daily Democrat*, April 4, 1907; "Mr. Flagler's Wonderful Work in the Development of Florida," Jacksonville *Times-Union*, March 7, 1907.

59. "Facing the Question Squarely," editorial, Tallahassee *Morning Sun*, April 2, 1907.

60. John Cheney to Attorney General, April 3, 1907, *Peonage Files*, reel 14; J. M. Cheney to Attorney General, April 4, 1907, *Peonage Files*, reel 14.

61. "War on Peonage System," *Washington Post*, October 19, 1907; "Peonage Charges Dismissed," *Pensacola News Journal*, July 1, 1908; "Peonage Charges Fell Through," *Miami News*, June 22, 1908.

62. Quackenbos Report on FECR II, *Peonage Files*, reel 14.

63. Daniel, *Shadow of Slavery*, 104–106; "Can't Show Peonage in Flagler Road Case," *New York Times*, November 11, 1908.

64. Reports of the Immigration Commission, U.S. Senate, vol. 2, 61st Cong., 3d Sess., Document No. 747 (Washington, DC: U.S. Government Printing Office, 1911), 445–46.

65. Carper, "Martin Tabert," 116, 129; Mancini, *One Dies, Get Another*, 197; "Samuel D. McCoy, Reporter, 82, Dies," *New York Times*, April 11, 1964. McCoy's articles ran in the *New York World* from March 30 to May 30, 1923.

66. Musgrove, *Lost Suwanee County*, 147–48, is an exception. A recent robust

biography of Plant discusses his use of convict labor in only one paragraph and actually uses J. C. Powell's *American Siberia* to defend Plant. See Canter Brown Jr., *Henry Bradley Plant: Gilded Age Dreams for Florida and a New South* (Tuscaloosa: University of Alabama Press, 2019), 156–57.

67. Standiford, *Last Train to Paradise*, 110.

68. Bramson, *Speedway to Sunshine*, 72.

69. "Henry Flagler Biography," Flagler Museum, https://www.flaglermuseum .us/history/flagler-biography.

PART FOUR

Measuring the Cost

CHAPTER 10

Silencing a Generation

BLAIR LM KELLEY

At the turn of the twentieth century, there were hundreds of Black newspapers in the South, covering both small towns and big cities and growing out of Black fraternal orders and church organizations. However, Black journalists of this age existed in a world that provided little space to speak plainly about the erosion of their rights. Said simply, journalism in the age of lynching was dangerous work. Several turn-of-the-century Black editors, particularly those who spoke boldly about what was happening to African Americans who were challenging second-class citizenship and racial violence, had to run for their lives as their presses were burned or destroyed by white mobs.

Ida B. Wells, the outspoken journalist who first analyzed the dynamics behind lynching, was forced to flee Memphis after writing about the lynching of her friend Thomas Moss, a postal worker and owner of the successful People's Grocery. Moss was lynched along with grocery employees Calvin McDowell and Will Stewart simply because his store was economic competition for the local white-owned grocery.[1] Wells asserted that economics, not sexual violence, was at the heart of hundreds of lynchings. In response, the *Memphis Commercial Appeal* called for Wells to be lynched and for J. L. Flemming, her business partner at the *Memphis Free Speech*, to be castrated with tailor's shears and burned at a stake. Both escaped with their lives, but their press was destroyed. This was the second time Flemming had to escape a mob; his first newspaper, the

Marion Headlight in Marion, Arkansas, had also been targeted in a successful assault on Black voters in 1888.[2]

Alexander Manly, the editor of the Wilmington, North Carolina–based *Daily Record*, escaped a mob of white men and boys fomented by segregationist state leaders in November 1898. After suggesting that some of the Black men accused of raping white women were in fact involved in consensual liaisons that just happened to be discovered, he became the target of statewide leaders who wanted to silence Black voters, oust Black politicians, and permanently disenfranchise Black citizens. Manly, the son of mixed-race parents, had pale skin and light straight hair that allowed him to pass for white, so he was able to pass the men stationed on the road to try to capture him. So fooled was the mob that one man in the group grabbed two rifles and handed them to Manly, who carefully placed them in the back of the wagon while another man in the crowd said, "If you see that nigger Manly up there, shoot him." Although he successfully fooled the men, who didn't know that the "nigger Manly" had just rode past them, he lost his press and his property when the mob burned the offices of the *Daily Record* to the ground, posing for pictures in front of the smoldering heap.[3]

Beyond the Southern mobs, segregationist lawmakers also endeavored to silence Black journalists. The Reverend A. N. McEwen, the fiery editor of the *Southern Watchman,* had once been a stalwart voice of protest in Mobile, Alabama, encouraging his readers to boycott the streetcars after a new law segregated transportation. Although he once vowed that he would "fight and contend for equal rights and justice to all men in all parts of the South . . . until the sad news comes . . . that God is dead," McEwen was silenced by a 1903 anti-boycott law so sweeping that it forbade Black newspapers from even reporting on news of a boycott. A story about a protest was punishable by serving time on Alabama's deadly chain gang.[4]

Given the threat of both extralegal and state-sanctioned racial violence, it is impossible to accurately discern what the Black press during Jim Crow could have been if Black journalists had been allowed to freely tell the truth. In the years that historian Rayford Logan characterized as the nadir, or the lowest point, for Black rights after the Emancipation, most journalists danced a precarious line, turning most of their focus inward and remaining silent or coy about radical protests. Plainspoken accounts of lynching and racial violence, detailed discussions about what Black communities endured daily as Jim Crow segregation expanded to every area of life, and news of Black Southerners' valiant efforts to resist were dangerous to the status quo. Those who insisted on telling the whole truth paid a price. In a nation that prided itself on the constitutional foundation of a free press, the reign of white supremist terror that ruled the South also controlled the press. However, even in the face of terrorists, Black journalists laid the groundwork for movements that in the next generation would lead toward civil rights, reminding us that the will required to do this crucial work existed even if the political climate did not.

This chapter details the work of Jesse Max Barber, one of the most promising editors of this nadir generation of Black journalists. In an age of racial terror, Barber stood against injustice, fighting along with those who tried to maintain their right to vote and contesting the stigma of segregation and second-class citizenship. At a moment when Atlanta's white newspapers were full of mistruths designed to fuel mob fires and sell papers, Barber produced journalism in his *Voice of the Negro* that lived up to the ideals of American democracy. Barber too would have to run to save his life, because he published an honest account about the source of the brutality of the Atlanta Race Riot of 1906. The loss of his voice as a journalist is a sharp reminder of the profound cost this early Jim Crow generation bore to speak candidly about conditions in the American South.[5]

Barber's early career was emblematic of the tremendous potential of the first free generation after the Emancipation. Born in 1878 in rural Blackstock in the South Carolina upcountry to former slave parents, Barber was a talented student. He completed a liberal arts teacher training course at Benedict College, a school founded by the American Baptist Home Mission Society (ABHMS) in nearby Columbia, South Carolina, but his love of journalism was sparked while he was a student at another ABHMS institution, Virginia Union University in Richmond, Virginia. On this larger, more urban campus, Barber thrived as a campus journalist; he served as the student editor of the *University Journal* and president of the campus literary society.[6]

Beyond campus, turn-of-the-century Richmond was a perfect training ground for a young Black journalist like Barber. The city was home to several Black newspapers—most notably two papers that grew out of vibrant mutual aid societies: The *Reformer* published by the Order of the True Reformers, and the *St. Luke Herald*, headed by the Independent Order of St. Luke and edited by its national president, Maggie Lena Walker. In the face of increasing segregation and economic discrimination, *The Reformer* advocated Black economic independence, while in the pages of the *St. Luke Herald*, Walker took a different tact. She promoted economic independence but also a collective fight against segregation. Richmond was also home to the nationally renowned *Richmond Planet*, published by John Mitchell Jr., a staunch anti-lynching advocate whose agitation saved innocent Black Virginians from death at the hands of white mobs. As a student Barber must have been intrigued to see how the editors of these three newspapers pursued distinct strategies in their effort to contest the deterioration of African American rights.[7]

It was just this kind of model, blending distinct points of view within the Black community, that Barber hoped to present in the new Atlanta, Georgia–based, national journal, the *Voice of the Negro*. The gains of Reconstruction were eroding quickly for Black Southerners as disenfranchisement, new segregation laws, and racial violence left Black citizenship in peril. But even in the face of such injustice, the *Voice* featured the great African American minds of the time and did not shy away from presenting differing viewpoints—from educator and race advocate Nannie Helen Burroughs, to Howard University professor Kelly Miller, as well as Booker T. Washington and his young rival W.E.B. Du Bois. It was not the only Black magazine of its time; there was the *Colored American*, *Alexander's*, and Du Bois's *Horizon* and *Moon Illustrated Weekly*, but Barber's effort was distinct for its clarity of vision.[8] The visionary behind "the first magazine ever edited in the South by Colored Men," Barber was just in his mid-twenties, but his journal quickly developed a good reputation and a loyal readership. In the hands of this skilled young writer and editor, the *Voice of the Negro* became an honest and broad reflection of Black dissent.

When the journal first began, Barber hoped that the *Voice of the Negro* would be provocative and would shine a light on the bleak conditions African Americans faced throughout the nation: "There may be times when literature we publish will rip open the conventional veil of optimism and drag into view conditions that shock."[9] Barber also hoped to make the *Voice* a place where a new generation of Black intellectuals could discuss and debate the best way forward in difficult times. In just a few short years Barber's work made an impact; in an article recounting his experiences during a Southern speaking tour, Kelly Miller noted that there was "wide-spread circulation and appreciation of the '*Voice*.'" Indeed, by 1906 it grew to be the most important African American journal in the country, with a circulation of over fifteen thousand.[10] Black readers were hungry for information and in search of the best way to respond to the growing injustices they faced daily.

The *Voice* covered it all. The inaugural edition announced that 1904 was "the herald of the Dawn of a new day," promising its subscribers "current history, educational improvements, art, science, race issues, sociological movements and religion."[11] Indeed, in the first issue, the venerable Atlanta educator John Hope wrote about the institutions of higher learning for Black students in Atlanta—including Atlanta Baptist Seminary (later Morehouse College), Gammon Theological Seminary, Spelman College, Morris Brown College, and Clark College—and suggested they all find their niche in order to further broaden educational opportunity for Black students. In the same edition, Miller argued that even as disenfranchisement, white primaries, and grandfather clauses left Black voters "eliminated as a factor in party management and party patronage," their contribution as workers made them "the greater part of the industrial strength" of the South and still left them with leverage and the collective strength to organize. Washington authored the article "The Negro's Part in the South's Upbuilding." In it he furthered his call for Black Southerners to make themselves of "real service to [the] community," insisting that "that service will not remain unrecognized." Black woman educator and clubwoman Fannie Barrier Williams exhorted the *Voice*'s readers to "become stronger in the virtue of patience, more efficient in good works, more deserving in our achievements, and more intelligent and co-operative in our contention for our rights."[12]

From the history of Black literature to contemporary achievements, the *Voice of the Negro* reminded readers that they had many reasons to be proud of African American success, but as time went by, Barber increasingly published stories that were not so uplifting. As his pen grew sharper, his crisp voice shone through in writing about the most difficult stories of his day. In an account of the execution of Jim Walker, a Black man accused of raping a white woman, who had been protected from a lynch mob only to be executed by the state in the most awful way in a violent and prolonged hanging, Barber boldly reminded his readers that even if Walker was guilty, there was no such justice for Black women who were similarly violated by white men. When reflecting on Walker's death, Barber wished that "every wretch, white or black, meet the same fate by the law." He went on to assert to his readers that no such equality under law existed as long as not "a single white has been hanged or will be hanged for committing the crime of rape against a black woman; and until that is done, the black people feel that there is no law in this land to protect their women." The *Voice of the Negro* would become an unwavering call for Black equality.[13]

Atlanta seemed like the ideal place to found such a journal. After all, it was home to several prominent Black colleges and a vibrant African American middle- and working-class community.[14] Barber hoped that a prosperous and growing Atlanta could be a laboratory for Black intellectual engagement like he had admired in Richmond and offered the space necessary to critique the growing calls for segregation and disenfranchisement. He strove "to give all sides free scope in our Magazine. . . . It is not our desire and has never been to appear one sided and narrow."[15] However, he may have overestimated his ability to balance the caustic political divides between African American leaders. And he definitely underestimated the dangers of speaking honestly about the growing racial divide on the pages of the *Voice*.

Remaining neutral in the shadow of Booker T. Washington's influence would be hard. The former-slave-turned-spokesman first came to national prominence after giving a speech at the Atlanta Exposition in 1895 in which he called for compromise on the question of Black citizenship. Washington did not publicly oppose policies of racial separation, arguing that accepting segregation would be the price of Black economic advancement. On the surface he was an educator—founder of the Tuskegee Institute, which became an industrial education stronghold for African American students in rural Alabama—but he was also a well-connected political mastermind, so much so that his opponents called him the Wizard of Tuskegee. Pushing well beyond questions of education, Washington sought to have sway in nearly every aspect of Black public life, including political appointments and organizational leadership, and behind the scenes he influenced a cadre of wealthy white philanthropists who gave to Black causes. Away from the public eye, Washington was complex. For example, contrary to his accommodationist approach, he secretly funded a court challenge to debt peonage, a system that crippled Black sharecroppers in the rural South. He pushed for the expansion of Black educational institutions of all kinds and supported Black newspapers with funds from his white benefactors.[16]

While Washington was publicly open to compromising with white segregationists, he rejected any public opposition from other Black leaders. Washington's powerful sway within Black life was difficult to avoid or contest. The broad community of African American activists and their white allies carried out a rich and wide-ranging debate over strategy, but Washington strove to make sure that only those beholden to his influence had a platform that could reach a mass audience. Barber, young and unaware of Washington's web of control, fell under his influence at the magazine's inception.

Barber founded the *Voice of the Negro* in partnership with John A. Hopkins, a friend and fellow Virginia Union senior. In addition to being a student, Hopkins served as a sales agent for J. L. Nichols and Company, a white publishing house that would later become Hertel, Jenkins, and Company. The firm had published the first and less-well-known ghostwritten account of Washington's life, *The Story of My Life and Work*. Although Washington wasn't happy with this first go at an autobiography, it did sell well; more than 120,000 copies were sold to Black readers throughout the South by Black agents like Hopkins. Because of the success of the Washington autobiography, the publishing house had a built-in sales base, which made it a perfect platform for an African American monthly. Thinking along such lines, Barber and Hopkins met with the vice president, Austin N. Jenkins, pitching the idea of the journal with Black voices backed by the white publishing house's infrastructure, start-up funds, and distribution. Jenkins was enthusiastic about the opportunity and the *Voice of the Negro* was born. Considering Barber's talent along with an established sales network and an initial investment, the journal was poised to be a success.[17]

Given the company's ties to Washington, Hopkins approached the Wizard of Tuskegee to ask for a word of support on their new efforts. Hopkins must not have fully understood Washington's desire for complete control over the narrative about Black politics. His decision to reach out to Washington proved to be a fateful error. After hearing from Hopkins, Washington immediately wrote to his secretary, Emmett Jay Scott: "I am very anxious that you have a good confidential talk with Hopkins and be very sure that we get an influence with this magazine that shall keep it working our way or at least not against us." Always the savvy businessman, Washington immediately recognized the *Voice*'s tremendous potential for success. Washington hoped to control the publication's tone, describing Hopkins as a "very sensible fellow," but went on to warn Scott that they "want to be sure that he does not get under wrong influences, which is easy to be done in Atlanta." Scott's talk must have worked; Hopkins and Barber partnered with Washington to garner his support. In exchange for his endorsement, Washington insisted that the *Voice* install Scott, his longtime and serially duplicitous secretary, as a perfunctory and part-time associate editor. Washington also installed his associate and fellow educator J.W.E. Bowen as a senior editor. Barber did not know that this endorsement would eventually make it impossible to amplify dissenting voices and hone his own critical voice.[18]

Washington was right about the *Voice of the Negro*'s potential—it was a resounding success from the start—but he was wrong to think he could temper Barber's fire. In the pages of his new journal, the young editor sounded important warnings about the spread of segregation, disenfranchisement, and lynching throughout the New South. In the years after the U.S. Supreme Court upheld legal segregation in *Plessy v. Ferguson*, segregation mapped a trail around every public space in the urban South. Barber's adopted home of Atlanta was no different. White suffragist and antiracist organizer Mary White Ovington noted that "Atlanta's color line was drawn 'more rigorously . . . with more gusto than in less commercial southern cities.'" The municipality had even passed laws that forbade Black and white passengers from sitting next to each other in the front seat of an automobile. Atlanta University educator George Alexander Towns had been arrested for riding alongside his wife, who had been mistaken for a white woman by the police. The two could have been servant and employer, but the appearance of an interracial husband and wife was just too much. Barber hated the illogic of Southern segregation policing every realm of public life in his adopted city. Such thinking irritated him so much that when Ovington visited Atlanta to see Du Bois, Barber defied the local laws and sat next to the white woman in the car. Ovington characterized Barber as a "dare-devil," but he just wasn't willing to bend without a fight.[19]

Barber knew he wasn't the only Black Southerner who detested segregation. Despite Washington's insistence on racial accommodation, he and thousands of other Black Southerners were determined to resist at every turn. So when Southern state legislators and local municipalities began to pass new laws and reinterpret old ones to segregate streetcars in the 1900s, African Americans throughout the South challenged the laws by pressing legal suits and boycotting the cars. These protests, both grand and small, peppered the urban South, taking place in at least twenty-five cities, collectively representing the largest popular effort to resist Jim Crow segregation in its time.[20]

Barber made the *Voice of the Negro* the voice of the boycott movement. Noting that "the spread of the Jim Crow idea is simply alarming," the editor warned his national audience, "The craze for separate street cars is spreading all over the south. Mere separation does not hurt the colored people half so much as the unjust discriminations imposed."[21] Although the boycott in Atlanta faltered because of trickery and competition between rival streetcar companies, Barber became an advocate of public protest. And the updates he received from readers revealed widespread support for the strategy.[22] The scope and scale of the boycotts reported in the pages of the *Voice* suggests that most African American Southerners from all walks of life believed that Jim Crow cars were degrading and unnecessary barriers. Thousands of Black Southerners in cities across the American South, in the words of Du Bois, "refuse[d] to allow the impression to remain that the Negro-American assents to inferiority, is submissive under oppression and apologetic before insults."[23]

In the pages of Barber's journal, readers broadcast their opposition to the offensive new laws in their own cities. They stayed off the cars, walking to and from work, to mark their belief that the color line was worth fighting. Barber chronicled the difficult conditions on streetcars, now ruled by "obnoxious . . . class-laws" designed to "give special privileges to the whites and to withdraw certain rights from the blacks." Inequitable treatment on segregated streetcars was designed not just to separate but to stigmatize Black customers, unfairly targeting all Black patrons with possible policing by white conductors.[24] Barber hoped that segregation laws dividing Southern streetcars would inspire waves of protests; he knew that the offensive laws had "fanned into a flame" "the spark of manhood in the breasts of the masses of colored people." Streetcar boycotts would be the best way to "make the white man pay for his prejudices."[25] The *Voice of the Negro* and other independent Black newspapers would help to spread the news about protests throughout Southern Black communities, providing insight and advice on how boycotts had been successful in other cities. Barber's words are also a vital testimony to character of a popular radical protest in the South after 1896. In the face of disenfranchisement, lynching, and race riots, the streetcar movement was difficult to maintain, but it would have been impossible without the voices of radical Black journalists.

The *Voice* painted a portrait of the movement in the midst of the nadir: African American Southerners of all walks of life risked their lives and their livelihoods to assert their own visions of the meaning of citizenship. For example, residents of Anderson, South Carolina, protested when their city's streetcars were fitted with seats that were facing backward in the back so that white passengers who boarded did not have to look Black people in the face. In response to this demeaning setup, Barber encouraged Anderson residents to continue a silent boycott; Black residents "quietly refused to be thus humiliated" and "either walk[ed] or [rode] in their own buggies" when traveling through the town.[26] Small, quiet boycotts like those held in Anderson and more-visible vocal efforts in large cities also took hold throughout the urban South.

In the pages of the *Voice of the Negro*, Barber took special note of the protests in Richmond after Virginia Passenger and Power began to enforce a voluntary state segregation law in the spring of 1904. Black city leaders, including newspaper editors John Mitchell Jr., and Maggie Lena Walker, were outspoken critics of the attempt to segregate the cars. On the pages of the *Richmond Planet,* Mitchell encouraged everyone to "stay off the street cars" and use their "big feet" to put economic pressure on the company. Boycotts would be "agony produced on the white man's nerve center, which is his pocket." Connecting this struggle to their historic fight for the end of slavery, Mitchell boomed from the pages of the *Planet* that "independence and liberty are sweet and the day of the time-server is past."[27]

Black Richmond's response was quick. Thousands of residents from all walks of life who once had used the cars daily stayed away from the segregated cars, many wearing buttons that read, "I will walk."[28] Participation in the protests came at a high cost; working-class Black Richmonders, particularly washerwomen and maids, used the cars to travel to white households far from their own neighborhoods. For washerwomen in particular, the streetcar was an opportunity to rest from carrying heavy bundles of dirty garments to their homes on Monday and returning them on Friday. Working-class Black men who worked on projects in far-off parts of the city also had to walk or find rides. The *Planet* reported that "it [was] a common thing to see wagons on their way downtown carrying three to six laboring men free of charge." Mitchell wrote that it was so effective that it left the once-bustling Clay Street line appearing as if "the colored population had left the city."[29] Both the middle class and the working poor valued the dignity of riding the streetcars without stigma.

Barber highlighted the success of the Richmond boycott in the *Voice*, telling thousands of readers that "in Richmond the Negroes are walking. It looks rather strange to see great crowds of colored people walking all the way to Church Hill or Manchester from the Western part of Richmond on Sunday mornings when the sun seems to shine particularly hot; but the colored people would rather do that than compromise their self-respect."[30] His reporting helped Richmond protesters garner praise from anti-segregationists across the country and spread the news of their success. Letters from places as far off as Chicago, Illinois; Mt. Vernon, New York; and rural Texas arrived at the *Voice* in support of the city's "walking Negroes." Black people across the South were driven into action; as one Black newspaper editor from Arkansas suggested to his readers: "Don't begin crying, but walk. Negroes everywhere are walking."[31]

Their walking was successful. In August 1904 Barber reported that Richmond protesters had been able to force a strike-weakened Virginia Passenger and Power "into the hands of a receiver." Citing the financial blow of a workers' strike in 1903 and the devastating blow of the boycott, which had "over eighty per cent of the colored people . . . walking and sweating," Mitchell was also sure that the laws would change.[32] Indeed, company records show that the streetcar company was operating in deficit before the boycott; their desire to enforce a voluntary law had come at a cost. Barber wrote that the bankruptcy was inevitable, commenting, "It is no surprise to us," and he "congratulated" Black Richmonders on their ability "to teach such a lesson and administer such a rebuke to violent race prejudice."[33] Even the broader political landscape encouraged Barber's support of the boycotts. In August 1905, in a delighted tone,

Barber provided the details of a 1905 Chinese boycott of American products. The editor highlighted the protests as "a measure of retaliation," a way to gain "more respect," and a way "to touch the heart of the white man . . . [by pulling] his purse strings." Barber hoped that what was working for the Chinese might bear fruit for Black Americans.[34] He followed this account of the Chinese protests with a report about the first meeting of Du Bois's Niagara Movement.

For Barber, the Niagara Movement confirmed the spirit of defiance in defense of Black citizenship he had already been encouraging in the pages of his periodical. He believed that Niagara was a new opportunity: a space for Black people to "contend and work openly and aggressively for equal civil and political rights." Niagara's "advocacy of high ideals" would serve to "strengthen the moral fibre of the race and the nation."[35] Barber used the *Voice of the Negro* as a forum for support of Niagara and the boycott movement. It became the only national journal that supported both protests. For Barber, the two efforts were interconnected. Unfortunately, his advocacy of Niagara assured that Washington would try to silence his dissent.

As Barber's political consciousness and, by extension, his support for Washington's opponents grew, so did Washington's desire to silence his protests.[36] Barber first fought back against his intrusion in 1904 when Washington offered unsolicited criticisms of Barber's commentaries and his use of honorific degrees for the people who were profiled in their pages. Barber countered by letting his publisher, Hertel, Jenkins, and Company, know that Washington was bankrolling their competitor, the *Colored American*, from Washington, D.C. Hertel, Jenkins responded by removing Scott from his role as associate editor. Scott was angry about being axed and lashed out at Barber, blaming his "malevolent spirit," his "affectation of superiority," and his "overweening egotism and acceptance of everything as an insult" for their falling out. Washington scolded his secretary for publicly arguing with Barber and the publisher, saying, "I do not think it ever pays to deal with a little man." Washington vowed that he would "find a way, however, very soon to show [Barber] his place."[37]

Washington's response to Scott's dismissal is revealing. It shows how the Tuskegee educator used the many newspapers he controlled to police the Black public sphere by eliminating opposing voices.[38] Even as editor Benjamin J. Davis claimed that his *Atlanta Independent* was "neither Washingtonian nor an anti-Washingtonian journal," the weekly reprinted every recrimination that Washington launched against his foes and benefited from Washington's financial support.[39] Although he sounded like a militant on some fronts, Davis's loyalty to Washington left him vacillating from protest to accommodation. Davis opposed the Atlanta streetcar boycotts and warned his readers not to engage in public protests. He chastised their impatience: "As a race we are always complaining about our political rights," the *Independent* declared. "Let us exercise the rights we have and their manly exercise will add to us many of the things we contend for on paper."[40] After Scott's dismissal from the *Voice of the Negro*, the *Independent* launched a public campaign against Barber, the streetcar boycott movement's greatest South-wide advocate.

With Washington's encouragement, the *Independent* mischaracterized Barber's partnership with the white-owned Hertel, Jenkins, and Company and accused the *Voice of the Negro* of secretly operating as a front for a white publisher. The claim was ludicrous because the partnership wasn't a secret; the Hertel, Jenkins firm was listed on the masthead of Barber's journal. Additionally, the company had long shown itself to be friendly to Black causes, particularly through their work with Booker T. Washington. The *Independent* also tried to shame Barber for publishing the *Voice* in a segregated building, quipping that he had to take the freight elevator up to his own office. Davis questioned how Barber could be the fiery advocate in the fight against Jim Crow he claimed to be when he accepted being demeaned in his own workplace.[41] Davis's accusations closely mirrored those Scott had made on Washington's behalf. However, in the end it wasn't Washington's opposition that effectively silenced Barber. It was white supremist violence.

As Black protests spread throughout the South, the racial tension in Atlanta grew worse. The city had once seemed to offer the possibility of safety and success for its African American residents, but in 1906 conditions rapidly deteriorated. Two white journalists were running for governor that year—Clark Howell, editor of the *Atlanta Constitution* and a New South segregationist who favored corporate interests, and Hoke Smith, former editor of the *Atlanta Journal*, who had served as the secretary of the interior under President Grover Cleveland. Although both had once taken a slightly more moderate tone on the question of race, these candidates chose to ride the eroding racial climate in the wake of the failure of cross-racial Populist coalitions in the 1890s and run race-baiting campaigns. Howell and Smith competed to deliver the most virulent, violent attacks against "Negro domination"; both men ran on the promise to disenfranchise Black voters after the election. Choosing between the two segregationists, white voters favored the harsher anti-Black rhetoric doled out by Smith.

Coupled with this toxic political climate was a growing anger about Black liberty in urban spaces. The presence of Black people—on streetcars, city sidewalks, as business owners, and as opinionated political citizens—irritated white Atlanta residents. Black and white working-class men competed for jobs.[42] White discontent about sharing their city with Black citizens was brought to a head in reports of a series of supposed assaults against white women by Black men. Newspapers reported that Atlanta's white women were under attack from every side, leading to a panic. Such a toxic climate made everyday occurrences into dangerous incidents. If a Black man accidently bumped into a white woman on a crowded sidewalk or brushed her skirts while moving to exit a packed streetcar, the contact was characterized as attempted rape. Story after story of white women terrorized in the city or near their suburban homes appeared in the pages of competing newspapers vying to sell more copies.[43]

The Decatur Street district where both Black and white men frequented interracial saloons and gambling dens served as a perfect foil for the angst of white residents about Black liberty. White Atlanta blamed Black "vagrancy" and "vice" for this scourge of attacks on white women. Black-owned establishments there were regularly raided by vice squads, arresting Black owners and patrons while sending white patrons on their way unscathed. The police reported to the press the presence of "pictures of nude white women"—which were actually liquor advertisements distributed by the companies featuring images of scantily clad white women—as evidence of the connection between Decatur Street and the "crime wave" against white women. The city's white newspapers characterized these Black revelers as criminals who were driven by animalistic desires to rape white women.[44] Barber also condemned vagrancy in the pages of the *Voice* but asserted that "there are vagrants of almost every race in Atlanta, and particularly obnoxious and dangerous is the white tramp." He asserted that much of the crime wave that was blamed on Black men actually involved white men who "lurk about bridges and viaducts and commit daring hold-ups" and "paint their faces black and, thereby, throw the police off their tracks."[45] Such a story of a white man blackening up in the style of a minstrel to disguise himself was reported by David T. Howard, a Black undertaker who received the body of a man killed by white mob violence who, upon examination, was revealed to be a white man who had blackened his face with makeup.[46]

After months of the city's white newspapers fueling racial antagonisms with provocative and unfounded rape allegations, anti-Black hysteria reached a fever pitch. On September 22, 1906, in response to a poster calling for "K.K.K Action," hundreds of white men and boys gathered in the Five Points area of downtown Atlanta and began to terrorize Black residents.[47] The Ku Klux Klan would not be officially revived as an organization for another ten years, but Thomas Dixon's play *The Clansmen* had been staged in Atlanta a few months before the riot, reviving the organization's spirit of violent reprisal that had animated the South after the Civil War.[48] For two days and three nights the mob targeted any Black person they could find, grabbing Black passengers on passing streetcars at Atlanta's Five Points interchange; attacking working Black men and women at barbershops, the post office, and the train station; destroying Black businesses; and planning coordinated attacks on Black neighborhoods. The killings were grisly, with members of the mob battling one another for bits of their victims' clothing or flesh; their victims' ears or fingers became totems of their participation in the murderous rampage. Official city records recorded that more than thirty Black men and women were shot, stabbed, or stoned to death on the streets of Atlanta during the riot; the number of killings reported by Black residents was much higher. When the city's mayor was asked how best to quell the riot, he sided with the lawless mob, saying, "As long as the black brutes assault our women, just so long will they be unceremoniously dealt with."[49]

Throughout the riot Barber stayed at the helm of the *Voice of the Negro*, residing temporarily at his office downtown so that he could more accurately report on white violence and Black resistance to the mob. His own investigations revealed that none of the reported accusations of rape by Black men targeting white women published in local papers could be verified. In fact, one investigator privately shared with Barber that bloodhounds traced the trail of one rapist back to the home of a white man who had disguised himself as Black.[50]

In the days after the riot, Barber grew incensed as white journalists continued to push false stories and Black apologists begged Black residents to be quiescent. After John Temple Graves, one of the white journalists who had fomented the riot, placed an article in the *New York World* insisting that the mob was justified because it involved "a carnival of rapes" of white women by Black assailants, Barber felt compelled to respond. The editor telegraphed an anonymous firsthand response to the *New York World* countering the falsehoods pushed by Graves. Calling the mob "lawless and godless," Barber laid the blame for the violence at the feet of Hoke Smith, the governor-elect who rode into office by stoking the fires of white supremacy, and the *Atlanta Constitution*, the *Atlanta Journal*, and the *Atlanta Georgian*, all of which had published fear-mongering stories even in the midst of the riot, simply to sell newspapers. Barber signed his report, "A Colored Citizen."[51]

The article caused a stir in Atlanta, and local officials soon discovered that Barber was the author, probably, according to Booker T. Washington's sources, through officials at the telegraph office.[52] For the crime of accurately reporting that "sensational newspapers and unscrupulous politicians" were to blame, Barber was told to prove that he "did not write the letter or get out of town." In a perversion of the ideal of being innocent until proven guilty, Barber was told by city officials that if he wanted to prove his innocence, he'd have to be questioned by an all-white grand jury, then publish articles in local papers denying his authorship, and finally report in the pages of the *Voice of the Negro* that the "Colored Citizen" article was full of lies. If he were found guilty, he would have been sentenced to Georgia's chain gang, a virtual death sentence in 1906. Knowing that there was no real chance for justice, Barber chose to escape to Chicago rather than face the threat of time on a deadly Georgia chain gang for simply telling the truth. He wrote his full account of the riot in an angry edition of the *Voice*, the first published in Chicago. Just as Wells had asserted years before, Barber questioned the false accounts of rapes by Black men, accurately determining that it was white politicians and white newspapermen who had fanned the flames of racial violence in the city of Atlanta for political purposes. Like Wells, Flemming, and Manly had done in the decade before, Barber, because he dared to tell the truth about racial violence, escaped with little more than his life.[53]

In that post-riot edition of the *Voice*, Barber used segregated streetcars in the New South as an example of the difficulties of racial politics in such a bleak time. He acknowledged the debate within the Black community between those who, out of fear, acquiesced to separate streetcars and those who bravely continued to demand fair treatment on racially integrated cars.[54] The cars became symbolic of their larger struggle. Barber asserted it was not "a humiliation for black men to ride with black men" but humiliating, rather, "when, because we are black and for no other reason, we are denied our rights, robbed at the ballot-box, driven out of courts with lynch justice, refused common civic treatment that belongs to decent men and loyal Americans." Worn down by his former outspoken stance and by the trials of being driven out of the South, Barber argued, "If it will conduce to the peace of society and to the protection of our women from the insults of white men and to the comfort of all parties concerned, we say it deliberately, 'as for me and my house,' give me a separate car or a trailer." In the effort to create spaces where African Americans, particularly Black women, could avoid white threat and violence, Barber argued in favor of all-Black cars, despite his years of protest to the contrary. "A separate car will save our ladies from the insults of white men and give us men passengers decent seats and guarantee to us protection." In his bitterness, Barber wrote, "This is the dictum of self-respect. We are not clamoring to ride with white men; but we are clamoring to ride with decent men." However, Barber set clear terms under which such compromise would be possible: "Frame the law in such a way that no white man shall be allowed upon the car set apart for the Negro race and the conductor shall be liable to a fine . . . for permitting a violation of the law." Barber, who had consistently asserted that segregated conditions always implied Black inferiority and degraded the humanity of all African Americans, concluded by rejecting any acceptance of separate cars. Instead, he reminded his readers that "if nobility of character, decency of person, purity of life and genuine gentlemanship and womanly deportment count for anything," African American Southerners were more than worthy of inclusion.

Washington haunted Barber even after he was forced to leave Atlanta in the wake of the race riot of 1906, sending an anonymous letter to the *New York Age* shaming him for leaving Atlanta, saying he was "disappointed in Mr. Barber's bravery and sense of loyalty to the race," implying that he was a coward for "desert[ing] the people" and for having not "stood [his] ground." Barber tried to revive the *Voice*, but every connection he tried to make to investors or supporters was challenged by the Wizard of Tuskegee.[55] In attempting to destroy Niagara and its ardent and articulate defender, Washington also silenced a leading voice of the streetcar boycott movement, undermining an important hub of communication about protest in the nadir. The Northern-based *Voice* was soon out of print. Its talented editor was trailed by Washington, hounded out of journalism, and forced to go to dental school and settle in Philadelphia in order to find a profession he could pursue that Washington did not control.[56]

It is difficult to assess what Barber could have accomplished if the *Voice* had continued, and it is impossible to know what could be known about this generation of dissent had the attack on Barber by white supremacists in Atlanta and by Washington's campaign of manipulation had not occurred. In the end, Barber sold his valuable *Voice of the Negro* subscription list to Du Bois for just twenty-five dollars. Du Bois would go on to use this list to propel the *Crisis*—the National Association for the Advancement of Colored People's journal. Perhaps, then, it is a fitting legacy to think of the *Voice of the Negro* as the forerunner of the *Crisis* in much the same way that historians consider the Niagara Movement to be the forerunner of the NAACP.[57] But beyond the question of his legacy, we ought to pause to consider the tremendous price paid by Barber and other journalists driven into silence.

Like Barber, in his life after white mob violence, Alexander Manly served as an activist, helping to found Philadelphia's Armstrong Association, a forerunner of the Urban League, but also like Barber, he never returned to journalism. He built a thriving painting contractor business only to lose his new fortune again during the Great Depression. His son said he never recovered from losing everything a second time in his lifetime. While J. L. Flemming did not return to journalism after running for his life a second time, Ida B. Wells continued to dissent in her writing and her organizational work but outside of the South.

In this political moment there are renewed conversations about reparations that first began at the turn of the twentieth century. Then and now there were those who were striving to calculate the value of the loss borne by the enslaved and those who suffered through segregation, but how can we begin to calculate the loss of free Black voices? These journalists suffered the loss of capital in the value of their presses, yes, but there was a greater cost, both personal and historical: the cost of silencing a generation of the most radical activist journalists and stifling the dissent of those who remained. How might you measure the cost?

Notes

1. "The Mob's Work," *Memphis Appeal-Avalanche*, March 10, 1892, 5.

2. Ida B. Wells, *Crusade for Justice: The Autobiography of Ida B. Wells* (Chicago: University of Chicago Press), 66.

3. There are several accounts of how Alexander Manly and his brother Frank escaped the lynch mob in Wilmington; the one recounted here is from his son Milo Manly, which he said he remembered his father telling him as a young man. His interview is an excellent source about Alexander and his outlook. See Milo Manly, interview by Charles Hardy III, September 11, 1984, "Goin' North: Tales of the Great Migration Oral History Project," Louie B. Nunn Center for Oral History, University of Kentucky Libraries; 1898 Wilmington Race Riot Commission, *1898 Wilmington Race Riot Report*, May 31, 2006, North Carolina State Documents Collection, State Library of North Carolina; David Cecelski and Timothy Tyson, eds., *Democracy Betrayed: The Wilmington Race Riot and Its Legacy* (Chapel Hill: University of North Carolina Press, 1998).

4. *General Laws of the Legislature of Alabama*, Act 329, H 518; Blair LM Kelley, *Right to Ride: Streetcar Boycotts and African American Citizenship in the Era of* Plessy v. Ferguson (Chapel Hill: University of North Carolina Press, 2010), 2–3.

5. Blair LM Kelley, "Protest in the 'Age of Accommodation': J. Max Barber and the *Voice of the Negro*," paper presented at the annual meeting of the 95th Annual Convention of the Association for the Study of African American Life and History, Raleigh Convention Center, Raleigh, North Carolina, November 27, 2014.

6. Louis R. Harlan, "Booker T. Washington and the 'Voice of the Negro,' 1904–1907," *Journal of Southern History* 45, no. 1 (1979): 45–62.

7. For more on Richmond's newspapers, see Kelley, *Right to Ride*, 126–37; Ann Field Alexander, *Race Man: The Rise and Fall of the Fighting Editor, John Mitchell, Jr.* (Charlottesville: University of Virginia Press, 2002); and Raymond Gavins, "Urbanization and Segregation: Black Leadership Patterns in Richmond, Virginia, 1900–1920," *South Atlantic Quarterly* 79 (Summer 1980): 257–73.

8. Washington historian Louis Harlan described the *Voice of the Negro* as the "most promising of those short-lived enterprises. Harlan, "Booker T. Washington and the *Voice of the Negro*," 45.

9. J. Max Barber, "The Morning Cometh," *Voice of the Negro*, January 1904, 37–38.

10. David Fort Godshalk, *Veiled Visions: The 1906 Atlanta Race Riot and the Reshaping of American Race Relations* (Chapel Hill: University of North Carolina Press, 2005), 31.

11. *Voice of the Negro*, January 1904, 2.

12. John Hope, "Our Atlanta Schools, *Voice of the Negro*, January 1904, 10; Kelly Miller, "The Negro as a Political Factor," *Voice of the Negro*, January 1904, 17; Booker T. Washington, "The Negro's Part in the South's Upbuilding," *Voice of the Negro*, January 1904, 28–30; Fannie Barrier Williams, "The Negro and Public Opinion," *Voice of the Negro*, January 1904, 31–32.

13. J. Max Barber, "A Brutal Hanging of a Negro," *Voice of the Negro*, January 1906, 61.

14. Godshalk noted, "A select group of elite African Americans achieved a measure of respectability and wealth as educators in Atlanta's prestigious black colleges and as ministers, teachers, and journalists. . . . By 1905, aggregate black property values in greater Fulton County [where Atlanta is located] approached $1 million." Godshalk, *Veiled Visions*, 20.

15. J. Max Barber, "The Morning Cometh," *Voice of the Negro*, January 1904, 37–38.

16. For more on Washington's influence, see Louis R. Harlan, *Booker T. Washington: The Wizard of Tuskegee, 1901–1915* (New York: Oxford University Press, 1983).

17. Harlan, "Booker T. Washington and the *Voice of the Negro*," 46.

18. "Booker T. Washington to Emmett Jay Scott, November 4, 1903," *Booker T. Washington Papers*, vol. 7 (Urbana: University of Illinois Press, 1977), 328–29; Emmett Jay Scott to Booker T. Washington, December 10, 1903, *Booker T. Washington Papers*, 7:364–65; Harlan, Louis R. "Booker T. Washington and the *Voice of the Negro*," 46–49.

19. David Levering Lewis, *W.E.B. Du Bois: Biography of a Race, 1868–1919* (New York: Henry Holt, 1993), 350.

20. For more on the streetcar boycott movement, see Kelley, *Right to Ride*.

21. J. Max Barber, "The Aggressiveness of Jim-Crowism," *Voice of the Negro* 1, no. 6 (1904): 216–17.

22. "There is in Georgia permissive legislation which allows cities to separate the races on street-cars by giving the Negroes the rear end of the car, and the whites the front. This is, however, seldom enforced, as the self-interest of street-car com-

panies forbids it. Recently, however, we have had a curious experience in Atlanta. The old street-car line which covered the main part of the city was thought to be getting rich, and the city council chartered a rival line. The rival line bid for public favor by announcing that it would follow the state law, and separate the races on its cars. The only effect of this at first was to drive the Negro patrons to the old line. Then the new line, which had meantime 'influenced' a few extra councilmen, put through a city ordinance compelling all street-cars to discriminate." W.E.B. Du Bois, "The Negro South and North," *Bibliotheca Sacra*, vol. 62, July 1905, 500–13, reprinted in *Writings by W.E.B. Du Bois in Periodicals Edited by Others*, ed. and comp. Herbert Aptheker (Millwood, NY: Kraus-Thomson Organization, 1982), 250–56.

23. W.E.B. Du Bois, "The Niagara Movement: Declaration of Principles, 1905," Du Bois Papers, reel 1, Special Collections and University Archives, University of Massachusetts, Amherst Libraries.

24. J. Max Barber, "Execute the Law," *Voice of the Negro* 2, no. 2, February 1905, 126–27.

25. J. Max Barber, "Nashville's Revolt against Jimcrowism," *Voice of the Negro* 2, no. 12, December 1905, 827–30.

26. J. Max Barber. "A Progressive Little Town," *Voice of the Negro* 2, no. 11, November 1905, 754.

27. "'Jim Crow' Street-Cars," *Richmond Planet* 21, no. 17, April 9, 1904, 4; "Colored Folks Yet Walking: More Trouble—The Rule Very Annoying," *Richmond Planet* 21, no. 21, May 7, 1904, 1.

28. "Trouble at Newport News," *Richmond Planet* 23, no. 6, January 13, 1906, 4.

29. "The Streetcar Company's Troubles," *Richmond Planet*, July 2, 1904; "'Jim Crow' Streetcars—Citizens Act," *Richmond Planet*, April 16, 1904.

30. Barber, "Aggressiveness of Jim-Crowism," 217.

31. "Walking Everywhere," *Appreciator* (Fort Smith AR), reprinted in *Richmond Planet*, April 30, 1904, 4.

32. "The Street Car Co. Here Busted," *Richmond Planet*, July 23, 1904, 1.

33. "A Rebuke to Jimcrowism," *Voice of the Negro* 1, no. 8, August 1904, 302; Virginia Passenger and Power Company, board of directors and stockholders minute book, 1903–1904. The decision that made Northrop's receivership permanent outlined that "upon his [William Northrop's] coming in, and through the instrumentality of those who caused him to be connected with the company, large pecuniary assistance was rendered the company, by reason whereof its financial disaster was for a considerable time averted." *Bowling Green Trust Co. v. Virginia Passenger and Power Co.*, 133 F. 186 (1904).

34. "The Chinese Boycott," *Voice of the Negro* 2, no. 8, August 1905,522.

35. J. Max Barber, "The Niagara Movement and Harper's Ferry," *Voice of the Negro* 3, no. 8, August 1906, 402–411.

36. Lewis, *W. E. B. Du Bois: Biography of a Race*, 319.

37. Emmett Jay Scott to Hertel, August 4, 1904, 38; Booker T. Washington to Emmett Jay Scott, August 9, 1904, *Booker T. Washington Papers*, 41.

38. Louis R. Harlan, "Booker T. Washington and the Voice of the Negro, 1904–1907," *Journal of Southern History* 45, no. 1 (1979): 45–62.

39. "Booker T. Washington and His Critics," *Atlanta Independent* 1, no. 35, March 26, 1904, 4.

40. Editorial Notes, *Atlanta Independent* 2, no. 10, August 20, 1904, 4.

41. "The Voice of the Negro," *Atlanta Independent* 2, no. 41, April 8, 1905, 4.

42. Godshalk describes this riot as "an attempt by white[s] to cordon off the center city as their own" and "an attempt among white men to claim the physical territory of downtown Atlanta as their own space." Godshalk, *Veiled Visions*, 107–108.

43. Tera W. Hunter writes, "By sounding the clarion for black male castration and female sterilization in its stories leading up to the riot, the newspaper had induced the mob to link racial and sexual hysteria." Tera W. Hunter, *To 'Joy My Freedom: Southern Black Women's Lives and Labors after the Civil War* (Cambridge, MA: Harvard University Press, 1997), 127.

44. Godshalk, *Veiled Visions*, 85; Mark Bauerlein, *Negrophobia: A Race Riot in Atlanta, 1906* (San Francisco: Encounter Books, 2001), 141–42.

45. J. Max Barber, "The Menace of Vagrants," *Voice of the Negro*, July 1906, 475–76.

46. Bauerlein, *Negrophobia*, 176.

47. Godshalk, *Veiled Visions*, 85.

48. Bauerlein, *Negrophobia*, 34–35.

49. "The Atlanta Riot," *New York Times*, September 25, 1906, 8. For a full account of the riot, see Godshalk, *Veiled Visions*, and Bauerlein, *Negrophobia*.

50. J. Max Barber, "Why Mr. Barber Left Atlanta," *Voice of the Negro*, November 1906, 470–71.

51. Ibid.

52. Booker T. Washington to Henry Hugh Proctor, October 1, 1906, *Booker T. Washington Papers*, 9:80–81.

53. Ibid.

54. J. Max Barber, "Where Are Our Friends?" *Voice of the Negro* 3, no. 10, October 1906, 437–39.

55. Booker T. Washington (unsigned) to the Editor of the *New York Age*, October 1, 1906, *Booker T. Washington Papers*, 9:82–83; Louis R. Harlan provides a poignant description of Barber's struggle to fight off Washington's campaign to silence him as journalist. Harlan, "Booker T. Washington and the *Voice of the Negro*," 45–62. For a description of the negative press releases, see p. 55.

56. Ibid.

57. J. Max Barber, Letter from J. Max Barber to W.E.B. Du Bois, November 18, 1910, W.E.B. Du Bois Papers (MS 312), Special Collections and University Archives, University of Massachusetts, Amherst Libraries.

Journalism and the World to Come

KATHY ROBERTS FORDE
AND SID BEDINGFIELD

The Civil War was a struggle between two competing ideas of the United States, Jill Lepore says, one liberal, the other illiberal. Liberal nationalism, associated with the North, construed the nation-state as conferring "the same set of irrevocable political rights" on all citizens. Illiberal nationalism, associated with the South and the Confederacy, embraced a nation-state built on a white ethnic supremacy that excluded "the negro" from citizenship and the rights it bestowed. Liberalism may have won the war, but the forces of illiberalism never accepted defeat. They continued the struggle, Lepore argues, and their cause gained new adherents in the North and West.[1]

Journalism and Jim Crow tells the story of the illiberal white supremacist Democrats who overthrew Reconstruction in the South and joined with industrialists, railroad companies, and other New South allies to impose a one-party kleptocracy and brutal racial caste system that came to be known as Jim Crow.

Southern white Democrats launched their campaign against Reconstruction from the only institutions they still controlled after the war: their newspapers. These papers did more than support the party in print and spread its propaganda across the region and country. They also served as base camps, ammunition depots, and command-and-control centers for white supremacist gangs that attacked African American communities, disrupted elections, and fomented chaos to undermine Reconstruction governments. Once they had "redeemed" the South, white editors and publishers of urban dailies worked with Democratic Party operatives, officeholders, and business leaders, in local contexts and across state lines, to build the white supremacist political economies and social orders of the New South. But their success in building the world of Jim Crow was not preordained. The forces of illiberalism faced widespread opposition, led by voices in the Black press and, for a brief moment, joined by a feisty and colorful white populist press. In its most radical form, this biracial populist movement fought valiantly in the 1890s to create a pluralist liberal democratic future for the South.

The white Democrats won their quest to shape an illiberal New South, and their newspapers enjoyed the spoils of victory. While the Black and white populist press faded quickly, the white Democratic papers that did so much to create the world of Jim Crow lived long and prospered across the twentieth century. They became some of the most famous names in Southern journalism: the *Atlanta Constitution*, the *Atlanta Journal*, the *Charleston News and Courier*, the Raleigh *News and Observer*, the *Montgomery Advertiser*, the Jackson *Clarion-Ledger*, the *Mobile Daily Register*, the *Tennessean* (formerly the *Nashville Tennessean* and the *Nashville American*), and the *Florida Times-Union*. As the age of professional and independent journalism emerged after World War I, they publicly declared their allegiance to the norms of objectivity and impartiality, and some developed a patina of respectability within the profession. Nonetheless, they continued the battle on behalf of illiberalism. For most of the long and disastrous reign of Jim Crow, these leading lights of Southern journalism worked diligently to preserve anti-Black racism in the South and to facilitate its growth in the North and West too.

In 1920, for example, after D. W. Griffith's noxious film *The Birth of a Nation* spawned a revival of the Ku Klux Klan, it was the *Atlanta Constitution*'s former religion editor, Edward Young Clarke, who turned the struggling organization into a national success story. With the support of his brother, the *Constitution*'s managing editor, Clarke carried the Klan's racist and xenophobic message of "pure Americanism" to every corner of the nation.[2] Outside the South, newspapers that denounced the Klan on the editorial page nonetheless granted the racist organization credibility in their news coverage. Increasingly committed to the new norm of objectivity—defined as detached, disinterested, and politically neutral reporting—professional journalists often treated the Klan as simply another political interest group. A *Washington Star* analysis of 1924 election results declared that "an outstanding feature of the election was the success in many states of the candidate endorsed—directly or indirectly—by the Ku Klux Klan."[3]

By the early 1930s, when popular opinion had turned against the Klan and Congress was considering federal anti-lynching legislation, Southern editors changed tactics. They claimed they had always opposed mob violence and only wanted what was best for their African American neighbors. The conservative *Charleston News and Courier* said its readers "want to protect the Negro. . . . They want to improve their health and give them education. . . . But they do not propose to invite Negroes to take part in government, and when anyone asks this, the South is going to oppose with a solid and unyielding front. The question whether we are right or wrong in this attitude, whether or not it is savage or civilized, we decline to discuss."[4]

Across the 1930s, a new breed of Southern journalist began to soften the *News and Courier*'s defiant tone. Led by Mark Etheridge of Louisville, Virginius Dabney of Richmond, John Temple Graves II of Birmingham, and Ralph McGill of Atlanta, these self-proclaimed Southern liberals condemned violence and mistreatment of African Americans and called for more spending on education and improved economic opportunities for the Black community. In the 1940s, however, their tone changed when they were confronted with more-assertive Black voices during World War II. No power in the world "could force the South to the abandonment of segregation," Etheridge declared. McGill agreed: "There will be no social equality measures. Now or later," the editor of the *Atlanta Constitution* wrote. Summing up a common view held by Southern liberals, Graves wrote, "The Negro needs much and is promised much but there is no hope for him unless he gets along with white men of the South."[5]

Graves and his Southern liberal peers benefited from the wave of "Lost Cause" nostalgia that accompanied the South's decades-long reconciliation with its old foes in the North and West. The paternalistic tone of the Southern journalists connected with a national audience that had been inundated with images of a mythical Old South where slave owners were honorable and kind and their Black chattel acquiescent and appreciative. Griffith's movie had helped popularize this depiction of Southern slave society, but the Lost Cause mythology reached new heights in the 1930s with the multimedia success of Margaret Mitchell's *Gone with the Wind*.

In the *Chicago Defender*, Black activist William L. Patterson said the movie version of Mitchell's Old South soap opera had "lied about the Civil War" and "twisted the history of the era which saw democracy fighting for its life." But the popularity of *Gone with the Wind* overwhelmed what little Black criticism found its way into the white mainstream press. The movie broke box office records and transformed Dixie into a pop-cultural phenomenon. Confederate battle flags were flying "everywhere along the Atlantic seaboard, from New York to Miami, and westward," a *New York Times* columnist reported more than a decade after the movie opened. The flags were merely "a fad," not a political symbol, he assured his readers. They were "simply another of those novelties that somehow becomes a rage." Black activists knew better. The Confederate flag's surprising popularity was evidence of illiberalism's enduring strength in the United States. The white South "lost the war of 1861," Patterson wrote in a letter responding to the *Times* article. "But who can deny that they won the ideological struggle."[6]

Among the Southern liberal journalists, McGill's view would evolve, and by the late 1950s he would embrace the civil rights movement. But Dabney and Graves would never cut ties with white Southern journalism's illiberal roots. Joining such firebrands as James K. Kilpatrick of Richmond and Thomas R. Waring Jr., of Charleston, they would play instrumental roles in fomenting massive resistance to Black civil rights in the years after the 1954 *Brown v. Board of Education* ruling declared segregated schools unconstitutional. And they would find allies in a new conservative movement emerging in the country. In 1957 William F. Buckley Jr., editor of the *National Review*, declared his opposition to Black voting rights in the South because, in his view, whites were "the advanced race" and "the claims of civilization supersede those of universal suffrage." Waring hailed these "brave words . . . uttered by a respected northern journal," and he and Buckley joined forces to bring white segregationists into the new conservative wing of the Republican Party.[7]

The Northern mainstream press is lauded for its coverage of Dr. Martin Luther King Jr. and the African American mass movement that dismantled Jim Crow laws in the 1950s and 1960s. But it is important to note the role of Black journalists such as L. Alex Wilson, Moses J. Newson, and Simeon Booker, whose aggressive coverage often influenced the white press. It is equally important to note the brave and often unrecognized work of Black community organizers across the Jim Crow South. Charles M. Payne describes the mainstream media's coverage of the civil rights movement as "overwhelmingly sympathetic and a crucial part" of its success. Nonetheless, he says the national press presented a distorted view of civil rights activism by focusing on national leaders, major events, and white participants while ignoring the long struggle of Black organizers who made the movement possible. Because of this blind spot, Payne argues, mainstream reporters missed the rising anger and frustration among young Black organizers in the mid-1960s and failed to provide context for the emerging Black Power movement. Their superficial coverage presented a false dichotomy between King's call for peaceful reform and the radical revolution envisioned by Stokely Carmichael. They used different rhetoric, but by the time of King's death in 1968, their views of what needed to happen in America were not dissimilar.[8]

After Black rage over persistent police brutality spilled into the streets of Watts, Detroit, Newark, and other urban areas in the mid-1960s, the Kerner Commission—a blue-ribbon panel commissioned by President Lyndon Johnson—issued a blistering critique of mainstream journalism. The news media have "failed to report adequately on the causes and consequences of civil disorders and on the underlying problems" that African Americans face in the United States, the report stated. They have "not communicated to the majority of their audience—which is white—a sense of the degradation, misery and hopelessness of life" for many Black Americans. The Kerner Commission called on news organizations to diversify their newsrooms, hire more journalists of color, and promote African Americans into management jobs that shape news coverage.[9]

In the 1970s sympathetic news executives declared their intention to achieve these goals. Under the leadership of Eugene Patterson, editor of the *St. Petersburg Times*, the American Society of Newspaper Editors (ASNE) launched an ambitious plan to increase minority hiring in newsrooms. But the industry's Project 2000 campaign faced immediate and enduring opposition from editors who claimed hiring more journalists of color would undercut quality in the newsroom. In 1997 the ASNE conceded that its diversity drive had been an abject failure. At that time, nonwhites accounted for only 11.35 percent of the industry workforce, less than half the percentage of the minority population nationally. Today nonwhites account for merely 24 percent of newsroom employees, although they are roughly 40 percent of the national population. Only about 7 percent of these newsroom employees are Black.[10]

From the founding of the first Black newspaper in 1827 through at least the civil rights movement of the 1950s and 1960s, the Black press and the white press operated in largely separate Black and white public spheres in the United States. Perhaps an integrated press would have paid attention to the systemic racism that greeted African Americans making the Great Migration from the South during the early to mid-twentieth century. Such a press might have documented residential segregation across the United States and shown that it was not simply the result of individual choices, the prejudice of realtors, and discriminatory mortgage lending practices known as redlining. Rather, as Richard Rothstein brilliantly shows in *The Color of Law*, it was the result of systematic public policy at the local, state, and national levels. These policies were unconstitutional violations of various prohibitions in the Bill of Rights against government treating citizens unfairly. An integrated press might also have noted anti-Black provisions and practices in critical New Deal public policies such as the Wagner Act and Social Security Act of 1935, as well as the Home Owners' Loan Act of 1933. It might have exposed and fought more effectively against school segregation and gerrymandering meant to weaken Black voting power in the North and West. It might have lifted the veil on what Brian Purnell and Jeanne Theoharis have called a Northern Jim Crow that "hid in plain sight."[11]

It is much harder to imagine an integrated press in the South before the victories of the civil rights movement. Despite Henry Grady's soaring rhetoric and industrial fantasies, the New South turned out to be a weakly industrialized syndicate of Southern states built on racial caste and terror, a near-totalitarian society operating for generations within the greater United States. Like all totalitarian states, it maintained power through a news system essentially controlled by those in power, with white press leaders working hand in glove with the Democratic Party to craft and maintain white supremacist political, economic, and social orders. These white leaders built a world that was inhospitable to Black aspiration, opportunity, and dignity, and they built it on stolen or exploited Black labor. It was a world that silenced a generation of Black journalists in the South who tried to keep this world from being built. As Blair LM Kelley observes in chapter 10, the personal, collective, and historical costs of this silencing are incalculable.

Yet it's a calculation any American interested in repairing and advancing liberal democracy would do well to ponder, especially given the discomfiting reality that every generation of Black journalists has struggled to be heard in America beyond the Black public sphere. In the summer of 2020, journalists across the country—indeed, across the world—covered the Black Lives Matter protests that blanketed the United States and spread to countries on every continent. Prominent Black journalists in the United States, many of whom came of age covering the Ferguson, Missouri, protests in 2014, publicly criticized their newsrooms for hewing to notions and practices of normatively "white" objective journalism that often prevented frank, clear descriptions of racism or, in the case of Senator Tom Cotton's op-ed in the *New York Times* calling for the use of military force to put down protests, allowed racist views to be aired in elite opinion pages. Some Black journalists who commented on anti-Black racism on social media were prevented from covering the protests,

yet these journalists and their allies pushed some of the most elite news outlets in the country to begin to reckon with and dismantle structural racism in
their own newsrooms.[12]

Some historically white newspapers have apologized for their roles in building and maintaining white supremacy. In 2005 the *Raleigh News and Observer*
apologized for its central role in the Wilmington Massacre of 1898. In 2006 the
paper published a special insert detailing its role in the corrupt North Carolina
election of 1898 and the violent overthrow of Wilmington's biracial Fusionist government. In 2018, when the National Memorial for Peace and Justice
opened in Montgomery, the *Montgomery Advertiser* apologized for its past
racist coverage of Black life and indifference to lynching. In 2019 the *Orlando
Sentinel* apologized for its racist coverage of the Groveland Four rape case in the
mid-twentieth century. In 2020 the *Florida Times-Union* apologized for failing
to cover a vicious 1960 Klan attack on teenage lunch counter demonstrators
with ax handles. (However, the paper failed to mention its support of Flagler's
racist labor practices at the turn of the century.) Also in 2020 the *Kansas City
Star* apologized for its prodigious history of anti-Black reporting, including its
support of redlining and countenance of racial violence. More apologies will
almost certainly appear, but apologies are hardly enough.[13]

What will news leaders and journalists do about the racism that continues
to structure American newsrooms and news content, especially coverage of
Black life, the criminal justice system, policing, racial justice, and Trumpism's
illiberal and racist values and political programs? What are the possibilities
in our own moment that journalism can be remade to serve the values of a
multiracial and just democracy, thereby perhaps even remaking the country
itself as a "new America?"

We hope historians will continue the line of research we've begun with *Journalism and Jim Crow*. For example, we know relatively little about the role of
the white and Black press as the border state of Kentucky transformed from a
Union to a Lost Cause society after Reconstruction. Historians have described
Henry Watterson, editor of the Louisville *Courier-Journal* for fifty years and
New South booster, as a paternalistic moderate on matters of race. But after
supporting the Reconstruction-era amendments, he went on to oppose Black
suffrage, hew closely to Democratic Party orthodoxy, and sign his editorials, syndicated in newspapers across the country, with the pen name "Marse
Henry." He was also a longtime supporter of (and recipient of a loan from)
the Louisville and Nashville Railroad, which made abundant use of convict

leasing to build its power and wealth. Dr. Henry Fitzbutler, a Black physician trained at the University of Michigan, opposed Watterson repeatedly in his sideline vocation as editor of the long-lived Black weekly *Ohio Falls Express* (1879–1904). He also hosted the National Convention of Colored Men in Louisville in 1883, where Frederick Douglass gave what became a famous keynote speech. Fitzbutler frequently opposed William H. Steward, editor of the Black weekly *American Baptist*, adviser on Black affairs to elite whites, and friend of Booker T. Washington. What's more, the convict leasing literature has barely touched Kentucky, although it's clear the system was used, abused, and controversial, with Watterson showing keen interest. These are just a few useful threads to pull in researching Kentucky.[14]

Louisiana is another state that requires close attention. Lawyer Louis Martinet founded the Black paper *New Orleans Crusader* and the Comité des Citoyens to agitate for equal citizenship and fixed his efforts on Louisiana's 1890 Separate Car Law. He was a critical actor, along with white author, lawyer, and ally Albion Tourgée, who wrote a column for the Chicago *Daily Inter Ocean*, in planning and executing the challenge to the law that eventually became *Plessy v. Ferguson*. We know that Democratic white newspapers in New Orleans and across the state supported segregation and white supremacy, but what were their roles in the *Plessy* struggle? And what role did newspaper leaders play in the brutal racial violence that was endemic to the state post–Civil War? And in the convict leasing system that built the state's railroads and levees and worked the Angola plantation? And in party politics that built Jim Crow in Louisiana?[15]

In 1883, fifteen years before Democratic newspapers helped wrest power from the Fusionists and carry off the Wilmington Massacre in the North Carolina election of 1898, the Democratic Party did something similar in Virginia. The biracial Readjuster Party had gained control of the state in 1879, and the majority-Black town of Danville, a vibrant tobacco center, soon had its own Readjuster government. White Democrats were determined to rid the state of Readjusters and restrict Black political power, and they used the specter of "Negro domination" to drive a wedge between the Black and white Readjuster coalition. A key tool was "the Danville Circular," a broadsheet published by the Democratic Council of Danville purporting Negro misrule and insolence in the city. Officially titled "Coalition Rule in Danville," the circular traveled widely around the state in the days before the election, republished in Democratic newspapers. Throughout election season, the Democrats had incited racial animus through inflammatory reports and commentary about "Negro misrule" in newspapers across the state, using an unofficial campaign strategy called "incorporating the color line." The stage was set for an armed conflict on the streets of Danville, started by white Democrats, blamed on Black Readjusters, and resulting in the murder of six Black men. News of the "Danville Riot" spread rapidly across the state and served to shift large numbers of white Readjusters to the Democratic Party. Historians have barely examined the role of newspapers in the political battle in the months leading up to the Danville Massacre and the Democratic defeat of the Readjusters in Virginia. It's time to tell this story.[16]

Additionally, much is known about Booker T. Washington's influence among Black press leaders in the South and across the country, including his efforts to undermine those he viewed as radical, like William Monroe Trotter and W.E.B. Du Bois, as well as his subsidy and part ownership of Black periodicals. But we know only bits and pieces about Washington's relationships and work with white press leaders. We need to know more. Given his regional and national role as the Black voice of the New South, we also need to understand more fully his role in the New South program beyond the 1895 Atlanta Compromise speech. Brian Kelly has convincingly argued that Washington's program of accommodation actually served up the "'cheap, docile, black labor'" that white New South elites required, noting that Louis Harlan once described Washington as "a black counterpart of Grady." We need a focused study on Washington's relationship with the press of his era.[17]

Finally, as historians continue to expand our understanding of the "Jim Crow North," it will be important to examine whether white press leaders beyond the South played roles in building Jim Crow societies and policies in other parts of the country. We know that many Northern white news leaders, both publishers and editorial writers, played prominent roles in U.S. political life, serving in office, advancing political agendas, and advising politicians throughout the early and mid-twentieth century. But we know very little about their involvement in the significant racial issues of their eras and their relationships with Black press leaders. We hope scholars of the Jim Crow North will take up this subject.[18]

Final Thoughts

We also hope newsroom leaders and journalists across the country will read, discuss, and reflect on what *Journalism and Jim Crow* teaches us about the past: the roads not taken, the opportunities missed, the compromises made with tragic and enduring consequences for democracy and justice. Voting and public faith in free and fair elections require rational public discourse based on trust in facts and a consensus notion of truth. Yet our news media ecosystem and democracy itself have been hacked by illiberal actors, including some masquerading as journalists and journalistic institutions, threatening our society's ability to inform the electorate, protect voting rights for all, and engage in good-faith public debate.

In their efforts to cover the Trump administration and Trumpism, journalists learned a great deal about the limits of democratic norms to rein in dishonest and corrupt governance. They learned the limits of journalistic norms too. How should newsrooms have covered a president who spewed lies, misinformation, and conspiracy theories; groped and insulted women; made common cause with white supremacists; engaged in racist rhetoric; corruptly pardoned friends and allies; used the highest office in the land for self-dealing and grift; courted and kowtowed to the most dangerous dictators in the world; seriously undermined public health officials' efforts to control the coronavirus pandemic; and sought to overturn the results of the most secure U.S. presidential election in history? How could journalists avoid amplifying Trump's dishonest tweets and other public statements? How could they have avoided letting Trump's agenda shape news coverage? How could they have avoided normalizing his antidemocratic behavior?

A first step might be to admit that in the United States, journalism has always been a political activity and journalists have always been political actors. Professional journalists have often been loath to admit this reality; too often, they have pursued neutrality at the expense of fact-finding and treated political reporting as something akin to political stenography. But this view of journalism has been thoroughly debunked during the Trump era. It is high time the news industry and the academy undertake the serious study of the news media in American political and social life.

Journalists should finally vanquish the misguided view that objectivity demands rigid neutrality. This journalistic norm has, across time, facilitated disinformation campaigns and played into the hands of white supremacists and other illiberal forces. One of us, Sid Bedingfield, worked in daily journalism for more than twenty-five years, and he concedes he was not always immune to the siren call of "balance" as a means of signaling fairness and placating political pressure groups. But the objectivity that Walter Lippmann and others first articulated in the 1920s did not mean balance or neutrality. Objectivity was a method of rigorous, transparent, and self-reflexive research that could empower journalists to interpret events and draw conclusions based on irrefutable evidence. Journalists helped shape public opinion, Lippmann argued, but they relied too heavily on personal bias and were too easily duped by politicians, business leaders, and other powerful forces. In the increasingly complex and interconnected world of the early twentieth century, Lippmann believed journalists needed new analytical skills that would allow them to deliver independent, evidence-based reporting, interpretation, and opinion. Those skills are even more important today.[19]

American journalism also needs to institutionalize the lessons learned from covering the Trump administration and reflect on what could have been done better. It is terrifying to imagine what might have happened had we not had a free and honest press, committed to the principles of liberal democracy, covering the Trump administration. Along the way, the press learned the importance of calling out lies; identifying disinformation campaigns, fakes, dishonest news brokers, and conspiracy theories; and devising new methods for investigating the abuse of power in the highest levels of government.

Finally, and importantly, American journalism needs to dismantle the systemic racism that continues to shape newsroom hiring, editorial decision making, and news content. Most newsrooms in the United States are predominantly white, and as Wesley Lowery pointed out in a widely discussed *New York Times* op-ed published at the height of the summer 2020 protests, this largely white press "has allowed what it considers objective truth to be decided almost exclusively by white reporters and their mostly white bosses." Such journalism has often ignored or misrepresented Black communities, issues, and perspectives. It has too often fallen prey to the perils of mistaking objectivity for neutrality, with editors making coverage decisions they believe will appear fair to a "theoretical reader, who is invariably assumed to be white." When a public official or figure trots out racist rhetoric or supports a public policy that disadvantages people of color, call it racist, Lowery suggests. When a police officer shoots someone, avoid newspeak like "officer-involved shooting." Hire Black journalists and other journalists of color, and give them positions of power in the newsroom. To Lowery's suggestions we simply add the following: news leaders and journalists should make it a point to learn about the history of white supremacy in American journalism and discuss it in open forums as they do the important work of pulling it out by the roots.[20]

Journalism and Jim Crow reveals that the problems that vex us now have always been with us. The bitter forces of illiberalism have waxed and waned across time, but they remain ever present, waiting for the right demagogues to activate their fury. When a rabid mob sacked the U.S. Capitol and briefly halted the certification of President Donald J. Trump's electoral defeat in January 2021, President-elect Joe Biden described the violence as un-American. The "scenes of chaos in the Capitol do not reflect a true America, do not represent who we are," Biden said.[21] It was an aspirational claim, not a declaration of historical fact. Just as Lincoln appealed to our "better angels" on the eve of a gruesome Civil War, Biden called for unity at a moment when illiberal extremists—fueled by lies from the president, Fox News, and its journalistic imitators—were on the march.[22]

Those who would attack pluralism and liberal democracy are ever ready to be summoned. And the problem is not solely American. "For the first time this century," Timothy Garton Ash has observed, "among countries with more than one million people, there are now fewer democracies than there are nondemocratic regimes."[23] If we are to rebuild liberal democracy and create the conditions necessary for it to withstand challenges from demagogues and antidemocratic forces, we must reimagine and remake journalism too. The world to come depends on it.

Notes

1. Jill Lepore, "A New Americanism: Why a Nation Needs a National Story," *Foreign Affairs* 98, no. 2 (2019): 10–19, quote on 13. See also Jill Lepore, *This America: The Case for the Nation* (New York: Liveright, 2019); Jill Lepore, *These Truths: A History of the United States* (New York: Norton, 2018); and Heather Cox Richardson, *How the South Won the Civil War: Oligarchy, Democracy, and the Continuing Fight for the Soul of America* (New York: Oxford University Press, 2020).

2. William F. Mugleston, "Julian Harris, the Georgia Press, and the Ku Klux Klan," *Georgia Historian Review* 59, no. 3 (1975): 284–95; Linda Gordan, *The Second Coming of the KKK: The Ku Klux Klan of the 1920s and the American Political Tradition* (New York: Liveright, 2018), 13–14. In the early 1920s, daily and weekly newspapers across Georgia either openly supported or remained silent about the new KKK, with one prominent exception—the *Columbus Enquirer-Sun*, edited by Julian Harris, son of author Joel Chandler Harris.

3. On the rise of objectivity in journalism, see Michael Schudson, *Discovering the News: A Social History of American Newspapers* (New York: Basic Books, 1978); David T. Z. Mindich, *Just the Facts: How "Objectivity" Came to Define American Journalism* (1998; New York: New York University Press, 2000); Richard L. Kaplan, *Politics and the American Press: The Rise of Objectivity, 1865–1920* (New York: Cambridge University Press, 2002); Andrew Porwancher, "Objectivity's Prophet: Adolph S. Ochs and the *New York Times*, 1896–1935," *Journalism History* 36, no. 4 (2011): 186–95. For more on the debate over objective journalism, see Thomas Na-

gel, *The View from Nowhere* (New York: Oxford University Press, 1986); Jay Rosen, "The View from Nowhere: Questions and Answers," *PressThink* (blog), November 10, 2010, http://pressthink.org/2010/11/the-view-from-nowhere-questions-and -answers/; G. Gould Lincoln, "Coolidge Margin Grows; GOP Gains in Congress," *Washington Star*, November 5, 1924.

4. Untitled editorial, *Charleston News and Courier*, May 30, 1930.

5. John T. Kneebone, *Southern Liberal Journalists and the Issue of Race, 1920–1944* (Chapel Hill: University of North Carolina, 1984), 4, 198; John Temple Graves, "The Southern Negro and the War Crisis," *Virginia Quarterly Review* 18, no. 4 (1942): 500–517; Morton Sosna, *In Search of the Silent South: Southern Liberalism and the Race Issue* (New York: Columbia University Press, 1977), 190–207.

6. William L. Patterson, "'Gone with the Wind': A Review," *Chicago Defender*, January 6, 1940; E. John Long, "Conquest by Bunting," *New York Times*, October 14, 1951; William L. Patterson, "Not 'Fad,'" *New York Times*, October 28, 1951.

7. William F. Buckley Jr. "Why the South Must Prevail," *National Review*, August 24, 1957; "A Courageous Stand," *Charleston News and Courier*, August 28, 1957; Sid Bedingfield, *Newspaper Wars: Civil Rights and White Resistance in South Carolina, 1935–1965* (Urbana: University of Illinois Press, 2017), 182–86.

8. Charles M. Payne, *I've Got the Light of Freedom: The Organizing Tradition and the Mississippi Freedom Struggle* (Berkeley: University of California Press, 1996), 392; Gene Roberts and Hank Klibanoff, *The Race Beat: The Press, the Civil Rights Struggle, and the Awakening of a Nation* (New York: Random House, 2006), 86–108.

9. *Kerner Commission Summary Report*, prepared by the National Advisory Commission on Civil Disorders (Washington, DC: Government Printing Office, 1968), https://www.hsdl.org/?abstract&did=35837.

10. Gwyneth Mellinger, *Chasing Newsroom Diversity: From Jim Crow to Affirmative Action* (Urbana: University of Illinois Press, 2013), 2; Elizabeth Grieco, "10 Charts about America's Newsrooms," *FactTank*, April 28, 2020, https://www.pew research.org/fact-tank/2020/04/28/10-charts-about-americas-newsrooms/; *ASNE 2018 Newsroom Employment Diversity Survey*, https://members.newsleaders .org/diversity-survey-2018-tables.

11. Richard Rothstein, *The Color of Law: A Forgotten History of How Our Government Segregated America* (New York: Liveright, 2017), vi-xii; Brian Purnell and Jeanne Theoharis, introduction to *The Strange Careers of the Jim Crow North: Segregation and Struggle Outside the South*, ed. Brian Purnell and Jeanne Theorharis, with Komozi Woodard (New York: New York University Press, 2019), 2–17, quote on 6.

12. Mathew Ingram, "Black Journalists Face Challenges That Stem from Systemic Racism," *Columbia Journalism Review*, July 9, 2020, at https://www.cjr.org/the_media _today/black-journalists-systemic-racism.php; Wesley Lowery, "A Reckoning over Objectivity, Led by Black Journalists," op-ed, *New York Times*, June 23, 2020; Ben Smith, "Inside the Revolts Erupting in America's Big Newsrooms," *New York Times*,

June 7, 2020; Clark Merrefield, "Race and the Newsroom: What Seven Research Studies Say," *NiemanLab*, July 22, 2020, https://www.niemanlab.org/2020/07/race-and-the-newsroom-what-seven-research-studies-say/.

13. Editorial board, "An Ugly Chapter," Raleigh *News and Observer*, December 17, 2005; Timothy B. Tyson, "The Ghosts of 1898: Wilmington's Race Riot and the Rise of White Supremacy," Raleigh *News and Observer*, November 17, 2006; Editorial board, "Our Shame: The Sins of Our Past Laid Bare for All to See," *Montgomery Advertiser*, April 26, 2018; Editorial board, "To the Community and the Families of the Groveland Four: We're Sorry," *Orlando Sentinel*, January 10, 2019; Editorial board, "An Apology for Failing to Adequately Cover Ax Handle Saturday," *Florida Times-Union*, August 21, 2020; Mike Fannen, "The Truth in Black and White: An Apology from the Kansas City Star," *Kansas City Star*, December 20, 2020.

14. Anne E. Marshall, *Creating a Confederate Kentucky: The Lost Cause and Civil War Memory in a Border State* (Chapel Hill: University of North Carolina Press, 2010); Daniel S. Margolies, *Henry Watterson and the New South: The Politics of Empire, Free Trade, and Globalization* (Lexington: University Press of Kentucky, 2006); Maury Klein, *History of the Louisville and Nashville Railroad* (Lexington: University Press of Kentucky, 2003), 382–83; Marion B. Lucas, *A History of Blacks in Kentucky: From Slavery to Segregation, 1760–1891* (Lexington: University Press of Kentucky, 2003), 319–20; "Colored Citizens," Louisville *Courier-Journal*, September 5, 1883; George C. Wright, *A History of Blacks in Kentucky: In Pursuit of Equality, 1890–1980* (Lexington: University Press of Kentucky, 1992), 19–20; Robert Gunn Crawford, "A History of the Kentucky Penitentiary System, 1865–1937" (PhD diss., University of Kentucky, 1955).

15. In *The African American Newspaper: Voices of Freedom* (Evanston, IL: Northwestern University Press, 2006), Patrick S. Washburn neglects to mention, in his discussion of newspaper response to *Plessy v. Ferguson*, the essential role of Creole Black newspaper editor and lawyer Martinet in spearheading the case. Blair LM Kelley, *Right to Ride: Streetcar Boycotts and African American Citizenship in the Era of* Plessy v. Ferguson (Chapel Hill: University of North Carolina Press, 2010), 76–81; Nathan Cardon, "'Less Than Mayhem': Louisiana's Convict Lease, 1865–1901," *Louisiana History* 58, no. 4 (2017): 417–41.

16. Among the newspapers that appear to have played key roles are the *Danville Times* (editor Powhatan Bouldin) and the *Danville Register* (editor Abner Anderson), both Democratic papers; the *Richmond Dispatch* (editor Charles Cowardin), the leading state Democratic paper; the *Richmond Whig* (editor William C. Elam), the leading Readjuster paper; the *Richmond Planet* (editor John Mitchell Jr.), which became a powerful Black newspaper; and the *Lancet* (editor George W. Bragg Jr.), a Black newspaper in Petersburg, Virginia. Three white press leaders in Danville (Bouldin, Anderson, and John Taylor Averett, editor of the *Tobacco Journal*, leader of the Danville Democrats, and key supporter of the Danville Cir-

cular) served as secretaries for the Committee of Forty, a group of leading white men in the city who issued a report blaming the riot on Black citizens of Danville. Jane Dailey, "Deference and Violence in the Postbellum Urban South: Manners and Massacres in Danville, Virginia," *Journal of Southern History* 63, no. 3 (1997): 553–90; Steven Hahn, *A Nation Under Our Feet: Black Political Struggles in the Rural South from Slavery to the Great Migration* (Cambridge: The Belknap Press of Harvard University Press, 2003), 364-411; Hampton D. Carey, "New Voices in the Old Dominion: Black Politics in the Virginia Southside Region and the City of Richmond, 1867–1902" (PhD diss., Columbia University, 2000), 82–83; "The Danville Riot: Congressman John B. Wise on the Stand," *Richmond Dispatch*, February 26, 1884; "The War of Races in Virginia," *Republican Chronicle* (Knoxville), November 14, 1883; Jack Irby Hayes Jr., *The Lamp and the Cross: A History of Averett College, 1859–2001* (Macon, GA: Mercer University Press, 2004), 32–35; Henry Lewis Suggs, ed., *The Black Press in the South, 1865–1979* (Westport, CT: Greenwood Press, 1983), 16, 389.

17. August Meier, "Booker T. Washington and the Negro Press: With Special Reference to the *Colored American Magazine*," *Journal of Negro History* 38, no. 1 (1953): 67–90; Kerri K. Greenidge, *Black Radical: The Life and Times of William Monroe Trotter* (New York: Liveright, 2020); Brian Kelly, "Sentinels for New South Industry: Booker T. Washington, Industrial Accommodation, and Black Workers in the Jim Crow South," *Labor History* 44, no. 3 (2003): 342.

18. Michael Schudson, "Persistence of Vision: Partisan Journalism in the Mainstream Press," in *A History of the Book in America*, vol. 4, *Print in Motion: The Expansion of Publishing and Reading in the United States, 1880–1940*, ed. Carl F. Kaestle and Janice A. Radway, 140–50 (Chapel Hill: University of North Carolina Press, 2009).

19. See Walter Lippmann, *Public Opinion* (New York: Harcourt, Brace 1922), 317–67; Walter Lippmann, *Liberty and the News* (1920; repr., Mineola, NY: Dover, 2012). See also Tom Rosenstiel, "Thread in response to @wesleylowrey's powerful essay in the @nytimes on objectivity," Twitter, June 24, 2020, https://twitter.com/TomRosenstiel/status/1275773988053102592?s=20.

20. Lowery, "Reckoning over Objectivity."

21. Transcript: Trump Sees Special People, Biden Sees Extremists," *Associated Press*, January 6, 2021. Transcript of President-elect Biden's comments after the assault on the U.S. Capitol, January 6, 2021, https://www.yahoo.com/lifestyle/transcript-trump-sees-special-people-231743284.html.

22. First Inaugural Address of Abraham Lincoln, March 4, 1861, Lillian Goodman Law Library, Yale Law School, https://avalon.law.yale.edu/19th_century/lincoln1.asp.

23. Timothy Garton Ash, "The Future of Liberalism," *Prospect*, December 9, 2020, https://www.prospectmagazine.co.uk/magazine/the-future-of-liberalism-brexit-trump-philosophy.

Contributors

SID BEDINGFIELD is an associate professor in the Hubbard School of Journalism and Mass Communication, University of Minnesota. He is the author of *Newspaper Wars: Civil Rights and White Resistance in South Carolina, 1935–1965,* winner of the 2018 South Carolina Historical Society Book Award.

BRYAN BOWMAN is a fellow in Middle East policy for the Friends Committee on National Legislation and was previously a reporter for the *Globe Post.* He is a 2018 graduate of the University of Massachusetts Amherst.

W. FITZHUGH BRUNDAGE is William Umstead Distinguished Professor of History at the University of North Carolina. He is the author of *Lynching in the New South: Georgia and Virginia, 1880–1930* and *The Southern Past: A Clash of Race and Memory,* winner of the Southern Historical Association's 2005 Charles Sydnor Award.

KATHY ROBERTS FORDE is an associate professor in the Department of Journalism at the University of Massachusetts Amherst. She is the author of *Literary Journalism on Trial:* Masson v. New Yorker *and the First Amendment,* which won the 2009 Frank Luther Mott-Kappa Tau Alpha Book Award for best book in mass communication and journalism.

Contributors

ROBERT GREENE II, a scholar of intellectual history, is an assistant professor of history at Claflin University, in Orangeburg, South Carolina. He is the author of "The Newest South: African Americans and the Democratic Party, 1964–1995" (dissertation, 2019) and "Where Do We Go from Here? The Implications of Black Intellectual History in the Modern South," in *Navigating Souths: Transdisciplinary Explorations of a U.S. Region* (2017).

KRISTIN L. GUSTAFSON is an associate teaching professor at the University of Washington–Bothell and a scholar of journalism history and practices, ethnic and community media, and archiving. Her work appears in *Columbia Journalism Review, American Journalism, Journalism, Journalism History, Newspaper Research Journal,* and *Visual Communication Quarterly.*

D'WESTON HAYWOOD is an associate professor of history at New York City's Hunter College and the author of *Let Us Make Men: The Twentieth-Century Black Press and a Manly Vision for Racial Advancement* (2018). His research also involves what he calls "Sonic Scholarship." His first project in this arena is "The [Ferguson] Files: A Sonic Study of Racial Violence in America."

BLAIR LM KELLEY is an associate professor of history and assistant dean for Interdisciplinary Studies and International Programs for the College of Humanities and Social Sciences at North Carolina State University. She is the author of *Right to Ride: Streetcar Boycotts and African American Citizenship in the Era of* Plessy v. Ferguson, winner of the 2010 Letitia Woods Brown Best Book Award from the Association of Black Women Historians.

ALEX LICHTENSTEIN (Preface) is a professor of history at the University of Indiana. He is the author of *Twice the Work of Free Labor: The Political Economy of Convict Labor* (1996) and editor of *American Historical Review.*

RAZVAN SIBII is a senior lecturer in the Department of Journalism at the University of Massachusetts Amherst and a scholar of media, identity construction, and discourse. He is the author of "'You Can Be a Good Romanian, but not a Romanian': A Critical Discourse Analysis of the Romanian History Textbook Narrative" (dissertation, 2019) and "Imagining Nation in Romanian History Textbooks: Towards a Liberating Identity Narrative," in *The New Politics of the Textbook: A Project of Critical Examination and Resistance* (2011).

Index

36; censuring of, 38; collusion with Brown, 38; governorship of, 36; involvement in convict leasing, 39

Columbia (SC) Daily Register, 169; support for Farmers' Alliance, 174

Columbia (SC) *State*, 165; start of, 175; on Tillman, 163

Columbus Enquirer-Sun, on Ku Klux Klan, 316n2

Colyar, Arthur S., *plate 9*; advocate of protectionism, 246n10; Alabama and Tennessee Coal and Iron Company presidency, 231; on Black Confederate soldiers, 250n63; and Bourbon Democrats, 247n10; on business/government relationship, 230, 248n24; business ventures of, 226, 251n79; in Confederate Congress, 227; convict leasing advocacy of, 12, 20, 227, 228–35, 242; convict leasing debate with Haselton, 231–35, 240, 249n52; death of, 243; Democratic-Conservative leadership of, 227; early life of, 226; editorials, 238–41, 251n70; editorship of *Nashville American*, 226, 238, 241, 251n75; engagement with press, 245; gubernatorial candidacy (1870), 229, 246n10; on "hierarchy of labor," 235–38; on interracial harmony, 237; interviews with, 245; legal practice of, 226; legislative investigation of, 240; multiple roles of, 243–44; New South ideology of, 20, 227; newspapers of, 16, 225–26, 238; in Panic of 1873, 248n33; paternal advice from, 237; political career of, 227, 237; railroad holdings of, 227, 228, 251n75; railroads' backing of, 238, 251n75; representation of TCI, 242; representation of Tennessee penitentiary, 239; Sewanee Mines of, 39, 226; slave ownership, 226, 236; on state immigration office, 248n25; Tennessee Coal and Railroad Company presidency, 230; on Tennessee labor force, 230; in Tennessee legislature, 227; warnings to Black Americans, 237; Wells on, 250n70

Comité des Citoyens, 312

Commission on Interracial Cooperation (CIC), investigation of lynching, 106

Confederacy, illiberal nationalism of, 305

Confederate flag, popularity of, 308

Confederates, former: monuments to, 129; in post-reconstruction South, 11; in Tennessee politics, 246n10

Constitution, U.S.: Reconstruction amendments, 9–10, 11, 12, 179, 237, 311. *See also* Fifteenth Amendment; Fourteenth Amendment

contract labor, 186n58; escape from, 180–81. *See also* convict leasing; debt peonage

Convention of Colored Newspapermen (Cincinnati, 1875), 120–21

"The Convict Catechism!" (1880), 39

convict leasing, 275n21; in Alabama, 136, 141–42, 149–52, 225, 231, 248n33; Alston's report on, 34–36; in Atlanta, 229; benefits to private persons, 234; benefits to state, 234–35; Black journalists on, 13; Black protests on, 42–43; Colyar's advocacy for, 12, 20, 227, 228–35, 242; competition with free labor, 240; corruption in, 142; cronyism in, 40; demise of, 142, 150, 241, 243, 250n56, 272; duration of, 41; Flagler's use of, 12–13, 20, 261–62, 272; in Florida, 254, 258, 260–63, 272, 274n13, 276n23; in Georgia, 12, 34–45; Grady and, 38–45; Haselton debate over, 231–35, 240; historical literature on, 273; investigations of, 41, 44, 150; journalists' denunciation of, 241; legality of, 225; legislation, 13; Louisville and Nashville Railroad's use of, 12, 311–12; mechanisms of, 20; moral foundations of, 235; in New South, 6, 7, 13; in New South industrialism, 20; Northern knowledge of, 46; Plant's use of, 255, 258, 261–62, 272, 281n66; populist opposition to, 241; press exposés of, 262–63; prison reform and, 240; profit from, 234–35, 264; public opinion on, 233, 236, 238, 242, 245, 263; railroads' use of, 12, 15–16; at Sewanee Mining Company, 230–31; silencing of protest on, 42; in South Carolina, 168; in Southern political economy, 7; *State* ex rel. *Warren v. Jack* on, 225, 243; subleasing of, 225; in Tennessee, 20, 225–45; by Tennessee Coal, Iron, and Railroad Company, 12, 141–42, 225, 239–40, 243, 252n79; by Tennessee Coal and Railroad Company, 230–34; Tennessee newspapers on, 238–39; women's opposition to, 42–43

convicts: death of, 41, 263, 276n23; disproportionally Black, 235; escapes of, 276n23; free miners and, 233–34, 241; increase in number of, 235; mechanical training for, 234; murder of, 263; mutiny by, 44–45; public auction of, 264; punishment of, 40–41, 260, 261–62; shackling of, 264; "water cure" torture, 40; working conditions, 42, 261–62, 263. *See also* convict leasing

convicts, women: brutalization of, 40, 42–43

Corrections Corporation of America (CCA), privatization of Tennessee corrections, 244

The University of Illinois Press
is a founding member of the
Association of University Presses.

———————————————

University of Illinois Press
1325 South Oak Street
Champaign, IL 61820-6903
www.press.uillinois.edu